THE MAN WHO ATE TOO MUCH

THE MAN WHO
ATE TOO MUCH

The Life of JAMES BEARD

JOHN BIRDSALL

W. W. NORTON & COMPANY
Independent Publishers Since 1923

For information about permission to reproduce selections from this book, write to
Permissions, W. W. Norton & Company, Inc., 500 Fifth Avenue, New York, NY 10110

For information about special discounts for bulk purchases, please contact
W. W. Norton Special Sales at specialsales@wwnorton.com or 800-233-4830

Manufacturing by LSC Communications, Harrisonburg
Book design by Marysarah Quinn
Production manager: Anna Oler

Library of Congress Cataloging-in-Publication Data

Names: Birdsall, John, author.
Title: The man who ate too much : the life of James Beard / John Birdsall.
Description: First edition. | New York, NY : W. W. Norton & Company, 2020. |
    Includes bibliographical references and index.
Identifiers: LCCN 2020015582 | ISBN 9780393635713 (hardcover) |
    ISBN 9780393635720 (epub)
Subjects: LCSH: Beard, James, 1903–1985. | Cooks—United States—Biography. |
    Gay men—United States—Biography.
Classification: LCC TX649.B43 B57 2020 | DDC 641.5092 [B]—dc23
LC record available at https://lccn.loc.gov/2020015582

W. W. Norton & Company, Inc., 500 Fifth Avenue, New York, N.Y. 10110
    www.wwnorton.com

W. W. Norton & Company Ltd., 15 Carlisle Street, London W1D 3BS

1 2 3 4 5 6 7 8 9 0

For Pat Matera and Lou Barker, my long-ago spirit uncles, who taught me how love could bloom behind walls. And for my husband, Perry Lucina, who showed me how to take the walls down.

CONTENTS

PREFACE

In the beginning, there was James Beard. Before Julia, before barbecuing daddies..., before a wine closet in the life of every grape nut and the glorious coming of age of American wines, before the new American cooking, chefs as superstars, and our great irrepressible gourmania... there was James Beard, our Big Daddy.

—GAEL GREENE

IF YOU LIVE IN the United States and believe in local food, rely on farmers' markets and produce stands to supply flavor and seasonal delight to your cooking; if you take for granted access to milk, butter, and cheese produced in human-scale lots, bakers who employ patience and their hands, and American wines expressive of soil and tradition, you owe a debt to James Beard.

Born in Portland, Oregon, in 1903, Beard came of age when the industrialization of American food was well underway. Starting in about 1940, Beard, in cookbooks and magazine articles and live cooking demonstrations, preached resistance to the dumbing down of food by commercial interests. At a time when the food press was largely a PR wing of manufacturers aligned to profit, Beard argued for taste.

Throughout most of the twentieth century, Americans believed that fine food was synonymous with delicacies imported mostly from France: canned truffles, foie gras, and pâté; wines, often cooked en route, that had endured Atlantic crossings without refrigeration. The nascent American gourmet food movement of the 1930s and 1940s was enthralled with imports. In the 1950s and 1960s, however, Beard gained an appreciation for the beauty and vividness of American foods—of smokehouse hams from Kentucky, wines from California, cheeses inoculated with mold and left to ripen in Iowa caves, and fruits and vegetables grown with an appreciation of the soil of the region, by farmers and orchardists who valued flavor more than expediency.

In 1949, he urged city dwellers to grow baby corn on their fire escapes so they'd know the pleasure of freshly picked ears. A decade later, he tried to convince New Yorkers it was worth sourcing eggs from farmers who raised chickens free to roam small-scale poultry yards on the fringes of the metropolis's sprawl.

Starting in the late 1970s, Beard became a mentor to a new generation of chefs yearning to cook in regional idioms, with ingredients culled from the landscapes where they felt themselves rooted. Beard was an inspiration to chefs in the 1980s cooking under the banner of New American. Larry Forgione, Alice Waters, Jeremiah Tower, and Bradley Ogden all looked to Beard as someone who remembered what food tasted like before the supermarkets killed off local butchers and produce stands.

He was also a national character, instantly recognizable to most Americans from the 1950s until his death in 1985. At six-foot-three and hovering around three hundred pounds, James had an enormous physical presence. He was usually genial in public, prone to cornball puns and a folksy delivery that tended to make his audiences lose their anxiety about making a proper soufflé or buying a bottle of wine. Beard made it look fun. He embodied America's culinary identity for most of the second half of the twentieth century. James Beard *was* American food, its pleasures and excesses, its beauty and simplicity.

He was one of the most famous people in America, and he was terrified that the public would find out who he really was. To the small circle of New York's food world, the fact that James Beard was gay was an open secret. To most everyone else in America in the 1950s and 1960s—the people who bought his cookbooks and read his articles and showed up to his cooking classes—his queerness would have been problematic, to say the least. No ecstatic gospel of taste, no wisdom or charisma, would have made the man most Americans had invited into their kitchens—even into their national identities, the man who embodied pleasure in food in a uniquely American way—anything but a pariah.

:::

IN 2013, I pitched an essay to the quarterly magazine *Lucky Peach*, for its gender issue, about the closeted male food writers who defined American cooking in the twentieth century. My stimulus was rage.

Lucky Peach was a representation of America's chef culture, a space where queerness was allowed to flicker only at the margins. A code of straightness ruled the nation's restaurant kitchens, an ethos oozing corrosive gender tropes. If you were queer in the kitchen, chances were you didn't dare let your guard slip all the way down—an injustice still aching within me, a gay veteran of those battle zones, years after I'd left cooking to become a writer. *Lucky Peach* had built an arena for chefs, yet queer voices didn't rise there. The silence flooded me with grievance—especially since every chef I knew wanted to win a James Beard Award.

Didn't they realize Beard was gay? Couldn't they see the irony of thirsting after a medal molded with his image, these chefs for whom homophobia was a scar on the face of kitchen culture? And so I pitched my story to *Lucky Peach*. Chris Ying, an editor, emailed to say he'd take it. I wrote furiously, on a short deadline. I called it "America, Your Food Is So Gay."

While it's common knowledge today that Claiborne, Olney, and Beard were gay, the details of their queer lives—the complexity of experience in the lives of these architects of American food—are still misunderstood. In my *Lucky Peach* essay, I talked about my own experience growing up in a world of gay men living in and out of the closet, having a coded existence around food, my gay "uncles" Pat Matera and Lou Barker, who helped raise me in my conservative California suburb, where they lived quietly. Men for whom food was a language that defied the ordinary coding of the closet, and who used food as public expression, a matrix of color, feeling, and pleasure, the exuberance of intimate lives they couldn't otherwise reveal to the world.

And even after my essay appeared in print; even after I won a James Beard Award for it in New York the following year, draped with a medal bearing his image, Beard continued to be the member of my trio who haunted me. I kept thinking about the complicated ways Beard lived a gay life, closeted and afraid, like most of his gay contemporaries in the decades after World War II, a period of brutal oppression for queer Americans. How did Beard, at precisely the same time, become the joyful face of American food? It was a question I felt a responsibility to answer. Because most of the detail of Beard's life as a gay man had been suppressed, compromised, or erased, I felt I had to give it voice; to trace over the things that Beard himself, with the help of friends and enablers, tried to wipe from the official record of his life.

Two earlier biographies—*Epicurean Delight* (1990) by Evan Jones, and *James Beard: A Biography* (1994; retitled *The Solace of Food*) by Robert Clark—did an impressive job of tracing the events of Beard's rise in American food, and, in the case of Clark's, of understanding his complicated persona. And even though Clark surfaced many details of Beard's private gay life, I felt that a deeper understanding of queerness in his biography would illuminate so much of his extraordinary career and, by extension, the history of American food in the twentieth century.

Queerness wasn't just an interesting footnote to Beard's life; queerness was its central principle, the fact around which Beard organized his existence. "His entire life was gay," Carl Jerome, Beard's assistant from 1972 to 1976 told me. "It was governed by his sexuality." And yet, said Marion Cunningham, Beard's teaching assistant and close friend, "it was a part of James Beard's life he chose to keep very quiet." This was the central paradox of Beard's life: to be a beloved national figure, someone every American cook invited into their kitchen and felt a certain intimacy with, and yet hide who he was. At a time when kitchen bibles, encyclopedic recipe collections such as *The Joy of Cooking*, were dominant, Beard longed to write in a personal narrative style. He looked to Alice B. Toklas as a hero for the way she blended recipes and memoir in *The Alice B. Toklas Cook Book* of 1954, yet Alice was a legend and an eccentric—her well-known lesbianism seemed to many an endearing literary quirk. With Beard, a man in the prime of life in 1954, any hint of his sexuality had to be denied. Any memoir of Beard's would have to be semimythical, to fill in the parts he couldn't tell.

Queerness and food were indistinguishable in Beard's life. As a young man at Reed College in Portland, Oregon, Beard experienced trauma through his sexual life, an incident that dictated the way he expressed his queerness for the next sixty-plus years, until his death in 1985. Those were amazing decades in LGBTQ history. They included the loosening of gender roles during World War II, the persecution of homosexuals during the McCarthy purge and the Cold War, the nascent queer civil rights movements of the 1950s followed by Stonewall, the sexual revolution, Gay Liberation, the rise and assassination of Harvey Milk, and the first years of the AIDS pandemic. Through it all, Beard remained officially closeted, minding his Reed scar, cautious and afraid.

From the outside, Beard's life looked rich and happy. Secretly, he suffered from loneliness and depression, struggled constantly with doubts about his work and constant worries about money. Depression plagued him all his life. Travel usually made him happy and more relaxed, more himself. In the fifteen years following the end of World War II, France and Spain, in particular, offered relative freedom for queer travelers. Living in virtual exile during that time exposed Beard to recipes and eating traditions that contributed to his ethos of American food.

And his experience of being an exile at home caused him to turn away from much of mainstream society, especially the dominant culture of magazine editors and cookbook publishing. At a time of strict gender roles, he was a man in a woman's profession. His size and other physical realities made him feel ugly and unlovable. He expressed the deepest part of himself in silence.

Beard knew rejection from an early age, and it made him embrace food and fame in a unique way. Though he was always present in American kitchens, Beard carried himself like an outsider, an alien with a secret, a man on a lonely coast who told us we could find meaning and comfort by embracing pleasure.

For a biographer, Beard is a challenging figure. He concealed so much of his private life from view, destroying letters he thought were too revealing, incriminating, or embarrassing. Instead, he turned his public history into myth, and he did it with such force of conviction that it's tempting to take all of it as true.

Brooklyn artist and social activist Avram Finkelstein asserts that to be queer is to be an archaeologist. "To find traces of ourselves in a world that prefers us hidden," he writes, "we excavate."

This biography excavates the story of Beard that he and those close to him tried to destroy. Where documents don't exist, I studied old photographs and contemporary records to animate Beard's life. I kept returning to a quote by Jean-Yves Tadié, from the introduction to his biography of Marcel Proust. "Even if we knew all the facts about [a subject's] life," Tadié writes, "and had heard all the testimonies, we would still have to interpret them. It is here that a biographer's task resembles that of the novelist, because it is a matter of delving beneath appearances, of providing . . . sense and meaning."

Today, we often seek a human connection through cooking, look on recipes and cookbooks as a window into other lives and experiences. Ironically, given that he had to hide so much of his authentic self, Beard was a pioneer in using food to communicate a lifestyle. He made food central to American identity.

This is the story of the architect of that identity, a man most of us know as an institution, fixed on a medal like a soul trapped in a mirror, restless to be freed.

PART ONE

CHAPTER I

THE SWADDLED HAM

$$\cdots \quad \underline{\hspace{8cm}} \quad \cdots$$

1913

WITH A FIDGETY MIND, the boy silently reeled off names of the stops in front of them, depots strung along the rails running south from where the river started. *Warrenton. Columbia Beach. Carnahan. West Gearhart. Surf. Seaside.* The ten-year-old knew the list by heart: half a dozen stations along the fifteen-mile Clatsop Beach Line on the Astoria and Columbia River Railroad, last leg of the five-hour journey from Portland. The boy and his mother would get off at West Gearhart, which everybody called Gearhart Park: ticket men and porters, and the women shouting above the rumble and roar of the day coaches, acquaintances of his mother's who'd likewise started out on the No. 29, the early beach train from town. With each stop, James's picture of their house on Salmon Street would grow blurrier, its sadness and sharp edges dissolving under the promise of summer and release. With each slowing, each lurch to a halt in a new station, another piece of him would jostle free.

This was James's escape, a journey he and Elizabeth took three times a year. In the weeks till August gave out, he would try to evade her jurisdiction—not difficult, since she would have a hundred daily preoccupations, as usual. For the next three months, James would keep as much as he could to the shelter of knolls and dune hollows, of old pathways and unfathomable forests at the top of Tillamook Head, and to the cold embrace of the ocean (even now he was a strong swimmer), paddling far out, deaf to cries from shore. For the next three months, his favorite taste would be of oysters, hauled down from shoals above the terrifyingly wide mouth of the Columbia and fried in an abundance of butter. He knew the sound they'd make, hissing and foaming, edging into brownness, with a scent so rich it would seem capable of tinting the air gold.

James's father rarely joined them at the beach. John Beard almost always stayed behind on Salmon Street with James's older half-sister Lucille (a schoolteacher) and her husband, Clarence. John seemed a man invariably absorbed in his work as chief examiner of goods from China and Japan, squinting over wrenched-open crates of import merchandise at the US Custom House in Portland. With James and Elizabeth gone, John would have unchallenged dominion over the dark rooms on Salmon Street. The boy knew that in place of the taut silence that reigned when the family was together, the house would soften under the influence of John's odious smells: balsam hair oil; cigarettes; boiled pork side meat. Yet the trying things about home would recede further and further from James's thoughts as the train headed toward the coast. From his stool on the deck of the observation car (two coaches behind Elizabeth, who rode on green plush), James watched dull-black coal smoke erupt from the locomotive and fog the cars behind. It curled around the edges of the train and faded, like the after-flourish in a magician's vanishing trick.

At Columbia Beach, James watched the train disgorge flushed women lugging valises, and children reeking of sour sweat and drooled stick candy, a rabble as eager as he was for summer to start. Porters hauled off steamer trunks and sacks of letters that had packed the cars' vestibules since the train crossed the long, rickety-scaled rail bridge at Astoria. Mothers yelled to their broods to step lively crossing the tracks before scrabbling off to the shade of scalloped overhangs slumping from depots not much grander than sheds, set on one long, south-yawning plain, damp with the breath of ocean. They were so unlike James and his mother, these frazzled women and their horrible offspring. James was a precocious boy, raised to air his opinions, no matter how disagreeably. Elizabeth had seen to that.

Even at this age, he found opera divine. Elizabeth took him to hear *Madama Butterfly* when he was five, and the beauty of it made him weep. His ardor ripened in the parlor recitals he and his mother attended in the houses and boarding-hotel rooms of friends his father avoided: actresses who laced their tea with brandy; men who winked at James and gave him sticky homemade marshmallows or nougat. Today the wail of cast-iron wheels at each curve along the rails rang in his ears like the cry of Violetta in *La Traviata: É strano! É strano!*—How strange! While the cry of the steam whistle sounded back *A diletti sempre nuovi*: Always new to delight.

They'd started from home that morning just after seven, in a hired cart with their hoard of trunks, hand luggage, and hatboxes; a summer's worth of library books, stacked and tied with sash cord; and a large, unwieldy, and thick-reeded picnic hamper. Elizabeth had swaddled the cooked ham like an enormous baby (first in waxed paper, then canvas), but James could smell it leaking through the wicker—cedar smoke fused with the mustard and molasses-sugar of the glaze, acrid and sweet. James had barely finished his breakfast tea and coddled egg and toast fingers. The aroma of ham left him hungry again.

They jolted westward across Portland's shiny, still-new Hawthorne Bridge, above a Willamette riverfront clotted with double-decked ferries and billboards vaunting sacks of High-Flight flour, bottles of Coca-Cola, and Preferred Stock in cans: the fascinating things James's mother thought too vapid or vulgar to allow through the screened back porch to her kitchen.

At forty-seven, Elizabeth had a plush figure and a biscuit-dough complexion. Her forehead was broad, above a powerful nose and eyebrows so fine and pale they looked transparent. They gave her a blank expression—guarded, scoured of passion—except that the combination of a taut mouth below cautious, heavily lidded eyes made her appear perpetually skeptical. Though she had lived in Portland for thirty years, her English accent persisted, the skimmed consonants of an impatient Londoner extracted from a gentle Wiltshire burr.

This morning she wore a hat trimmed with small crepe roses and a brim that cantilevered out to her shoulders. A long-skirted traveling suit fell from her hips and flared under a knee-length summer coat in sandy linen already creasing at the elbows. She was a barricade of fabric and flesh.

James was encased in the blue serge suit with long pants he'd begged Elizabeth to buy. (She'd balked at the twenty-five dollars it cost, but when she learned John also disapproved, she bought it, if only to needle her husband and prove her independence.) On James, the jacket bulged around the seams of its sewn-in belt, refusing to cinch like the ones in the *Morning Oregonian* ads. James's eyes were guarded and delicate, sunk in a face as plump and pale as milk-poached meringue. Under the flat cap he wore tipped back, James had groomed his thick brown hair to lie flat against his forehead, a look more awkward and innocent than the glinting comb-backs on the boys who posed in smudged newspaper ink.

At 8:15 their train, the northwest-bound No. 29 to Astoria, juddered out of Portland's red-brick North Bank station, the passenger terminal for the Spokane, Portland & Seattle Railway. It rocked along at twenty miles an hour on steel rails quivering in bright, cloud-filtered light, tracing the south bank of the Columbia River. In the southeasterly distance, the solitary twisted fang of Mount Hood dissolved in haze. Soon even Portland—the frieze-topped hotels downtown and houses poking corbelled mansards through the trees of the western hills—petered out. First myrtles and spruce, then forests swallowed the riverbank's roads and rail yards, its icehouses, and eventually its salmon canneries, before which Chinese workers paused on planks strung across rough piers to watch the train lurch by in a burgeoning black chrysanthemum of coal smoke.

James's eyes settled on one man, smoking as he loitered outside a salmon shack perched on stilts in the wide river. Wearing boots and a long rubber apron slicked with scales and guts, he raised his hand to wave at the boy in the blue suit, seated on a campstool on the awning-sheltered platform behind the observation parlor car, the train's last. James waved back, and for a half-second thought it was Jue Let, the Beard family cook (recently departed), whose tea cakes and curries, Welsh rabbits and roast ducks, were even now the vivid memory pictures in a fairy story of life on Salmon Street that existed far from reality. But the man with the cigarette, disappearing now as the train banked along a bend in the tracks, was a stranger, whose wave was nothing more than a curious, ultimately disinterested hello.

: : :

FROM THE OBSERVATION DECK, James followed the rise and fall of scenery beyond the spill of the city. He knew it all, every mile, just as he knew the hinged tableaus in a well-loved pop-up picture book: the river's curves, scribed along the south bank in sagging telegraph wires strung from stripped pines; the fenced pastures and farmhouses with here and there a huffing smokehouse; the slovenly shacks and prim white Rural Gothic churches. Their pointy narrow windows looked to James, if he squinted, like ears of corn in the husk.

First stop was St. Helens, a town at the northern tip of Sauvie Island, where Multnomah Channel cleaved apart from the Columbia. James could just make out the arctic dome of Washington's famous dormant volcano, in the boy's imagination a hibernating mastodon the world had left to sleep.

Next was Rainier, a lumber boomtown strung up on forested hills. Below the railway lay the riverbank, frenzied with lumber mills' churning smokestacks and new boards stacked high into megaliths, pale as tender flesh in the intensifying daylight. (For a hundred years, Portlanders' faith in the ability to grow their city had been as infinite as the surrounding trees, and the building frenzy of the 1905 Lewis and Clark Exposition had hoisted optimism and an appetite for virgin forest all the way to the ridgetops.)

Like James, Elizabeth relished their spring migration from Portland. Travel made her independent again, a woman of her own affairs, as she once had been, a person of business. She had friends in Rainier, people she'd known years ago in Portland when she was unattached, a widow from her first marriage, mistress of a proper boardinghouse and not just a housekeeper for Lucille, whom she always disliked, and Lucille's lunkhead husband. Elizabeth had written to her Rainier friends to say which train she'd be on. They were in the station to meet it, and in the few minutes of its loitering would gab with Elizabeth about how well she looked, how much James had grown since last year, and about the warmth of the spring so far and the early peas they reckoned were only days from harvesting.

The locomotive lurched and rolled again. (*É straano! É straaano!*) Dogs, making the summer migration to the coast with their families, yapped and nipped at children. Freed from leash-holds, they nosed around the day coaches, lifting legs to doorway edges and unlucky trunks in the vestibules. Sweating porters picked around them while scuttling through to deliver wax-papered chicken sandwiches and stoneware bottles of ginger beer. This was a midweek train at the start of summer vacation, so almost all the passengers were women and kids en route to beach cottages and hotels. They'd spend the weeks till September teetering in the frigid ankle-waves of the Pacific, weighed down by heavy woolen bathing suits with modesty skirts, larking about at strawberry-gathering parties and ice cream socials, and above all picnicking, braced before the soft, wind-protected humps of the dunes. *A diletti . . . sempre nuovi.*

The Saturday morning run to the coast was dubbed the Daddy Train. Husbands and fathers like John Beard, who stayed in town to work, would ride out for weekends and make the five-hour return on Monday mornings. James's father made the journey only once or twice all summer. He cited social obligations in town he couldn't ignore, since he owed his position at the Custom House in part to being in good standing with the heirs to his political patron, the late General Owen Summers (James's godfather). Besides, the beach was Elizabeth's realm, a place to entertain her women friends without the demands of Salmon Street, and to resume her catering business, an enterprise that earned her money she could save or spend as she liked.

Elizabeth and James always rode the train apart: she in the bustling day coach filled with gossip and sociability, he in the open, amid the blasting solitude on the deck of the observation car. It was the only place the boy would sit, willingly and without throwing tantrums. Securing space there was why he and Elizabeth needed to arrive early at the station, to tip a porter to slap the dust off a campstool, cover it with a napkin to protect the boy's blue serge, and set out a little table to hold his boxed snack.

James folded himself into the landscape and the rush of wind, the smell of countryside between cindery blasts of locomotive smoke. He almost relished the fine grit of coal dust on his neck, face, and hands and even loved clinkers, the fused shards of molten rock and coal shoveled from the engine's firebox as they built up and flung from the side of the train off a shovel's tip. The clinkers rode the headwind down along the cars to the observation deck, to glance like dull needles off the boy's skin, a sensation rippling with excitement and danger.

Alone on the observation deck, as soon as the tracks banked away from the Columbia toward the low green clearing of Clatskanie (last stop before Astoria), James would open the paperboard box he'd set on the floor back at North Bank station. It was his snack, something Elizabeth always prepared to hold him over between breakfast and luncheon, which they would have at their cottage in Gearhart Park. Inside were butter-and-marmalade sandwiches: his mother's own bread, with bitter-orange marmalade cooked in the big copper boiler, and butter from Grace Harris, a special friend of Elizabeth's who lived with a cruel husband on a farm at the pasture's edge of Oregon City. There was a hard-boiled egg and some of the first cherries of the season from the Salmon Street garden: pinkish-yellow Royal Anns, tender and sweet. There were cookies—small, buttery, and crisp, the way Elizabeth insisted cookies should be—everything concealed in its own packet of wax paper, folded with exacting efficiency, all of it lavish yet constrained.

James had grown up with a sense of his mother's impatience with him. He knew she would have preferred him to be an adult, not a boy who needed things, became sick and disrupted the household order, or cried some nights until his tears soaked the feathers in his pillow. As long as James could remember, Elizabeth had wanted him to be a partner, an ally in her endless simmering war with John. But now, with summer and the beach so close at hand, all James wanted was to disappear.

:::

TO SKIRT THE FISHHOOK turn of the riverbank, the train ran for miles along a low trestle bridge over open water, a wood-stilt structure fording the Columbia's shallows west from Tongue Point clear through to the main harbor. Once the train crossed the John Day River and the tracks veered northward, James glimpsed the thickening cluster of boats and pilings and knew they were close: Astoria, city of salmon!

On the bankside south of the trestle bridge, low boathouses with pitched roofs stretched from shore on jetties running perpendicular to the tracks. They came within spitting range of any train running the track. Through the windows of the boat shacks, James could see gill-netters blued by tobacco smoke mending their seines; other nets, drying under the bright-white sky, hung limp as dead fish from poles sunk in the muddy bottom.

As the Columbia yawned wider, James felt the river's spray from waves, looking more and more like ocean whitecaps, slapping trestles beneath the train. Off in the channel, he spied four-masted old battle frigates converted to salmon seiners; closer in, the hulking offshore cannery of the Union Fishermen's Co-Operative, top-heavy on chopstick stilts. Men here dragged huge fish from the water, silver bellies flashing, the way James had scooped pollywogs from Clackamette Park pond in his tiny muslin net. Astoria was a town built on plucking things out of this confluence of river and ocean. (In 1811, from far-off New York, town namesake John Jacob Astor had shanghaied the area's hordes of otters for his empire of fur.)

Sturdy Finnish and Norwegian gillnetters strung their seines on anchor poles arrayed in circles and filled the holds of their boats with thumping cargoes of freshwater silvers and huge, hideous Chinooks, crook-jawed and nail-toothed like Punch and Judy faces. Here Chinese workers gutted and skinned these seasonal hauls and canned the rich, oily meat to ship all over the nation, but especially to the Northeast, where once-teeming spring salmon runs were already trickling out.

James found joy in Astoria, in the whirl of its sawmills, canneries, and factory smokestacks; in its forest of telephone-cable poles; in the street-cars with slender connector arms gripped to floating electric wires, as if dynamism hovered in the air; in its elegant city hall with columns that appeared piped from buttercream, its oyster parlors, its boardinghouses fronting the piers with signs hawking rooms and home-cooked meals. James adored the waterfront's clutter of advertising placards, the ones for cheap salmon-cheek suppers, whiskey, and beer in a glass some sign-painter Rembrandt had rendered frosty.

The grand part of town scaled the hills as if on risers, petering out before reaching the patchy border of firs and hemlocks on its scarred and craggy ridgeline. James spied tall mansions with ornate tracery, tur-rets sprouting black-iron finials, every window with its rippled curtain of ivory lace. Yet beyond the edges of Astoria's elegance, a frontier raw-ness persisted. Down where the train rumbled through to its termi-nus, past the rough and graceless municipal docks, Astoria's perennially chill and humid air was heavy with the charred-wood and fish-oil pun-gency of smokehouses, the tannic smell of creosote in wooden trestles, and the hot-iron tang of wheels grinding on rails (*é strano*). Suffusing everything were salt gusts of ocean, the boy's first tastes of summer.

Like Lewis and Clark a century before them, James and his mother were finally—at last!—in sight of the Pacific, closer than ever to Gear-hart Park. Soon they'd lose sight of the wide Columbia, where tree-covered bluffs stepped back to give the river room enough to meet the ocean. From there, the ocean carried river waters far out to a world the boy longed to see and supposed he someday would.

The train stopped at Astoria station—it was red brick and bulky, with huge circular windows like Chinese moon gates, closed up by a jumble of small panes. Mrs. Beard and her son didn't have long. In only fifteen minutes, James and Elizabeth would have to hustle from the cars of the Spokane, Portland & Seattle, dodging children and dogs, flag-ging a porter to make sure their trunks, valises, books, and above all the picnic hamper, with its large and fragrant ham, would be transferred properly to the new train, the six-car Astoria and Columbia River Railroad, bound south for Seaside and all stops between. Just as at Rainier, friends of Elizabeth's say hello. Harry Hamblet, a local real estate speculator, and Peter Grant, who was in the canning business, trundled her and the boy quickly into a new coach.

The train then skulked across the slender, squat, and dainty-looking trestle bridge that spanned Young's Bay, a connector so long, across a body of water so wide, that passengers could feel as if they were hovering above the sea itself, drifting toward a new continent. Once across, the train picked up speed as James silently recited the stations to come like an incantation: *Warrenton . . . Columbia Beach . . . Carnahan. . . .*

Finally the rails left the wide, unending meadow, above which it rumbled on a flattened spine of dune. The train slowed as it entered a familiar stand of Douglas firs and Sitka spruces (to James, an enchanted forest) and rolled to a stop in a clearing: Gearhart Park. The station was small and clapboarded and stood to the side of a bare-dirt platform beneath a high wooden roof forming a shallow V. It always looked to James like abstract hands touching at the wrists, splayed beneath the pale sky.

They'd arrived at last: the place James had fantasized about all through the long days of April and the first weeks in May. He and his mother had been here only two months earlier, for the Easter holidays, when the rain didn't stop and they holed up in separate corners of the cottage with books, listening to the eaves drip. Already that felt like last year.

The conductor was eager to push off toward Seaside (destination for most on the train), but Elizabeth was not to be hurried. While Gearhart Park's old stationmaster (who doubled as the high school teacher) struggled with a large wooden hand truck, ferrying luggage and the picnic hamper onto the platform, Elizabeth stepped off the coach with the poise of a star aware of her audience. She let the conductor reach for her gloved fingers at the bottom of the steps, and paused to wave to those she knew who were still on board, as if she were Mary Garden, the world-famous Scottish soprano, emerging from her first-class carriage at the Gare de Lyon, as James had seen her do in a photograph in the *Oregonian*. In that photo, she was in the act of turning back, as if to acknowledge the fans crowding the windows of the second- and third-class coaches before facing the dignitaries waiting on the station platform to welcome her. Though for Elizabeth, the only people there to bid her welcome were the stationmaster and the manager of the local livery stable—Elizabeth had written them to meet her on arrival.

A diletti sempre nuovi . . . A diletti! The locomotive shot a white plume from its smokestack. *É straano!* The engineer sounded the whistle. With a rumble and the hiss of steam, the train rolled toward Surf, and beyond that to the crowds and automobiles and ice cream cones of Seaside.

It was just after one-thirty, an inconvenient hour for the railroad men to schedule arrival. James and his mother would have to scurry to the cottage for luncheon, though he doubted she'd let him run on ahead, alone.

::::

JOHN TYBERG, the stable man, loaded the Beards' luggage on his wagon and set out on Railroad Avenue, heading north to Summit. He would cross Neacoxie Creek (brown and smooth as glass) at Gearhart Lane, then turn south to trace the eastern flank of the golf course on Cottage Avenue, straight on to E Street and the Beards' cabin. Elizabeth and James would go by foot. Though the social pages of the *Morning Oregonian* and the *Morning Astorian* might report in a week or so that the Beards had opened their cottage for the summer (part of a long list of seasonal arrivals), there was no good reason for Elizabeth to delay advertising her presence. The former proprietress of the Gladstone boardinghouse was available to hire for beach picnics and parties.

There were so many parties in summer: strawberry-picking socials in the troughs behind the dunes, everyone sprawled on blankets for a boxed-lunch picnic; organized clamming in the early mornings, followed by a beach breakfast of hotcakes, bacon, and eggs fried over a driftwood fire. Hostesses had to write early to engage the services of Mrs. Beard, whose plump son sometimes helped her. You could arrange for her to cook a private luncheon or supper in the Beard cottage: razor-clam chowder, delicate biscuits, and some of the petite local peas suffused with the mineral sweetness of Clatsop soil, lavished with butter churned nearby at Henry Ober's dairy farm.

Elizabeth and James walked from the station along a narrow-plank pedestrian boardwalk named Pacific Way, though everyone called it the Boulevard. It ran west through hemlocks and spruces to the old Gearhart Hotel and the Chautauqua Hall, the green and barren golf course, and eventually to the great ocean and its horizon, so vast it seemed infinite.

They turned south at Cottage Avenue, the primary north–south road, which ran along the ridge of a larger dune sprouting roomy summer houses. They had weathered shakes and dormers, and west-facing porches, places for teacup socializing and naps beneath open numbers of the *Seaside Gazette*, shelter from the prism glare of sunsets.

For centuries, Clatsop Indians trudged along the shoulder of compressed dirt and sand, in bare feet or in deerskin moccasins, sheathed in tule-reed capes when it rained. The road James and his mother walked was a native highway between winter and summer settlements. Lengthening days drew them to the Clatsop Plain, its hollows and creeks, river and beaches, for camass roots and razor clams; huckleberries, thimbleberries, high-bush cranberries, dewberries, and wild grapes. Above all, it called to them for salmon: Ten varieties of the sacred fish offered themselves for harvest in the southern estuary and its feeders.

James knew that tomorrow morning by five, if the tide was low, his mother would be on the beach in her best bathing dress, with a shovel in one hand and a bucket in the other. She'd join others up and down the vast expanse of mud-colored sand, as pale-gray morning broke, shoveling sand before kneeling to dig for razor clams with bare hands. Most clammers were men, digging in rolled shirtsleeves as dogs barked and wrestled and rolled on washed-up skate carcasses to pick up the stink. Only a handful of women would be on the beach, mostly to watch, scarves tied at the chin against the wind, in mutton-sleeve coats so long the hems grazed the sand. Elizabeth was different. After an hour or two of clamming, she'd walk back along the dune path, toting as many as six dozen razors in a bucket that must have weighed thirty pounds.

This was a place where food—the search for it, the killing and plucking and skinning and roasting of it, the drying and smoking of it—ruled life. It occurred to James that food must have been why the Russians and Scandinavians and Americans had come in, learned from the Indians, and then brutally choked them out, because anybody who came to this rich place of eating would surely wax greedy and plot how to seize it. The train that brought Portland families to Gearhart Park and Seaside for summering in cottages or chic, rambling hotels or boardinghouses smelling of boiled cabbage was merely the trailing shadow of an old and irresistible longing.

: : :

GEARHART PARK SAW its first, studiously pastoral cottages rise early in the 1890s, just after the tracks that James and Elizabeth so recently arrived on were laid. The colony's founders were a canned-salmon baron and his wife, an apostle in the Christian temperance movement.

Marshall and Narcissa Kinney conceived of Gearhart as a place of American optimism, dedicated to a worshipful pursuit of leisure. Astoria, fourteen miles to its north, was a dank and rusted town, ruled by shipping, sawmills, and the Iron Chink—the salmon-butchering machine that replaced Chinese workers—where, to the Kinneys' minds, the detritus of old worlds (Finns, Russians, Chinese, Swedes) washed up to grasp at dollars, only to squander them on liquor and other transgressions.

The Kinneys envisioned a New Jerusalem in the trees, a white utopia consecrated to a rapturous, wholly decorous appreciation of God's handprint on the land. They sought to rededicate Oregon's coastal frontier to pioneer values, a place where whiskey and vice would find no sanction and where Christianity and the restrictive deed covenant reigned.

In 1851, a settler, Philip Gearhart, paid a thousand dollars for squatter's rights to native land in the Clatsop Plain, ultimately acquiring almost two thousand acres. By 1880, a small summer resort called Sea Side had sprouted just south of Gearhart's holdings, in view of

Tillamook Head's brooding grandeur, with a beachfront of fine sand. Getting there from Portland, however, required taking a long, bilious journey by stagecoach or paddleboat.

Sensing opportunity, Marshall Kinney bought up acre after acre from Gearhart's heirs. In 1888, he founded the Astoria & South Coast Railway. As owner of the land under which future trains would run, Kinney deeded the transit pathway to himself for a fat sum. In 1890, the first train lumbered south from Astoria to the still-new resort with a freshly squeezed-together name: Seaside. Soon, Kinney and his wife were drawing up plans for a rival vacation colony with a name reminiscent of a British country estate: Gearhart Park.

Narcissa oversaw the platting of Gearhart Park's two hundred acres and the drafting of its charter. An ardent officer in the Woman's Christian Temperance Union, she decreed that no alcoholic beverage was to be fermented, distilled, brewed, or sold within municipal limits for a hundred years. Unlike Seaside, which had turned its beachfront into a carnival jumble of souvenir picture studios, ice cream parlors, oyster shacks, and saloons, Gearhart would keep its coastline pristine. Cottages would keep to the interior dunes and meadows and appear modest, rustic, and tasteful, lit by oil lamps and candles instead of the electric glare of Mr. Edison's bulbs, which must, surely, dim the stars.

At the edge of a meadow, the Kinneys built a large and comfortable hotel in Queen Anne style, with a façade of gables, bays, and sunbursts formed of wooden spindles. Nearby, in a clearing of pines and spruces, was the center of Narcissa's grand vision: the assembly hall of the Chautauqua Literary and Scientific Circle. It was a large auditorium of unvarnished wood, with clerestory windows and soaring, cathedral-like arches.

In its prime in the 1890s, Gearhart Park's Chautauqua was a jamboree ground for American energy and optimism, awash in the fervor of bootstrap capitalism. Its rafters rang with shouted speeches declaring the moral vibrancy of a nation of white pioneers (distinct from those with origins in wretched swarthy lands) eager to export its ideals on the wings of imperialist adventure.

Then came the Lewis and Clark Centennial and American Pacific

Exposition and Oriental Fair of 1905, marking the hundred-year anniversary of the fateful expedition. Over nineteen weeks, more than a million and a half visitors surged through the grounds at the northwest edge of Portland, then rising in a curve of the Willamette River. By 1910, a hundred thousand new residents had settled in Portland. The city had become irreversibly fixed in the American imagination.

Theodore Kruse bet that the Lewis and Clark Exposition would be a boon for the entire region, and especially the picturesque coast south of Astoria. Kruse was a German who'd jumped ship in Alaska and found his way to Portland. In 1906, the year the expo closed, Kruse acquired all of Gearhart Park, including its hotel, from Marshall Kinney. (Kinney became a widower in 1901, when Narcissa, just forty-six, heeded her untimely summons to heaven.) Kruse's purchase coincided with the year Elizabeth and James, a shaggy blond toddler of three, took their first holiday in Gearhart Park in a rented cottage, and four summers before Elizabeth built them a place of their own.

: : :

THE BEARD COTTAGE STOOD in a neighborhood called the Meadow, a grid of raw streets on a field of undulating green. There were widely scattered residences with picket fences, yards with young pines and ancient black spruce scribing jagged outlines against the sky. Compared with the respectable homes of Cottage Avenue, the Beard place was a shack: a box twenty by twelve, with a porch in front and a roof with a high peak that sought to lend the place a greater presence. The house was hardly adequate for two. It had a kitchen, a combination dining room and parlor, and a pair of small bedrooms. Outside, it was covered in unpainted cedar shingles; inside, it had tongue-and-groove fir, oiled to keep the grain visible.

The Meadow was beyond the formal boundary of Gearhart Park, though within its communal realm. Lots were cheaper here than in Gearhart proper. Harry Hamblet, husband of Elizabeth's friend Polly, had a real estate office in Astoria. He found Elizabeth her plat on E

Street, negotiated the purchase (the deed listed Elizabeth's name alone, without John's), and hired and supervised the builder.

James disliked the cottage. It smelled like turpentine and there were spiders. The kitchen was so small that all the work except the cooking took place around the table in the central room. The stove itself was tiny, barely big enough to hold Elizabeth's capacious iron chowder kettle. It burned wood, and to James it seemed capable of only one temperature: blasting. Only Elizabeth knew how to bake in it.

Many families entrusted John Tyberg with a key. They would write him in advance to open their cottages on the day they arrived, as he'd done for the Beards that morning: swept the front steps, then pried the boards from the door and the shutters from the windows. There had been a rash of fires and vandalism lately at empty cottages, no doubt perpetrated by anarchists or tramps. Tyberg had pushed open the windows to let air in, and filled the stove with logs and kindling. Elizabeth immediately set to boiling water for tea.

: : :

AT THE TIME he acquired Gearhart Park, Theodore Kruse owned a well-known restaurant in Portland, the mirrored, palm-filled Louvre. It had a scandalous reputation, a record of liquor-law violations, and reports of immoral behavior on its premises. It was said that Kruse himself turned a blind eye to the circle of so-called inverts, homosexuals who gathered in the Louvre's men-only grill room. Elizabeth was a regular at the restaurant, despite John's angry disapproval. She would take James to dine and make him be polite to gentlemen in tight trousers with velvet jacket lapels and ladies who ate and drank with abandon.

Kruse directed town officials to rezone Gearhart, opening Narcissa's pristine beachfront to development and imposing new plats onto the original grid. Speculators shoehorned bungalows and hulking Dutch colonials onto the crowded heights of the western foredune, now with the grand name of Ocean Avenue. A strip with magnificent views of the sea, it was sited just outside the Alcoholic Beverage Covenant zone. It would come to be known as Gin Ridge, a name of cruel irony to rattle Narcissa's ghost.

Summers became a whirl. The beach pages of the *Morning Astorian* noted the arrival of the celebrated and the well-off who journeyed by train or steamer from Portland, Seattle, and San Francisco, even from as far away as Baltimore and New York. Men in woolen bathing tunics and bowler hats mugged for portraits in camera studios, frozen in he-man flexes in front of canvases painted with ferocious curling white-caps. At night there were dances at beach-facing villas with carefree, romantic, or cheeky Indian-lodge names: Tillzeronia, Ivanhoe, Sleepy Hollow, Uneedarest, Takit-Eezy. Parties spilled out to cottage gardens trellised in clematis and climbing roses.

In 1910, after months of publicity in the Portland papers, a brash new beachfront hotel welcomed its first guests. Designed by Portland architect Morris H. Whitehouse, Kruse's Beach Hotel was a wonder, with a porch like a colonnade, showy awnings to shield guests from the lowering sun, and a shocking green carpet of lawn spread across a berm flanking Gearhart Park Beach. The hotel's roof, in tiles of zinnia red, was a complicated arrangement of dormers and gables cutting into the pastel blue sky. Likewise beyond the western limit of the dry zone, Kruse's new hotel was awash in liquor.

Kruse had met Elizabeth many times at the Louvre, and he must have known her reputation as the capable former mistress of the Gladstone. At the beach, on nights when there were multiple banquets and parties at the hotel and Kruse needed someone with an eye, a palate, and a calloused pair of hands, he would send word to Elizabeth (discreetly, almost as a friend) to take charge.

In the evenings, in the hotel ballroom, women showed off dresses trimmed in flowers, the younger ladies in princess gowns with unpadded hips, a silhouette still daring in Oregon. Couples twirled to the "Merry Widow Waltz" near the romantic crashing Pacific, even though the blare of Kruse's orchestra nearly drowned out the ocean. A hulking natatorium eventually rose next door, making the ocean more or less irrelevant. It became scenery, like the backdrops in photo studios.

In time, even Narcissa's precious Chautauqua succumbed to this new Gearhart. It began showing motion pictures. In the weeks after James and Elizabeth arrived in the summer of 1913, vacationers (some undoubtedly with liquor on their breath) packed the wooden benches to watch the lurid and thrilling *Dr. Jekyll and Mr. Hyde*, starring chin-dimpled King Baggot; and *The Girl and the Greaser*, with hot tomato Charlotte Burton. Electric lights, brighter now than even Edison's filament bulbs, had been strung along the Boulevard so the crowds could make their way home in the dark. If the lights outshone the stars, nobody seemed to mind.

:::

ELIZABETH DIRECTED TYBERG to muscle the wicker picnic hamper into the kitchen first, before stacking trunks and suitcases onto the tiny porch, making it barely passable. When he'd gone, she set about making lunch. She got out the canister with the tea leaves she had blended to her liking, a large tin of crackers, a lump of Grace Harris's butter wrapped in paper, and straw-sheathed jars she had filled with apricot-pineapple preserves, thumb-size cucumbers pickled in olive oil with mustard seed, her precious white asparagus—enough jars to give them a start, not last all summer.

James helped her lift the swaddled ham from the basket. The canvas was stained where the mustard and brown sugar glaze had begun to seep. Elizabeth unwrapped it, carefully, peeling away the waxed paper where it had stuck. With James's help, she set it on the freshly scrubbed board stowed next to the stove. She removed a slicing knife (wrapped in canvas and tucked in the hamper) and, for their lunch, cut thin slices of the enormous dark and sticky and beautifully shiny thing she'd glazed only yesterday.

Every year, Elizabeth received two smoked hams, each weighing nearly twenty pounds. They came from John's sister's ranch in eastern Oregon: hogs slaughtered in the fall, their haunches cured in salt and hung up for weeks in the smokehouse—the Beards, after all, could trace their people to Kentucky. Blackened, hard, and moldy, the hams arrived at Salmon Street at winter's end. James sometimes went to the cellar to smell them: to close his eyes and catch the ghost of burning alder (earthy-sweet, like overripe bananas) from branches culled on his aunt's ranch; the mineral whiff of salt; and a goading tang of rot.

Cooking a ham for the journey to the coast had become a ritual for Elizabeth, and James was her eager altar boy. It had to be soaked for days in the tin baby's bathtub she kept for poaching salmon, then scrubbed with a stiff-bristled brush (James's task) to remove most of the ashy mold. It simmered for hours, also in the tin tub, in water and vinegar and a small sheaf of bay leaves, until the liquid turned the color of strong tea. After fishing the ham from the tub and cooling it, Elizabeth baked it for several hours. At last it was ready for painting with a slurry of English mustard powder and water. Elizabeth would pack it with a mix of sieved brown sugar and fine breadcrumbs, heave it with James's help, now that Let was gone, into a fast oven, and bake it until the surface looked like burnished saddle leather.

Her hat and jacket now off, Elizabeth cut thin slices on the oblique. And she and James, also in shirtsleeves, sat at the parlor table, bathed in the sun reflecting off the raw wood walls, and ate what was always the first meal of their Gearhart summer: cold ham with buttered crackers, oil-cured pickles, and a little reconstituted English mustard that burned in the nose like coal fire. They drank their tea neat—they'd buy milk from Henry Ober when next he rattled down E Street on his cart.

The ham was salty and pungent. Its smokiness and moldy specter would linger as the first taste on the coast, its flavor the threshold onto an existence reset to a familiar rhythm. In the next few days, thick slices would fry in the cottage's black iron skillet. They'd push sunny-side-up eggs to the rims of Elizabeth's beloved Blue Willow plates, chipped and therefore banished to the coast. Later the boy would shave off chewy bits as snacks, to push into split biscuits or between slices of bread, both of which his mother could coax from the edges of her blasting oven. Elizabeth would turn the minced leftovers into ham cakes held together with flour and egg and fried crisp in the skillet. She'd press the wrack of ham pieces into boiled and crushed potatoes—the little yellow ones from the farm at the coast road—to make hash. Finally, she'd crack the bone into pieces small enough to fit the kettle, and extract from them a broth that recalled the flavors of the vanished meat. It would seep into chowders, made from razor clams dug on the beach just across the final dune before you came to the Pacific, on broad, wind-carved sands that James almost never stopped imagining.

:::

AFTER LUNCH, there was the hurly-burly of emptying the trunks and cases. James, however, moved the collection of blue-green and drab gray Chinese ginger jars, carried from Salmon Street after Let drained their contents for cakes and other things, from shelves to the table. He told Elizabeth he needed to gather flowers from the weedy trough that ran between beach berm and foredune. He hurried out before she could order him to stop.

He walked the short distance on E Street west to the dune, past the Marias's cottage and up the road to Ocean Avenue, where Harry Hamblet was building houses far grander than the shoebox Beard cottage. Below him in the hollow was a low thicket where wild iris, Indian paintbrush, and flowering currant grew, and native strawberries stretched in angled chains across a mix of dirt and sand. From there, he could take in summer's most crucial vista: Tillamook Head, rising from its southern sweep of beach beyond the mouth of the Necanicum River.

Millions of years ago, Tillamook Head was the last great bloody-red blob of lava to heave out of the earth in what is now Idaho, then to surge through the Columbia River Valley and push to the Pacific. In 1806, Meriwether Lewis and William Clark heard rumors of a whale beached south of their expedition's camp, near what is now Astoria. Determined to hack oil and blubber from the carcass, Clark, with Sacagawea and a small party, climbed Tillamook Head and traced its pathways south. They noted five Indian lodges on the molar-surface plateau thick with trees before reaching the mouth of a creek called Ecola, *whale* in the language of the Tillamook.

One day, Clark looked down on the wide flank of the Pacific: at the rocks rising like the peaks of mountains from the ocean floor, at the far-off outcropping from the water (later named Haystack), and at the vertical plunge of cliffs into waves. He declared that he "beheld the grandest and most pleasing prospects" his eyes had ever seen—this from a man who had traced most of the northern tier of a continent! As though merely taking in a landscape, being in the thrall of a particular place, living off its berries and its fish (which Clark had learned from the Indians to roast leaned up against a fire) had changed him.

James Beard would absorb the history in these landforms: William Clark's sense of wonder; Narcissa Kinney's reverence for place; Theodore Kruse's flamboyance and love of pleasure. They would coexist in James.

The next three months would bring days of escape and discovery for the boy. In the gaps between his mother's orders, her picnic jobs and parties, he'd find freedom enough to dawdle on the beach; to swim. To go out during slack tide (the moment when the tidal stream goes still, before the flow reverses) armed with a garden rake for catching shy, vulnerable summer Dungeness crabs buried at the margins of beach, not far from the inlets and tide pools where they feed, keen to the movement of water. To wade up creeks with Mary Hamblet (Harry's little girl) and pick huckleberries that stained his fingers, and then stop on the way back to eat ice cream and pickles (both technically forbidden). Mornings to troll the Necanicum River above the estuary at the foot of the Meadows, dangling in the water scraps of beef liver tied on string for luring crawfish; afternoons to fish for trout. Hours to read and study the clouds through the pines on Strawberry Knoll, whose needle-cluster branches breathed in wind sucked from far out in the ocean and exhaled in swirls that would rustle the pages of his book and trouble his hair.

He scrambled into the hollow to gather flowers as fast as he could, before his mother's anger surged to dangerous. She was a woman who would brook no disrespect. James knew from her stories, which she told endlessly, that she'd lived through too much to stand for that.

CHAPTER 2

MANGOES IN PANAMA

1861–1903

THE BABY ARRIVED RED-FACED, fat, and squalling to Elizabeth's bed on Salmon Street. When it was time to weigh the newborn, the nurse who accompanied the doctor discovered she'd failed to bring her scale. Let was summoned. In a few minutes, he arrived at the bedroom door with the kitchen scale, its tray lined with an old damask napkin. Though exhausted, Missy (Let's name for Elizabeth) would have been furious, he knew better than probably anyone, had he allowed a decent one to be soiled.

The scale's needle wrenched and fluttered beneath the squirming baby. At last the point settled on a number: thirteen pounds! The doctor declared the boy fine and healthy; the attending nurse, who recorded the weight in her daybook, raised her eyebrows and declared she'd never seen so large an infant delivered. John Beard's daughter, nineteen-year-old Lucille—called Lucy Bird—took the swaddled infant from Let and set him in a bassinet. A kind of glowing halo crowned Elizabeth: her hair in its customary large bun, frayed and glistening with sweat.

On a dark morning in this same bed last February, Elizabeth had seen the slack body of her stillborn boy wrapped entirely in a blanket—legs, arms, face. This time, she had made sure to fatten the child in her womb: on roast chickens with cream gravy, Let's Welsh rabbits and apple charlottes, and a daily tumbler of beer. Elizabeth, forty-two, was at last a mother—of a plump, towheaded boy with skin folds so extravagant he looked regal. After all, it was the reason she'd even agreed to marry John five years and one month ago, so she would conceive and bear a child. They had said she was too old. This baby showed they should never have doubted her.

She kept her Episcopal prayer book on the bedside table. Still, she appealed not to God but to a fate that had been mercurial enough to deliver her, a poor English girl, to this raw and restless place, this Oregon.

The next day, Wednesday, May 6, 1903, the *Morning Oregonian* ran a single birth notice.

BORN.

BEARD—May 5, to Mr. and Mrs. John A. Beard,
749 E. Salmon St., a son.

At Trinity Episcopal Church, they'd christen him James Andrews, the middle name for John's father, Andrew Francis Beard, as well as John's middle name, so the "s" made it plural. Besides, *James Andrews* sounded lordly.

The bearer of this name with the majestic onus would come to know this about his mother's life: that it was a never-ending revolt against anyone who ever tried to enclose her.

:::

ON JANUARY 7, 1861, in a small village near Westbury in Wiltshire, England, Mary Elizabeth Jones took her first furious breaths. She was one of twelve children born to Charlotte and Joseph Jones. Though not desperately poor, the Joneses brought Elizabeth, as she'd be called, into a world of limited prospects. Maybe she'd grow up and hope to marry a farmer; maybe go into service, become a domestic for a rich family as did her father, who was a gamekeeper at a great country house. With luck, she'd wed a man with a skilled trade (perhaps a fine, sturdy blacksmith) and produce a dozen children of her own.

Westbury nestled under the cliff of Salisbury Plain. On the weekly market day, stalls splayed out before its austere town hall, built of buff stone. In the distance lay the famous white chalk horse, tattooed on the green flank of a hill, with graceful spindle legs and bottleneck muzzle. Tourists assumed it to be the work of industrious Druids, but for centuries it had been re-scribed and altered by restoration until the Westbury White Horse likely bore little resemblance to the image the ancients had cut. It was as if mythmaking—a culture of shameless reinvention—manifested on the very landscape into which Elizabeth was born.

The Joneses were restless. When Elizabeth was still only a toddler, the family moved to Hawarden Castle, Prime Minister William Evart Gladstone's country estate in Wales, where Elizabeth's father had secured a berth.

As gamekeeper, Joseph was allowed a cottage to live rent-free on the estate grounds. Every eight or ten days, the Jones family received an allotment of large, craggy Coburg loaves fired in the estate's oven. Young Elizabeth's diet didn't stray far. Most days she ate stale bread: crusts, days old, pulped in boiled water so they softened and swelled into a rough, sticky porridge. Her father's position gave the Joneses privileges. They kept a garden just big enough to grow cabbages and onions, got an occasional egg and an even less frequent hen. The bird would be too old for laying but was ripe for neck-wringing, plucking, and boiling. Handfuls of flour bullied the cooking water into a thin and copious gravy, which, ladled over more crusts, yielded a gray, stringy dinner for Sundays. Elizabeth was obstinate in her hatred of it.

By the time Joseph found a new position at a country house in Ireland, to which the Joneses trekked across the sea, Elizabeth had found the will to escape. She learned to wander off in the evenings, at suppertime, to the cottages of Irish workers on the estate, for bowls of steaming potatoes they shared with her. (In the hierarchy of country houses, a gamekeeper had status; it wouldn't do to shoo away his child.)

Elizabeth loved potatoes, desired them boiled so the skins burst and the flesh cracked open and crumbled a little. Their texture was plush and floury, the flavor like clean, sweet dirt. The woman of the house, if she were kind, dribbled on some rich and slightly tangy milk (once, on some saint's feast day, Elizabeth even received some salt herring). These illicit potatoes had a vividness she did not find at home. One of her siblings would always have to find her and drag her back home.

The Joneses' condition was untenable (too many mouths to feed on too little), and Elizabeth was proud, willful, and in need of taming. When the girl turned nine, her aunt Clara (reasonably well off and childless) arrived from London to take her to live in the city. She and Elizabeth's uncle, who owned a shipping company, would give her advantages. And they would make her yield to a more structured and purposeful life than Elizabeth had known as a semisavage country girl.

London in 1870 was a city of putrid fogs, choked with the soot and burnt-iron reek of more than three million daily coal fires that made every outdoor surface feel oily. At her aunt Clara's table, Elizabeth faced meals of paucity—not from lack of money but as a systematic way to constrain the girl's spirit.

Her new guardians were Christian fanatics, followers of the British Holiness Movement, modeled on American evangelism. (In 1878, English acolytes would found the Salvation Army.) Elizabeth was forced to memorize Bible verses and other pious texts, renounce stubbornness, kneel before an invisible Jesus. The food they gave her imposed virtue through mandatory thrift: funky smelling vegetable consommés (actually yellowish water left from boiling cabbage), thin soups of barley and scrags of mutton, and endless plates of kedgeree, with all manner of rubbish scraps fried up with the rice and oily fish. Laced into obedience, under heavy gored skirts and itchy, high-necked blouses, she pondered escape.

In 1878, seventeen-year-old Elizabeth spied a chance to free herself. By accident, she'd met a woman visiting London from Toronto; they'd stayed in touch by letter, and before long, Elizabeth became tenacious in her desire to get to Canada. Eventually the captain of a steamship in her uncle's line agreed to give her secret passage to Montreal on a steamship that carried emigrants westward across the ocean before returning to Liverpool with a cargo of timber.

It was a six-week voyage. Elizabeth endured the cold, the pitching of the boat, and the meals of bread or hard biscuit, oatmeal, and tea that tasted of tin.

In Montreal, there was confusion, a rush for the terminal and the Toronto train: darkness and cold, the shouting of porters and screaming of children, masses of people packed together. Elizabeth waited on the freezing platform. There was no waiting room for those traveling emigrant class, and the train's cars were locked until just before leaving.

Toronto was a hive of new-brick houses, raw in sunrise. There was the smell of burning wood, not coal, and rutted streets as yet unpaved, choked with mud and carts. She arrived at the house of the lady she'd met in London, her deliverer. The woman offered Elizabeth a bedroom and told her she could stay as long as she cared to. Meals were copious. Elizabeth gorged on pork, corned beef, and potatoes; on buttered muffins, and cakes spread with cream and jam—luxuries previously unthinkable. Even the bread, made of flour milled from Alberta wheat, was astonishing. What other pleasures might this vast continent reveal?

At eighteen, Elizabeth landed her first position: as governess to the family of a military officer and his wife. They were about to embark on a long tour of the United States and needed someone to manage the children during the trip. For the next two years, then, Elizabeth would see the northern half of America, its states and territories, through the windows of trains that jagged westward. Her view of this startling new country would be from the narrow, plush chairs of day coaches, with one eye on the young ones in her charge, in a welter of soot and the grit of plowed-up prairie sifting in through the open ventilators.

:::

THE CITY ELIZABETH SAW from the deck of a steamer, as it heaved through the waters of the Willamette River in 1882, was green but hardly pastoral, a place where an imperative of progress cut as deep as mole plows through wetland prairie. Portland was not so much a city as a coalescence of wooden structures. Houses rose on dank ground, amid the stubble of tree stumps. The din of nails pounded into wood continued after nightfall, and everyone was feverishly converting into US greenbacks the boundless yields of timber and salmon, and harvests of orchard fruit and wheat from soils unsapped by intensive farming.

North Street downtown had well-set brick façades, under Gothic pinnacles and Italianate domes, but when the masonry ended Portland still felt like a settlement. With a population of 18,000, it was smaller than Salt Lake City or Poughkeepsie, but its numbers had more than doubled in the previous decade and would do so again in the subsequent one. Across the Willamette in East Portland, beyond the trestled streets crisscrossing sloughs and creeks, new clapboard houses stretched along grids planted with elm and sweet-gum saplings. Snow-flanked Mount Hood seemed to step back to make room for new arrivals hustling for work in logging camps or on scine-haulers, and those who scrambled for provisions before spreading out to claim their 160 cleared acres under the Homestead Law.

At the boardinghouse where the family settled in for a long stay, Elizabeth ate vegetables like none she had tasted, most bought from the Chinese truck farms on the west side, down behind the shanties in the bend of a creek. There were turnips so delicate and crisp Elizabeth ate them raw, like apples, savoring the feral sweetness and mustard bite—she had only ever known turnips as large watery things boiled into pulpy submission. There were fine red carrots and celery, white with a faint cast of green, blanched in black alluvial soil. She gorged on extravagantly musky late-summer strawberries so ripe, and with so much intrinsic sweetness, that all they needed to reach transcendence was a dribble of Guernsey cream, hauled across the Willamette from East Portland.

Then bad news arrived by letter: a death in the family of Elizabeth's employers. They would have to begin the return journey at once. Elizabeth, though she had little money and no friends, decided to remain in Portland—this wild, fertile place of energy and ambition.

She took small jobs to get by. She found a family, the Maxwells, who needed a governess for two young girls. A. L. Maxwell was high up in the Oregon Railroad and Navigation Company. He was big and buttery, with a Prince of Wales beard—a gentleman, in other words—and Mrs. Maxwell was kind. The Maxwells were closer than any family she'd known.

In 1885, thinking she might marry a man she'd known as a girl, twenty-four-year-old Elizabeth returned to London. After seeing him, however, all she wanted was to escape England again. She traveled back across the Atlantic, back to Portland and the Maxwells.

In 1886, Mrs. Maxwell told Elizabeth that a woman she knew, Lizzie H. Curtis, was looking for someone to help manage her stylish boardinghouses in San Francisco. The girls were old enough to board for their schooling; there was little for Elizabeth to do. Mrs. Maxwell thought it was a fine plan for her to live in San Francisco for a time and learn how to run an elegant house, especially since Mrs. Curtis wished someday to open one in Portland. Elizabeth would be perfectly situated then for the position when the time came.

In San Francisco, Mrs. Curtis's main house (twenty-four rooms, a mix of singles and bay-windowed alcove suites) was on Post Street near Polk. She operated a second, more select house on Sutter just east of Larkin: large private suites smartly furnished, with an attached stable for residents who kept private carriages. The quality of the cooking made her houses stand apart from the throng of competing residences. "Superior table," Mrs. Curtis stressed in advertisements placed in the *San Francisco Chronicle*. "Excellent board."

San Francisco's boosters called their city the Paris of the West. In 1886, it was the undisputed economic and cultural center of the Pacific Coast and an epicurean capital with a surplus of French chefs and Italian pastry cooks. Elizabeth oversaw a dining room where residents savored plates of roast veal tongue, the slices drenched in rich, mahogany-colored brown sauce. They were treated to chicken braised with ham and mushrooms, the cooking liquid reduced and enriched with cream; to chowders made with clams carted down from Bolinas Bay, and salads of local crab dressed with olive-oil mayonnaise rich in egg yolks. They gloried in terrapin stew and mock turtle soup braced with sherry or Madeira, and wiped their bowls with swabs torn from hot rolls. They paused to breathe in steam rising from brandy-laced soufflés rushed from the oven and took extra helpings of pound cake sliced to reveal a terrazzo pattern of candied citron and glacé fruits.

With notebook and a pencil at the ready, Elizabeth diligently kept track of menus and whatever recipes she managed to wheedle from the cooks.

:::

YEARS LATER, James would wish he'd listened more closely to his mother's stories of how she met Stella Chase Ainsworth. Perhaps at one of the San Francisco theaters she talked about: the Moorish Alcazar or majestic California; the ornate Baldwin or perpetually crowded Tivoli Opera House, with its fearsome lobby panorama of the Siege of Vicksburg.

Stella Ainsworth, twenty-four, made her acting debut at the California Theatre as Juliet. She had a high forehead and dark eyes, full lips, and a thin nose that ended abruptly in an uptwist. She'd grown up in a prominent Illinois family; her great-uncle was the late Supreme Court Chief Justice Salmon P. Chase. She moved west to Oakland to marry Edward Ainsworth, scion of a well-off family in the grocery business. Despite becoming Mrs. Ainsworth, Stella harbored dreams of the stage, of landing in the stock company of one of the big New York theatrical outfits, perhaps Augustin Daly's or Wallack's. After her honeymoon, she took acting lessons. *The Daily Alta California* theater critic's take on Stella's debut turn as Juliet was less than ecstatic. She pressed on anyway.

In May 1888, not long after she and Elizabeth would have met, Stella received some longed-for news. The impresario John Augustin Daly invited her to New York that September to audition for his stock company. Stella asked Elizabeth to travel with her. Stella planned to sail to Panama on the Pacific Mail steamship *Granada*; from there, she would take the train north across the isthmus to Aspinwall (now Colón) on the Caribbean and board a connecting steamer, the *Acapulco*. Once they reached New York, Elizabeth could return to California by rail. It would be the adventure of their lives.

Elizabeth first needed Mrs. Curtis's permission to be away from the boardinghouse for six weeks or longer. In the end, she didn't ask. Elizabeth just . . . left. On the night of July 10, 1888, she and Stella set off together from San Francisco on the *Granada*: a grand lark. And an illicit one, since Stella was abandoning her husband and Elizabeth was disappointing not only Mrs. Curtis but Mrs. Maxwell, her patron, who had vouched for her. As the *Granada* pushed off from the pier at First and Brannan Streets, Stella and Elizabeth—as if one woman—undid their ties to respectability.

In later life, James spoke guardedly to his closest confidantes about his mother's sexuality. He knew she was queer, although he and Elizabeth had never spoken frankly of it. But in stories of their adventures, Elizabeth flashed the fact of her love for Stella like a signal she knew James would be capable of decoding. His mother was of a generation that conceived of sex in ways different than his. For Victorians, queerness was not an inherence, a gift (or a curse) at birth, but a moment's acquiescence to passion: a surrender anyone was capable of. For Elizabeth, queer liaisons were the result of circumstance and weakness, falling prey to a moment's foible. James would come to know his mother's sexuality—her love for vibrant, beautiful Stella—as a thing of both joy and sustained regret.

The *Granada* lingered a few days at San Pedro in Los Angeles. Stella and Elizabeth disembarked at Mazatlán, Manzanillo, and Acapulco to look around. At Panama City, they left the ship for good.

She and Stella rode out to where the old Frenchman Ferdinand de Lesseps oversaw the canal that men were clawing from collapsing mud. Surely it would never be finished. Strangest and most spectacular of all were the fruits they ate: ferocious-skinned alligator pears with flesh as smooth and rich as custard, pineapples ripened on the stalk, and succulent golden mangoes, with a fragrance finer than that of the ripest peach.

For years, Elizabeth would tell stories of Panama and the Caribbean: the Bahamas, St. Thomas, Key West. James understood it as the one time of pure happiness in his mother's life. He would think of Elizabeth's voyage in almost mythical terms, his mother's journey to discover foods of a vividness and intensity previously unimagined. It was a lesson James absorbed, if only unconsciously: how to ascribe to food all the thoughts and feelings too dangerous for one to avow openly.

::::

FROM NEW YORK, Stella was to travel upstate to see family in Hammondsport, on the shore of Keuka Lake. She would spend the weeks before her audition for Augustin Daly with relatives. It was unthinkable that Elizabeth, a single woman with no money, status, or family connections, would meet Stella's family, so she rode the train west to Portland and back to Mrs. Maxwell. But Elizabeth was quickly off again, to Kansas City to look after Mrs. Maxwell's ailing sister. Elizabeth would soon be thirty. Her situation was as tenuous as it had ever been. She made up her mind to do what every woman was expected to do. She resolved to marry.

She returned to Portland and found a husband, a man named John Brennan who had a shop and a consoling income. He also had the early signs of tuberculosis—"consumption," as it was known. Elizabeth adopted a role she knew well, the woman of brisk purpose and maximum efficiency. Fourteen months after becoming Mrs. Brennan, Elizabeth was a widow.

Just as Elizabeth again began to ponder her future, word came that Lizzie Curtis was finally preparing to open a boardinghouse in Portland. Portland was now a stop on the transcontinental Northern Pacific Railway, and the new residents who streamed in needed accommodations. Mrs. Curtis had sold her boardinghouses in San Francisco and put everything up for auction: the mahogany dressers, horsehair mattresses, and ladies' desks. She prepared to start fresh in Portland.

Though Elizabeth had deserted her three years earlier, Mrs. Curtis hadn't forgotten what a sharp manager she was, how she dealt with the residents politely yet firmly, understood good food, and assumed all chambermaids and cooks were merely waiting for a mistress's back to turn before sneaking off to nap in vacant beds or loiter on back stairs. Elizabeth never took her eye off anyone. Mrs. Curtis wrote to Elizabeth to say all was forgiven and to please come work for her again.

The Portland Curtis, managed by Elizabeth Brennan, opened in 1892 at the corner of Twelfth and Morrison Streets, four blocks from the stupendously chateauesque new Portland Hotel, and even nearer to the Empire and Bungalow Theatres. It was a moderately fashionable district, close enough to downtown to appeal to business and professional men. In ads, Mrs. Curtis appealed to bachelors and "transients" (short-term guests) who appreciated the kind of superior table she had perfected in San Francisco.

Before long, Elizabeth began calculating how she could open her own hotel, a place like the Curtis only better, if only because she, Elizabeth, would own it.

Her old mentor A. L. Maxwell was now speculating in real estate. With his help, Elizabeth purchased a building: a four-story Queen Anne boardinghouse on Thirteenth between Morrison and Yamhill, just two blocks from the opulent seven-story Hill-Ton.

It was shabby and needed work. Mr. Maxwell found her an architect. Elizabeth resolved to call her house the Gladstone, both for the eighty-one-year-old scarred lion of British politics and to honor her father's stint as a gamekeeper on Mr. Gladstone's Welsh estate. Besides, the Englishness of the name gave it a certain feeling.

: : :

THE GLADSTONE OPENED IN 1896 with two dozen guest rooms, some occupied by boarders Elizabeth poached from the Curtis. The common areas had the rich and fashionable glimmer of Carpenter Gothic in polished redwood: manor-house paneling in the drawing room, dados studding the walls and chamfers softening hard-edged trims, wallpaper patterns dissolving into shadows beneath the high ceilings, and fantastical knobby braces anywhere an archway yawned. In the drawing room, there were parlor palms in blue-and-white Chinese jars and ferns cascading in the front windows: adornments that flattered young couples harboring ambitions for the Hill-Ton or the Portland; the midlevel office men, accountants and managers who aspired to respectability; widows compelled to give up their own houses, who complained about the most trifling things; and fastidious single women in middle age, living off inheritances.

The mistress of a good hotel learned to keep her boarders' secrets, acknowledged by necessity the vast range of human appetites, and became an actor in little face-saving dramas. Gladstone residents included a lady who drank and liked to have a small table under her place in the dining room on which to set her brandy flask. (Throughout luncheon and supper, she would lower her delicate china tea cup out of sight for discreet spiking.) There was the bookkeeper fond of meeting young men in Lownsdale Square Park on Sunday afternoons and bringing them home to entertain with sherry in his room, and the retired factory manager getting more and more addled, whom Elizabeth would assist back to his suite while explaining he was merely tired from reading.

Managing, keeping her gaze on all the things perpetually at risk of coming undone, was what Elizabeth did best: the new waitress pocketing the silver nutcrackers, or the market girl sending scarred and desiccated asparagus when Elizabeth had taken pains to set aside the fattest and juiciest ones. Elizabeth had made sure everything at Mrs. Curtis's hotels ran smoothly, and she was determined to make the Gladstone do the same.

The problem was, Portland was not San Francisco. In the Northwest, there was no immigrant brigade of French and Austrian and Italian chefs jostling for places in restaurants. In the sprawling West, there were no finer restaurants than San Francisco's. European cooks needed a level of ambition to travel to the Pacific Coast. The ones who stepped off in Portland rarely stayed. They'd move on to San Francisco for status and a stellar wage, or to Dawson City in the Yukon to become rich fueling the appetites of the Klondike Gold Rush. As a result, Mrs. Curtis's Portland kitchen was in constant flux. It was no different at the Gladstone, where good chefs scattered like silverfish in the glare of a switched-on cellar light.

Even for Portland's middle class, Chinese cooks and servants were essential to a smooth domestic life. The Maxwells had "Charlie" (whatever his birth name was, Mrs. Maxwell thought it distasteful). He arrived at dawn or earlier each morning, in the dark, and stoked the fire in the range and boiled and strained the coffee, set up the dining room for breakfast, scrambled the eggs and fried the ham, shouted to the vegetable man Lam when his cart rolled in from the western truck farms. Charlie did everything diligently and cheaply, the cooking and pantry drudgery and the washing up, all day, until Mrs. Maxwell had her cup of tea sent up at ten each night.

In 1890 and still in 1900, Portland had the second largest Chinese settlement in the United States, smaller only than San Francisco's. Before and after passage of the Chinese Exclusion Act in 1882, San Francisco and other West Coast cities saw white riots against the Chinese—Celestials, as they were known—and even bloody massacres. Until 1900, Portland was relatively hospitable to men from China, thanks to the political influence of elites like the Maxwells who depended on cheap Chinese labor.

Ships from Canton arrived often at the Portland docks, disgorging a trickle of men who slipped off, disappeared into the tenement buildings and gambling parlors along Second Avenue in Chinatown, and then surfaced to look for work. Elizabeth resolved to find a Chinese cook who did as well or better than the French drunks who stole from her and inevitably cut out.

With the Gladstone and the social blessings of the Maxwells, Elizabeth achieved a kind of respectability. She made the acquaintance of Clara Summers, a small, wrenlike woman with severely smoothed-back hair and wire spectacles. Her husband, General Owen Summers, was respected in business, politics, and the local militia. Clara had an air of privilege tempered with a blunt sense of humor bred on the Midwest prairie where she had been raised. Clara knew of a Chinese-born cook named Jue Let who might serve perfectly for the Gladstone.

Jue Let helped out in the kitchen of the Summers residence whenever Clara needed to throw a big party. A man of middle age, he cooked with skill and composure. Elizabeth took him on. He soaked up every recipe in her notebook.

Let hired an assistant cook, a man named Gin. Then came a pastry chef, Poy, whose hands and timing were so deft his puff pastry rose in the oven like a bellows slowly expanding to fill with air. Poy's sweet, buttery tartlet shells had the delicate texture of crisply molded sand, implausibly holding their shape.

Clara showed Let how to make a properly gelatinous terrapin stew. It called for sherry and the diamondbacks' livers and small intestine and eggs, if the cow turtle shipped to you happened to have any of the latter. (The reptiles had become fiercely expensive; by the mid-1890s, the wild ones, sent on the train from Savannah via New York, had been almost entirely fished out from the brackish marshes.) Terrapin meat simmered in stock until it relaxed to jelly, after which Clara made a liaison with chicken eggs and cream to thicken the poaching liquid. The addition of sherry both acidified and perfumed the rich sauce.

It was likely that Let already knew how to cook a turtle with rice whisky and medicinal roots and herbs, a traditional Cantonese tonic for health and longevity. Clara's tutorial was on how to cook terrapin so it would be acceptable to white families—a dish in the canon of American food—though the tradition of cooking turtles in Guangdong, where Let came from, was far older and more complex than that of the American South.

And so the legend at the Gladstone became that the adept Jue Let learned from the wife of General Summers her secret for perfect terrapin stew. The dish did not find definition in Let's skill so much as in Clara's pedigree, and her kind patience in communicating what she knew. In truth, the Gladstone's terrapin stew showed how Let, like other immigrant domestics in Portland, had learned to survive: by choosing not to challenge a narrative about his presumed ignorance.

: : :

By 1897, Elizabeth was attending services at Trinity Episcopal Church, a structure that appeared to be the work of Gothic forest gnomes: slender pointed arches and a spire-topped tower with a finial cross vaulting high above the canopy of red alders and bigleaf maples. Trinity's parishioners were some of Portland's oldest pioneers, those like Clara

Summers, who boasted of her family's journey along the Oregon Trail. Clara made it her mission to find a new husband for the widowed Mrs. Brennan.

Owen Summers was wiry and white-haired, with a mustache he displayed like an animal trophy, the ends waxed into tusklike points. As a young man in Illinois, Summers had fought with a Union cavalry regiment in the final months of the Civil War; later he fought the Sioux in Minnesota and the Dakotas. Eventually Summers settled in Portland, started a crockery business that made him rich, and scared up a volunteer militia that eventually would become the Oregon National Guard. As with most of Portland's elite, his politics were Republican. Because of that, and since Summers knew the import market (especially Chinese porcelain), President Chester Arthur appointed him United States appraiser for the port of Portland, where most West Coast–bound ships from China docked.

In 1893, the general appointed a thirty-four-year-old assistant, a man who seemed capable enough and loyal, though lacking the kind of ambition that might pose a threat. Likewise a Republican, John Andrew Beard had enough political savvy to have been elected mayor of Lebanon, a flour-mill town in Linn County eighty miles south of Portland, though he was born in Scio, a village of sheep ranchers.

Clara came to see her husband's assistant as a man assailed by tragedy, with a broken heart. In 1896, John lost his wife, Emma, and before that a daughter, Genevieve, though he had another who survived, thirteen-year-old Lucille. Clara sensed a perfect match: the solid, faithful John, so besieged by melancholy, and the lively widow Elizabeth. The charming Mrs. Brennan, fastidious in the running of her boardinghouse, and with a figure she showed off through fine corseting, would surely bring John happiness and comfort.

This seemed especially true since John always looked so rumpled and perspiring, with a stiff, too-small collar he wore in obvious agony. In theory, his mustache was as thick and commanding as General Summers's, but it was limp and untrimmed, as Clara noticed when she had him for tea (not long after he started at the Custom House). It was a mustache easily glazed with milky tea and readily clotted with crumbs from her best seed cake. And for the hour he endured Clara's company, with her ceaseless clucking about her pioneer ancestors and civic exertions, John had worn a serious and at times sour expression, as though it pained him to do anything else but think of his work. Clara knew he needed a woman's graces, just as she knew that Elizabeth would blossom under the rigorous attentions of a good man.

Elizabeth still wanted a child. She was thirty-six; time was weighing on her. Clara happened to mention that John's salary was $1,800, a plush yearly income—a figure that could give a couple some independence from one another. Perhaps Elizabeth could tolerate another husband after all.

:::

THE NEWSPAPER CALLED IT one of the prettiest weddings of the season, though that was part fawning, since there were notables from society and politics in attendance. At 9:30 on the morning of April 12, 1898, General Owen Summers, soon to leave with the Second Oregon Volunteer Infantry Regiment for the Philippines front in the Spanish-American War, walked Elizabeth down the aisle of Trinity Church to her waiting groom. Elizabeth's matrons of honor were Clara Summers and Mrs. W. T. Gardner, a prominent committeewoman for the Boys and Girls Aid Society. The bride wore not some joyful flowery ensemble but rather a plain traveling suit. After the service, the new Mr. and Mrs. John Beard retired from the church to the organ strains of Mendelssohn's "Wedding March." They honeymooned around Puget Sound and on a few islands in British Columbia and were back in Portland within two weeks. Elizabeth had far too much to do at home.

Even before the ceremony began, Elizabeth knew she was making a mistake.

John and Lucy Bird moved into the Gladstone. Their presence proved impossible for Elizabeth. The girl made petulant demands of the waitresses, things Elizabeth wouldn't tolerate from a paying boarder. It turned out that John had eight blood siblings and as many half-brothers and half-sisters. Nearly all of them showed up at the Gladstone, a crush of Sarahs, Williams, Elvas, Marthas, Charleses, and Freds. They came to make wedding calls and sample the hospitality of the new Mrs. Beard. Elizabeth thought they were boors and yokels and ate like farmhands.

Lucy Bird demanded a new wardrobe of fourteen dresses. When she didn't get her way, she "borrowed" a silk petticoat from Elizabeth's room. When she walked out into the street, it slipped from her waist and dropped around her ankles. The mortified girl stepped out of it and hurried away. A friend of Elizabeth's watched it happen. She retrieved the crumple of taffeta and returned it to the Gladstone. For Elizabeth, it was the final outrage. Less than a year after her wedding, and only three years after she opened it, Elizabeth put the Gladstone up for sale.

Besides Elizabeth's frustrations with her new husband, by 1899 the Gladstone's neighborhood had become more competitive than ever for boardinghouses. Mrs. Curtis became fierce competition after she and a partner leased the Hill-Ton and renamed it the Hobart-Curtis. The handsome Romanesque highrise boasted an elevator and a wide front lawn, a chandeliered dining room looking onto the trees and mansion turrets of Vista Ridge, and Mrs. Curtis's signature fine board. Next to all that, the Gladstone seemed old-fashioned and small.

Elizabeth found buyers for the Gladstone: Mrs. Cornell and Miss Murphy. Perfectly pleasant ladies, Elizabeth noted with satisfaction, though completely in over their heads. Jue Let quit. He told Elizabeth he'd work for her again anytime she might need him, though because he refused to tell her exactly where he lived, she would have to leave word for him in Chinatown.

John, Elizabeth, and Lucy Bird took an apartment on Main Street near Fifth, not far from John's office. It was close, too, to Chapman Square, a park reserved for women and children, next to men-only Lownsdale Park. (The gender segregation, intended to ensure propriety between the sexes in a frontier town, dated to the 1850s, when the parks opened.) Suddenly with no occupation, save the unpleasant one of raising Lucille, Elizabeth was lost. That fall, she walked in the square with her umbrella, dodging rain, nodding to women, and watching the park's exclusively female gingko trees turn spectacularly golden. She pondered what might come next.

"I'm going to build a house," Elizabeth announced to John one evening. "You may live in it, but we're independent." She would repair her mistake in becoming Mrs. Beard by carving out a life for herself within the confines of her marriage.

Meanwhile, Portland's eastward sprawl was expanding. The city had annexed the town east of the Willamette River in 1891, and the Morrison Bridge had been free of tolls since 1895. There was money to be made in buying and reselling land across the river. With Mr. Maxwell (now a real estate speculator) to guide them, and with the profit from unloading the Gladstone, Elizabeth began to buy up empty lots, ten acres in all. She bought on the east side near Belmont Park; north, where the Columbia merged with the Willamette, in St. Johns; and far out in the southeast suburbs beyond Mount Tabor.

In the spring of 1900, Elizabeth began to sell. John's younger brother Fred bought some of Elizabeth's lots, and with John as his partner, he built rental cottages.

But there were four small adjacent lots in Hawthorne Park that Elizabeth didn't sell. They were on East Salmon Street at the corner of Twenty-Second, behind a row of curbside saplings. They faced south along a gentle rise, with plenty of air and light. Elizabeth must have pictured the house she would build here, the garden she could plant and manage with the efficiency and bravado she'd exercised at the Gladstone. She could hire Let to be the family cook. She could host ladies'-committee teas and invite Clara and Mrs. Gardner—with the proper arrangements, even Stella might visit and sit in the shade of the arbor Elizabeth imagined she'd build and nurture. It would be a proper house for raising a child.

And so, on May 5, 1903, Elizabeth's red, round, thirteen-pound baby wailed his first cries in her room in the comfortable and rangy, shake-covered bungalow she built on Salmon Street, with a separate bedroom for John.

CHAPTER 3

JUE LET'S TRUE ESSENCE
OF CHICKEN

1911–1919

JAMES'S EIGHTH BIRTHDAY PARTY was planned for Oaks Park in Sellwood, on the eastern bank of the Willamette. Portlanders called the six-year-old amusement park the Coney Island of the Northwest. In summer, the interurban trolley unloaded throngs of children, long-suffering mothers, and amorous couples. They might take in the diorama of Chilkoot Pass, the fearsome Golden Stairs leading straight up and over to the Klondike goldfields, ride the Whirlwind, or splash around in the natatorium.

On a Saturday morning in early May, the trolley carried James, Elizabeth, and about twenty of his classmates from Hawthorne School. They lugged a picnic in Elizabeth's enormous wicker basket. Actually, it was a two-part picnic—lunch and afternoon snack—which Elizabeth supervised and Let cooked and assembled. It included James's monumental birthday cake, set in its own hamper. Elizabeth entrusted it to a couple of strong-limbed boys to ease it into the trolley car and protect it with their lives.

James told Let he wanted a White Mountain cake (also known as a Colorado), with beaten egg whites for softness and lightness and the palest, fluffiest crumb. It was spectacular: four stacked layers diminishing in diameter at the crown, heaped with white frosting like the snow cloaking Mount Hood and dredged in coconut, James's obsession. And because the boy adored flowers of all kinds, Let raided Elizabeth's hawthorn tree, just then exploding gloriously into blossom. He clustered the sprays around James's cake, masses of white flowers with greenish-yellow centers and an exuberance of black-tipped pistils.

Other children wanted birthday cakes bristling with candles. Mrs. Pamelia Benson, mother of James's friend Chester, made famously gaudy cakes with multicolored layers: one year green, yellow, and blue, the next year pink and white, smelling of strawberry juice and rose extract. The finished cakes were thick with swirls and swags of icing, shimmery and sweet from dustings of crushed rainbow candies.

By contrast, James's cake was one any bride would have cherished, the envy of the Hawthorne School girls. Though boys like Lester, Morris, and Virgil Coomer, James's next-door neighbors on Salmon Street, might laugh at his extravagantly pristine and floral cake (free of candles, since James thought they spoiled the effect), James was not embarrassed.

Where the Coomers roughhoused and went trolling in streams for sucker fish, hideous monsters with loose, fleshy mouths, James preferred to read or knit, a skill he was learning. Elizabeth cultivated in her boy an exquisite sense of preference, fearlessness in expressing himself, sensitivity to taste, and an unabashed regard for his own opinions.

Elizabeth had wanted a child; she was raising a physically immature adult. Elizabeth and John both separately read Dickens to James, starting when he was a toddler. The stories described human folly and the vicissitudes of fate, randomly elevating or indiscriminately cruel. Elizabeth taught James not to bother with childish things but to be more like a friend, someone to sit with her in the dressing room during corset fittings and say which style best showed off her figure. Above all, Elizabeth raised him to be her ally in ongoing fights with John and Lucille (still living in the Salmon Street house), with Let, and against strictures of all kinds.

Elizabeth didn't banish the boy from rooms where adult conversations occurred, talk that might have proved racy even for most grown-ups in Hawthorne Park. James heard sexual transgressions alluded to: insatiability, infidelity, inversion. Elizabeth had several friends and acquaintances who led unconventional lives.

She sometimes took James along to meet friends in "fast" places such as Theodore Kruse's Louvre and James Falt's Quelle Café on Sixth at Stark. Elizabeth knew Mrs. Falt quite well. She had a house of her own up the Columbia. Elizabeth visited there frequently, sometimes taking James. The Quelle was famous for crawfish, crab, and oysters, both Eastern and Olympia. Its private dining rooms were notorious for alleged debauchery. And though James Falt was said to pay off the police, vice men occasionally hauled him in front of a judge on charges of immorality, or of thwarting the Sunday liquor ban by serving gin in teapots—Falt's "special blend"—an off-menu house special.

James grew up as an accessory to Elizabeth: her plump Little Lord Fauntleroy with a petulant face who'd say what he thought of the oysters and make everyone howl. Once he met a woman Elizabeth often gossiped about, passing along rumors of how she'd cheated on her husband. "I suppose you've been keeping busy," James said to the lady, as gasps and barely suppressed chuckles rippled through the room. Elizabeth made a show of scolding him for his cheek, though James suspected she was secretly delighted. He was that most charming of small guests for afternoon tea: an innocent corrupted.

Most children avoided James. He had a temper and a nasty tongue; he criticized their rooms, clothes, and toys. When Elizabeth took James along to call on a friend, the woman's children might be absent, with vague or flimsy excuses given in explanation. James would be left to sit at the edge of a roomful of grownups, handed plates of sandwiches and sweets to keep him occupied. He'd have nothing to do but think about what he was eating, as when a regal friend of Elizabeth's who once lived in Vienna gave him tea with a float of schlag. She'd folded crushed praline into the whipped cream. It stuck in his imagination.

: : :

JAMES DID HAVE FRIENDS, mostly girls. Esther Kelly, who was older than James, lived in the house opposite and called him Baby Beard. The Kan girls, Grace and Miriam, lived in the nearby Mount Tabor neighborhood. As a young man, their father, Andrew Kan, had emigrated from Fujian Province in China, before the Exclusion Act. He weathered racism and the obstacles it enshrined in the law to become well known as an importer of goods from China and Japan: embroidered silks, Peking furs, fireworks, dishes, curios. He had shops and a warehouse downtown, also a large hopyard and truck garden south of the city. Kan's friendship with the customs appraiser John Beard was a strategic one. He urged his wife, Minnie, to send Grace and Miriam to Salmon Street often to play with James. The children spent hours together in the backyard playhouse.

Elizabeth liked having the Kan girls around. She instructed James's Chinese nanny—his amah, Thema—to dress him like a Qing Dynasty princeling. The boy's fine, sandy hair was done up in Buster Brown style—a pudding-basin cut, heavy bangs sitting low and straight across his forehead. Thema dressed him in Chinese suits of silk pongee, little embroidered coats that buttoned on the side and had frog closures at the shoulder. In summer, his suits were of Japanese loose-weave cotton, cool though scratchy; in other seasons, he wore Chinese linen with short pants in blue or white.

For breakfast, Let served him fruit and tea in the Cantonese manner, congee (rice porridge) if it was chilly, and sometimes Guangdong steamed salt fish or one of Elizabeth's English kippers. James had his own collection of ivory chopsticks that fit his small hands, gifts from his merchant Chinese godfather (another strategic affiliation), a counterpart to General Summers, the boy's white godfather.

Elizabeth had begun collecting pretty things from Andrew Kan's cluttered so-called Japanese Bazaar on Morrison Street. Hatred of the Chinese exploded in Portland after 1900, so labeling the shop Japanese was certainly an act of self-preservation for Kan. It had a mezzanine and a large American flag tacked high on the back wall, as if to assure Portlanders that Kan was a loyal, patriotic neighbor. Elizabeth displayed the treasures she bought at the Japanese Bazaar in her Salmon Street parlor: courtesans painted on silk, fans revealing floating landscapes when opened, mirror frames with imperial scrollwork in carton-pierre, screens of delicate rosewood tracery, and Canton jugs emblazoned with blue pagodas. All of it provided proof of a distant world where beauty and strangeness mingled, far from Portland's glooms, its drab minds and dripping streets.

Stella always wrote to Elizabeth from far-flung places where she ventured: Honolulu and the South Sea Islands in 1908, and seasons in Europe almost too numerous to count. Elizabeth, in turn, would have shared with Stella descriptions of her latest acquisitions from Kan's.

James wished he'd been born a Chinese American boy. He adored Thema and Let; likewise Billy, Let's friend and the chef of House's Restaurant downtown. Billy was famous for his coleslaw, lavished with cream and dotted with tiny salty shrimp or flakes of crab. It had the majesty of the ocean James knew stretched from Gearhart Beach all the way to the shores of China. It matched the cool serenity of the Kan residence in Mount Tabor, where James sometimes went to see Grace and Miriam, and for a time their cousin John Kan, staying with them in Portland while his parents, Christian missionaries, were off converting Chinese souls in country towns beyond Mount Hood.

James loved listening to the eldest of the Kan children, Andrew Junior, practice at the piano in the lace-curtained parlor. It gave James a feeling of beauty, in the same way Mr. Kan—elegant, ebony-haired, and slender—was beautiful. There was no other word to describe him.

The entire Kan family was cultured and kind. It was obvious they cared for one another with a warmth the Beards were unable, or unwilling, to beget. Nor did Elizabeth and John, with their separate interests, and friends who rarely mingled, spend much time with James as a family. But the Kans, and their house of music and children and delicious smells from the kitchen: how James yearned to belong.

There was one Salmon Street memory James would forever keep close. He was three and sick with malaria. Portland was in the midst of a summer heat wave, and the old swamp districts on the east side were incubators for the disease. James's limbs ached, and he had shivering fits. He despised the taste of stomach bitters his amah dissolved in water to make him drink; his tongue felt so thick he didn't have the will to swallow. One afternoon, the primrose-dotted curtains in his room were drawn to keep it cool, and a fly buzzed at the open window. He could hear the Coomer boys thwacking a can with sticks and whooping, and Mrs. Coomer stomping out to the yard to shush them.

And then Let appeared at the door, holding something and entering without words. In the darkened room, James caught the white flash of his long changshan, heard it rustle around his legs in motion. The bed slumped as Let sat beside him. James noticed his bare, work-scarred forearms and saw that he was bearing a saucer, with a spoon and a small crock of something the color of weak tea, though it didn't move like liquid. Gently, Let cradled James's head to raise it, dipped the spoon in the crock, and brought it to the edge of the boy's lips. He allowed Let to place it in his mouth: its coolness against his inner lip gave instant comfort. It was jelly, salty instead of sweet, and with the flavor of roast chicken and giblet gravy. It clung to the roof of James's mouth and tickled it. When he flexed his tongue—pressed the jelly to his bony palate— it became slippery, easy to swallow. It cooled his throat, and conjured the richness of the world beyond his primrose curtains.

Patiently, spoonful by spoonful, Let fed James until the crock was empty—the first act of tenderness James would remember, and the one that would stay with him for the rest of his life. He studied Let's face, still close on the bed: the deep lines framing his mouth, pursed in a half-smile above the exuberant patch of whiskers sprouting from his bottom lip; his high forehead and soft, dark eyes. Of all the fine and elaborate things James would recall eating at his mother's table—the oyster patties and roast beef, Parker House rolls and braised ducks— Let's subliming of chicken to become rich golden jelly was somehow the purest and yet most complicated.

Let returned every afternoon for nearly two weeks with his crock, spooning cold elixir into James's mouth like a father robin tending a nestling, until he was again able to feed himself, submit to being dressed, and return to the whirl of his mother's dominion.

: : :

JOHN SPENT LONG DAYS away from Salmon Street, at work behind the heavy iron gate of the appraiser's storeroom in the Custom House. It was a ponderous heap of masonry, with bars at the windows and a brooding courtyard. Within its fortresslike walls, he pored over the contents of sample crates from ships loaded with cargo from Chinese and Japanese ports, anchored at the Willamette docks.

As assistant appraiser for the District of Portland, John assessed the value of Asian imports for the US Treasury Department to assign a duty, payable before a cargo was released to its owner. He was diligent. He passed his days squinting through a magnifying glass at the bottoms of lotus bowls and teacups, decoding brushstrokes and factory marks. He trained an electric light onto brass figures of sages, goddesses, and beasts of the zodiac to gauge the percentage of copper in their alloys. He sifted through medicinal herbs in search of smuggled contraband, unraveled silk to assess the grade of its floss, and counted fibers in cotton embroidery and sakiori weavings—some of the very objects Elizabeth would later buy at Andrew Kan's shop, or receive as gifts at banquets hosted by the merchants and brokers whose cargoes John appraised.

While she treasured her pictures and knickknacks for the distant places they opened in her imagination, John regarded them as subjects for material analysis, free of prejudice, emotion, or fancy. James found himself fixed between both.

At home, John hid his own desires, his delights and passions. To James, he was a man of invisible currents. Besides Elizabeth's bitter complaints about her husband—his crudeness, his coveting of what she thought of as *her* money—what James knew of his father was the self-portrait John displayed to the world. He painted himself as a man of essential American character and pioneer roots; a person of ruggedness and self-reliance, conversant with things of the wild. At the Custom House, he was a bureaucrat whose position depended on political alliances within the local Republican Party—a civil servant, not a federal appointee like his patron, boss, and protector, Owen Summers.

His protection couldn't last forever. After Summers died in 1911, John was vulnerable, his position tenuous. Oregon's congressional delegation in Washington didn't put forth John's name for the job of chief appraiser. In the year and a half it took President William Taft to appoint a new man, as he mulled whether to kill the federal position altogether (Portland's ship traffic had dwindled, compared to newly booming ports like Tampa and Detroit), John worked harder than ever to prove his value. He kept an even greater distance from Elizabeth.

James knew his father mostly as a noisy shadow: the sound of drawers opening and closing in the small back bedroom as John dressed for work, the pop of an errant cuff link hitting the floor, the clank of the iron skillet against the range early in the morning, and the rich, slightly scorched, flour-and-bacon aroma of his Sunday-breakfast fried chicken.

On chicken mornings, John rose early. He added wood to the live embers in the range's firebox, carried a muslin-wrapped side of smoked bacon from the pantry and skived off several pieces. These he sliced in thin strips, which he then tried out in a deep skillet set on the range's relatively cool zone. As pieces of bacon crisped, he removed them to a plate; into the hot grease he slipped (gingerly, to keep the grease from splashing) the chicken (sometimes two), hacked into ten pieces and floured. He covered the pan and moved it to a cool edge of the range to simmer, then lifted the lid and moved the pan to the hot zone so the skin would crisp.

Once he removed the chicken and poured off most of the grease, he made cream gravy in the skillet: a heaping spoon of flour stirred up with the recalcitrant leavings and diluted with butterfat-rich milk, then simmered, salted, and peppered. Meanwhile, Let would have made biscuits for sopping up the gravy.

It was all too rustic for Elizabeth's tastes. It annoyed her that John never closed the kitchen door when he cooked, and thus allowed insinuating odors of bacon and frying to seep into the parlor and taint her pretty things. What stood out for James was his father's precision in what was essentially an intuitive process, grounded in weekly practice. John cooked in Elizabeth's kitchen with a vengeance and seasoned ferociously with black pepper—acts of subversion the boy would not forget.

::::

JOHN WAS BORN IN 1861 in Iowa, a midway point along the family's arc of migration. His father, Andrew Francis Beard, was a stable keeper from Kentucky (originally the Carolinas), pappy to sixteen children, all told, conceived with two wives. John was five when Andrew once again uprooted his clan to seek material uplift on the Pacific Coast. They traveled west in wagons along the Oregon Trail, which had begun to peter out ever since the route across Panama opened a decade earlier. When the first locomotives rolled along the Transcontinental Railroad, in 1869, the wagon route to the Northwest was little more than a deeply rutted ghost track. In time, John's journey westward took on the shape of legend—the covered wagon that jolted him across Kansas, the shoot-outs with natives on the Plains—pioneer credentials that gave him status in Portland, a place steeped in a founding myth of Lewis and Clark and the intrepid white settler.

By 1880, the Beard clan had settled sixty-five miles south of Portland, in a farm and ranching village in Linn County named Scio, a flat place cut through with roads, all leading somewhere else. The town had a white clapboard church and a pharmacy where nineteen-year-old John became a druggist's apprentice. He washed bottles and learned to compound simple medicines, a grounding in rudimentary laboratory methods that trained him for work as an assessor.

In 1881, twenty-year-old John married Emma Clifford Biggers. In 1884, they had a girl, Lucille Bird (James's half-sister). Two years later, Emma gave birth to another girl, Genevieve, but at the age of four, only months after John and Emma moved their young family to Portland, the small, sickly child went up to heaven to live with the angels. In August 1896, Emma died of consumption. By Christmas, when Trinity Church choir gave its annual carol recital and General Summers, wearing the Santa Claus suit he donned every year, showered gifts and candy on the children of political allies, Clara Summers had already begun to scheme.

Before the new year was old, Clara convinced the still-mourning John that Mrs. Brennan, handsome mistress of the Gladstone boardinghouse and likewise bereaved, would not look askance at Mr. Beard's request for her hand in marriage.

John had loved Emma. The grief of losing both a wife and a daughter within the same year had made him vulnerable. When it came to the movements of his heart, John's skills of analysis, so keen in his work at the Custom House, deserted him.

After marrying Elizabeth and moving into the Gladstone with Lucy Bird, John's brothers and sisters paid their wedding calls to congratulate him on crossing a new threshold, witness the start of his reinvigorated life, and help lay Emma and Genevieve to rest at last. The new Mrs. Beard was having none of it.

Elizabeth rudely implied they'd all only showed up at the Gladstone to take advantage of her: use up the hot water, devour all the rolls and butter, and pocket the silver. She seemed to take particular delight in turning them out in the most public way possible, in front of the Gladstone's residents. Far from finding peace, the ghosts of John's departed wife and daughter were doomed to go on haunting him.

He found comfort in work and its social demands. He went on men's retreats with bureaucrat colleagues to St. Martin's Springs on the Washington side of the Columbia, for mud baths and bonding over whiskey, firing buckshot at deer in the woods, and long, improbable tales about sex. He joined a fraternal lodge and mutual benefit society, Multnomah Camp No. 77, Woodmen of the World. He anchored himself to the bedrock of its mystical pioneer values and un-churchy Christian philosophy and cut loose at its hee-haw gatherings and secret initiations around the bonfire—excuses to drink and cuss with other men.

In time, he'd become an officer of the organization. And though it was a motto the Woodmen reserved for the rusticated gravestones of felled brothers, "*Dum Tacet Clamet*" (in jokey jackass Latin, "Though silent, he speaks") seemed especially fitting for John. Even though he was a scant and mostly silent presence at Salmon Street, the awkward fact of his existence echoed through the house like a roar.

Elizabeth and James cleared out of Salmon Street when John threw his annual holiday whirl for local Treasury Department men and other useful Republicans. There were Tom and Jerrys for John's braying, shoulder-slapping guests: a dollop of egg-butter-sugar batter, with cinnamon and allspice, diluted with hot water and whiskey. All was vigorously stirred in the glass with fingers, a spoon, or, for the critically drunk, a cigar, until the sticky liquid overflowed onto shirt cuffs and dripped onto Elizabeth's Peking carpet: a mess, it's true. Yet it was the only time in the year when the house ever thumped with crowds or was unself-consciously alive to joy.

:::

ELIZABETH STAGED RETREATS of her own. Twice in 1915, during San Francisco's Panama-Pacific International Exposition, she sailed south with James from the Astoria pier. Other years, they traveled by rail—Southern Pacific's Shasta Limited—to spend a week or more in the city James came to think of as his dream place.

They stayed at the Palace Hotel or the St. Francis. They dined in the winter-garden opulence of the Palace's Garden Court, James in a double-breasted suit and the overly meticulous grooming of a boy eager to look smart in the glamorous city he'd heard his mother describe with longing and nostalgia. They shopped and went to the opera, took in plays. Above all, they ate: Marquard's for the luncheon and hors d'oeuvre buffets; Tait's at the Beach for its dark-paneled rooms, high-walled Japanese garden, and theatrical clientele; Jack's for abalone and calf's-head vinaigrette; Solari's and the Fly Trap for veal chops and sand dabs.

Stella Ainsworth was still on the stage in New York. She traveled every year to California to visit her sister, married to a judge in the farming town of Woodland, northwest of Sacramento. James knew she was a great friend of his mother from the constancy of their letters, but mostly from Elizabeth's stories, things he'd heard dozens of times about their travel together in Los Angeles and Panama, New York City, and of course in San Francisco.

On one of James and his mother's trips to the city, strolling in Golden Gate Park with no particular destination, Elizabeth spotted a woman and a man on horseback. James noted the woman's beautifully tailored black satin suit, and especially her pretty shoes. "What a surprise!" Elizabeth said to James. "This is Stella, my actress friend that I am always telling you about."

After Stella and the man rode off, something in the way Elizabeth acted made the boy think that perhaps this surprise meeting wasn't entirely by accident.

:::

THE BEARD HOUSE on Salmon Street looked cheerful enough from the sidewalk. It stood two stories tall, under a low-pitched roof with dormers, six steps up from a barren street garden. The porch had plain stick balusters and windows with unfussy trim. The front door, flanked by a fern in a basket and a rope-hung swing with a settee of white canvas, displayed a homey flash of curtain through its central pane. A stranger walking past might think a conventionally happy family lived here, maybe even a boring one. It wasn't so.

Loneliness hovered in the high ceilings of the kitchen, where, on most nights, James ate by himself. He was free to study in solitude the cream wallpaper with red polka dots, the immense black wood-burning stove that also heated the room. Of course Elizabeth kept everything well ordered: cuts and joints set away in the meat safe or hung in the basement (along with the stove wood and baskets of onions and potatoes) to age and ripen; jars of pickled lambs' tongues, white asparagus, and Seville orange marmalade on pantry shelves, above the tin baby's bathtub used for poaching whole salmon too long to fit the regular boiler. There were stacks of dishes—Chinese Peach Blossom and Blue Willow—as if the house might be expecting a horde of guests to descend. But there was never company for dinner. Even James and his parents seldom ate together.

The Beards occupied the kitchen in shifts. John had early mornings when Elizabeth was out, dressed in a fedora and divided skirt on her bicycle for exercise. John cooked breakfasts of bacon or fried ham with eggs for James, Lucy Bird, and her husband, Clarence Ruff. He sent trays up to their rooms. The young woman who helped out—paid help to succeed Let, who had disappeared in 1913, at the peak of Portland's anti-Chinese fervor—delivered them.

After John departed for the office, Elizabeth took possession. She had her baking day, her annual weeklong mincemeat and fruitcake offensives. She fussed, preserved what needed putting up, checked her stores, and marketed or dealt with the tradesmen who rang at the back door. She made lunch for a close friend or two and served it in the kitchen, something simple and often cold: Billy's coleslaw or pickled salmon and toast, maybe chilled stewed tomatoes and a poached egg, followed by scones or macaroons and pots of tea. The Ruffs ate their dinner apart from the Beards. Some nights, John did not even get home until late, after everyone was asleep.

A spirit of paucity ruled the Salmon Street kitchen, yet an almost absurd abundance surrounded it. The backyard was a tangle of perfumed and edible things in a perpetual state of flower and fall. In February, wild sour grass, aka clover-leafed oxalis, clustered at the fence line. In spring, the lilac that leaned against the screened back porch made the kitchen ache with fragrance. For two weeks in June, the magnificent quince was a lacy mass of pinkish blossoms. When the pomes came in, fuzzy, whorled, and deeply perfumed, Elizabeth piled them—as many as eighty!—in bowls at the center of the big oak kitchen table.

Later in spring, branches on the Lambert tree bobbed with clusters of blackish cherries, the Royal Ann with yellow-pink ones. A May Duke tree and a Montmorency yielded sour cherries for pies. There was yet another cherry tree, whose name James always forgot, that produced fruit with pits that practically slid from the flesh. Who would eat them all?

Three large Gravenstein apple trees spread their branches at the foot of the garden. By midsummer, they were heavy with fruit in vivid stripes of orange and parakeet yellow, fragile and crisp by late summer's peak. In fall, when the apples turned mealy, Elizabeth cooked them to a jelly in a pinkish shade of amber. Sometimes she spooned it into a mold to set and then turned it out onto a cut-glass dish and placed it on the kitchen table, where it shimmered in the light of the overhead lamp. Alone, James helped himself to great spoonfuls of it, and doused the mound with cream. Eating without the distractions of company had its consolations.

After October's rains, Elizabeth would wade through tall weeds in Hawthorne Park's empty lots—ghostly white with field mushrooms at dawn—toting an empty ten-pound lard pail and bring it back full.

For weeks in autumn, the basement was a gallery of dead birds—gifts from friends and John's colleagues who hunted, which was all of them—hung to dry and ripen the meat. Pheasant, geese, quail, and ducks (teal, mallards, canvasbacks); also venison—Elizabeth had learned from her father how long to hang each one. As a young boy, James had learned from Let how to pluck and singe the birds; how to draw entrails and excise bitter gall sacks. He knew the peculiar tangy odors of game as it aged, the trill of richness and rot that time produced.

There were only five people living on Salmon Street, all working out daily routines for avoiding one another. It didn't stop Elizabeth from provisioning as though she were the mistress of a great house—still presiding over the Gladstone—directing a fantasy in which food was the center of a shared life.

: : :

"LOOK AT THIS, WAITER," James said furiously. "*Look at this!* What is it, what is it—in my glass?"

"It's only a fly, sir," replied the waiter, in the best Cockney accent a sixteen-year-old Portland boy with a penciled-on mustache could manage. "It'll do you no 'arm: It's quite dead. Shall I take it out for you?" The boy shoved his thumb and forefinger into the glass, displacing water. James sputtered with outrage.

"Take your fingers out of that glass, at once, at once, at once!" James bellowed. He rose from his chair. He lifted his foot to stamp in protest, but as his shoe came down against the stage, it crushed his bowler hat.

James was on the stage at Washington High, in a student vaudeville show to raise money for decorating school floats in the Rose Festival Parade, just weeks away. He was playing the role of Mr. Jabstick, a rich, fat old gentleman lunching with his daughter (played by the popular

Billie Fenimore) at a Soho café, in a one-act Scotland Yard slapstick, *The Crimson Cocoanut*, by English writer Ian Hay Beith. Sixteen-year-old James (class of January 1920) wore smears of red greasepaint on his cheeks and chalk dust in his hair and eyebrows. He'd swiped a stiff shirt collar and silk tie from John's dresser; another student had borrowed her father's boxy double-breasted suit coat for James's costume. As a corpulent old prig, James was a natural—he didn't even need to pad his suit. The audience (students, teachers, and parents) adored him.

"Confound and dash it!" James roared. Laughter surged through the auditorium—James could feel it as much as hear it. It sent an arc flickering up his spine, as though something in him had been switched on—electrified. He didn't want to go dark again.

"James Beard nearly rivaled Miss Fenimore in his general popularity and extent of the undertakings," read an item in the paper next day. "He was easily the star of the young men. He played the heavy part." (Few could ever resist making jokes about James's size; even then, he was remarkably large.)

The students raised $250 for floats: a triumph, and for James an overdue premiere. Washington High was a four-story Romanesque fantasy at Southeast Fourteenth and Stark, faced in ponderous gray stone, with dark halls and four flights of pitched stairs. Its classroom wings flanked a central steep-roofed campanile that glowered and seemed to hint at future doom. James's first two years of high school had been trying.

When President Woodrow Wilson led the United States into the Great War in April 1917, a rush of enlistments followed. Junior and senior boys disappeared from school—Washington's class of January 1919, the one above James, was nicknamed "the war class." Then, in the summer of 1918, news seeped into Portland's dailies of a deadly influenza outbreak in Boston. In September, the so-called Spanish flu broke out at Camp Lewis, Washington, thirty miles north of Portland, following a troop transport from New England. And in October, Portland's City Health Officer asked theater owners to eject anyone who coughed or sneezed. Panic gripped the Rose City. The Civic Auditorium became a hospice ward for terminal cases. People avoided streetcars, pool halls, bowling alleys, lodge meetings, and parades. When Mayor George L.

Baker ordered the schools closed, all extracurricular activities ceased too. There were no football or basketball games (the fit boys had all enlisted anyway), no dances or assemblies. Student plays were canceled. James was no stranger to loneliness at home. War and a global pandemic made him feel it everywhere.

Schools reopened in December 1918. Days later, Washington High's five English classes performed its long-delayed musical, a fundraiser for new library books. It was a comedy, a classical burlesque titled *The Olympiadical Operatic Myth*, with students portraying ancient Roman deities in singing tableaus. James wasn't in the cast, but he reviewed the show for *The Lens*, the school journal. "How everybody laughed at Jupiter with his deep and sonorous voice," he wrote, "perched on his mountain top (we were afraid it would fall down). . . . The flying Mercury was beautiful in symmetry, his black, gold, and apple green blending harmoniously with the surrounding." The boy had an eye for beauty, a feel for aesthetics. And Elizabeth had taught him long ago to voice his opinions boldly, with a performer's flair.

As the school year began, James was elected to student government— sergeant-at-arms, tasked with keeping order at meetings—or, as *The Lens* put it, poking fun at his size, "the 'most' sergeant-at-arms." He joined the Hi-Y Club, a student service group for boys. At the new-member meeting, they initiated him as Jimmie Beard, played the palm-stinging slap game "hot hands," and snacked on cheese and cider. The new fellows gave short speeches about themselves and Jimmie, of course, knew how to make everybody laugh.

Performance allowed James to become Jimmie, the boy who was funny, likable, social, and fully alive—strong enough to push off from the sadness yawning at home. Normally his body was an object of casual ridicule, but Jimmie the performer embraced his size, his height, his chins, and his softness around the middle. He made them into the things everyone loved about him; his body was the source of his power to command attention, and if there was anything James craved, it was attention.

Acting would be James's life. It was the only thing that created a reason for his differentness, his dispensation for being something other than typical Washington High boys, who hutted footballs in some muddy, rain-washed field or stood around stiffly and stupidly with girls who were James's closest confidantes.

For his class's salute in *The Lens*, each graduating student officer got to write a motto next to their portrait. "Actors," James wrote for his, "are born in the best of regulated families." It was a quote he misremembered from a small book of Elizabeth's, something she'd picked up on one of her trips to San Francisco: *The Entirely New Cynic's Calendar of Revised Wisdom for 1905*. It was a rather daring book, full of adult bons mots in the style of the late Oscar Wilde.

"Knowledge is power, if you know it about the right person."

"You may lead an ass to knowledge—but you cannot make him think."

And one James found dangerous: "Tell the truth and shame the—family." (A twist on "Tell the truth and shame the devil.")

James altered one of the sayings to describe himself. "Actresses will happen in the best regulated families," went the original, a witty twist on a line of Wilkins Micawber's from *David Copperfield*, which he knew well: "Accidents will happen in the best regulated families." James merely changed the gender, from "actresses" to "actors."

He knew he was different. He realized at the age of seven that he liked boys. He was drawn to beautiful things: flowers and art; pretty clothes and ravishing cakes. Being an actor might prove to be his salvation, a plausible reason for his difference. It set him apart. He could explain his delicate tendencies as being the innate sensitivity of an artist.

"Hard on the Eyes," was the headline of a jokey item in *The Lens*. It listed the most hilarious and grimace-provoking things no one ever wanted to see, including "Fat" Hickman in BVDs and Jimmie Beard in a bathing suit. In the same issue, in a farewell to the class of January 1920, each student named someone famous they aspired to be. James chose the late Edwin Booth (brother of John Wilkes Booth), the best-known American Hamlet of his generation, a man with an axe-chipped profile and eyes that seemed to tunnel into some deep well of suffering and spirit. Together, the two *Lens* items expressed the paradox of James's existence. Through performance, he gained the attention that lifted him from isolation and depression, but instead of becoming the handsome idol he wanted to be, James had a physique that doomed him to bluster through comedic parts. He'd always be Mr. Jabstick, sitting down to a farcical lunch that might never end.

CHAPTER 4

CECIL FANNING'S TEA CAKE

1920–1921

As HE ENTERED REED COLLEGE as a boarding freshman in September 1920, one of eighty-five first-year students, James had new confidence in himself. His favorite look included a thick navy-blue cardigan. It stretched to engulf his stomach, something a blazer couldn't do, with brass buttons and pockets capacious enough for his hands. He wore straight neckties under floppy collars. He combed his fine hair—sandy after a summer's bleaching at the coast—with a dramatic side part and a high sweep across his forehead. He was six feet three, two hundred forty pounds. He could look in the mirror, see his cherub's face with its wicked smile and fading sunburn and almost believe he was handsome. At seventeen, and for the first time in his life, James felt a sense of ease someplace other than the beach.

Other men in the class of 1924 stood nearly as tall as James. None exuded his presence or carried themselves (walked or laughed or buttered their toast) with quite as much character. To the women who became his instant friends, he was a gossipy girlfriend and a wisecracking brother rolled into one. To men—fellows with muscles, tanned faces, and thick, brilliantined hair, who played football and canoed on Crystal Springs Lake—James was a hulking, high-voiced clown, the fatty who made everyone laugh, and flaunted the things that made him different.

He and Reed seemed perfect for each other.

:::

SIMEON GANNETT REED WAS a well-off young man from Massachusetts who trekked to the Pacific during the California Gold Rush. In Oregon, he made his own fortune in transportation—first in river shipping, later in railroads. When he died in 1895, he left his widow Amanda with millions, along with a behest that she find some way to spend them on the improvement and edification of the citizens of Portland. By the time she died, in 1904, she hadn't fulfilled his wishes, though four years later trustees of the institute established in the Reeds' name announced they would use Simeon's bequest to build a liberal arts college. And after the son of Simeon's former business partner donated forty acres of farmland in the Eastmoreland district of southeast Portland, not far from the Willamette, Reed College was fit to rise in fields that not long before had known the plow.

To serve as president of this new institution—a beacon of enlightenment for the people of Portland—the trustees recruited a serious young academic, William Trufant Foster, thirty-one, from Bowdoin College in Maine. Under Foster, Reed would be anti-elitist, free of class, anti-Semitism, sex discrimination, and what the new college board called "highbrowism." It would be unlike the corrupt and aristocratic institutions on the East Coast—Harvard, Princeton, Yale—that bred and coddled what reformers branded an arrogant ruling class. Instead, Reed's curriculum would incubate a new society, full of the vigor and openness of the West, based on the lessons of literature, science, and art.

Everything about Reed would be different. There would be no intercollegiate sports, only intramural ones; no fraternities or sororities, nothing to distract from learning. All courses would be electives; teachers would assign grades secretly, sharing them only later, after students graduated (assuming they did). In their third year, students would have to argue why they should be granted a fourth. And there would be no formal honor system, nothing legalistic and therefore easily broached in spirit (as at Ivy League schools), but something deeper: a *principle* of honor and personal purity that would apply to every part of college life.

Reed's first semester opened in the fall of 1911 with forty-six students. Half were women. Foster would tell the *New York Times* that, on its first day, Reed was the only American college "that had made no mistakes, [and] that had no alumni of which it might be ashamed."

For all its iconoclasm, Reed clung to the comforting optics of an old and hallowed English university. Its insignia was a griffin, a creature that appeared to be liberated from shield-bearing duty on a baronial coat of arms. There was morning chapel, nonsectarian and voluntary, but Reed encouraged students to attend, since it offered "regular provision for religious thought and aspiration." The heart of the campus was the Old Dorm Block of brick and stone tracery, built in 1912 ("old" was pretty much just a mood). Its Tudor arches, bays, and heraldic reliefs could have been pried off an outbuilding of Hampton Court Palace in London. Rising above a green commons ringed with towering Western red cedars like sentinels, it fronted a forested canyon.

On wet evenings, the campus felt like a setting for some brooding neo-Gothic romance. "Glance at the old rickety bridge"—the one that spanned Reed Lake, behind the Old Dorm Block—read the *Griffin* yearbook of 1921 (James's first). "Time has clothed it with romance. To appreciate the spot you must have night with the great branches shimmering in the water while the moon rides along in the depths of the lake." It was a place where a boy, released from the rules of home and the gaze of family, could imagine falling in love.

At the start of James's freshman year, Reed's student newspaper had a message for the entering class of 1924. It described the special bond—the spirit—that developed with a teacher for any student willing to yield completely. "You are entering Reed in a year destined to distinction," ran the item in the *Quest*. "Many of you will catch the spirit this first year, for the faculty is 'at least as strong' as at any time in Reed's history." In its tenth year, Reed had a large slate of novice teachers, and two new departments.

"And when you have a real teacher," James read in the *Quest* that September, "a man whose good fellowship and physical vigor are sufficient to make his scholarship attractive and stimulating, you cannot help yourself. You become enthusiasts for learning without a struggle."

:::

A FEW WEEKS INTO the fall semester, Reed held student elections. James was voted freshman class treasurer (he had just one opponent: Alvin Hawks), responsible for fundraising and party planning. Also on the ballot: whether first-year Reedies should take up the sophomores' challenge in the annual interclass tug-of-war. The freshmen voted to accept, and in early October, on a cloudy day with a raw wind blowing, teams assembled on each edge of a shallow finger of Crystal Springs Lake, fifteen men per side. James took up the anchor position, farthest from the fulcrum point, which hovered, taut, above the water.

The whole school had trudged to the lake to watch, said a reporter for the *Quest*: students, faculty, maids, kitchen workers, even the gardener. The whistle blew, "the rope pulled taut, women cheered, coaches yelled and the sophomores pulled the freshmen thru [*sic*] the lake. . . . James Beard, 240-pound end man for the freshmen, ended the contest by splashing into the pond. Sputtering, gasping for breath, choking on duckweed. . . ." The sophomores had won, though James, on the losing team, was the star. The reporter even had a nickname for him: "Sliver" Beard, a burn on his size ("sliver" being slang for toothpick).

Portland's afternoon paper, the *Oregon Daily Journal*, also sent a reporter, who fudged some of the details to heighten the comedy of a fat kid flailing in the water (upping James's weight by ten pounds; saying he was first, not last, to hit the lake). Any night, Reed students could take the streetcar up to the Palm Theatre on Hawthorne and, for a nickel, watch a mugger hilariously fleece Roscoe "Fatty" Arbuckle in *Life of the Party.* Arbuckle shivered in the cold on screen, his coat stripped to reveal his helpless, doughy body straining the seams of a Buster Brown suit. In James, Reedies had their own life of the party.

He quickly became a running bit in the *Quest.* A story about a campus straw poll before the 1920 US presidential election, in which Reedies voted overwhelmingly for prosperity candidate Warren G. Harding, made up a quote as a gag. "Reed Straw Vote Successful," a headline blasted. " 'No More Lean Years,' Says Beard." Another item had a history professor asking, "What made the tower of Pisa lean?" and James replying, "I don't know—if I did I might try it."

:::

REED COLLEGE WAS in trouble, though.

Besides tuition, the school's survival depended on community support: convincing enough ordinary Portlanders to donate to an institution that enriched the life of their city. But how to keep popular support, in a conservative region, for such a singular and progressive college? From the beginning, William Trufant Foster knew he would have to convince the city at large that it *needed* the college, not just as a place to learn but also as a guardian of ethics and culture; that Reed couldn't keep to its Tudor fastness among the trees of Eastmoreland and play out private rituals. So in theaters downtown, the college's drama club put on plays, the chorus gave recitals, and teachers delivered public lectures. Foster worked to plant an idea of Reed as essential to the intellectual and moral life of Portland.

Foster even came up with a mystical name for the fellowship of students, teachers, and civic allies he envisioned taking up this mission of learning and morality stretching beyond campus lines. Together, they were Comrades of the Quest.

Except most Portlanders didn't particularly care for the college, much less tbecoming Foster's comrades. Reed plays and recitals were always fun, but the school didn't even have a football team to root for. Foster's talk of quests sounded like academic claptrap, the thoughts of a man out of touch with ordinary working people. Portlanders' financial support—vigorous at the beginning—withered. Only five years after Reed rose in the fields of Eastmoreland, the institution was at risk of sinking.

By 1919, the year before James entered Reed, most of the original faculty had scattered. When Foster offered his resignation, the board of trustees didn't object. As 1920 dawned, Reed lacked a president and had just eight faculty members and a librarian. Still, sacrificing President Foster seemed to work. "The regents are persuading the city that Reed is truly its college," the *Quest* reported. "And the college in turn is striving to serve the community in every way possible." Would Portlanders be willing to give Reed a second chance?

"Reed college opens its tenth year . . . under unusually auspicious circumstances," the *Oregon Daily Journal* reported, a day before James became a freshman. "The appropriation of $75,000 from the general educational fund has been matched by Portland subscriptions, and the college budget for 1920, including faculty salaries, pay for student labor, building expense, and appropriations for research has reached the highest point."

That summer, the acting administration made fifteen faculty hires. Among them was the head of the new German department, who would also be codirector of the drama club (Reed lacked a dedicated theater department). He was a tall, dark-haired, twenty-eight-year-old bachelor who'd grown up in Wichita, Kansas. His name was Edmund Carl Bechtold. James thought it might have been fate that assigned Professor Bechtold to live in the same dorm where he, James, was to stay: House I, Reed's newest.

: : :

OTHER STUDENT RESIDENCES clustered in the Old Dorm Block. Each was segregated by gender. House I, a clapboard farmhouse with a crisp white porch, on a grassy slope, was just off campus, across Woodstock Road from Reed proper. It housed ten men, all in modest-size single bedrooms. (Herman Kenin, likewise in the class of '24, had the room next to James's.) The boys took their meals in the commons, on campus, since House I had only a small kitchen, just adequate for making toast or tea. There was a phone in the hall, which always seemed to be in use (James called Elizabeth on Sundays).

There was already a resident parrot, Feathers, donated by Ted Eliot, the house prexy (president). Feathers could only screech "Ar-r-r-rk," though every man in the house tried teaching him a vocabulary. House I's formal mascot was a black cat, which ruled over its "mystic lair," according to *The Griffin* yearbook, and "many a midnight revel." Prohibition had begun in January. An abiding aim of the men of House I was to sneak in liquor under Professor Bechtold's nose.

Edmund Bechtold was born in a Kansas farm town, the son of a German-speaking minister. As a student at the University of Kansas in Lawrence, he acted in performances of the German dramatic club. Then came Columbia University and a brief flirtation with Broadway; then the Great War, during which he served as second lieutenant in the air services. Back in Kansas, Bechtold taught high school, even rose to become principal, but he was restless. By 1920, he was off again, this time to Pocatello, Idaho, and a job as a newspaperman. A mere two months later, however, the *Oregon Daily Journal* was introducing Bechtold as founding director of the new German department at Reed College. "He has the reputation of being one of the most capable school men of Kansas," the *Daily Journal* reported—which was curious, since he'd only ever taught in a single rural high school. Clearly, he knew how to make a good first impression.

Portland was lucky to have landed such a bright new academic star, one who also promised to electrify the city's cherished amateur dramatics. His talents spanned the campus and the city; the local papers were already intrigued. Reed needed good press and Bechtold seemed the perfect man to get it. And this was the part that seemed to James like fate, since getting Professor Bechtold to notice him was the key to landing a meaty role in a big play downtown. Since they lived under the same roof, James had a leg up.

It wasn't long before the men of House I came up with a nickname behind his back: "Becky" Bechtold, half affectionate, half mocking—

also a joke, given his impressive height and piercing intensity. A girl's name was just so wrong it was funny.

Bechtold had a strong face, brutal at certain angles, commanding rather than handsome. His head looked large for his lean body, as though his brain was so big it needed extra skull. He combed his dark hair back from a widow's peak trespassing onto his high, smooth forehead, above a frank and forceful nose. He wore wire-rimmed glasses with clinically round lenses and stiff Oxford collars with points partly concealing the plush, dimpled ties he favored. In conversation, he had a pet expression: *old chap*. "Chapel in ten minutes, old chap," he'd say to Floyd Woodings, usually the last man to straggle down the stairs in the morning. "You don't want to be late." Or "Thanks, old chap," when Harry McCoy handed him his umbrella as he prepared to dash out in the rain to cross Woodstock Road.

When some of the men asked about this, Bechtold said it was likely a phrase he picked up at Columbia, where he pursued postgraduate studies and sought the company of theater men. (He'd tried out for Charles Frohman's famous New York theatrical company, and even made it to the stage in a small role.)

James found it thrilling, the stories of New York and Broadway and "old chap." Bechtold was worldly in a way that surpassed his mother's friends, even Stella. He'd seen and done things far from the dripping trees, muddy fields, and small minds of Oregon, even farther than San Francisco. James was getting desperate to leave Portland, to get out into the world. To follow in "Becky" Bechtold's footsteps to New York, and beyond.

∷

JAMES WAS GETTING SOME good press of his own. The great Neapolitan baritone Antonio Scotti of New York's Metropolitan Opera assembled a company for a tour of the Western states. Scotti's ensemble was to sing three complete operas in Portland, in the Romanesque splendor of the Heilig Theatre. To Reed went an audition call for supernumeraries (aka supers), actors who could, without speaking parts, mill around the stage during crowd scenes.

James was one of thirty-two men chosen—he nabbed the role of the bishop in Puccini's *Tosca*. (In 1901, Scotti had premiered the role of Scarpia in the opera's Met debut.) For James, it was a thrill: to smear on the stage makeup and shimmy into a sour-smelling black robe and fake-ermine cape; to hear the performers clear their throats and warm their vocal chords off stage; to wait in the wings for his cue to walk on and silently bless the chorus of Italian peasants.

James and the other Reed supers were each paid a buck. On the streetcar back to campus, he and the other budding singers terrorized passengers with displays of coloratura. "It is said," the *Quest* joked, "that one Woodstock conductor has requested a quiet transfer to a quiet owl line." The article called James "super of supers"—a weak crack about his weight—but it didn't matter. It was enough for James to have made an impression.

Other possibilities then opened. For the first time in his life, he was not in Elizabeth's house, either in town or at the beach. At the freshman Halloween dance—the Bumpkin Ball—James showed up at the autumn-leaf-and-cornstalk–decorated gym in drag: one of Elizabeth's old hats, a pair of tablecloths borrowed from the commons, draped like a slouchy Russian peasant tunic and skirt and tied at the waist with a cord and paper roses. James was among the party's "naughty children," the *Quest* noted, yet he acted the perfect lady and won second place in the costume contest. (First prize went to Ann Shepard, who'd fashioned a gown from burlap sacks.) Away from home, James was feeling freer and more open than ever before. His friends encouraged him to be outrageous. He began to think of himself as a rebel.

As 1921 arrived, so did the baritone Cecil Fanning. He'd come to Portland with his piano accompanist, Mr. H. B. Turpin, to perform an evening of favorites from Handel's *Messiah*. Fanning was known for making melodramatic arm gestures during recitals. Critics said his singing could be toneless; to James, he was a transcendent star. One afternoon, he showed up at Fanning and Turpin's hotel room (the bridal suite at the Mallory) and introduced himself as a hopeful young tenor eager for training. Fanning and Turpin were "special friends," as Elizabeth called them, men of the theater, like the ones she'd known at Theodore Kruse's Louvre. James flirted with Fanning, who asked him to stay and chat over tea. Fanning, pale and sensitive looking, with deep-black beagle's eyes, flirted back, though Turpin looked as though he wanted to throw the boy out. Fanning asked James to sing.

James struggled through "E lucevan le stelle" from *Tosca* (he'd studied it since hearing Scotti the night he supered). James's voice was loud and uncontrolled, though, and at times he fought to find the melody. Turpin winced and rolled his eyes. Fanning was unfazed.

Fanning told James he was a born Heldentenor: big, high, and dramatic. And perhaps James should consider finding a teacher in New York. Herbert Witherspoon, maybe?

Yes, James answered, as he reached for more tea cake. New York was always where he imagined his future.

: : :

IN MARCH, the papers were buzzing. Professor Bechtold had unveiled plans for an artistic spectacle the likes of which Portland had never seen. It would happen in three months, during Reed's commencement week.

DANCE DRAMA IS BECHTOLD PLAN, shouted the headline in the *Quest*. They called it "Reed's most stupendous dramatic [and] aesthetic dancing attempt, and the first of its kind to be staged in the northwest." The *Sunday Oregonian* had details: "Edmund C. Bechtold of the department of Germanic languages has written the drama, entitled 'The Swan Knight,' gathering his material from old French, English and German legends of Lohengrin. The entire presentation will be in pantomime in three cycles, with interpretive dancing by the principals and a chorus of 30."

The Swan Knight promised to be Wagnerian not only in theme (the *Quest* called it "a gripping tale of tenth century knighthood") but also in scale. And since no indoor theater would be able to do it justice, Bechtold was planning to mount it outside, on the heavily wooded peninsula jutting into the northern end of Crystal Springs Lake and in the lake itself.

The experience of twilight amid trees and shadow was sure to evoke an almost mystic feeling in the audience. "After surveying the location," the *Quest* reported, "Mr. Bechtold declared that nature must have created it for the dance spectacle." More than fifty students would be needed for the cast of dancers, singers, and musicians. Miss Anna Nilson, instructor of physical education, would lead the dance rehearsals.

Word spread fast. The *Quest* noted that it caused "considerable stir among dramatists, dancers and musicians of Portland. Offers of aid are pouring in, and some of the foremost dancing instructors of the city have even offered to take the leads." But Bechtold and Nilson were not to be persuaded: Students alone would play all parts. In the cold mornings, under the eyes of Miss Nilson and Mr. Bechtold, the cast of flower girls and boy knights would learn their moves in the gym, and every afternoon at four it would fill again with "the sprightly figures of the dancers" rehearsing their parts. Excitement followed the casting of role after role: the villainous Duke of Brabant, the Court Fool, Elsa, even Lohengrin himself.

Even beyond the planned dance drama on the lake, Professor Bechtold was bringing new luster to Portland theater. He decided to direct the Harold Brighouse comedy *Hobson's Choice* at the Little Theatre downtown (James was in the stage crew), and he sent to San Francisco for costumes. "The production will have touches of professionalism," according to the *Quest*, "very seldom found in amateur performances." In April, Bechtold took the stage himself, playing the part of Prospero in Shakespeare's *The Tempest*, in which the cast wore historically accurate sixteenth-century dress. Everything Bechtold touched seemed to shimmer.

As excitement mounted for *The Swan Knight*, new details leaked. The audience would be seated on the lawn, amid giant evergreens. A boat would be decorated to look like a large swan, for the hero to arrive on Crystal Springs Lake. "Lohengrin, born on the lake," the *Morning Oregonian* reported in late May, "arrives on the back of a swan." The paper noted again that Bechtold's great pantomime dance was the first of its kind to be presented in the Northwest. The performance was less than three weeks away. A reporter from the *Quest* saw final rehearsals and called them very promising.

And then, suddenly: nothing. In the Portland papers, in the *Quest*—not a word of Professor Bechtold's never-seen Wagnerian extravaganza on Crystal Springs Lake. In late May, about the time the students were in final rehearsal, a small item appeared in the student paper: "The announcement that Mr. Edmund Bechtold will enter the business field at the conclusion of the present semester came as a surprise to his Reed friends today. Mr. Bechtold has as yet made no binding connections, but he hopes to remain in the Northwest, with headquarters possibly in Portland." The German department was to be folded into Romance Languages under one head (to be named).

Bechtold had been at Reed only eight months. Inexplicably, his teaching career appeared to be over. For good.

The notice of the professor's departure ended with a businesslike farewell, striking for its coolness: "Mr. Bechtold's Reed friends wish him the best of luck in his future undertakings." Whoever his friends were, they didn't appear to include the administration. Nor did they include James, technically, since he had ceased, quietly, to be a student at Reed sometime in the middle of March 1921.

He was gone by April, when the yearbook photographer showed up at the farmhouse on Woodstock Road to shoot the men of House 1. The only evidence that he'd been a student that year lingered in the freshman class portrait, taken at the beginning of the fall semester, in a couple of Reed play credits, and in a memory of his dunking in the lake at the frosh-soph tug-of-war. James, never inconspicuous, had been all but erased.

::::

AT THE BEGINNING OF 1921, Reed was an institution acutely sensitive to Portland's politics. Many in the city had been wary of William Trufant Foster's moralizing and modern notions of social engineering. The college, which was just emerging from financial insecurity, was under public scrutiny.

Always staid, Reed was becoming conservative. Now, a different guest minister from one of Portland's churches would give a sermon in chapel on Fridays. And in February, after a yearlong search, the college's board of regents announced they'd found a new president, a man who would bring stability and a reinvigorated spirit to Reed.

Dr. Richard Frederick Scholz was a man of wisdom, family values, and steady demeanor. He wore a patchy mustache that made him look younger than his actual age (forty-one), and he had calm but determined eyes that peered through wire-rimmed spectacles. Scholz's formal tenure would begin April 1, but in mid-February—when James was feeling his most openly rebellious and Bechtold was starting work on *The Swan Knight*—Scholz paid an unannounced visit to campus. He stood in the commons, greeting students and faculty. Later he met privately with the trustees to discuss pressing business. Though it probably wasn't on the agenda that day, the reverberations from a nine-year-old gay-sex scandal in Portland were still rattling the windows of the Old Dorm Block.

On the night of November 8, 1912, Portland police arrested nineteen-year-old Benjamin Trout for suspected petty crime. Interrogating officers noted how frightened Trout seemed. Before long, he'd not only admitted the theft he was picked up for, but he'd also confessed he was part of a local subculture of homosexuals, with links to similar communities in cities up and down the West Coast.

Trout described performing sexual acts with several men in Portland, and not with the loggers, hobos, and immigrants the press often cast as degenerates lurking in the vice district. Trout revealed an invisible ring of respectable white men who were queer: shop clerks, businessmen, lawyers. Most shocking of all was disclosure that many rented rooms at the Portland YMCA, seemingly the most wholesome of residences for upstanding young men.

The local papers exposed this secret world of debauchery with screaming headlines. ROTTEN SCANDAL REACHES INTO THE Y.M.C.A., blared the front page of the *Portland News*, a muckraking populist daily. The story was shocking: An insidious ring of sexually deviant men—the so-called Vice Clique—had seeped into the city's institutions, corrupting good boys from decent families. These villains, enemies of Portland's values of honest work and progressivism, were impossible to spot. They moved freely, even at the highest levels of society. Most Portland voters ascribed to a brand of Republican populism that painted homosexual men as part of some corrupt liberal elite, rich businessmen and capitalists intent on exploiting an honest working class.

When Oscar Wilde went on trial in 1895 for gross indecency, the Portland papers pointed to it as proof of the moral decay of the Old World. Such crimes could never happen in America, least of all the Pacific Northwest, where the bracing wind of a brash and energetic young society, faithful to industry and worship, starved the ancient vices of their putrid air. Our Morals Are Better Than Europe's, claimed a headline in the *Oregon Sunday Journal* in October 1912, weeks before the YMCA scandal broke. At least Americans, the newspaper's editors argued, "have the grace to be ashamed of their sins."

What if there were truly shameless men with easy access to the innocent young, though? What would happen if members of this Vice Clique infiltrated schools and colleges, inculcating this deathly culture of sin in a new generation?

: : :

To evade police, men tagged by informants as members of the Vice Clique scattered as far south as Los Angeles and as far north as Vancouver, British Columbia. Some fled all the way to New York City, where they hoped to find anonymity. In Portland, there were roundups at the Bohemian Restaurant, where Elizabeth sometimes took James. A Hungarian violinist, Jansci "Gypsy" Rigó, on an extended engagement from Paris, was arrested at Theodore Kruse's Louvre. (Six months later, the scandal-plagued Louvre closed for good.) Sixty-eight men were implicated in the scandal. Several men picked up by the police received sodomy convictions; most served long prison sentences. Those lucky enough to be fined, or even acquitted, struggled to repair their shattered reputations. Moving and changing one's name seemed to be the only solution.

William Allen, a fifty-one-year-old single businessman who lived at the Portland Y, botched a suicide attempt. Swept up in the raids, he wasn't charged with any crime, but the mere taint of suspicion got him fired from a job he'd held for twenty-seven years. Someone leaked his suicide note to the *Portland News*. The paper ran it with the headline, SCANDAL MAY BRING DEATH.

"I am innocent," he wrote, "but the disgrace is more than I can bear. There are circumstances that look unfavorable, but there are any number of young men who can tell of my helpfulness to them. Any way I see it, my life is ruined. I have tried to do my best." Even a shadow of suspicion branded a man for life. It made him an outcast.

At the age of eight—about a year after he realized he liked boys— James heard about the scandal from his mother. Two friends of Elizabeth's had been swept up in the furore. James would overhear her discuss it with her friends in lowered voices, and the conclusion was always the same: One could do as one liked, as long as one lived within the social conventions. The important thing was never, ever getting caught.

When the Vice Clique scandal broke, Reed president William Trufant Foster took immediate action. Like other enlightened people, Foster believed that any innocent could succumb to the lure of homosexual acts. Few of us were actually born depraved. Any young man, through proximity and weak resolve, could catch the disease of degeneracy, a contagion like any other. The solution was disinfectant, in the form of education, liberally applied. A young man must be taught the proper use of sex in marriage. Or, if he were to remain a bachelor, how to manage—alone—this evolutionary imperative to carry on the species.

In 1913, Foster and eleven other distinguished speakers presented a lecture series, "Sexual Hygiene and Morals," at a downtown Portland hotel. These became the seed that would grow into public schools' sex-education curriculum—focused on the proper, lawful use of sex between men and women—begun in Oregon as a response to the Vice Clique scandal. For many years, authorities in Portland were concerned with making sure that the evil of homosexuality would find no welcome in their city.

Elizabeth attended a few of these lectures, one of which held up masturbation as a mechanism to keep young men from giving in to homosexual temptations and other forms of vice. At the Gearhart Park cottage one day, after James turned fourteen, she asked him whether he ever masturbated, and she insisted that if anyone ever told him he'd grow hair on his hand from the practice, he was not to believe them. Embarrassed, James lied. He told his mother he would never even consider so dreadful a thing as masturbation. Frankly, he told her, it sounded awfully boring.

:::

At about the time Richard Scholz was arriving at Reed with his wife and three young children, Oregon's legislature passed a eugenics law. All men convicted of sodomy—"moral degenerates and sexual perverts"—would undergo forced sterilization. (Oregon's law would stay on the books until 1983. Over the course of enforcement, 2,648 people were known to have been sterilized: 1,713 women and 935 men. The law applied to three groups: the mentally and physically disabled, those convicted of three or more felonies, and so-called sexual deviants, of whom homosexual men made up the largest group.)

Even if Scholz had been sympathetic, personally, to the case of a popular freshman boy caught in an act of oral indecency with a professor in his room in an old farmhouse where every sound carried, and on a Sunday when the two offenders thought they'd be undisturbed, apart from a parrot squawking at every creak of a bed, it was a case that had to be dealt with decisively. If the Portland papers ever caught a whiff, suspected even a hint of scandal, it could imperil the already tenuous existence of Reed College. The populist tide was against sympathy.

When it came to students mingling with faculty, maybe the Reed that Scholz inherited was too permissive. A spoofy item in the *Quest* told of a student who transferred to Princeton. "While yet unfamiliar with the local color and eastern social custom," the story read, "he entertained his major professor in his room. The Reed man was immediately viewed askance by his fellows, and eventually ostracized for his daring unconventionality. Reed," it concluded, "is singularly free from the bondage of conventionality." Scholz's task was to make his institution more conventional. He had to deal with this sensitive disciplinary item at once, and do it quietly, without any notoriety.

Besides, private justice would be nothing new for Reed. It happened in the case of a facilities engineer, a man who'd worked at the college for five years and was entrusted with keys to all the locks on campus. The engineer was found to have stolen kitchen supplies, a Liberty bond (from one of the gardeners), cash, and even candy from the student co-op. Instead of alerting the police, Reed administrators required the man to find a new job off campus and pay fifty dollars every two weeks until he made full restitution. Why wouldn't the college deal extrajudiciously in a far more delicate case? In the furious antihomosexual climate of Portland, a quiet solution may have been the most progressive one.

James's expulsion happened so quietly it almost seemed he chose to leave, drifting invisibly off, as though one day he'd decided to move home and stop going to class. If anyone ever raised questions, there'd be a formal record of insufficient performance, dated to January 1921 (before the new term started). As for the professor, his firing would have to be handled even more delicately, delivered to the papers as a sudden decision on the man's part to leave academia behind. Forever.

And so the incident at Reed came noiselessly to an end. Dr. Scholz embarked on a well-publicized train blitz through the West to find new teachers. The Rockefeller Foundation had given the college a grant, on the condition that it meet a high minimum from local endowment drives. For the college to survive, then, its local standing would have to stay lofty.

: : :

EDMUND BECHTOLD STAYED in Portland, still active in theater. He was elected president of the Portland Players, an amateur drama group. He became an ad man and started his own agency, Edmund C. Bechtold and Associates. With his commanding looks and theatrical training, he was a popular speaker at advertising club luncheons in towns across the state.

James moved back to Salmon Street. On the afternoon he arrived, with the clouds so thick it seemed like night had fallen outside the screened back porch, he sat with his mother at the kitchen table. He told her everything. For the first and only time as an adult, he cried in her presence. Elizabeth was angry at James only for having succumbed to such a foolish indiscretion. She was furious with Reed. They agreed not to tell John, only to give him the official explanation that James's grades had been poor. She asked James how he would live, now that college seemed unlikely. He said he wanted to pursue theater, perhaps learn to become a great tenor from the teacher Cecil Fanning had recommended.

Years later, a friend would observe of James that he hated being gay. Perhaps what he really hated was bearing the wounds of being gay in a world that never let them scar over. The college imprinted itself on him in a short time. He resented Reed, or at least its cowardice in offering him up for sacrifice to suit political expediency. And yet James considered Reed his alma mater, the institution that cemented his sense of himself as a Westerner, free of snobberies and pretension, full of vigor and democratic ideals. Like Gearhart, Reed College was a place where James felt a deep sense of belonging. Being forced to leave it would haunt James for the rest of his life—as if he were Lohengrin in the swan boat on a dark lake, except that James was being ferried to a shore he feared he'd never reach, and without a chorus to mark the journey.

CHAPTER 5

EARLY PEAS AND OTHER PRIVATE PLEASURES

1923–1933

SHE WAS NOT A SHIP to stoke romantic notions of travel on the high seas. The *Highland Heather* was a serviceable old tank: an old-fashioned pair of masts, a single smokestack painted in red and black stripes, and only the most basic passenger amenities. She was a slow-moving tank, plowing south through the warm Pacific somewhere off the tropical coast of Mexico.

And she reeked of apples—hundreds of thousands of apples. If James never ate another, it would be too soon.

Except that food on the ship was so dreary, the cooking a daily onslaught of gray provisions, all of them boiled—beef, cabbage, dumplings. An apple, peeled and cut up with a pocket knife, was the only gleam of luster. James had only ever traveled on statelier steamships (to San Francisco with his mother, exactly twice), where the cooking was decent even in tourist class. On the *Highland Heather*, food was merely something to keep the thirty paying passengers alive until they all debarked in England, six weeks after leaving Portland.

On the first day of February 1923, they pushed off from the Willamette River dock, bound for Southampton via the Panama Canal. The *Highland Heather* originated in Seattle, where workers loaded into the ship's refrigerated hold sixty thousand boxes of Washington's finest apples for the European market. Another sixty thousand were hauled aboard in Portland.

The *Highland Heather* dated from the previous century, when she hauled beef from Argentina to London; later she was armored and pressed into service in the Great War. The Huns torpedoed her, though not fatally. After the armistice, the Royal Mail Steam Packet Company patched her up and put her back in the water. She plied the only direct passenger route between British ports and the Pacific Northwest, with stops in San Francisco and Los Angeles.

Twenty-year-old James bunked with John V. Bennes Jr., twenty-one, son of a well-known Portland architect. They knew each other well, having performed in amateur drama leagues together, and shared a small cabin in the spartan "intermediate" class. Both carried letters of recommendation from George Natanson, director of one of those drama leagues, the Red Lantern Players. In London, Natanson's letters were to be presented to the head of vocal training at the Royal Academy of Music, one of the world's finest institutions for musical study. Both James and Bennes were seeking opera training. Both dreamed of becoming stars on the world stage.

Though the *Highland Heather* was nothing more than a rusty apple tank with bad food and a crew of men from all over Europe, including a Dutch cook and British scullery mates, it represented James's best hope for redemption.

It had been almost two depressed years since James's exile from Reed: two years in which he seemed to be doing little else but marking time. It wasn't just the de facto expulsion that stung. James might have recovered relatively quickly were it only that. It was the erasure that came with it: hardly a word about him in the yearbook, a cruel wiping of James from the record. And because of what? Yielding in a moment of weakness? Trusting a man who was supposed to protect him?

Before being banished, James's momentum had seemed inevitable. He had always been an awkward boy, assertive—mischievous and even joky—on the outside, while inside suffering from loneliness and self-doubt, long spells of unshakable sadness. The stage had taught him to show himself, to vanquish self-consciousness by magnifying who he was and to raise his voice. He'd learned how to act the confident rebel, striding toward an inevitable future on the New York stage. All that had been wiped away.

That year, James went to live at the beach alone, weeks before his mother arrived. The journey in the day coach was quiet so early in spring, plus the highway between Portland and Seaside was all but completed. For those who had one, an automobile was now the preferred transport to the coast, despite the last few jolting miles of dirt road. Progress seemed to conspire with circumstances to leave James behind.

At the cottage, he cooked clam hash and baked biscuits in the treacherous range he tried to master. He was used to eating by himself; living alone at the beach in the quiet season gave him time and room to reflect. Gearhart's community of year-rounders, however, was tight-knit. If grocer Jim Cutler asked why he'd come to the beach before the end of the term at Reed, James would have been forced to lie and say he'd finished early and been given permission to leave. James sought to avoid anyone he knew. He climbed Tillamook Head, and even though the humiliation of having been caught was still fresh, he strolled at night through Strawberry Knoll, where solo men loitered in the hope of meeting interested strangers, and where James had given up his virginity years earlier.

He read Turgenev and Tolstoy. He swam daily, disappearing under the waves far from shore. Someone took his picture on the beach in front of the Gearhart natatorium. James is in his bathing suit, which is still wet. Even as he smiles, he looks pained, as though worried his thighs are lumpy and too large, his hair in need of combing. It's the photograph of someone who fears he's revealing too much; of a young man trying to look affable, though in fact he's acutely uncomfortable in his flesh.

James was physically unlike other men, and not just because he was husky and tall. He knew it from a young age, when he'd go skinny-dipping with Gearhart boys in shallow stretches of the Necanicum River.

Other men had equipment that seemed to work differently than his; had male parts that *looked* different than his, in all their lovely hugeness. The trouble was, the tender skin that sheathed James's never grew as it should have. It did not keep up with the growth of James's body—almost as though it had gotten stuck at a particularly obstinate stage of development and refused to budge. And when his penis was mature enough to react spontaneously to excitement, the tightness in the skin didn't ease, so that whatever pleasure James felt always registered through a filter of pain. In the complicated realm of sex, maybe his destiny lay in giving pleasure to others; his reward would be the feeling—a sense of satisfaction—that he'd made another happy, and to feel love, which he knew so little of and must, surely, have craved.

:::

JAMES RETURNED TO Salmon Street weeks after the summer season ended. His father was away, making a tour of customs houses for the government. In fall, along the banks of the Willamette not far from Reed, geese fly south in darkened skies swirled with clouds. There are whiffs of smoke, smoldering piles of leaves raked from beneath maples and sycamores. Everything in the landscape, even the air itself, evokes change and a sense of inevitable movement, of a narrative that has turned. Thoughts of the school term well underway surely troubled James. Did anyone at Reed still remember him?

James tried reviving his burgeoning career in theater. He had already started doing charity shows, entertaining residents at a home for the destitute called Multnomah Farm. He and the other performers called themselves The Joy Club. James sang. One of The Joy Club's female members read O. Henry stories. Afterward, they served refreshments. It was hardly a matter of picking up where James left off, but he had to start somewhere. Momentum is a force that won't reactivate at will.

Elizabeth prodded him to join a committee that was planning a dance for young people in the parish house at Trinity Church. He auditioned for a lavish new play that would be performed before the General Convention of the Episcopal Church. Titled *A Sinner Beloved*, it was a dramatization of the story of the Prophet Hosea. James got a non-speaking role as one of the sinners, a seller of slaves. The auditorium where he performed wasn't even full.

"Hosea of old was a prophet of fierceness," explained the review next morning in the *Oregon Daily Journal*, "holding that God was severe and the punishment of the sinner would be without mercy. Gloomy and wrathful he spread gloom over those who surrounded him." Charity acts and church pageants: They felt to James like rites of penance the world expected him to perform.

James's deliverance came from George Natanson, founder of the amateur Portland Drama League and its spinoff, the Red Lantern Players. In the spring of 1922, Natanson cast James at Turn Verein Hall in *This Way, Please*, a one-act drama by a local playwright. Natanson saw more of what James could do a few weeks later, on St. Patrick's Day, when James wore a leprechaun costume and sang Irish songs at a PTA benefit. In May, Natanson gave James his most prestigious role yet, in the drama *Nothing But the Truth*, costarring the celebrated actor Earle E. Larrimore.

Natanson liked what he saw in James, the young man's mix of energy and bravado. All he needed was finessing, under a teacher who could help him harness his natural instincts. James could go to New York and find a good teacher there—someone who could work on both his voice and his acting. Or he could look higher.

Natanson was a good friend of Carl Denton, conductor of the Portland Symphony Orchestra, who had studied at the Royal Academy of Music in London and cited his education at the conservatory as exceptional. Not only that, Denton had been honored as the academy's official representative in Portland. Why, Natanson wondered, couldn't James pursue his training there? Why shouldn't Portland be the western capital of musical theater, with a constellation of rigorously trained young stars?

Elizabeth needed no convincing. She, too, was still smarting from James's expulsion, still eager to prove to Reed College—and the world— that her son was a budding artist far too great for a town as provincial as Portland. Besides, London would be good for the boy. He could stay with her brother Fred and his wife, in their flat.

It wasn't possible to enroll at the Royal Academy from a distance of five thousand miles. James and another of Natanson's Red Lantern protégés, John Bennes Jr., would need to travel to London to audition for places in the summer session. So Natanson wrote letters of recommendation and vouched for James to the Secretary of State in Washington, DC, on his passport application, supporting James's request to go to Europe to pursue vocal studies.

And so, somewhere off the Pacific coast of Mexico, on an old steamer with a battered, sour-sounding piano in the lounge, James worked to memorize his audition piece: Puccini's "No! Pazzo son!" from *Manon Lescaut*. Trying to ignore the reek of apples.

: : :

THE *HIGHLAND HEATHER* reached St. Thomas in the Virgin Islands at the end of February. The town of Charlotte Amalie rose from the harbor as a stack of pastel stucco houses behind white-painted wood verandas. They clustered within a vertical rise of low palms, the fronds splayed and drooping in the heat. Behind them sprawled a wider landscape of soft, barren hills. The ship had docked in the quiet harbor for an afternoon of provisioning. In dripping humidity, a human chain of loaders (women in long skirts, men in stained undershirts and rolled-leg trousers) portered sixty-pound baskets of coal on their heads, promenading up the gangplank to add their cargoes to the ship's bunker.

James and Bennes had debarked and ambled through the port, past sweaty US sailors in dungaree suits and slouchy white caps. They climbed the main street to the colonnaded Grand Hotel and its dim dining room troubled with flies. There they ordered a luncheon of gristly entrecôtes and potatoes fried in questionable oil. Nothing was delicious, but it was a relief to be eating away from the ship. A waiter rolled up with a cart of rattling bottles and fixed them drinks known as Swizzles: dark St. Croix rum, juice of sweet Spanish limes, Cointreau, and sugar, mixed in glasses of slushy ice by means of a wooden molinillo, which the man twirled between his palms. Thank God that Prohibition, with its throat-scouring gins and beers like water squeezed from washrags, was behind them.

After lunch, the men split up. James strolled aimlessly, tipsy from rum and heat. A street opened to a throng of locals, natives of color: a girl goading an unfazed donkey saddled with baskets of coconuts, men with flat caps and rolled sleeves, women in wide-brimmed hats of woven palmetto and forearms laden with baskets, dogs scratching at fleas or sleeping fitfully in the roadway—an outdoor food market. It stretched along a raised concrete platform in a clearing of houses, under a swooping canopy like that of a train station from the last century, held aloft by cast-iron columns of Greco-Roman design. Dozens of women selling fruits and vegetables squatted on low stools, shooing flies with palm fans. James saw his chance and seized it. He bought two baskets.

One he packed with a mix of small pickling cucumbers and deep-red, musky, juice-filled tomatoes no bigger across than the length of his pinkie. Into the other basket he wedged clusters of tiny fig bananas, pygmy pineapples, Spanish limes like the ones at the restaurant, and cashew apples with the nuts—kidney-shaped brown drupes—still dangling. He selected melons: compact and orange-fleshed, with a perfume so strong it had a hypnotic effect on James, blotting out every other field of his attention. He loved the market women, how they laughed with good nature at his curiosity, joked about his size and supposed appetite. They told him how to eat the curious things called ackee and what to do with cassava. They pulled his sleeve so he'd come see what fruits they'd spread out on old coffee sacks: guavas and tamarind pods, star apples and noni fruit. There were greens called callaloo he'd never seen at home, and christophenes (chayotes) shaped like clenched fists. He was curious about it all. He regretted there was only so much he could try.

He hauled his baskets on board the ship. For the next ten days, until the *Highland Heather* puffed into the harbor of Ponta Delgada in the Azores, James and Bennes and another passenger, Charles Woodhouse, a baker from Liverpool likewise unimpressed with the ship's cooking, ate through James's island larder. They had salads of cucumber and tomato that James cut up with a pocketknife and dressed with lime; desserts of banana, pineapple, and cashew apple, doused with the earthy island rum that Bennes had picked up.

James marveled at how the fruits and vegetables that grew in a place—the ones that gave it a particular flavor—amplified his experience of having been there. How taste made the vividness of certain landscapes resound, long after he had left them. How the truck-farm ingredients of a place, sold by poor women with cracked hands, could be so rich and expressive.

:::

JAMES REACHED LONDON at the end of March. For three weeks in the front parlor of his aunt and uncle's flat in West London, he rehearsed Puccini. At last, on the day he had to sing for the opera admissions panel, everything went wrong. It was a rainy April morning and he left his umbrella behind in the crowded Underground car, so he was wet when he arrived at the recital hall. The room—with its chandeliers and cream moldings, its vast vaulted ceiling—intimidated James, making him feel like a Portland boy dropped into a thrilling but unsteady dream, confused about how he'd gotten there. Then the pianist's tempo was half a beat too fast, and James became flustered. He struggled to reach even a middle C.

The panel rejected his application.

He asked whether he could try again, but that was explicitly against the rules. James was humiliated, demoralized. What's worse, John Bennes's audition went spectacularly well.

James wrote to Elizabeth with the sickening sense he'd been through this before, after the doors to Reed College slammed shut behind him. James was embarrassed. He feared he was worthless, incapable of securing a future for himself. He hadn't booked his passage back home, assuming that after studying at the conservatory he'd stay in London to begin a career on the stage. Now what? Rush back home on another broken barge in defeat?

To feel better, he took himself to the downstairs bar at the Ritz. Because he didn't know what else to ask for, and because he'd read about them in magazine stories about England, he ordered whisky-soda, a boring drink.

He'd noticed a woman at a table nearby, sitting with two young men, both with sleek, shining hair. One man flashed a slightly lingering look at James, who thought perhaps it was because he, James, was dressed wrong: in a darker, heavier suit than spring warranted. The woman, maybe in her early thirties, had a rather long, elegant face, dark eyes, and beautifully sculpted cheeks. She kept erupting in laughter. Soon, James realized they were talking about *him*. The other man, the one not glancing at James, rose and approached his table. Saying that James looked awfully lonely, he asked if he'd care to join them. The woman introduced herself as Helen Dircks and said she hoped he didn't mind them staring, but he looked so much like a lost little American boy in need of a good drink.

Helen was a writer, author of two books of Imagist poetry, both fairly well received, published during and just after the war. Her father was Will H. Dircks, the distinguished drama critic and editor. When James met her, she'd just divorced the novelist Frank Arthur Swinnerton. Because she needed a job, she'd recently become an advertising copywriter and publicist for The Palladium, the West End variety theater with a grand classical façade, all Corinthian columns and statues throwing heroic poses along the pediment.

Helen moved in a circle of theater people, artists, and interesting characters, chaps who loitered in cafés and small restaurants in Soho. Many, like the men James met that night at the Ritz, were queer. By the time the evening ended, and James headed back to Uncle Fred's in Acton Vale, he'd become Helen's little project: the funny, corn-fed nineteen-year-old from Portland, Oregon (she said it like *Orry-gawn*), a stranger in the cruel British metropolis, who dreamed of becoming a great singer and needed some nice English boys to play with. She'd have to see what she could do.

Oh, and it was *essential* that she teach him how to order a proper cocktail.

: : :

UNDER HELEN'S WING, James came to adore London. He so loved the view from Victoria Embankment, on a Sunday afternoon when the sun made the river turn the oxide green of old window glass, afloat with orange tugs and coal barges in lazy flotillas. The haze through which any glimpse of London was filtered—its skyline of spires and shipping cranes, the Houses of Parliament and Big Ben—made the city feel edged with cashmere. Men in soft-shouldered suits with fawn caps or light-brown fedoras; women in pale, pleat-skirted springtime coats and cloche hats of delphinium pink or blue: London had a scale and a smartness James never dreamed existed. It made even Meier & Frank, Portland's most stylish department store, seem dinky and provincial.

In James's eyes, Soho was nothing short of magical. Helen took him to lunch at Gennaro's Rendezvous on Dean Street. It was there, in the faux–Olde English farmhouse dining room, with its black ceiling beams, bank of small-paned cottage windows, and high-backed rush-weave chairs, that Helen ordered James his first London dry martini (three parts gin, one of vermouth). They ate sole Rendezvous (in white wine sauce) and soufflé Gallina (named for the restaurant's previous owner), with brandied cherries and an amber puddle of Cognac, flambéed at the table with high theatrics. James was enraptured. James was drunk.

Through her gay friends, Helen gave James an entrée into London's discreet queer subculture, something he hungered for without even daring to hope that such a thing *could* exist, or what it would feel like, what its rules and language were. Queers in the other great European capitals flaunted their existence. There were drag balls and openly gay beer bars in Berlin, and male hustling on radical display in the Left Bank cafés of Paris. London was different. Police raids were constant. The queer city blossomed at night, in the dark. London's gay scene operated more like a network of speakeasies. One had to be tipped off about where to find the alley tea shop of boys in berets and colored sweaters, some wearing rouge and lipstick; or the basement bar of quiet yet purposeful men in crisp suits and bowler hats with tightly rolled umbrellas. The hunt for these places alone was thrilling.

The hotspots were usually takeovers of existing places: the monumental marble bar at the Trocadero; the basement bar at the Criterion Hotel in Piccadilly Circus. Queer men had been stopping in for drinks at the Criterion, amid the neo-Byzantine splendor of its mosaics and arches, almost since the death of Queen Victoria more than two decades earlier. (It had camp nicknames: the Witches' Cauldron for its bitchiness; or the Bargain Basement, since the men could be had so cheaply.) Another place, though James didn't know it the night he met Helen and her friends there, was the downstairs bar at the Ritz. Gay regulars called it l'Abri, the Vault, a place locked away from the dangers of the nonqueer world. Subterranean bars were London's queer cocoons, incubator sites for pleasure and discovery, as remote as possible from the cruel and risky street. James found recognition and safety there. He learned the culture of cocktails, and of camp.

Even the galleries off the rococo lobby of the Palladium, Helen's client, were places where men found each other; where they could lock gazes and discreetly grope beneath raincoats folded over arms, especially during the blare and pyrotechnics at the climax of the popular *Rockets* revue, when the audience's eyes would be focused on the stage. The body language in these establishments, the queer code, was subtle but undeniable. Even on the streets of the West End, a daring man might telegraph his queerness by walking with his overcoat slung behind one shoulder. One simply had to know how to read the signals.

Besides, London was a city of nearly invisible secret pleasures. James stumbled on Covent Garden Market while en route to the Royal Opera House. After that, he returned again and again in the early mornings to see it bustling with Cockney sellers who haggled with customers, drily roasted them sometimes, and even clapped the rude ones out of the market entirely. In May, Early Warwick peas came in: crates of them from Sussex, small and shining when you stripped open a pod. The strange thing was, in the two weeks they appeared at Covent Garden, James never once saw them on a restaurant menu, certainly not on his uncle and aunt's table, where only sulfurous cabbages and sprouts, obliterated to almost-mush in the boiling kettle, represented all of the vegetable kingdom besides potatoes. *Someone* in London was eating those peas.

James bought a large basketful. Following the advice of a market woman, he left them whole and boiled them quickly, lifted each by the stalk end to gave it a dip in melted butter before sucking out the peas. They were extraordinary, as good as (or better than) ones he knew from the coast of Oregon. He imagined thousands of others doing the same thing that night, quietly, at kitchen tables across the vast city, from sacks of early peas bought from greengrocers: a map of cravings satisfied in private.

:::

JAMES OWED HELEN a huge debt, too, for salvaging his hopes for operatic training. She dropped a line to Gaetano Loria, a vocal teacher she knew, asking whether he'd be willing to talk to a promising young American arrived in London to become a tenor. Just shy of fifty, Loria was a Sicilian with a questionable past, though in England he'd built a reputation as a great impresario of Milan's La Scala, a maestro who groomed singers for glory.

Loria grew up in a village on the slopes of Mount Etna. In Milan, he was secretary to the soprano Ada Giachetti, who in 1910 ended a long, illicit liaison with Enrico Caruso. After the breakup, Giachetti sued Caruso for compensation, and in a messy, complicated trial, Caruso accused Giachetti, Loria, and an associate of extortion and slander. A court in Milan absolved Loria of perjury but found he'd bribed witnesses. He was ordered to pay damages. The trial exposed Loria as a money-grubber and a snake. And it revealed he'd once begged Caruso to hire him as his secretary, but he was so incompetent the tenor had no choice but to fire him.

Hoping for a new start, Loria moved to England in 1914. He advertised himself not only as the great Caruso's onetime personal secretary but also as the master of bel canto, a man who'd trained some of the greatest singers who appeared at La Scala. He landed a job teaching elocution to officer cadets at Sandhurst Military College. Someone noticed him and thought there might be a chance he could help the Duke of York, Britain's future King George VI, a man desperate to overcome his stammering and fear of public speaking. He did not cure the duke. For Loria, it was a great success anyway, since the fact of royal patronage gave him status, along with the ability to charge his pupils almost whatever he liked.

The man James went to see was short, round, and jovial. Loria had prospered in England. Six months earlier, he had moved from Notting Hill Gate to a studio above Wigmore Hall, the esteemed chamber music and vocal concert venue in Marylebone, an address that only added to his luster. He took pupils in London and once a year opened a temporary studio in Manchester.

James and the self-styled maestro came to an agreement. For the next two and a half months, he would have twice-weekly private lessons on the production of voice, as well as the diction and interpretation of English, French, and Italian songs and operas. Madame Loria, her husband's manager, demanded the first month in advance before scheduling James's first appointment. After James paid, Loria suggested they celebrate their felicitous new arrangement by having James take them to luncheon at one of Loria's favorite restaurants in London: Gennaro's in New Compton Street.

As a restaurateur, Gennaro (who also owned the Rendezvous) was an impresario. He'd been a dancer in Milan, but now his restaurants were his stage. Since his days of performing in ballet tights, he'd grown large—weighing well over two hundred pounds and wearing a tuxedo. He shaved his head bald and shiny with a razor. He had a prominent mustache, eyebrows died raven black, and a sharp little nose that angled down, like the beak on a mask for *carnevale*. Gennaro had a film actor's control over his facial muscles, raising a single eyebrow, for instance, to greet a distinguished guest like Signor Loria, accompanied by his newest pupil. When a lady entered, no matter where Gennaro was in the dining room, he'd pivot with practiced grace and virtually glide across the floor to the restaurant's small foyer, where he'd present her with a single carnation. He was famous for presenting one to every woman who entered, which Gennaro called out in advertisements. "The restaurant," read one ad, beneath a photograph of the mustached proprietor embracing a lady wearing a Spanish mantilla and gripping a lace fan, "where you are greeted with a smile and a flower."

James found the lunch astonishing. It was his first taste of Italian food outside Portland or San Francisco. Milanese cooking, for the most part, though tailored for English people: no garlic, or only a whiff, and nothing too vivid. (Italians, however—singers performing at Covent Garden, such as Mattia Battistini, the aging King of Baritones, and the great tenor Beniamino Gigli—did dine *a Gennaro*. For them, the chef cooked dishes not on the regular menu.) It was an antipasto freddo that made the strongest impression on James: a chilled tomato, skinned and hollowed out, filled with a thick chunk of cold lobster, a poached egg with the yolk just set, and a spoonful of mayonnaise.

The brilliance of Gennaro's wasn't so much the food as it was the performance, an actor spinning magic so convincingly that the audience came to believe in his mastery. Not just the cooking; that, plus the smile and the flower and the maestro's unchallengeable air of authority. Gennaro made an indelible impression on James.

The Royal Academy of Music had been a bust, but James had found something better, he wrote his mother: personal instruction from a man who'd worked side-by-side with the genius Caruso and had mentored an actual royal. Elizabeth's money (which, incidentally, she'd need to wire more of) was not going to waste—which she'd be able to judge for herself, she wrote back to say, since she'd booked passage to Southampton on the Canadian Pacific Line steamship *Melita*, leaving from Montreal and arriving the first of June. She was interested to hear what James had learned from this shockingly expensive Signor Loria.

:::

ELIZABETH CAME AND WENT. She told him she approved of Loria, whom James now called Tano. He'd studied about a dozen baritone roles (a new one every week), including Schaunard from *La Bohème*, Escamillo from *Carmen*, Tonio and Silvio from *I Pagliacci*, Ford from *Falstaff*.

James took his mother to Gennaro's for the stuffed tomato, which she adored as he knew she would, since she loved simple cold dishes. She spent most of her time with her brother Fred. James rode with her on the train to Wiltshire one Sunday to visit her sister (his aunt) and have tea: currant-studded buns, homemade bread with butter as good or better than Grace Harris's and wild bramble jam. It was impressive and stupefying.

Elizabeth, who'd once spurned her siblings, embraced them in old age. She wept when she and James left to catch the train home. Soon Elizabeth was off to stay with another sister, who lived in Kent, in the port town of Folkestone on the English Channel. James was impatient for her to leave, impatient to resume his life in the West End. It was agreed he'd take some weeks to visit Paris, after his lessons with Tano had ended. Elizabeth gave him some money. She warned him it would be the last. And yet she wasn't done trying to prepare for his future.

At the end of July 1923, the music page of the *Oregon Sunday Journal* ran the item LONDON HEARS PORTLAND BOY IN CONCERT. It reported that James had sung five numbers in front of an audience at Wigmore Hall. Though eleven of Loria's students sang that night, James—perhaps because Loria didn't think James's vocal skills reflected well on the master—wasn't one of them. And Elizabeth, home from abroad, would have found it easy to send a bogus notice to the music editor of the *Sunday Journal*. Who would know it was false? Elizabeth and James both had too much pride to let something as insignificant as facts keep them from telling the truth as they saw it.

: : :

JAMES'S STRUGGLE FOR a life in theater was fruitless and frustrating. He would explain away his operatic failures as bad luck. In London, he said, he'd developed nodules—growths like callouses—in the folds of his vocal chords, a result of working too hard, too fast. That Loria had pushed him to learn the role of Wolfram in *Tannhäuser*, James would explain, pushed him and pushed him until he had an overworked voice and reached a state of exhaustion. That Loria had decided to make James a Wagnerian tenor in the mold of Lauritz Melchior, but alas:

nodules. James would say he'd proven himself a good singer; that his performance at Wigmore Hall had been a complete success. What more could he have done? He had an alibi.

The truth nagged him nonetheless.

There was no night of triumph at Wigmore Hall, no training at the Royal Academy, no Melchior path to glory. After Elizabeth left him in London, he'd taken the money she gave him and drifted across to Paris for six weeks, ostensibly to meet up with a vocal teacher who could ease his troubled chords. In fact, James wanted to taste his freedom even more completely than he'd done in London, where he got the flavor of the queer city lurking just beneath the conventional one. There, he was staying with relatives for those four months, still under the gaze of family. In Paris, city of legendary pleasures, he knew no one, which gave James a thrilling sense of possibility. All he had were the names and telephone numbers of men Helen Dircks had told him to look up, a pair of English friends not much older than James. She said he'd get on with them. She said they'd show him around.

He stayed at a *pension* on the Left Bank's rue Jacob (near rue Bonaparte), a street of four-story houses with garrets and rather rickety-looking shutters flanking the tall windows. His room had a narrow balcony above the street, from which drifted the strangely delicious-smelling blue smoke from the tailpipes of lorries. He wasted a precious chunk of his funds on dinner at Maxim's with one of his Helen-endorsed acquaintances. It was a deflating experience: mediocre food, and service that let him and his new friend understand they were nobodies. As if James needed to be reminded of that.

James preferred the food at his *pension*, where board was included. Every night brought a different cheap expression of *cuisine bourgeoise*, real-housewife dishes: boeuf bourguignon; pot-au-feu; thickly sauced blanquette de veau, which robed cheap bits of meat in glory; calf's feet coated in the sauce called poulette, an emulsion rich with egg yolks and chicken broth, cooked down to concentrate the flavor. In another *pension* around the corner, where they let nonresidents buy single meals, he ate cold slices of a mosaic of pink-and-white ham cubes fixed in a mortar of parsleyed jelly, vibrant, fresh, and surprising. Each morning's breakfast—hot chocolate with a spume of bubbles and madly buttery rolls, shattery outside, gently elastic and yeast-scented within—brandished richness yet seemed unfazed by excess. Every dish broke open a vista. Still, twenty-year-old James hadn't come to Paris in search of cuisine.

His new English friends said they'd take him south of the city to Plessis-Robinson, a forested suburb where outdoor taverns were built into ancient chestnut trees, rustic vertical pavilions overlooking terraces with music for dancing—real French guinguettes, something out of Renoir. And when it got late, it was possible to wander off into the woods and have charming adventures with men.

One night they took the train south and climbed the narrow, uneven stairs to a treehouse platform in one of the taverns. They ate roast chicken, cold and dry and with rubbery skin, hoisted up in baskets, and drank bottle after bottle of wine. When they finally sauntered into the forest, they became separated in the dark. Eventually James found his way back to the station alone (no sign of the English boys) and took the early train back to Paris. He reached rue Jacob just as dawn was breaking. He stood on his tiny balcony smoking, listening as the sweeper scraped his shovel up the curb, babies in the houses began to cry, and the din of traffic rose with the sun.

Another night his friends took him to a queer brothel in Pigalle that looked like a bathhouse. In a locker room, they stripped and donned bathrobes. Then they sat on benches facing inward in the tiled main room, as gigolos wrapped in short towels, black satin masks concealing their faces, sauntered past, here and there pausing to flirt with a patron or talk into his ear. A few patrons opened their robes when they saw something they liked. If you fancied a private massage from one of the boys, you gave the bath attendant a few francs; he'd show you to a niche and pull the curtain closed. James tried to absorb every detail so he'd remember later: the whispers and laughter, moans and an occasional slap, a gigolo's yawn.

Before he left France on September 7, 1923, sailing on the SS *Paris* from Le Havre to New York (a splurge, though he shared a cabin), James did have a brief affair. It was with a boxer—a *prizefightairr*, the man said in his husky accent. They met on the street and went to a hotel the man knew about. James paid for it.

And while his six weeks in Paris had given James his first taste of caviar with blinis, and of exquisite little mille-feuilles and éclairs, it was his *prizefightairr* who had given him his first truly astonishing, never-to-be-forgotten taste of possibility in a world he was only beginning to understand.

::::

WHEN HE ARRIVED in New York the first time, after the SS *Paris* docked at the Chelsea Piers in late September 1923, following his five and a half months abroad, James was eager to find his milieu in New York, but the manic city proved indifferent to him. London teemed, but order prevailed; shops and cafés had decorum. Parisians were uninhibited, once you breached their walls, yet polite in their own way. New York was an arena, where everyone constantly elbowed each other out, grasping for the smallest scrap of comfort, wealth, or advantage. On the subway, someone was always eager to seize your grip space if you took your hand away from the support pole for even a second.

James meant to stay as long as he could, possibly forever. He couldn't face Portland. He'd persuaded Elizabeth to give him an allowance (enough for a furnished room in Chelsea with board—it wasn't much) while he searched for auditions. He wandered the city he'd long imagined. He stood in the lobby of the Waldorf-Astoria, awed by its grandeur, the rich fabrics and the Victorian paintings; the ironwork and epic columns. He returned a week later to treat himself to lunch in the restaurant—he'd had a tooth pulled that morning and needed coddling. He ordered Waldorf salad: apples, celery, and walnuts in mayonnaise dressing. He'd seen the name so many times and supposed it must be wonderful in its birthplace. It was not; the apples were mealy, past season, and the dish was expensive: a simple thing gotten needlessly wrong.

He went to Times Square, to the old Astor Hotel and its bar, infamous as a rendezvous spot for men. On one side of the long bar, the sexes were mixed; the other side was the male realm. It was darker there and stifling, not chatty or cheeky like the subterranean queer hotel bars in London, but serious. James found he preferred the Astor's actual beef to a bull on the hoof. He discovered he enjoyed dropping in on the hotel's café before a matinee at a Midtown theater for the cold boiled-beef salad, while watching anxious gentlemen scuttle to the bar. When it came to sex or sourcing decent apples, New Yorkers had no patience.

The only real place in Manhattan where James found peace and a sense of recognition was Greenwich Village. Once he left the clattering, soot-caked Sixth Avenue El behind, the city opened to the western sky, the clouds bobbing above the Hudson like chipped, weightless meringues. The metropolis reoriented here. The buildings were on a more human scale, and the streets veered charmingly off-kilter. It seemed sequestered. It felt safe.

James finally got his casting break, from the actor-impresario Walter Hampden. The previous fall, his repertory company had mounted a production of *Cyrano de Bergerac* at the National Theater. Hampden was taking it on the road for the 1924 fall season, and word was he was seeking actors of all sizes to populate his spectacle. James wrote to Hampden, describing himself as large but not colossal. He auditioned and landed a nonspeaking role in the chorus.

Logistics for the seven-week tour were mad: an eight-car train—one just to transport the pair of horses appearing in the show, three sleeping cars, a day coach for the actors, and three baggage cars—eighty-one cast members, thirty-seven crew and mechanics, wailing child actors and stage mothers. The road production of *Cyrano* opened in St. Louis in October 1924, and the train rolled on to Cincinnati, Boston, and Philadelphia. The show closed at Brooklyn's Majestic Theatre on December 1.

It was the highest-profile engagement of James's stuttering career. And yet what stuck with him was the daily ritual of the show's female lead, the London-born Jeanette Sherwin Jolley, who played Roxanne. She drank bootleg liquor ceaselessly, scurrying from the train wherever it made a morning stop, and into a restaurant or hotel dining room, demanding in Lady Macbeth tones a large soup plate of cold, canned tomatoes: balm for her hangovers.

In every actor was a deep well of need, a brokenness that vanished when they were playing a part. James was a silent extra whose only value in the theater was as a body that stood out even from the cheap seats. What part was he playing? When the tour wrapped, he booked a sleeper on the train home to Portland, a one-way ticket back to Salmon Street.

:::

IN THE SPRING OF 1925, James took a job in the interior decorating department of Portland's stiff and bourgeois Meier & Frank store. He returned to local dramatics, as a player in several productions in the city's booming Little Theatre Movement. They called it the Broadway of Portland.

Bess Whitcomb, a producer and director, liked James and took him on. He found an acting mentor in Whitcomb, and, because she was a lesbian, a sense of recognition. That fall, James quit the department store after landing work as a drama teacher at a private girls' school, Gabel Country Day in Southwest Portland, where he organized a Christmas pageant. To the girls, James was a star.

He got announcer gigs on local radio. In the fall of 1926, James landed a plum stage role, Father Hyacinth in *The Swan*, by the Hungarian Ferenc Molnár, in a production by the new Portland Art Players. James played a grizzled monk who served up a stew of comedic and melodramatic lines to the young romantic leads. Anyway, he looked right in the robe.

Prohibition, begun in 1920, still reigned. On occasional Sundays, James got together with female friends to make bathtub gin and drink themselves stupid. It took all day: mixing alcohol, distilled water, and aromatics in a friend's bathtub, as her mother hovered nervously on the other side of the closed door. They transferred the searing liquor to a wooden cask and rolled it around the bathroom floor to help it "age." As night fell, it was ready to fuel a sloppy party, with shrieking and dancing to orchestra music blasting from the radio.

One day, James's father gave him a large package wrapped in paper. It contained dozens of flat cans of contraband Russian vodka, smuggled in on a ship from China. "Drink this instead of bootleg whiskey," John told him. It was James's first taste of the spirit: a revelation.

James made another discovery that winter. He learned that for several years—since James was a small boy, at least—his father had kept a mistress, and that together they'd had a child. Essentially, John had a parallel family. It explained his absences, his distance. Elizabeth knew about it. They had long ago erected an iron partition between their lives.

In a way, it made James appreciate his mother more. James had little affection for Elizabeth, but he admired the rational arrangement she'd forged with John, one they'd kept for so many years. After this, James thought of his father in a different way. He felt sorry for him, for marrying a woman who actively hated him. As the reality of it settled in, John's other family made sense to James. He hoped his father was happy in his shadow home away from Salmon Street.

:::

JAMES THOUGHT OF BREAKING into pictures. In 1926, he found a cheap room in Hollywood, in a house where he met another aspiring actor, Paul Claude Fielding. Born in India, Paul had a nice face and a proper English public-school accent. They drove to Tijuana together in Paul's car and had a picnic on cold chicken fried in olive oil. Paul got a small part in a Rex Ingram picture, *The Garden of Allah*. And while James was neither as handsome nor as lucky as Paul, he did land a place as an extra in a crowd, a Roman soldier in the crucifixion scene of Cecil B. DeMille's *The King of Kings*.

James got a nod to costume up for another crowd scene in 1927, for Erich von Stroheim's *Queen Kelly*, starring Gloria Swanson. Since the picture was never released in the United States—only in Europe and South America—James was doubly invisible. Hollywood was a daily crush of hopeful extras in studio casting lots, eating wax paper–wrapped sandwiches they'd stuffed in jacket pockets and playing cards to cope with boredom.

In 1931, James moved to Seattle to audit classes in the University of Washington's theater department. After a semester, he was accepted to Pittsburgh's Carnegie Institute of Technology (the future Carnegie Mellon University), where he took classes in costume and set design and became friends with John Ashby Conway, a young instructor of theater design visiting from the University of Washington. Late one night after a party, as they stumbled home along Pittsburgh's frigid Fifth Avenue, both men opened their coats to flash anyone unlucky enough to be shuttling past.

After the first semester, James—still restless—returned to Portland and Salmon Street in January 1931. He acted in local theater and cooked for dinner parties at friends' houses. His fellow actor Agnes Crowther, an interior decorator just starting out, persuaded some of her clients to hire James to teach them how to cook a few simple dishes in their newly done-up kitchens.

By 1932, James was directing a small repertory theater company that performed plays—one-night engagements, usually—in towns throughout northwest Oregon. In Salem, they had their biggest opportunity yet: two performances of Shakespeare's *Cymbeline* for residents of the state capital. James had played the lead role the previous year in Seattle, in a traveling production with Portland's Dufwin Players. Now, James was directing and starring. For days before the one performance, the Salem paper was buzzing: Professional actors from Portland promised to put on a first-rate show.

But the reviews next morning were no better than lukewarm. Critics praised the female lead, Genevieve Thayer. Everything else about opening night, however, had seemed outdated and stagey. James read the review at Genevieve's parents' house in Salem, where everyone in the repertory company was bunking for the week, sleeping in pinned-together blankets on Mrs. Thayer's parlor carpet. James was pushing thirty. Salem seemed far from the fabulous life in the theater he'd imagined for himself.

What was it James hadn't liked about New York City? He struggled to recall. Maybe if he worked for a couple of years more and put some money aside, he'd have enough to give Manhattan a second shot—even working at a department store there would be better than languishing here among the provincials.

If one had to accept being a nobody, one might at least try to have some fun.

PART TWO

CHAPTER 6

THE DUCHESS OF WINDSOR'S CORNED BEEF HASH BALLS

1938–1939

JAMES BARLOW CULLUM JR. had a well-fed look, not heavy but plumped: on roast beef and Château Latour; on hominy spoon breads and lemon meringue pies his housekeeper Dora made when asked; on Beefsteak Stanley at the Algonquin and ice cream churned from the rich, pale-yellow milk of his family's prize herd of Pennsylvania Guernseys. A man of thirty-seven, with a wide face and dark hair that seemed to be making an amiable retreat from his forehead, Cullum had learned to cultivate an expression of subtle amusement and unshakable calm. This was partly a professional demeanor, since he worked as an analyst for an investment bank on Wall Street. Still, Cullum enjoyed an extravagantly padded life, busy with charity balls at the Ritz-Carlton and dinner parties at the Viennese Roof Garden atop the St. Regis; cocktail gabfests with the Young Republicans and Sunday spins out to Montauk in the apple-green Rolls-Royce convertible he kept parked in the garage. It all tended to keep a man appearing unfazed in public, never mind the things that dogged him in private.

Cullum grew up in Pottsville, Pennsylvania, the son of a man who

became wealthy in the gilded age of iron and steel and bought a mansion ringed with porches and gardens. His parents sent him to West
Point and arranged a wedding to a distant cousin, old-money style,
though in 1931, after nine years of marriage, the young Mr. and Mrs.
Cullum took a train to Reno and divorced. In 1936, as if resigned to
bachelorhood, Cullum leased a large apartment for himself just east of
Washington Square, at 14 Washington Place, a twelve-story highrise of
buff brick wrapped around undistinguished art deco bones. Two years
later, in the summer of 1938, Cullum asked James Beard to move into
his spare bedroom.

They were unlikely acquaintances, much less roommates. Cullum
was rich (or rich enough—he received an inheritance after his father
had died some years back, and he earned a cushiony annual four grand
on Wall Street) and socially connected in both New York and Philadelphia. He didn't *need* to economize, certainly not by taking on a
roommate, least of all a thirty-five-year-old failed baritone and actor
struggling to pay rent, whose most recent address was on West Forty-
Ninth Street, in Hell's Kitchen. It was a district said to be crawling with
queers from the world of the theater.

After a year in New York, James had given up on trying to find stage
work, jobs in the scenery or costume departments. At the start of the
academic year, a friend got him a position teaching English, French,
and social studies to a small class of girls at the Buxton Day School in
Short Hills, New Jersey. The commute by train was an hour and a half
each way, and the salary wasn't making him rich. But then, James had
trouble paying his rent, and teaching was a desperation gig. Cullum
offered rescue.

They met through Hattie Hawkins, a friend of James's from Portland who'd moved to New York in 1936, a year before he did. Hawkins
lived at Fifth Avenue and Eleventh, in a residential hotel for women
where Peggy Martin, Cullum's girlfriend, had a room.

Peggy was Cullum's front, his public girlfriend, the woman he
escorted to the balls and dinners he was obliged to attend. She was
young—only a year out of college—and therefore perhaps naïve enough
to miss the nature of Cullum's interest in her. With her copper hair,

Peggy was striking as she stepped out of the Rolls and waited for Cullum's arm before entering the Plaza together. Peggy diverted scrutiny from Cullum, who used her radiance as a shield.

Meanwhile, James had gained a reputation in Hattie Hawkins's circle for his divine touch with parties. Friends would ask him to manage the cocktails and edible tidbits for their dos that, though modest—in packed apartments hazy from cigarettes—were always fabulous when James was involved. Through Peggy, the word got around to Cullum, who noted the name of this entertaining whiz. Because Cullum had become interested in throwing parties—lots of them.

James and Cullum had no interest in each other as boyfriends (certainly not), but they were compatible in one crucial way. James understood the level of discretion Cullum needed to maintain in order to act on his queerness; to meet interesting men and have a social life he actually enjoyed, rather than one he kept up for considerations of family and position.

Cullum was seeking someone to orchestrate the kinds of parties he hoped to host at 14 Washington Place.

After Prohibition ended in December 1933, New York's State Liquor Authority (SLA) implemented new rules for conduct in bars. Any behavior deemed disorderly could result in the SLA revoking an establishment's license. Authorities made it clear that the mere presence of known homosexuals (or those perceived as queer) qualified as "disorderly" under the new rules. As the 1930s advanced, bars like Gloria's on Third Avenue and Fortieth Street, a queer gathering place, were compelled to refuse service to homosexuals—not just to surveil *conduct* on their premises but also to eject patrons who dressed or talked in ways that didn't fit the narrow normative gender reckoning of the SLA.

For affluent gay men in New York City (those the playwright Arthur Laurents dubbed "silver and china queens"), private cocktail gatherings—apartment parties—were their primary points of contact. Some men hosted nearly every evening at five: drop-in gatherings with drinks and hors d'oeuvres, where consequential men like Cullum could mingle with handsome young newcomers. A man might have tickets to the theater that night and invite a new friend to accompany him, or retreat for dinner and private drinks elsewhere, or merely jot down a telephone number in his pocket address book before leaving for another engagement. James became Papa, the house factotum for Cullum's affairs. He made the martinis and old-fashioneds, passed the nibbles he'd prepared—sometimes something substantial, such as battered and crumbed fried squab pieces and thin bread-and-butter sandwiches—emptied the ashtrays, and peppered the polite talk with jokes. Sometimes a guest stayed so late it was better if he spent the night rather than trying to get a cab, and Papa would be up early to make breakfast.

Small-framed, slender, and with an Andy Hardy freshness, Horace Gibson was a twenty-one-year-old queer Southern boy who'd come to New York for art school. On New Year's Day 1940, Horace ended up at a gay party at 14 Washington Place. The host was Herbert Weinstock, a balding, bespectacled, stick-thin musicologist with a zeal for Italian opera. He was also an author and editor, eventually of poet Wallace Stevens's books for Knopf. Herbert had a boyfriend, Ben Meiselman. After a while, Herbert and Ben ducked out of their own party to take Horace to one that Jim Cullum was having in the same building, to meet their friend James Beard.

They found Papa in the kitchen, making jam with the fruit left in the brandy-and-Champagne punchbowls from Cullum's New Year's Eve bash the previous night. James was practicing household economy in an apartment that needed none. Still, it was his job, as the resident manager of James Barlow Cullum Jr.'s discreet cocktail and hors d'oeuvre salon.

: : :

IN NOVEMBER 1938, James noticed a couple at one of Jim Cullum's parties. Obviously brother and sister, he in his early thirties, she older. He was dark-haired, pale-skinned, gorgeous—maybe the most beautiful man James had ever seen. He had large black eyes that smiled on their own, autonomously from his mouth. A single-breasted suit tailored to show the pinch of his waist, a breadth of shoulder suggesting he'd rowed crew in college and never lost the muscle. James approached with a tray of radishes, an hors d'oeuvre he'd learned from Peggy (sweet butter spread around the middle of each, cinched with an anchovy, pinned closed with a toothpick).

He had the barest of accents. Bill Rhode (pronounced "Roda") and his sister Irma grew up in Berlin, in an aristocratic family with a clergyman father, the Reverend Rudolph Rhode. Irma had been forced to go to a genteel household school in Badenweiler, for girls to learn the lessons of homemaking. (The school's director, Princess Hilda of Nassau, the last Grand Duchess of Baden, was good-natured despite her fate of serving as an obsolete pedigree's dying ember.) Irma passed on to her little brother everything Hilda taught her about cooking. Then, instead of getting married and becoming a housewife, Irma pursued a doctorate in chemistry at the University of Kiel and went to work extracting aluminum from clay.

Bill and Irma left Germany in the mid-1920s, fleeing the Weimar Republic and hyperinflation. Bill, who had a photographic memory and an extraordinary grasp of English, went to Hollywood to try screenwriting. Since then, he'd been working on a sprawling encyclopedia of food and drink he hoped someday to publish. Meanwhile, Irma got a job on the team planning the Tennessee Valley Authority project, but now it had ended.

Bill had written a cookbook, published only weeks earlier, called *Of Cabbages and Kings*. Three days before that, the *New York Times* announced that Bill and a droll fraternity of writers and others (Gelett Burgess, Rex Stout, G. Selmer Fougner, Achmed Abdullah, Walter Slezak, Ford Madox Ford) had launched the Society of Amateur Chefs. They would get together on stated Thursdays, "the traditional housemaid's night off," according to the *Times* story, and "demonstrate their skill in the male interpretation of good cooking."

Bill was sexy, forceful, and charismatic. (And though he was not queer, he knew the effect he had on a party like this; why else would he bring his older sister to Cullum's, except as a buffer for ravenous gazes?) Bill was searingly brilliant, had experience of the world and a talent for spinning—maybe he embroidered his stories a little, but so what? He made them believable. James started the night wanting to go to bed with Bill; after hearing him talk for a couple of hours in Cullum's living room, he wanted to *be* Bill. The other guests filtered out to the elevator. Finally it was just the three of them: James, Bill, and Irma and a bottle of Cullum's best Scotch, talking late, about food and New York and how to get rich. As they left James to face the ashtrays and glasses, Bill remarked on what a good night it had been. He joked that the three of them should go into business together and throw parties like this for the right people, that it could be like finding the goose that laid the golden egg.

The next day, James walked to the bookshops on Fifth Avenue and found *Of Cabbages and Kings*. It was brash yet suave, outrageously theatrical but practical in its own way. Bill obviously knew food and how to cook. But then came all the gossip about European nobility: the late Queen Victoria of Sweden's love for stuffed cabbage; King Nikita of Montenegro's favorite stuffed eggplant; the fried corned beef hash balls (with a bit of pickled onion pressed inside) that Wallis Simpson, the newly minted Duchess of Windsor, served. It was all absurdly like a Greta Garbo costume flick about court intrigue in old Sweden, or some such candelabra fantasy. His storytelling—the bravado behind the invented anecdotes—breathed life and drama into the recipes.

The food made easy shifts between high and low: rich pheasant cooked with common lentils; pressed duck à la Tour d'Argent in Paris served with fried hominy squares, browned and crisp; a whole chapter devoted to hash! Framed with stories of Prince Charles of Belgium and Mary Pickford in a little café in Hollywood eating a midnight snack of corned beef hash, or the veal hash in a Paris restaurant beloved of the exiled King Manuel of Portugal. It was all as dazzling and yet as carnal, as casual and down to earth, as Bill seemed. *Of Cabbages and Kings* had a central message about balance in food: about texture and contrast, luxury and simplicity, seriousness and camp.

With scant tools—a limited repertoire of homely dishes and a knowledge of cooking gleaned from his sister—Bill had perfected the art of seeming fabulous. All it took was a set of dramatic flourishes, a lack of shame in spinning fantastic stories, and deep conviction in his own powers of charm. James took note.

: : :

WHAT HAD STARTED AS a weary joke in the cigarette-stale small hours after the Cullum party in November—the one about James and the Rhodes starting a cocktail catering business—took serious form only two months later. James quit the girls of the Buxton Day School in December 1938, after only one semester, and in January 1939, the new partners christened their new catering business Hors d'Oeuvre, Inc. with a bottle of Champagne. Bill, with his social connections, had worked out a plan to get a juicy piece of the cocktail party business on the Upper East Side: to win over hostesses with confidence and a well-bred European's taste and sense of social ease. Bill would be the handsome, rather flirtatious face of Hors d'Oeuvre, Inc.; Irma and James would work behind the scenes, in the production kitchen, cooking and, eventually as they expanded, overseeing the prep for multiple simultaneous parties.

Bill found an office and kitchen convenient for staging: space in the former Oliver Payne carriage house on Sixty-Sixth Street near Lexington. It was a substantial old structure, built in 1890s Romanesque Revival style, pale brick with brownstone and terra-cotta, converted to use as a garage, with living quarters above.

Hors d'Oeuvre, Inc. had a small office in the corner of the garage with a room behind it for food assembly. James and his partners outfitted it with a large old-fashioned icebox, the kind chilled by blocks of ice, since Bill thought mechanical refrigeration killed the soul of food. They bought a machine to slice breads for canapés, and an hors d'oeuvre assembly table. The workhorse kitchen of range and refrigeration and ingredient storage, where James and Irma would spend long days, was in the basement. The garage had space for an old delivery truck Bill found.

Bill's sales pitch to hostesses was iconoclastic. The food at most cocktail parties relied on cheap, starchy fillers and bland spreads: finger sandwiches on cottony white bread overloaded with cream cheese; heaps of potato chips for jabbing into dips of indifferently flavored sour cream. Drinks were no better: assembly-line old-fashioneds slopped into glasses with too much ice, and pitchers of poorly blended martinis. Hors d'Oeuvre, Inc. would bring an epicurean sensibility to parties, a worldly inventiveness equal to the cooking at New York's finest hotels. Their finger foods had stories and a pedigree attached, a shimmering aura of celebrity and fun.

Guests at an Hors d'Oeuvre, Inc. party might nibble on fried corned beef hash balls, a recipe said to come from the private recipe book of the Duchess of Windsor, the woman who made a king give up his throne for love. They might sip demitasse cups of vichyssoise, the chilled potato–leek soup chef Louis Diat had made a sensation at the Ritz. Bill Rhode told hostesses that Hors d'Oeuvre, Inc.'s vichyssoise stretched all the way back to the court of the paranoid Louis XIV, where the potato soup had to circulate among so many royal tasters that by the time it got to the king, it would be deliciously ice cold. Hors d'Oeuvre, Inc. served party food with style and panache, and it *was* inventive and flavorful.

In 1939, international glamour was just what hostesses on the Upper East Side wanted. New York City was getting ready to premiere the World's Fair out in Flushing Meadows, and King George VI and Queen Elizabeth were expected to visit the British pavilion in June. Especially with the troubles rattling Europe (Hitler deciding to take Czechoslovakia, and just like that it was part of Germany), New York seemed more and more the city of the future. Bill Rhode's boutique cocktail parties were all part of the new spirit of modernity. Even its name, with that funny businesslike "Inc." tacked on, was a refreshing change from other caterers.

And the food James and Irma, along with an old friend of James's from his Seattle days, Mack Shinn, were producing in the carriage-house basement did have flair and a focus on fine ingredients. James and Irma spent hours in shops and markets all over Manhattan, sniffing out dark sourdough breads from German and Russian bakers; marble-size tomatoes for stuffing with chopped ham or chicken; Genoa salami slices twisted into cornets and filled with cream cheese so dense with herbs it was electric green; tender calf's tongues poached and shaved, the delicate curls wrapped around balls of creamed Roquefort.

By the spring of 1939, Bill had worked his charm on New York's highest tastemaker. On the morning of April 29, James read Lucius Beebe's *Herald Tribune* column on Bill Rhode, "culinary scholar," whose new catering company had "turtle livers flown in from Florida, the finest of Danish hams and caviars, anchovies, lobsters and game pastes in every known combination."

What a load of shit: turtle livers James's ass. No mention (not one word!) of Bill's partners. "It's a brand new sort of gastronomic agency and already shows signs of being a minor Klondike." Beebe, the most lecherous old queen in New York, obviously had it so bad for Bill he was embarrassing himself. James could already hear the phone upstairs, rung by matrons in Lexington Avenue penthouses with the morning paper still open, maids reading out the number from the telephone directory, hot to book Mr. Rhode's new catering concern for their next cocktail do.

James knew one thing: He sure as hell wasn't going to be scuttling around a basement like an oversize rat forever.

: : :

THE WINE AND FOOD SOCIETY OF NEW YORK was a young organization struggling to find its legs. The International Wine and Food Society sprang up in London in 1933, founded by the eccentric, proudly snobbish, French-born British epicure André L. Simon. The society's first events calendar came together under Simon's pen at the table of the Dowager Lady Swaythling, a name not invented by the Marx Brothers for their recent picture *Duck Soup* but one attached to an actual person. Simon was unabashed about the patrician nature of his organization of amateur gourmets. He made an evangelizing sweep of the United States in 1934, blessing the launch of chapters in Boston and Chicago, and within two years in San Francisco, Los Angeles, and New Orleans. New York proved slippery, though it did take root in 1934 at the hands of Crosby Gaige, theatrical producer and connoisseur of wines, assisted by Republican antitrust attorney Henry Waters Taft, brother of the late President William Howard Taft.

The food scene in New York had proved slightly more dynamic and populist, somewhat less mesmerized by France than Simon might have liked. He abhorred cocktails, for instance, or any beverage besides wine. In his heavy French accent, he told an American reporter how much he despised the rush of life in America; how he abhorred the kind of man who wolfed down an overcooked cutlet in a restaurant so he could scurry back to the office. "Does he once think of the sleeping beauties that lie in the soul of the cutlet," Simon told the reporter, "waiting for the magic of the chef to wake them?"

:::

NEVERTHELESS, by 1936 and 1937, the Wine and Food Society of New York had found an identity through a series of buffet-style tastings, events for members to try twenty-two Champagnes, for example, and nearly as many Alsatian Rieslings; to sample eleven different varieties of Long Island oysters; even critique eggnog recipes and oolong teas.

These tastings—seven a year, at revolving locations on a short list of Manhattan's posh hotels—kept members' palates educated. They served a commercial purpose, too: as a space for wine and caviar importers and cheesemakers, caterers, and smokers of meats to reach New York's small but influential circle of gourmets and, even more important, the food press. "This gang of eating and drinking exquisites," wrote the *Poughkeepsie Journal's* Alice Hughes about Wine and Food Society members, "serves as a liaison agent between wine, liquor and food companies and the people who insist that their browsing and sluicing be correct, and just exactly right in taste and punctilio."

In May of 1939, the New York chapter was to host a big reception at the Waldorf-Astoria's still-new Starlight Roof in honor of the International Wine and Food Society. It would show off the local organization to Simon and the traveling members and be the young chapter's biggest showcase so far for the New York press. Among the providers of hors d'oeuvres would be Bill Rhode's celebrated new company. The president and secretary of the New York chapter, and the woman coordinating with Hors d'Oeuvre, Inc., was Jeanne Owen.

Jeanne was forty-five-ish (her confessed age varied) and a self-styled "gourmette." Her signature, apart from the silver timbre of her voice, was her hair. Prematurely white, fine and flossy, she had it marcelled in a style that never varied: not in the usual serried waves but as a pattern of dimples, giving Jeanne a chic, dappled look. It softened the long, elegant line of her jaw, her pert, pointed chin, turned-up nose, and brows penciled on as triumphant arches—a French face, with a perpetual look of wry amusement, under a white hydrangea puff of coiffure.

She was French—well, born Jeanne Le Provost to French parents. They moved often. Jeanne spent a stretch of her childhood in San Francisco and a span of young adult years in the South of France. She studied theater, and in the fall of 1925 landed the biggest role of her life: Diana Trapes, a smart, self-serving madam, in forty-three performances of John Gay's operetta *Polly* (his sequel to *The Beggar's Opera*) at the Cherry Lane Theatre in Greenwich Village. Since then, she had performed on radio. She had a voice for it, gorgeous and mature, all nasal vowels, cigarette huskiness, and a resonance seemingly capable of causing living-room consoles to vibrate.

Since 1933, Jeanne had been doing a weekly Friday-night musical comedy bit, *Just Relax*, broadcast nationwide on the NBC Red Network. Her cohost was Will Cuppy, humorist, author of satirical books. They'd begin with a subject—the cliché aversion to spinach, for instance, or eating crackers in bed—and depart on mad, looping conversations, marked by mild flirtatiousness and absurd leaps of logic, as a pianist noodled softly in the background. When *Just Relax* began, *The Forum* magazine's radio critic thought it might appeal to a small audience appreciative of "Miss Owen's blithe wool-gatherings and Mr. Cuppy's quiet, but florescent, meanderings among the gigantic daffodils."

Jeanne did meatier roles, too, such as Mrs. Malaprop in Sheridan's *The Rivals*, also broadcast on NBC. Jeanne was a star, a widow with two adult children. She was arguably the best-educated gourmet in New York City and a rare connoisseur of wine, ferocious achievements for a woman at a time when men supposed that female culinary ambition could rise no higher than unlocking the secret to perfect angel food cake.

When she dialed the exchange and number for Hors d'Oeuvre, Inc., however, to talk about the coming Starlight Roof event (which, like all food served at Wine and Food Society tastings, she expected the caterer to offer at a steep discount, if not for free), Jeanne was flabbergasted. Bill Rhode refused her offer to come display his well-publicized cocktail-food artistry.

A few days later, Jeanne called again, intending to underscore just exactly who'd be at the party, starting with Monsieur André L. Simon himself. Instead of Bill picking up the phone, it was James, who said he was Bill's partner. Why, of course, he'd consider it an honor to provide a generous assortment of nibbles for members of the society. He'd even be her liaison for the whole event, personally taking care of it. She shouldn't worry about a single thing.

Besides being a connoisseur of wines, oysters, and caviar, Jeanne was someone who appreciated men—bon vivants—especially queer ones who loved food and cooking. In a way, she collected them: fussed over them, mentored them, called them her Brotherhood of Bachelor Cooks. Sometimes she even found she had a crush on one.

: : :

WITH JEANNE, every door opened for James. Trailing her to Jack and Charlie's "21"—one of her favorites—they slid so easily up the stairs in the oily wake of the maître d'. Slipped so naturally into chairs pulled out by a pair of waiters in short white jackets and shiny black hair. Conversed so easily with Philip, the headwaiter, who would personally be attending to Madame and the gentleman this evening.

Food arrived so effortlessly, without their even ordering. Philip set before them the chef's best dishes: fried rosy-fleshed shrimp with Dijon mustard, crabmeat ravigote, paupiettes de sole anglaises, veal crown roast with truffled wild rice. Philip rested bottles on his upturned forearm for Madame to consider: Alsace Wilm Riesling with the sole? Pontet Canet Pauillac, such an inspired choice for the veal, Madame has excellent taste. A touch of Dom Perignon with the île flottante? Just a little—Madame must try it, compliments of the house. If Hitler made

trouble soon in France like some said he would, this could be the restaurant's last *cuvée véritable* for a while. Perhaps a touch more? Why not
make the night gay!

For James, it was a dream.

Jeanne's circle of gourmets included Lucien Prince, a legendary
wholesaler at the Fulton Fish Market. He was a member of the Thursday Club, epicureans who met every week in the restaurant at the Lafay-
ette Hotel in Greenwich Village, mingling with the bohemians and the
French immigrants. She took James to dine with them. Born in Paris,
Prince could keep a table rapt with his stories and reminiscences. He
knew more about seafood, about caviars, Hudson River shad runs, the
details of a proper bouillabaisse from Marseille, and the habits of flat fish
than anyone Jeanne knew. It was the start of James's serious education.

Jeanne took her new pupil to pay tribute to Crosby Gaige, founder of
the Wine and Food Society of New York and chairman of its executive
committee. Gaige was a fifty-seven-year-old theatrical producer—the
society's business took place in Gaige's office next to the Lyric Theatre
on Forty-Third Street, though that's not where she took James. They
took the train one Sunday to Gaige's country house, Watch Hill Farm
in Peekskill on the Hudson River, forty-five miles north of Midtown. It
was a regal white-board colonial set back from the road, amid lawns, a
grove of pines, and old stone walls.

Physically, Gaige had a consistent roundness: a bald head like a
sphere, circular tortoise-rim eyeglasses, and a fullness of face that
betrayed his love of indulgence. As a young man, he made a fortune on
Broadway producing hit shows. In 1929, before the stock market crash,
he was said to be worth $4 million (the equivalent of just under $60
million in 2019).

Gaige was a gourmet and a connoisseur. During Prohibition, he kept
a warehouse in London where he cellared thousands of wines awaiting
repeal, at which point he had them shipped to New York. The large
flagstone terrace behind the house at Watch Hill was the site of many
dinner parties with icons of the theater: Harpo Marx, George and Ira
Gershwin, Irving Berlin, the Barrymores, Jerome Kern.

Gaige's passions extended to printing and typography. He installed a high-quality press in the corner of a barn, imported paper from Europe, and developed a close and complicated relationship with a handsome younger craft printer and book designer, Frederic Warde, a man described as "an exquisite enigma." After Gaige's marriage ended in divorce in 1928, Warde came to live in one of Watch Hill's five bedrooms for several years. He and Gaige produced small runs of books with pristine design, including Virginia Woolf's *Orlando* and Yeats's *The Winding Stair*. Warde designed the gardens, including the large and encyclopedic one planted to culinary herbs, perhaps the largest of its kind on the East Coast. Together, Warde and Gaige distilled perfumes.

At the time of James's first trip to Watch Hill Farm, the guests on the flagstaff terrace had changed from the stars of New York theater to the elite of New York food and nightlife: Lucius Beebe, Richardson Wright, Lucien Prince, Mac Kriendler of "21." Gaige had recently written *The New York World's Fair Cook Book: The American Kitchen*, a regional overview of cooking in the United States, published in spring 1939, as the fair opened. As she did for restaurants, Jeanne gave James entrée into this rarefied world of power that moved easily between Manhattan and country houses, a nexus of theater and food where homosexuality found easy sanction, as long as it stayed enigmatic and implied, never crossing into messy or overt. He knew that from Jim Cullum's parties.

The Hudson Valley was a world of butlers rolling carts out to flagstone patios for hosts to mix cocktails as performance, and where the writing of cookbooks was a hobby, not a living. James would have felt more comfortable as the butler, but after all, he had experience on the stage, and, as everyone knew, ninety percent of fitting in was acting like you belonged. When someone asked James what he thought of the Meursault, all he had to do was swish it around his mouth, mumble, and arch his eyebrows in a way that suggested an important opinion, though he hadn't committed to one. Besides, if he waited a minute, Jeanne would subtly signal to him what to think of it.

: : :

THE 1939 WORLD'S FAIR in Flushing Meadows ("Flushing-on-the-Commode," as a friend of James's dubbed the 1,200-acre site in Queens) remade New York City in ways James found simultaneously sad and ripe with possibility.

Months before the fair opened on April 30 (exactly 150 years after George Washington's presidential inauguration in New York City), Mayor Fiorello La Guardia had ordered a crackdown, in the name of civic cleansing, that resulted in most of the city's gay bars being closed down. Even the well-worn cruising ground of Bryant Park, the small patch of green on Forty-Second Street behind the New York Public Library, was cleared of men. "Hardly a loafer lingered," as *Esquire*'s Carleton Smith observed two months before opening day. The scoured city braced for an invasion of tourists, and more permanent changes.

Days after his thirty-sixth birthday, James took time off from Hors d'Oeuvre, Inc. to stroll the fair with Jeanne, in the rather forbidding witness of the Trylon and Perisphere—the modernist spire and ball, icons of the fair—and the Soviet-scale statue of George Washington in a cape, all of it looking somehow molded out of compressed tooth powder. Machines milked two hundred cows simultaneously in the Borden Rotolactor, the sleek food factory of humanity's future; a bathysphere took you deep into the ocean to view the fish that would be filleted and quick-frozen, convenient whenever hunger struck; RCA's televising camera could show you a live, unedited movie of people in another part of the fairgrounds.

Westinghouse's planned electric kitchen of the future, with its promise of "electrical freedom," looked as hard-surfaced and shiny as a doctor's office: a refrigerator and cake mixer, a washing machine for dishes, all of it white, enameled, and antiseptic. The kitchen of tomorrow looked strangely absent of food—a bit of a con job, this gleaming, frictionless vision of a distant 1960, free of smells and muck and socks hung above the sink to drip-dry.

In the French Pavilion, though, was a different, far more fragrant vision of the possibilities of food. Jeanne was James's guide for lunch on the top floor of architects Roger-Henri Expert and Peter Patout's

French Modernist showplace, offering a panoramic view of Flushing Meadows. The French government was said to have imported sixty cooks and forty maîtres d's, captains, waiters, and sommeliers. The restaurant manager was Henri Soulé, squat and black-suited, with large Bakelite-frame spectacles that were his face's main source of expression. Jeanne had phoned to say the president of New York's Wine and Food Society was coming to lunch. Soulé treated her with deference. Madame Owen was not impressed.

High above Constitution Mall and the Lagoon of Nations, James was astonished. Waiters swooped in with trays of glass dishes filled with cold hors d'oeuvres: tiny cauliflower à la grecque, marinated in olive oil and lemon juice and covered with thick, yellow-green olive oil mayonnaise; celery root rémoulade; marinated beets; delicate green beans with olive oil and herbs; sweet-and-sour pickled onions with raisins; stuffed marinated artichoke hearts. There were varieties of sardines; three types of poached and marinated tuna; small pickled trout; shrimp salad; lobster mayonnaise. It was chic and easygoing, simple yet with style quite unlike the rustic hors d'oeuvres (the marinated herring and cold saucissons) from James's *pension* days in 1923.

After that, James took the long, ten-cent trip on the World's Fair subway line out to Flushing Meadows several times. He and Jeanne dined at the restaurant in the Belgium Pavilion. Once he rode out with Jim Cullum and Peggy Martin in the apple-green Rolls. They bought cheese at the Swiss Pavilion and vodka at the Soviet Pavilion and had dinner at the French Pavilion. In early spring 1940, James and Jeanne had dinner on the fairgrounds at the Ballantine Three Ring Inn, a place with an American menu of baked pigs' knuckle, Yankee pot roast, and Columbia River salmon, along with Ballantine's beer and ale for washing it down. They dined with Hub Olsen, an editor at M. Barrows and Company who'd recently tapped Crosby Gaige to write a book on cocktails, with a foreword by Lucius Beebe. Barrows was a scrappy publishing house that churned out a high volume of inexpensive, service-y books—titles on cooking, canning, dressmaking, housecleaning, baby rearing.

Over dinner, Olsen challenged James and Jeanne each to come up with an idea for a cookbook. Jeanne's was about cooking with wine. James thought of the thing he knew best, following months of Cullum cocktail parties and assembling tartar balls and cheese croquettes for the hostesses of the Upper East Side: a book devoted to hors d'oeuvres with a modern touch, as well as tips on throwing cocktail parties.

Olsen thought for a minute, counted the months on his fingers. Jeanne's book would need slightly more time for the recipes to come together, and anyway, it was a book with a longer life. James's was hot. Barrows would want to publish in October 1940, for the 1940 holiday season. It was now, what, March?

"How about getting a manuscript to us," Olsen said to James, as the apple pie with a softening slice of New York sharp cheddar atop the hot crust arrived, "in six weeks?"

CHAPTER 7

BRIOCHE EN SURPRISE

1940–1947

IN JULY 1940, James received a letter from his father, the first in James's almost three years in New York. Elizabeth's heart had long been prone to stuttering, episodes that made her flush and clutch her chest. In the past year, her heart had become even more violent and mercurial. For the past few months, her doctor had ordered Elizabeth to keep to her bed. Her heart was completely unpredictable, John wrote in his letter. It would beat rapidly for several minutes at a time, and the pills she was taking seemed powerless to control it. The doctor didn't expect Elizabeth's heart to keep going too much longer. The time had come to tidy her affairs and make arrangements for the end.

So after the last Independence Day party was loaded into the delivery van and rolled out of the sweltering carriage house, James said goodbye to Bill and Irma. He didn't know what he'd find on Salmon Street or how long he'd have to stay. He was quitting Hors d'Oeuvre, Inc. for good. A few days later, James boarded a train for Chicago, where he caught the Northern Pacific's Alaskan, bound for Portland.

He was no doubt grateful to have a reason for leaving, since things would soon be awkward with the Rhodes. In a few months, they'd learn that James had knifed them in the gut.

:::

IT HAD BEEN THREE YEARS since James was on Salmon Street. Elizabeth's Gravenstein trees had gone unharvested this year; birds had pecked at some of the greenish-yellow fruit James could see clustering among the leaves. Those apples had been Elizabeth's pride. Woe to anyone who failed to pick her precious apples when and how she decreed—James recalled the fierceness of her battles with Let about it! In truth, she was having trouble keeping up the garden even before James moved to New York. Whenever Clarence, Lucy Bird's husband, tried to help, she snapped at him.

What would happen to it all? John would keep living in the house, but someone would have to come in and do something with the garden. And what of his mother's collection of things, her bric-a-brac and Chinese treasures? She told James they were his, since John never appreciated them.

Even weak and straining to breathe, Elizabeth related stories from the past: of the great actors Hamilton Bodil and Hobart Bosworth, who both flirted with her outrageously; of the Maxwells, whose daughter Ruth was now more beautiful than ever; and of her dear friend Stella, gone these twelve years now.

Elizabeth's heart gave out on August 19, 1940. She was seventy-nine. Before she died, she told James she thought they might have been great friends if she hadn't been his mother. She said it with a sigh, an air of regret.

When he thought about it later, James supposed she'd paid him a compliment—God knows Elizabeth didn't suffer many people in the course of a long life marked by an incredibly restless youth. James felt only emptiness, the enormity of regret his mother had left as her legacy. Had she loved him? Probably about as much as she was capable of loving anyone. Though James had no particular feeling for his father, he was glad John had a woman who loved him.

After a month spent getting his mother's things in order—giving away her possessions and writing thank-yous for the flowers, condolence letters, and food that friends delivered—James returned to New York. He took only two things of Elizabeth's: a small stone Chinese chop stamp and her handwritten book of recipes.

His indelible image of her was at the beach, in her best wool bathing suit, crossing the foredune on her way back to the cottage, toting a shovel and a bucket of razor clams weighing thirty pounds if it weighed an ounce. Her hair was wet from the surf, and she was smiling.

:::

BILL RHODE'S FAME as New York's "hors d'oeuvre man," as the *Daily News*'s Danton Walker christened him in his popular "Broadway" column, was greater than ever. Bill was getting a radio food program. He and his charming wife had taken a lease on a large, handsome apartment on East Sixtieth Street. Soon the Rhodes were expecting a baby, or, as Walker phrased it for his readers, "anticipating a small caterer in their home."

Meanwhile, the large caterer toiling in the Hors d'Oeuvre, Inc. basement was envious and vexed. James had no real place of his own—he was still lodging at Jim Cullum's, in his ambiguous role of part friend, part paid help. Whenever Bill's name came up with Jeanne Owen, she vented her scorn (she hadn't forgotten Bill's slight of the Wine and Food Society). How could James still be working with that arrogant German bastard? He was forever slighting James, she said, never giving him credit for his ideas or his long hours.

James's revenge came on October 1, publication day for *Hors D'Oeuvre and Canapés, with a Key to the Cocktail Party*, by James Beard, published by M. Barrows and Company. Hub Olsen hosted a release party. Two luminaries from the magazine world showed up: Murdock Pemberton, *The New Yorker*'s art critic, and Alexander Lawton Mackall, *Esquire*'s wine and drinks writer. In the book, James touted his experience as a caterer, his "constant workouts with various types of appetizers," without once mentioning his business partners or acknowledging their contributions (or even authorship) of the recipes: a shocking silence.

James adapted Bill's corned beef hash ball recipe slightly, it's true, but his failure to acknowledge his ex-partner was glaring—especially since James took the trouble to acknowledge borrowing four of Jeanne's recipes, and even one of Peggy Martin's. James had felt exploited at Hors d'Oeuvre, Inc. He also resented Bill for his looks, and for his easy popularity with the tastemakers who took no interest in James. Erasing the Rhodes from his official narrative was James's act of revenge, an entire banquet served cold.

James's most appalling act of getting even was failing to credit the Rhodes for the dish that had made Hors d'Oeuvre, Inc. famous: a canapé called Brioche en Surprise. This "brioche onion sandwich," Clementine Paddleford wrote in the *Daily Herald*, "gives the palate its great moment." She described it to her readers, how it started with circles punched out with a cutter from slices of rich, buttery egg bread. A layer of good mayonnaise went on the circles, then a shaving of sweet onion (white, yellow Bermuda, or red), a sprinkling of salt, and finally a second brioche round, also moistened with mayonnaise. "Now each small sandwich," Paddleford explained, "gets a tight little squeeze until it oozes dressing." The mayonnaise-glossed edge was rolled through a bowl of chopped parsley, "a frosting of green curls," she wrote.

Boldness collided with delicacy in these sandwiches, which were the size of small biscuits and half an inch thick. They started with a common Jewish nosh from Central Europe—raw onion on dark bread plastered with schmaltz—and tweaked it with luxurious French ingredients, brioche and mayonnaise, plus parsley for freshness and a built-in breath sweetener to assuage worries about onion breath at a cocktail party. It's a recipe where charm and originality come from taking a traditional dish and swapping out its signifiers with ones that seem new—a skill James would learn to master, and eventually use to build a cuisine.

Years later, Irma Rhode would admit that, while the core recipe was Bill's, James had come up with the parsleyed edge, so the Hors d'Oeuvre, Inc. sandwich was a true collaboration. Bill, as he did for most recipes in *Of Cabbages and Kings*, came up with an apocryphal origin story, one that got hostesses to blush. He'd discovered them as a young man sowing his wild oats in Paris, he'd say. They were the specialty of a madam in a house that people in polite company didn't speak of: slices of brioche left over from breakfast, spread with mayonnaise and filled with onion, and served with aperitifs.

In *Hors D'Oeuvre and Canapés*, James came as close as he could, in all decency, to evoking Bill's mythical brothel. "Some famous French hostess supposedly started the fashion for these tiny bits of flavor," he wrote, "and created a sensation in her salon. I am sure a reputation and a leading position in any town can be built up if you serve enough of them."

James borrowed something else from Bill: worldly experience, knowledge of the wealthy and titled he didn't actually have. Pineapple scooped and filled with sugared strawberries or other fruits was an idea, James wrote in *Hors D'Oeuvre and Canapés*, inspired by "a famous English hostess who entertained a great deal in the summer at her large country place." He might as well have been playing a role, the sputtering Sir Simon Spatchcock in a drawing-room farce for the Portland Civic Theater, where the view out to the formal gardens through the morning-room window was painted on muslin. So much of James's book was stagecraft.

:::

BACK FROM PORTLAND and bracing for the release of the hors d'oeuvres book, James met with Hub Olsen to pitch a second title for Barrows. They decided he should write a book about cooking outdoors.

Barrows published *Cook It Outdoors* in June 1941. It's a book percolating with James's voice and personality and bristling with mentions of those who filled James's world. He gives Mary Hamblet's method for making mint juleps, and a Zombie recipe from Harold Grossman, drinks author and Wine and Food Society member. Jeanne makes more than one appearance; likewise Charlotte Adams, food editor of the New York paper *PM*. He passes along a recipe from Nancy Dorris, food editor of the *New York Daily News*, and one from Hy Frager, a restaurateur in Medford, Oregon, locally famous for his hamburger rarebit. James calls him "one of the really great hopes of the American kitchen."

James's language is playful and unabashedly queer. He calls a game stew recipe "Game in the Goo," and tosses off "chichi" and "doodadery" with abandon. His look at cacciatore includes the camp read that "practically everything but a henna rinse has been given the chicken which goes by this name."

He dishes Bill Rhode for namedropping Europe's crowned heads in *Of Cabbages and Kings.* James says his formula for Russian Salad is not "the original recipe of the Grand Duchess What What, nor the recipe of the royal family." And he teases an image of bedroom horseplay to explain the appeal of garlic. "No refinement here," he writes of the allium. "But like most of the roughnecks, it is fun to have around."

What makes James's voice particularly striking is that barbecue books were supposed to hew to caveman clichés of manliness. "The authors of cookbooks . . . had to be sure that their readers could not possibly doubt the masculinity of the man in the kitchen," writes Jessamyn Neuhaus in *Manly Meals and Mom's Home Cooking*, a study of gender in American food writing. James throws a bone to gender conventions at the start of *Cook It Outdoors*. "Primarily," he writes in the introduction, "outdoor cooking is man's work and man-sized menus and portions should rule." Yet James's voice subverts the role of the conventional male gourmet of the 1930s. He's neither the wolf who cooks to impress and seduce women, nor is he the gastronomic hobbyist husband who spends all of Sunday mounting a complicated glory dish. James's persona is that of a feminized man in the kitchen. Camp is where James's charm resides—it's the engine of his power.

Cook It Outdoors contains the first recipe of Elizabeth's that James shares, though he doesn't mention his mother specifically, instead referring to Oregon Clam Chowder as "our old recipe." And in describing the outdoor cooking gear of "two girls [who] wanted to see the Gaspé Peninsula," he introduces a lesbian couple who would have an enormous impact on his life and work.

James met Cheryl Crawford at a theatrical party he'd catered for Hors d'Oeuvre, Inc. Crawford was that rarest of things in New York:

a woman who produced and directed theater. Her range would span avant-garde productions and big Broadway musicals. With Harold Clurman and Lee Strasberg, Cheryl founded the Group Theatre. Later, she'd cofound the American Repertory Theatre and the Actors Studio. She was small and slight, wore her hair short and parted, and favored tailored suits with trousers.

Through her good friend, the writer Carson McCullers, Cheryl was a frequent visitor to February House, the queer bohemian co-op at 7 Middagh Street, a dilapidated house in Brooklyn Heights. Starting in 1940, the residents included McCullers, W. H. Auden, Paul and Jane Bowles, George Davis, Benjamin Britten and Peter Pears, and Gypsy Rose Lee.

Cheryl's girlfriend was Ruth Norman. It's likely they met through Janet Flanner, *The New Yorker*'s Paris correspondent. Ruth was a quiet woman with a gentle, nurturing personality, a talented amateur ceramicist who loved to cook. When James met them, Ruth had just moved into Cheryl's homey apartment in a highrise on East Fifty-Second Street, stuffed with books (mostly poetry, Cheryl's passion) and boasting a fireplace lined with Ruth's tiles, painted with commedia dell'arte scenes based on engravings by baroque printmaker Jacques Callot. Cheryl and Ruth spent summer vacations in the queer colony of Cherry Grove at Fire Island.

Here was a life James had been seeking in New York and hadn't found: a supportive queer circle, immersed in theater and food, more open, welcoming, and playful than Crosby Gaige, Lucius Beebe, and the snobs of the Wine and Food Society. They ate well and drank; they had fun—all the elements echoing in James's confident voice in *Cook It Outdoors*.

The only problem was Jeanne. She resented James's new self-confidence, his growing independence from her with his new circle of friends with whom she couldn't compete. She became possessive of James, wanted to know where he was all the time. They'd have dinner together and part. Jeanne would know, roughly, how long it would take James to get to his room at 14 Washington Place. She'd telephone to make sure he hadn't stopped anywhere. If he didn't pick up, she'd keep calling. She'd call James first thing in the morning to find out whether he'd spent the night in a bed other than his own; she'd call him five or six times during the day, just to relate some gossip or find out what he was doing. It was becoming unbearable.

The truth was he'd gotten what he needed from Jeanne: a chance to sit at the table with New York's food elite, an entrée to cookbook writing, scores of valuable connections, and a remarkable foundation in food and wine. But he wasn't Crosby Gaige, a gentleman gourmet eager for social connections. He'd refused to be Bill Rhode's lackey and he sure as well wasn't going to be Jeanne's queer nut to crack. James was determined to break out.

: : :

IN THE SUMMER OF 1941, not long after *Cook It Outdoors* appeared, Lucius Beebe recommended James for a consulting job in Putnam County, New York, fifty miles north of the city. The Bird and Bottle was a historic colonial inn in Garrison. Its new owners had restored it and wanted help with a menu delicious enough to draw weekenders from Manhattan. James gave them recipes for baked chicken, lamb curry, and shrimp remoulade.

In December 1941, when the United States entered World War II, queer Americans faced a dilemma. Before the war, the Selective Service System didn't screen out homosexuals, but in 1942, after consultations with psychiatrists, the Army and Navy put antihomosexual policies in place. Stories of men and women being discharged after disclosing their sexuality swirled in queer circles.

James was thirty-eight. He applied to both Army and Navy. With a body weight north of two hundred fifty pounds, he was obese according to qualification standards, and thus unable to serve. He tried to get into the Hotel Management Division of the Army Quartermaster Corps, the Army's logistics branch, an easier place than combat divisions for queer men to serve. He failed.

At last, in August 1942, the Army drafted James and sent him to Fort Dix, New Jersey, but they didn't enlist him in training. In December, he was assigned to the Army Air Corps at the Miami Army Airfield in Florida, where he at last had basic training. It lasted eighteen days.

On Christmas Eve, James was one of a dozen men assembled for a special assignment. A commander marched them to the mess hall. For the next six hours, starting at midnight, they were to carve almost four thousand pounds of roast turkey for the trainee pilots' Christmas dinner. It was exhausting; his back and his hands ached. The reek of turkey was nauseating. When dawn broke and it was over, the carving corps got leave as a reward. James escaped to a Miami restaurant and ordered steak tartare.

In January 1943, the Army sent James to cryptography school in Pawling, a town near the eastern border of New York, southeast of Poughkeepsie. The Army had taken over an old prep school for boys and ringed it with barbed wire. James completed the class, but the Army discharged him in February, on a miserable day when the mercury dipped to fifteen below zero. James was not being sent overseas.

The Selective Training and Service Act of 1940 gave men age thirty-eight to forty-four deferments if they pursued certain occupations in the national service. One of them was agriculture. So James wrote to Allan Cullum, brother of his old roommate Jim, and asked whether he could work on the family dairy farm in Pennsylvania. Cullum, happy for any available pair of hands during the wartime labor shortage, agreed.

Riveredge Farm spread beside the Schuylkill River outside Reading. Through the spring and summer of 1943, James kept milking records for the Cullums' herd of Guernseys. He learned to operate the butter churn machine and helped oversee cultivation of the sprawling vegetable gardens and orchards. On weekends, he took the train to New York. He saw the second performance of Rodgers and Hammerstein's *Oklahoma!* at the St. James Theatre on April 1, 1943.

In early June, James received a telegram from his half-sister Lucy Bird: their father had died at the age of eighty-three. James stayed on the farm. His father had meant little to him; he'd had a life quite apart from James and his mother. In many ways, John seemed a stranger. In September, Lucy Bird wrote to James: He needed to return to Portland to settle John's will, especially since Elizabeth had left the Salmon Street house in James's name when she died. James sold the house.

In October 1943, James returned to New York and found an apartment, a small second-floor walkup in Greenwich Village at the rear of 36 West Twelfth Street. The kitchen was a converted closet, separated from the bathroom by a partition. There was no kitchen sink. He washed dishes in the bathtub.

James became reacquainted with Horace Gibson, the art student friend of Herbert Weinstock and Ben Meiselman. "Do you realize," James asked Horace, "that you have never invited me to your house?"

Horace said he wouldn't dare cook for a gourmet. James told him not to be silly, that he liked him and he liked food, so why wouldn't he enjoy a blending of the two? Horace relented. They became friends. James took his young friend shopping at Jefferson Market in Greenwich Village and the Fulton Fish Market.

James reached out to Hub Olsen at Barrows, proposing to write another book. They agreed on his third title for the publisher, *Fowl and Game Cookery*. James spent two months testing recipes and writing.

What he produced was a book of just under two hundred pages, less carefree in tone than *Cook It Outdoors*. No doubt the death of John and saying good-bye to the Salmon Street house weighed on James. *Fowl and Game Cookery* would be his most revealing and autobiographical book until *Delights and Prejudices* two decades later. James described Jue Let's cool chicken jelly during James's malaria sickness as well as a detailed rendering of his lately deceased father's Sunday morning skillet-fried chicken ritual.

James wrote of his father that he "had many ideas and definite ones, about food and life. Not only did he have the ideas but he worked at them with a vengeance." If James intended this as an elegy, it was nothing if not ambivalent.

A friend he ran into in New York told James about the United Seamen's Service (USS), part of the War Shipping Administration. Like the

Quartermaster Corps, it provided logistics, except that the USS served the Merchant Marine, operating social clubs and dorm-type accommodations for traveling commercial sailors. James applied. In December 1943, he was accepted and took a training course in New York City.

In May 1944, the USS informed James of his first assignment: to open a new sailors' club in San Juan, Puerto Rico. Axis submarines were torpedoing American commercial supply ships headed for North Africa. James was tasked with opening a club and dormitory in an abandoned bowling alley.

In August 1944, James was on a PanAm flight to his second posting, Rio de Janeiro. The USS club was in an old baroque mansion, not far from the beach. He hired a woman named Manuela, who'd worked as a cook in Rio's foreign embassies. James himself often worked sixteen-hour days. On Christmas Day, he consoled homesick sailors, hanging out a shoulder, he wrote to a friend, "for about twenty young kids to weep on."

The next day, he worked eighteen hours at a party for 220 sailors: turkeys, hams, homemade rolls, an enormous coconut cake of Manuela's, and eggnog heavily spiked with cachaça.

He thought Brazil magical. "I have never found a place I loved so well," James wrote to his friend. He took a train into the Fluminense Mountains to see the city of Petrópolis, transferring to the old cog railway as the terrain became steep. At the station, boys were hawking bananas, bearing great trays on their heads, and calling out the varieties for sale: *banana d'oro, banana pronto*. The world was an aggregation of wondrous local landscapes, full of beauty and variety.

After Christmas, James was sent to Cristóbal in Panama. Then, at last, James got the assignment he wanted, at the American Seamen's Club in Marseille, France. In the week James turned forty-two, in early May 1945, he flew on a Douglas C-47 Skytrain—a Gooney Bird—from New York to Casablanca, with stopovers in Newfoundland and the Azores. He traveled to Marseille via Naples, where he was on May 8, V-E Day, when Germany surrendered to the Allies.

The Seamen's Club was in the old Hotel Continental, near the Vieux-Port de Marseille. It was a bustling facility during the weeks and months after the war officially ceased. James spent the next seven months in France, sneaking away whenever he could to sightsee: to Cassis and the Alps near Grenoble, and as far away as Paris, where he hadn't been in more than twenty years.

::::

IN NOVEMBER 1945, James's USS gig was over. He caught a transport ship home, a miserable voyage of thirty-six days, landing on December 23. A month later, he ran into Charlotte Adams, the food columnist for *PM* and a radio personality. She told James that a producer for WNBT, New York's NBC television station that had exploded in coverage since the end of the war, was looking for James. He wanted him to audition for a regular series of on-air cooking demonstrations. James auditioned. He got the job.

In April 1946, James debuted in *Radio City Matinee,* a twice-weekly magazine show with a cooking segment. James alternated segments with George Rector, the Broadway restaurateur. In June, James replaced Rector as the show's only on-air cooking personality. WNBT experimented with the time slot, sometimes broadcasting in the evening, when the audience in the New York area was assumed to be more male.

James oozed authority. When he baked a whole striped bass, he didn't dumb down his lesson. He stuffed an onion, parsley sprigs, and garlic in the cavity and splashed white wine in the dish. He left the head on. "The people who cook better than any other people," he told the audience, "the Chinese and the French, always serve their fishes like this, and why not follow their example?" Yet he wasn't pedantic— he tempered information with folksiness and self-effacing fun. He instructed viewers to close the bass's cavity with "those delightful little gadgets called toothpicks." He urged the people at home to be uncompromising, to seek out olive oil.

"It takes a little searching around town," James said, "under the Brooklyn Bridge and into Bleecker Street and other little crannies." He could guarantee viewers that it was worth the search. He came across as authentic. He came up with a tagline. "Yes!" he'd roar at the end of a live segment, "I love to eat!" A housewife watching during the day, or a businessman relaxing in his chair after work could look at James—his robust size—and *see* that he did. He was interesting to watch.

After a few months, WNBT rechristened *Radio City Matinee* with the name of an identical show it broadcast once a week in the evenings, *For You and Yours.* For the new season that launched at the end of August 1946, James got his own fifteen-minute weekly show— sponsored by Borden and named for his tagline: *I Love to Eat!*—one of the first regularly recurring cooking shows on television.

It broadcast in the New York area on Friday nights at 8:30, right after *Let's Rhumba,* a Latin dance instruction program, and before *The World in Your Home,* a series of educational short films. The highlight of NBC's Friday nights—*Boxing from Madison Square Garden*—came on at 9.

Cooking on live television was not for prima donnas. The lights were searing. The director thought James's head, bald except for the back and sides and a wispy gray poof on top, looked too large and white. Before each show, makeup man Dick Smith penciled more hairs onto his head before powdering him down to reduce glare. Within minutes, though, James would be shiny with sweat. Sometimes the food looked washed out, too. For a show featuring a wedge of Roquefort, the set designer inked veins on the cheese to emphasize the mold. For a program featuring indoor barbecued turkey, the oven broiler wouldn't work. Just outside the camera's frame, James used a blowtorch to blast the raw bird.

The Borden commercials were built into James's demos. He was required to mention "Borden's" in the name of dairy products, and each show had a gag that tied into Borden, often the appearance of Elsie, the company's cow mascot—as a puppet, or the voice of a telephone caller. James ad-libbed everything else about the demos.

He could be corny and hyper-theatrical, employing pregnant pauses, little vocal trills, and dramatic pronunciations. In some of his spontaneous vamping, James's real voice—the sassy voice of *Cook It Outdoors*— came through. In an episode on roasting a chicken with herb butter under the skin, James ad-libbed, "Chicken, I've got you under my skin."

When he told viewers that the best way to mix herbs into butter was with one's fingers, he suggested this might be something women could be squeamish about. "The female contingent is always afraid to get the fingers into the slurp, as it were," he said. When it came time to decorate the serving platter, he cautioned against getting too fancy, something he claimed women were prone to do. "Men," James said, "are a much better bunch of decorators than women."

WNBT renewed *I Love to Eat!* for the fall 1947 season, but by spring Borden dropped out as sponsor. Birds Eye picked up the show in April, expanding to thirty minutes and renaming it *Birds Eye Open House.* A month later, Birds Eye and the network switched off the lights for good.

James had shown the New York television audience—and potential advertisers—that he combined what had always seemed like contradictions. James was a Continental gourmet who spoke in American cornball vernacular. There was nobody like him.

Privately, beyond the glare of television, James moved in queer circles. In September 1947, he spent an evening out with Horace, Herbert and Ben, and forty-six-year-old Aaron Copland—the so-called Dean of American Composers, likewise queer—at a concert at the Second Avenue Ballroom. They heard New Orleans trumpeter Bunk Johnson, with Lead Belly on guitar. That season, James and Horace joined a few other friends to meet the young writer Truman Capote at his apartment in Brooklyn. The neighborhood was seedy. Truman was odd, and altogether marvelous.

: : :

GEORGES DUPLAIX LOOKED like a fox in a picture book of fairy tales: feral, mischievous eyes set in an inverted triangle of a face, ending in a goateed chin and a mouth frequently fixed in a smirk. In the 1920s, Duplaix migrated from Paris to New York, where he thought he might become a doctor, until a love of drawing and design spurred him to write and illustrate children's books. Duplaix got a job in the Manhattan office of Western Printing Company, a novelty publisher headquartered in Wisconsin. Eventually, he became the director of its New York–based creative book division, the Artists and Writers Guild, which in the late 1930s forged an alliance with upstart publisher Simon and Schuster.

In 1942, the first dozen titles in this pivotal collaboration landed in bookstores and the wire racks of drugstores across the country. They were called Little Golden Books. Each cost twenty-five cents, cheap enough so a child could drop one in the bathtub and their parents wouldn't be furious. Each was illustrated by one of Duplaix's keenly talented artists, many of whom were in New York as refugees from Hitler's war in Europe. Within five months the first volumes, including *Three Little Kittens* and *The Poky Little Puppy*, sold a million and a half copies, with another two million on back order in the United States. New York's notoriously anti-Semitic book-publishing establishment had sneered at the Jewish-owned Simon and Schuster. Now, the men in paneled offices on Fifth Avenue were forced to acknowledge the design and marketing brilliance of Duplaix and his Simon and Schuster partner, Albert Rice Leventhal.

In 1944, Simon and Schuster launched a new division, Sandpiper Press, which would work directly with the Artists and Writers Guild to produce books. Leventhal would oversee it; he hired Duplaix to run it. In January 1948, Duplaix and his wife, Lily (herself the author of a Little Golden Book, *The White Bunny and His Magic Nose*), had a flash of inspiration on the patio of their winter home on Jungle Road in Palm Beach, Florida. Amid the aroma of chickens turning on the outdoor rotisserie, they regarded their guest from New York—a large and affable gourmet with thinning hair plastered to his oddly tapering head—and it occurred to both that this might be the perfect man to write the cookbook Leventhal had been wanting Sandpiper to take a chance on: an illustrated picture book of food for grownups.

With a Champagne glass in one hand and a pineapple chunk impaled on a cocktail stick in the other, their guest was telling one of their rapt and rather shocked Jungle Road neighbors about a black market restaurant he knew in Marseille just after the war, where one feasted on illegal *grives* (thrushes) and feared arrest. Duplaix and his wife watched James Beard, a man who just might have the kind of cartoonishly outsize presence that could pull off a picture cookbook.

: : :

JAMES WAS IN PALM BEACH on assignment from *Gourmet*. Publisher
Earle MacAusland sent him down on the train to report on outdoor
grilling for the June issue. A friend of MacAusland's, a builder and con-
tractor who'd created a lush spread for himself, had an elaborate backyard setup MacAusland wanted James to see.

You could practically smell the postwar cash in Florida's breezes.
The afternoon James arrived in Palm Beach, the Breakers Hotel's Spanish Baroque towers shone white above its rows of royal palms, near a
parking lot full of pale, gleaming Cadillacs. He'd read that the Duke
and Duchess of Windsor were in town—maybe he'd be lucky enough to
glimpse them strolling the shops of Worth Avenue. Here on sidewalks
dappled with women in skirts of pleated linen and hatless, healthy looking men whose golf-course sunburns made them glow, the cold and gray
slush and lingering war depression of New York City seemed far away,

An acquaintance in New York put James in touch with Emilie
Keyes, who wrote a column ("Slightly Off the Record") for *The Palm
Beach Post-Times*. She invited him to her home for Sunday brunch the
day after he arrived. The food was a flop. The cheese soufflé she said
she'd made a hundred times refused to rise. James tasted a spoonful of
the warm, sticky mess and, politely but with obvious annoyance (he was
hungry), suggested she have her oven checked. Keyes was mortified.

To make up for the spoiled brunch, she offered James her services as
driver and local guide. He did not refuse. She took him to the still-new
Society of Four Arts to look at the paintings (he told her he was a devotee
of the School of Paris). She then delivered him to the home of MacAusland's pal, for the outdoor grill party staged in honor of *Gourmet*.

James mowed through plates of mediocre hors d'oeuvres and, with
a drink sloshing in his hand, poked around the four-foot-high brick
range on which steaks were grilling. He found it all rather dull: the
pompous house and obsessively trimmed garden, and the insufferably
smug host—naturally, since he was a friend of good old Earle, whom
James considered a son of a bitch.

What saved the night from being a complete bore was meeting Lily

Duplaix. She described to James the patio rotisserie she and her husband had imported from France. Georges was a French import too, she
joked, and most days just as temperamental; they both laughed. The
rotisserie was capable of cooking three chickens at once, and it filled
the garden with the most delicious smells of garlic and rosemary. James
simply had to come to dinner. Was he free on Tuesday?

CHAPTER 8

THE COUNTRY OMELET OF NEW CANAAN, CONNECTICUT

1948–1949

THERE WERE SNOW FLURRIES when James met Albert Leventhal in the Sandpiper Press offices at Rockefeller Center in late January 1948. Leventhal could warm a room, though. He had ageless varsity bravado, with his short hair and tennis physique, his striped silk ties and Upper East Side tailoring. Leventhal was confident in a way that threw James off, making him feel somehow less than worthy. He was amusing, easy on the eyes, and he spoke James's language. He told James how much he adored the almond soufflé at Gino and Bruno's (what regulars called Quo Vadis on East Sixty-Third) and daily martinis at his regular table in the bar at the Restaurant Mayan downstairs, where he could look its mangy, flea-bitten stuffed jaguar straight in the eye. He charmed James and seduced him into signing a contract for the picture book of food Georges and Lily Duplaix had described in Palm Beach: *The Fireside Cook Book.*

Sandpiper's *The Fireside Book of Folk Songs* was a national bestseller for Simon and Schuster in 1947. "Fireside" indicated a book for leisure reading, once you could flip through while lounging before a raging hearth, a radio concert on, as you lost yourself in the pictures. A fireside book on food would have to walk a careful line for a broad audience: practical recipes and informative descriptions for cooks, and lush language with evocative pictures for those who merely liked to eat.

James would write the text and provide a minimum of one thousand recipes, with shopping notes, a primer on wines and spirits, suggested menus, and a chapter all about the deep freeze, then the hottest subject in American food. All this for a flat fee of five thousand dollars (about fifty-two thousand in 2019 dollars)—flat, as in he would forgo all future royalties. He had just under eight months to deliver a manuscript.

It was sheer madness to sign; he could already hear Jeanne Owen's reasons for why he was a fool. James needed money. Since his television program went bust, he'd been living mostly off what he made at Sherry Wine and Spirits, Jack and Sam Aaron's shop at Sixty-second Street and Madison Avenue. James began working there as a part-time sales clerk in 1946. Two years later, the Aarons made him the manager of Alanberry's, a small gourmet food shop they opened next door—a promotion, but still: James wasn't getting rich. Five grand would see him through most of a year. (God knows he couldn't live off the dribble of royalties from his existing books.) Besides, perhaps this *Fireside* book would make his reputation and lead to some future cache of gold. If nothing else, Simon and Schuster's imprint would give his name luster and the book wider distribution, across all forty-eight states. Barrows couldn't do that.

James had written books on niche subjects: hors d'oeuvres, outdoor cooking, poultry. This would be his first kitchen bible, a sprawling manual on how to cook everything. The task before him was stupendous and exhilarating. If he managed to get all the recipes tested in his telephone booth of a kitchen, it would be a miracle. He asked Ruth Norman to help.

:::

In 1944, Georges Duplaix hired a deputy to help run Sandpiper Press. Dorothy A. Bennett was a thirty-five-year-old native of Minneapolis with quick eyes, a soap-and-water face, and short, sandy hair she combed simply, free of drama. Back home, she'd studied astronomy and anthropology and received a BA in English. In New York, she landed a job in the education department at the Museum of Natural History. She sat in on Margaret Mead's night classes in anthropology at Columbia and eventually took a job as curator at the Hayden Planetarium on Central Park West. Bennett was brilliant, loved the outdoors, and had a scientist's fidelity to order and precision. Also, she was a lesbian.

One day, Bennett and two female friends went to an auction, and, on a romantic impulse, bought a busted old covered barge on the murky Gowanus Canal, a slough of industrial-waste sludge in Brooklyn. They restored the boat with the assistance of Gowanus characters: retired sea captains, winos, junkies, and their assorted bohemian friends from Greenwich Village. Bennett and her friends lived on the canal until a storm sank their houseboat, sending it to rest in the toxic residue of the canal bed. She authored a 1940 memoir of the entire saga, published by Cadmus Books of Chicago: *Sold to the Ladies! or The Incredible but True Adventures of Three Girls on a Barge.*

At Sandpiper, she authored *The Golden Almanac* of 1944 and *The Golden Encyclopedia* of 1946. Albert Leventhal disliked her. He found her prickly and uncompromising, and her insistence on fixing small errors discovered late in the process had resulted in cost overruns.

In 1948, Duplaix let Bennett know she'd be responsible for a new project, another *Fireside* book, this one a cookbook by an author they hadn't worked with before but, Duplaix guessed from looking at James's books for Barrows, would need every bit of patience and precision Bennett could muster. Frankly, he told her, they were *une catastrophe*, a mess as bad as the Gowanus Canal.

: : :

THROUGH THE END OF WINTER and into the spring of 1948, James and Ruth cooked and typed the *Fireside* manuscript. At the end of summer, Cheryl and Ruth bought a weekend house in New Canaan, Connecticut, a small estate near the country place of Cheryl's good friend, the actor and Broadway star Mary Martin. Called Eastham, it consisted of two houses built about 1700 on Cape Cod. Someone in the twentieth century had had them shipped by barge to Connecticut and rebuilt as a single house on thirteen acres of garden and woodland. There was a stone-lined swimming pool set away from the house—perfect for skinny-dipping during summer visits from Cheryl and Ruth's queer friends, including Tennessee Williams and his boyfriend Frank Merlo, the composer Marc Blitzstein, and of course James.

At Eastham, James and Ruth finished the testing for *Fireside*. They braised ducks with canned pineapple and green bell pepper, others with red wine and canned cherries. They broiled ducks, poached and steamed them, roasted them both stuffed and naked, and made an Americanized, barely sweetened version of duck à l'orange, the famous French dish of roasted duckling with a classic brown sauce flavored with sour oranges.

They cooked three dozen recipes for beef, from minute steaks to braised oxtail, another two dozen for veal, including broiled and sautéed calf's liver, a blanquette, and a whole poached calf's head with sauce gribiche. They cooked dozens of recipes for pork in all its fresh and cured forms—from chops and spareribs to boiled pigs' feet and hocks (James's favorite), from homemade sausage and salt pork to glazed smokehouse ham.

They waited for vegetables to come in at Walter Stewart's. And as the frosts weakened and finally disappeared—and Cheryl Crawford's avant-garde play *A Temporary Island* closed in March after only six performances, and *Brigadoon* at last came to an end in summer—Eastham's vegetable garden (Cheryl's joy) came to life.

Though Duplaix and Leventhal wanted a recipe bible from James, a thorough compendium of home cooking, vegetables would be the heart of the book, his most expressive recipes.

He invoked the artichokes growing in great coastal fields south of San Francisco. He wrote about chayote, which he came to know in Rio de Janeiro during the war as *xuxu*—carioca slang, cooed between lovers. He recommended corn by variety, picked and eaten within half an hour: early producing Golden Bantam and Golden Cream; Country

Gentleman, a white shoepeg spun with knobby, irregular kernels; and, for city dwellers, midget cultivars to grow in a pot.

Still, Simon and Schuster insisted on a chapter about cooking with frozen vegetables, meats, and fish. "Not since the appearance of the first glacier," E. J. Kahn Jr. wrote in *The New Yorker* in 1946, "has there been any phenomenon to compare with the frigid giant that is now looming on the horizon of the American housewife, in the shape of the frozen-foods industry." In six months of that year alone, twenty-two shops devoted exclusively to frozen foods (some with windows flocked to look frosty) opened in Manhattan. By the end of the year, there were forty.

A 1949 survey revealed that three-quarters of American housewives had purchased frozen foods, and two-thirds of them served freezer food more than once a week. And it was affluent women, the ones who bought cookbooks, who relied on them the most. In 1946, Birds Eye, the company that traced its origins to Clarence Birdseye, inventor of the quick-frozen process, offered more than sixty types of frozen foods, from asparagus spears to mackerel fillets, and forequarter roasts of lamb to rhubarb.

In 1941, General Foods Company, Birds Eye's parent, published the *Birds Eye Cook Book*, a thick promotional pamphlet with recipes. It touted the miracle of strawberries in January and corn on the cob year round, a world of industrial marvels capable of erasing the seasons. Despite himself, James worked out recipes for frozen squash with oranges, frozen green bean and ham hash, and frozen three-fruit compote.

James already had a relationship with Birds Eye and the publicity director for General Foods, Marjorie Dean, since they did pick up sponsorship of *I Love to Eat!* after Borden bowed out. James was grateful to the company, even though frozen cobs of corn were a sad substitute for fresh ones. Besides, he didn't say that frozen ingredients were superior, only that they enabled "informal living": the ability to cook up crabmeat salad, for instance, when unexpected guests showed up. As for convenient freezer dishes such as stews, pies, and cakes, James traced a line in the slush. "I am obliged to withhold my enthusiasm," he wrote.

Unlike Jeanne Owen, who called for Birds Eye frozen raspberries in a recipe in one of her books, James didn't mention the brand, though he did pack his frozen foods chapter with Birds Eye marketing points (courtesy of Dean). Convenience, lack of waste, true economy, and the year-round blessing: They were all industry concepts, calculated to overcome doubts about quick-frozen foods, which didn't seem to many shoppers worth their elevated price. James sucked up his own ambivalence and skepticism, waded in, and borrowed freely from the language of the *Birds Eye Cook Book.*

A former sponsor, one that might prove useful in the future, was hardly someone to piss off. A boy had to eat.

: : :

THE PROJECT WAS almost too ambitious—he was under contract to deliver a thousand recipes! James took a shortcut he considered necessary for survival. He plagiarized himself.

Of the approximately twelve hundred recipes in the *Fireside* manuscript, more than a hundred were slight tweaks of ones published in James's three previous books, with perhaps only a single word altered. James cited permission from Barrows to reprint only one, the cheese croquettes from *Hors D'Oeuvre and Canapés.* The others—nearly ten percent of *Fireside*—were brazen acts of self-plagiarism.

Thanks to Dorothy Bennett's edits, *Fireside*'s "Outdoor Cookery" chapter is merely a refined new draft of James's nearly identical introduction to *Cook It Outdoors.*

With no acknowledgment, grilled turkey legs and Mabelle's Turkey Casserole (from James's Portland friend Mabelle Jeffcott) migrated straight from *Fowl and Game Cookery;* marinated steak and steak sandwiches from *Cook It Outdoors*; venison burgers from *Fowl and Game Cookery. Fireside*'s squab recipes were word for word the same as in *Fowl and Game Cookery.*

In some cases, James did update or refine previously published recipes, adjusting cooking times or bumping up serving portions of meat, now that wartime rationing was a fading memory. Vichyssoise is identical in *Fireside* and *Fowl and Game Cookery*, except that in the latter James spelled it *vichyçoise*, the way Jeanne Owen did in one of her books. Herb-stuffed broilers were a tweak of Léonie de Sounin's recipe in *Fowl and Game Cookery*. He added heavy cream and a pinch of thyme to *Fireside*'s clam chowder, otherwise it's identical to his mother's rustic original in *Cook It Outdoors*.

Still, why did Bennett and Leventhal turn a blind eye to James's self-cannibalizing? Surely they heard echoes—at least—from his earlier books.

And yet, in their hands—with recycled material—James was beginning to articulate an original concept, of a new kind of American home cooking built on the bones of French *cuisine bourgeoise*. Louis P. De Gouy, the French-trained American chef who was *Gourmet*'s recipe editor, approached something similar in his 2,462-recipe *The Gold Cook Book* of 1947 (the year De Gouy died at age eighty-eight). But where the chef saw a juxtaposition of French and American dishes— cooks who would master both Brunswick Stew à la Dixie and Coq à la Bourguignonne—James was feeling his way toward a fusion of the two.

James loved the hearty, unfussy traditional cooking of mothers and grandmothers in France: pot-au-feu, coq au vin, boeuf bourguignon. With *Fireside*, he began not only to use English names for some French dishes but also graft American ingredients onto the rootstock of French recipes. So he finessed a traditional French daube into *Fireside*'s Braised Beef, Peasant Style: in other words, pot roast, though with red wine, Cognac, and thyme.

This new American hybrid seems fully evolved in his Country Omelet: diced bacon fried with potatoes, onion, and parsley, added to beaten eggs and cooked to produce a flat omelet. James's inspiration was *omelette paysanne* ("peasant" or "farmer's wife's" omelet), made with *lard de poitrine salé*, salted pork belly, a French staple. With American smoky bacon and an English name to reorient it, James created something new in *Fireside*: a dish that seemed to have roots with farmers in the Willamette or Susquehanna Valley, not villagers in the Rhône. American food.

:::

THE MANUSCRIPT JAMES DELIVERED to the Sandpiper offices late in the summer of 1948 was sprawling and chaotic. It was up to Dorothy Bennett to subdue it, to shape it into coherence. She had to ghostwrite most of James's introduction in *Fireside* as though she were curating a food-history exhibit for schoolkids. Bennett combed through *Hoyt's New Cyclopedia of Practical Quotations* to find food-themed maxims to sprinkle throughout the book, from Claude Mermet—"Friends are like melons . . . to find a good one you must a hundred try"—to John Gerard's recycled Spanish proverb: "Four persons are wanted to make a salad—a spendthrift for oil, a miser for vinegar, a counselor for salt, and a madman to stir it all up."

It was Bennett, her mind grounded in scientific classification, who built a workable cookbook template for *Fireside*. It involved a basic master recipe (Plain Chicken Sauté, for example) with detailed technique notes, followed by variations, usually switched-out aromatics, cooking liquids, and garnishes (Chicken Sauté Italian, Provençale, Amandine, Herbed; with Mushrooms, with Paprika, and more).

When James finished, he had approximately eight hundred stand-alone or master recipes, with about four hundred variations on the latter. It was a revolutionary way to organize notoriously hard-to-use kitchen bibles. The lavishly illustrated *Betty Crocker's Picture Cook Book*, released almost exactly a year after *Fireside*, in September 1950, would use a system of master recipes similar to the one Bennett created.

Bennett shaped and polished James's voice, making him sound like a spirited yet pedantic professor, as when Bennett had him quoting the Catholic novelist Ernest Oldmeadow ("Both wine and cheese represent man's effort to transmute the perishable into the durable"). In his books for Barrows, James's writing voice had been flamboyant and opinionated, full of rapture, eye rolls, and sass; it captured his speaking voice, which is to say it resonated with queerness (as it did on television in *I Love to Eat!*). Bennett crafted the professional, carefully filtered writing voice James's future editors would preserve and continue to shape. For the myth, which would endure, of James Beard as an epicurean bachelor professor, Bennett delivered the rough cut. The cleaning and polishing of James into a commercial entity starts here.

The timing of James's de-queering in public was no coincidence. Since the end of the war in 1945, gender roles in America had acquired taut boundary lines, and the backlash against queers was sharp. Even in the 1930s, New York City—especially in the enclaves of Harlem and Greenwich Village, and in pockets of Brooklyn—was more permissive of homosexuals, including those who identified as "fairies," men who moved and talked, dressed and groomed themselves in ways that strayed from mainline American norms.

After World War II, though, the general tolerance for "pansies," men who read as "effeminate," withered in the Cold War's frost, a patriotic adherence to strict gender expectations. James was the male author of a book on everyday cooking, a space reserved for women authors. Men did write cookbooks, but they were assertions of traditional masculinity: cooking as a tool to get women between the sheets, as in *Wolf in Chef's Clothing*, a 1950 cookbook by *Esquire* food and drinks editor Robert H. Loeb.

It was no time to be anything but a sexless bachelor with a crisp, professional voice, too focused on work or the singular pursuit of fine living to think about marrying. And James, indeed, had been far too busy even to think about pursuing anything resembling a sex life. Perhaps when *Fireside* was all over, and he could travel. Sex was always easier abroad, in civilized places where people tended to shrug about such things. For James, harboring memories of the uninhibited city he tasted in 1923, Paris loomed as a place of release.

: : :

ALICE TWITCHELL MET Martin Provensen in Los Angeles in 1943. She was an illustrator at Walter Lantz Productions, home to Woody Woodpecker, Andy Panda, and Chilly Willy. Martin had worked for Walt Disney: drafting character studies for the "Dance of the Hours" in *Fantasia,* designing a Russian folk-art scheme for an early vision of *Peter and the Wolf.* Both worked in a pop medium that riffed on high culture, toggling between Americana and classical European motifs. The couple married in 1944 and eventually moved to New York City, where an old friend from Disney, Gustaf Tenggren, was doing contract work for the Artists and Writers Guild. Tenggren introduced the LA transplants to Georges Duplaix, who in 1948 tapped the Provensens to illustrate *The Fireside Cook Book*. Duplaix also enlisted French art-book designer Guiton Chabance for *Fireside*, which was to be printed in a large format, on heavy stock with a subtle sheen, and bound in lacquered cloth.

In their New York apartment, the Provensens sketched and painted more than four hundred line drawings and thirty-six full-page illustrations in their Disneyfied style, and they even tested many of James's recipes from the manuscript pages. For some chapters, they drew anthropomorphized animals as visual leitmotifs to unify the recipes: a dopey-looking turtle for Soups; a cuddly clone of the Easter bunny for Salads; and, for Poultry, a henhouse-raiding fox that looked suspiciously like Duplaix, with a snout as sharp as an awl and a taste for spit-roasted chicken. (The Provensens winked at Dorothy Bennett, too. In an illustration for cold-weather menus, a rainy urban streetscape features a billboard showing a woman rushing to the table, bearing a tureen for her waiting man. "Need a LIFT?" the billboard reads. "Bennett's Vitamin Enriched Soup.")

The Provensens also quoted from high art. They drew a leering troubadour composed of squashes, tubers, corn, and cabbages, echoing the creepy fruit and vegetable portraits by sixteenth-century Milanese painter Giuseppe Arcimboldo. They placed their edible troubadour in a starkly receding horizon that borrowed from the Surrealist Giorgio de Chirico. They painted Cubist collages worthy of Georges Braque and a Disney cartoon pastiche of Grant Wood's famous painting *Dinner for Threshers*. Every visual aesthetic seemed ripe for quoting: Parisian street tableaus from the belle époque, cowboy-film iconography, and Americana with the flavor of Lemuel Ayers's clapboard-and-windmill sets for the original production of *Oklahoma!*, still in performance at the St. James Theatre in Manhattan.

The glossy book jacket pays homage to nineteenth-century American trompe l'oeil painter William Harnett. Against the grain of a wooden cutting board, the Provensens designed each letter of the words *COOK BOOK* as a still life of twisted herbs, vegetables, or fruits anchored to stiffer props (a cinnamon stick; olives on the branch). A leaf ravaged by aphids clings to the stem of a bruised and burnished little delicious-looking apple. Cover lines ramble across what look like torn slips of paper.

The jacket opened to reveal a poster-size illustrated chart, the flap copy explained, "to decorate your kitchen or game room." It shows a lace-curtained window, through which a woman in a sunbonnet broadcasts feed to her chickens. In the foreground, fruit spills from bowls and baskets. All around them were lists of food categories: Meats, Vegetables, Pastry, Herbs and Spices, and more, an entire taxonomy displayed like a needlepoint sampler with quotes from English poet Matthew Prior and Edward Bulwer-Lytton. Both sayings are about finding joy through eating. Embedded in so much Americana, they imply that pleasure at the table is critical to American identity.

James found the book very pretty. It gave him a new public face. He was now a leading American authority on cooking and the good life.

When he wrote a piece on carving for *Gourmet*'s Thanksgiving issue of 1948, James felt emboldened to call out the phony gentility of the gourmet crowd—"those whose first idea is elegance rather than function"—and the idea that one should never touch food with bare hands. He gave readers permission to grab and steady small carcasses; to snip through bones with carving shears. James was in control now. He gave his readers permission to take off their jackets and roll up their sleeves. He was eager to flee old rules.

:::

SIMON AND SCHUSTER released *The Fireside Cook Book* on October 28, 1949. Albert Leventhal splurged for a celebration lunch at Jack and Charlie's "21," with Georges Duplaix, the Provensens, Dorothy Bennett, James, maybe a dozen in total. They crowded around two pushed-together tables, in a haze of cigarettes, with the light flashing off the old silver trays and baronial tchotchkes propped on the shelf above the dark paneling. Black-tied young waiters in epauletted Eton jackets hovered around Leventhal, holding lit matches to cigarettes and pouring seven, maybe eight different wines, each in its own glass. They all drank themselves silly. James was ecstatic. His euphoria didn't last.

Six weeks later, on December 10, *The New Yorker* published a devastating capsule review, unsigned but clearly by Sheila Hibben, the magazine's food writer and a powerful friend of Jeanne Owen. The review called *Fireside* "as beautiful and elaborate a picture book . . . as the season is likely to provide." That was the bright note; the rest was catastrophic.

She called it "enormously pretentious, repetitious, padded with bits of women's-magazine anthropology." It used bombastic language to cite platitudes about wine. The menus were absurd, mixing up hot- and cold-weather dishes. "The truth is," Hibben concluded, "Mr. Beard simply doesn't know enough."

Who else but Jeanne could have poked at Hibben to spew such venom, and to strike James so personally? She knew better than anyone the extent of his recycling and plagiarizing, the knowledge he'd faked, copied, or just made up. She'd even spotted Dorothy Bennett's rare mistake (the hot buttered rum and jellied broth business), when she didn't catch the transposed page headings for warm- and cold-weather menus. Someone had to have sifted through *Fireside* minutely. This was an orchestrated takedown—in the magazine read by anyone who mattered in New York. The author of *The Fireside Cook Book* was no better than an amateur, a man who could cook but didn't rise to the status of true gourmet: a *poseur.*

Hibben's proxy hit for Jeanne hurt, because James knew there was truth in it. Maybe he didn't know everything he claimed to know, but pretending was the game. The day after *Fireside*'s publication, the *New York Times* ran an interview with James by its food editor, Jane Nickerson. "Mr. Beard said that he came by his interest in cooking quite naturally," Nickerson wrote. " 'My mother operated a hotel, so even at an early age I felt very much at home in even a huge kitchen,' he explained." James hadn't *lied*. Elizabeth did operate a boarding hotel, though of course it was several years before he was born.

This business of being an authority was about acting the part. Jeanne and Hibben could go to hell. Besides, James was already onto something new, a stupendous project in Paris that would leave no one in doubt about his taste or expertise.

Although in truth, he'd be happy if it just paid his expenses to stay away from New York for a good long while.

PART THREE

CHAPTER 9

PHEASANT SOUVAROFF,
AN AMERICAN DISH

1950–1952

THE DUKE ELLINGTON ORCHESTRA sailed on the *Île de France* in April 1950. They were booked for nearly a week in the City of Light, to shake the walls of the stiff and blocky Palais de Chaillot, near the Eiffel Tower. Days before they arrived, Air France flew a Lockheed Constellation from New York's Idlewild to Paris's Orly Field in record time: eleven hours, eleven minutes, instead of the usual seventeen. Only four months into the new decade, the heart of the old world palpitated to the kick drums and turbines of the new.

James stepped off a plane not long afterward, descending the airstair to Orly's tarmac. Also on his flight were Gene Kelly and Hollywood producer Arthur Hornblow Jr., a year and a half before the release of MGM's *An American in Paris*. The French capital was already planning celebrations for its two-thousandth birthday in July 1951. James, with a flight bag over his shoulder, his suit jacket flapping open in the wind blowing across the plateau beyond the southern limits of Paris, was toting a sense of mission, a determination to excavate the past.

Brothers Sam and Jack Aaron, owners of Sherry Wine and Spirits on

Madison Avenue at East Sixty-Second, had sent James here. The Aarons had toyed with the idea of opening a Sherry store in Paris, a showplace for French wines close to the source. More and more American tourists were streaming into Paris, queuing at the Louvre to gape at the Leonardos and Vermeers recovered from pilfering Nazis. Why not also show them the Montrachets and Haut-Brions in the house of Sherry, where the sales clerks smiled and spoke English and could arrange easy shipping home to Cleveland?

Sam Aaron was a Francophile who needed no excuse for sending one of Sherry's men to Paris. Immediately after the war, he forged a friendship with the American wine writer and merchant Frank Schoonmaker. He took Sam on a personal tour of France's wine regions, and for the past few years, Sam and his wife, Florence, had dreamed of moving to Paris, ancient center of wine, art, and *joie de vivre*. Sending James, the Aarons' in-house bon vivant, to schmooze with restaurateurs and travel scribes and the wine elite could only build momentum for a Sherry flagship. Anyway, the Aarons weren't the only ones picking up James's tab.

After the war, Air France advertised its planes as chic, modern transport for Americans making pilgrimages to the motherland of cuisine. (A 1955 ad in *The New Yorker* showed none other than America's original gourmette, Jeanne Owen, her disembodied head floating above a sketch of Nice, endorsing Air France as her favorite carrier to the Côte d'Azur.) When James was able to land a first-class flight to Paris with a tacit understanding he'd describe the food and service in some future piece for *Gourmet*, the Aarons agreed to put him up at Sam's favorite small hotel off the rue de Castiglione, near Place Vendôme.

James had neither a checkout date nor a return ticket home, and he didn't plan to spend a minute more than he had to in his official capacity for Sherry. He had bigger plans.

:::

ONE NIGHT IN OCTOBER 1949, three weeks before Simon and Schuster published *Fireside*, James had what he thought was his best idea of all time.

James was in Paris, at the end of a long wine-tasting junket with a group organized by the San Francisco chapter of the Wine and Food Society. They'd assembled a group of members (and a few invited food writers) on a three-week tour of France's wine regions: Bordeaux, Burgundy, the southern Rhône, Alsace, Champagne. They met up with André Simon in Rheims and dined at Fernand Point's La Pyramide in Vienne. Louis Vaudable, director of the famous Maxim's restaurant in Paris, hosted a lavish farewell party for the group. Vaudable wanted to prove to his distinguished and influential American guests that, after war and Nazi occupation, Paris was open for business again, gleaming brighter than ever. Ironically, Vaudable himself had a brooding intensity. His long gangster's face, tanned and leathery from unshielded terrace time at his villa above Nice, reset to a naturally savage expression whenever he relaxed his professional obsequious smile. Tonight, he orchestrated a theatrical, sensually overwhelming feast with one aim: seduction.

There were huge platters of greenish claires oysters from the Marennes-Oléron beds in Charente-Maritime, served with a riveting 1934 Montrachet. The white Burgundy continued through the next course: *rouget en papillote,* red mullet baked in parchment. "The red fish made a most dramatic appearance," James wrote in a long, two-part report for *Gourmet,* "as they were rushed in encased in their voluminous paper coverings, and the aroma was overpowering as they were torn from their sheaths before eating." Next course was Pheasant Souvaroff, Maxim's glory dish with truffles and foie gras, baked in dough-sealed crocks cracked open at the table. Vaudable ensured that delicious smells would waft over the half-inebriated guests in waves. Waiters served a 1919 Château Haut-Brion, decanted from magnums. The taste seemed to reverse time, conjuring a France that existed before the war.

Before the Wine and Food Society trip, all James had had of Paris, foodwise, were aging impressions: memories from his six weeks there as a boy of twenty in the summer of 1923, before his food senses were keen. Then, James was more attuned to the astonishing freedom Paris offered, its indifference to shame in satisfying human appetites in a queer brothel or the nighttime restaurants near Les Halles, where butchermen in bloody smocks demolished plates of tripe and calf's brains, washing away thirst and the reek of carnage with entire bottles of cool, violet-scented Beaujolais.

The affair with his boxer—his *prizefightairr*—in the summer of 1923 remained the single most electrifying sexual experience of James's life. He'd relived hundreds of times in his memory the afternoon they had sex. The recollection was indistinguishable from Paris, the wider city: the strangely delicious blue smoke of buses; the early morning gossip and shrieking laughter of maids echoing down hallways in hotels of every class; the inextinguishable smell of ripened butter on one's hands after ripping through a basket of horn-shaped breakfast rolls called *croissants*, a word unknown in the US. Vaudable's operatic production— this *grand fête de séduction*—revived the scale of James's memories.

This Maxim's seemed a different place from the one he visited in 1923, when the fear of what it would all cost merged with the sneers of the waiters and the disappointment of the food. Tonight the restaurant looked exquisite, a kind of museum piece of the voluptuous grand époque Paris that Americans were suddenly eager to discover. The tracery of the windows and dark mahogany of the walls, so like Guimard; the nymph murals and plants in art nouveau pots.

That night at Maxim's, James met Alexander Stuart "Sandy" Watt, one of the Parisians Vaudable had invited to mingle with the traveling Americans. Forty-year-old Watt had a face like that of the actor Leslie Howard: long and pale, with brows cocked in perennial bemusement, set in a forehead so high it looked as though his features had all slipped down gently over time and settled in a sympathetic pile just above his chin. He was lean but had a fleshy sensuality James found enchanting. He loved the soft edges of Sandy's Edinburgh trill, his combination of wit and British public-school grooming.

Watt had spent nearly half his life in Paris. Like the fledgling American painter Richard Olney, the Iowa boy who would settle here in 1951, Watt loved French dishes both rustic and evocative of place—in Parisian terms, cooking expressive of its *quartier*, the neighborhood it simultaneously nurtured and helped define. He especially loved bistros:

small restaurants with a zinc bar and sawdust on the floors and a loose ambiance overseen by a mom and pop, *la patronne et le patron*, working as chef and waiter. They were restaurants *en famille*, the sort James had known and felt least intimidating back in 1923. A love for them was one thing (actually the only thing) James and Watt shared.

Watt was born in Edinburgh in 1909, a son of the distinguished portrait painter George Fiddes Watt. Young Watt was restless. With his friend Jack Cowan, Watt took to the road in the late 1920s. They were two dashing young men with no money, just energy and charm.

They lingered in Switzerland and France. In 1930, Watt settled in Paris. He tried to find work as a writer on the gallery beat, as commentator and critic. He befriended artists. He spent long hours in the galleries and studios of the Latin Quarter and Alésia, and in Montparnasse's quirky, squalid beehive of ateliers called La Ruche, where Modigliani, Léger, and Chagall had lived and worked. Paris was a laboratory of volatile ideas and expression: Surrealism, Dadaism, Cubism. In magazines (*Art and Industry*, *The Studio*, *Art in America*) and newspapers (*The Scotsman*, London's *Daily Telegraph*), Watt tried to make sense of these constantly changing movements for Anglo-American readers. And because bistros and cafés were where artists loitered, Watt got to know those, too.

"Before the war," Watt would write in *Paris Bistro Cookery*, "it became a fashionable pastime to 'collect' bistros, much as one collects postage stamps." In the 1930s, he began writing for the *Telegraph* about the places he'd collected, and he even plotted a gastronomic visitors' map of Paris for the French National Tourist Office. As Paris braced for war in 1939, Watt retreated across the English Channel. In 1944, when the Allies asserted that peace had returned to Paris, so did Watt. In the wake of Liberation, as Paris tried to remake itself as a tourist destination—a center of art, cuisine, and couture—and the boulevards bustled with civilian traffic, Watt chronicled the city's cultural reawakening.

And so, amid the fragrance of truffles and *rouget* released from the crimped-parchment balloons at Maxim's that night, James sniffed opportunity.

: : :

IN 1950, cultured Americans were hungry to taste the *real* food of Paris and the French provinces, dishes Continental restaurants could only approximate at best, even in Manhattan. Pâté en croûte, tourne-dos Rossini, bouillabaisse, soufflés: Americans had read about them in *Gourmet*, maybe even tried cooking one or two, using whatever substitute ingredients they could find (truffles from a can; fresh chicken livers instead of foie gras; good old cod for rascasse, Mediterranean scorpionfish). Americans in 1950 opened their pocketbooks to spend ten dollars (an almost shocking price) for ring-bound copies of *Betty Crocker's Picture Cook Book*. Those with refined tastes were also rushing to mail-order another ten for a cookbook from *Gourmet* weighing more than three pounds.

Published by the magazine, *The Gourmet Cookbook* was as thick and imposing as the New York Social Register. It had a vinyl binding with the texture of alligator skin, in library-shelf oxblood with gold embossing. You could personalize the cover with a monogram or a complete moniker, to save it from the indignity of being defaced inside with a scrawled name. Golden fleurs-de-lis floated across the endpapers. "Our recipes wear fancy dress," read an ad for the book in *Gourmet*, "and they're proud of it." *The Gourmet Cookbook* was unapologetically opulent. To many Americans, opulence was the same thing as Frenchness.

The United States had gone to war to preserve a Europe of independent nations, in which Paris—virtually intact, physically, after five and a half years of war—was the jeweled and filigreed crown. Americans—and not just rich Americans—wanted to take a look at what they'd wrested from Hitler. Trans World Airlines would begin selling tourist-class tickets from New York to Orly in 1952, and crossing the Atlantic by ship had never been cheaper. Most who got to Paris wanted real French cooking, in restaurants that wouldn't cheat them or try to pawn off horsemeat entrecôtes as beef. For that, they needed a guide. And Watt, it occurred to James that night at Maxim's, was just the person to write one—naturally, of course, in collaboration, since it would be a guide with recipes, with James Beard, author of *The Fireside Cook Book*.

The timing seemed excellent. More and more, American travel books were blending practical, on-the-ground information with armchair narrative. Publishers were seeking writers capable of telling entertaining stories, not just dredging up history and listing museum hours. "The fashion in guidebooks is surely changing," Samuel Putnam, author of the memoir *Paris Was Our Mistress*, wrote in his 1948 *New York Times* review of Horace Sutton's *Footloose in France*. "Time was . . . when these compilations sounded as if they had been written by near-sighted antiquarians for long-haired esthetes. . . . The trend now is in the opposite direction, away from the dry-as-dust and toward the bright." If anyone could tell bright stories about Paris, it was Watt, a writer connected to its artists and bohemians, its cooks and *patrons* who dispensed Pastis and café au lait from behind zinc bars.

So in April 1950, six months after that night at Maxim's, when James stepped off the plane and walked thickly on the tarmac at Orly Field, technically he was on assignment for Sherry and the Aarons. Sheila Hibben's stinging review of *Fireside* in *The New Yorker* still hurt. This book, James thought, would force them to eat a pointedly lavish dish of crow.

: : :

JAMES'S ENEMIES WERE powerful, and their numbers were growing. Jeanne Owen's proxy takedown via Sheila Hibben's pan of *Fireside* in *The New Yorker* had been egregious and appalling. Before James left for Paris, Earle MacAusland booted him from *Gourmet*. His February "Spécialités de la Maison" column (a roundup of old-fashioned chophouses in New York City, including Keen's and Gage and Tollner) would be his last. It was an outrageous expulsion, almost as painful as James's exodus from Reed College, and for a similar reason. MacAusland found James too brazenly queer.

One afternoon, James and some members of *Gourmet*'s staff were enjoying rounds of the Oak Room's famously stiff and delectable martinis downstairs from the magazine's offices in the Plaza Hotel. MacAusland wasn't there. Someone reported to him, though: James had talked too freely about being a homosexual. He lacked the proper discretion.

This was ironic, since the Oak Room was well known among gay men as a safe place to gather, albeit with the proper decorum, and even pick up other men, as long as it all happened quietly and nobody touched.

MacAusland had already found James a handful. His copy was atrocious and messy: single-spaced sheets of digressions, personal associations, and the flaunting of proudly held prejudices regarding food that wandered wide before looping back to the ostensible subject. James had personality but no discipline. He gossiped all the time and now this, this . . . acknowledgment of a subject people in decent society should never publicly avow. It could besmirch the magazine and taint MacAusland's personal reputation. James had to be cut loose.

Gourmet needed a cover story to explain James's dismissal. It arrived in MacAusland's mail: the Sherry Wine and Spirits catalog, featuring James Beard's report of his recent tour through the wine regions of France with members of the Wine and Food Society. James had plagiarized himself yet again, with some material identical to his story running that month in *Gourmet*! MacAusland had his pretext for firing James literally in his hands.

For James, exile from the magazine merely reinforced what he knew: that MacAusland was a miserable son of a bitch. One of James's closest gossip girlfriends, whom he spoke to by phone nearly every morning, was Ann Seranne, a bright, perky native of rural Ontario, Canada— James's equal in gab, likewise discreetly queer—and an executive editor of *Gourmet* who'd studied food chemistry. Seranne would continue to be his source of intel on MacAusland's movements: his alcoholism and yearly dry-outs at a dude ranch for reforming drinkers in Nevada; his affairs with women and battles with his wife. James found fresh delight in every report.

It was true, though: James struggled at the typewriter. His natural style was kind of monologist, explaining by accretion rather than paring down to an argument's salient points. After an editor was through with his copy, there were so many pencil notations (deletion, transpositions, inserted words and phrases) they sometimes resembled worksheets of physics equations. His magazine assignments began to pile up. He needed help.

It came in the form of an old theater colleague from Portland. Isabel Errington grew up in Portland, started performing at Baptist Church suppers, and studied in the theater department of a women's school, Mills College in Oakland, California. She met James after graduation in 1933, when both worked on productions for Portland Civic Theatre. James was working on costumes, Isabel in the properties department. One day at rehearsals, James fixed a snack for the crew in the backstage kitchenette: fresh peaches peeled, sliced, sugared, and inebriated with red wine (still technically illegal then, due to Prohibition). Isabel was amazed at how good and vaguely illicit the dish was, and how naturally and with what flair James seemed to toss it off. They became friends.

They worked together on several more productions, even had small acting roles in some of the same plays. Later Isabel wrote scripts for Portland radio dramas and directed James in a few performances of the Community Players before James moved east in 1937. Isabel moved to Chicago, where she helped produce a radio series for the Natural History Museum and married Ron Callvert, a writer, who landed a job in New York City, in the publicity department of AT&T. Isabel needed a job, too. When she looked up her old friend in Greenwich Village, James asked whether she might want to help with some magazine articles waiting to be kneaded into shape. He could pay.

If there was one thing Isabel Errington Callvert knew how to do, it was turning rambling rough drafts into scripts ready for the spotlight. She knew James's voice, his stage voice. She knew and loved who he was in private. (Gay men percolated through the Portland theater scene. Isabel had always been unfazed.) She became James's editor, which meant being his uncredited writing collaborator, which meant being a kind of stage director in print for the gourmet personality suddenly with a new masculine identity.

In late 1949, as *Fireside* was poised for release, James got a regular column in a quarterly journal published by the National Brewing Company of Baltimore, makers of National Premium and National Bohemian beers. Company president Jerold Hoffberger had some showy marketing ideas, including trotting out a one-eyed, thick-mustached mascot, Mr. Boh, and creating a coast-to-coast association of male gourmets under a wonky, comically ostentatious French name: La Société des Gentilshommes Chefs de Cuisine. He reached out to James to be a fixture of the society's journal.

James contributed stories on manly subjects that carried a sense of style: party snacks, pepper mills, sandwiches, chicken sautés (recycled *Fireside* recipes, of course). National Brewing's target consumers were reasonably affluent men who cooked as a hobby, their branding angle being that premium domestic beer could hold its own with French wine. This fit James's emerging profile as America's unfussy bon vivant, as much in love with a good club sandwich as he was with veal Oscar. The money was good (part of it was Isabel's now), even though the editors sometimes changed his recipes in ways that embarrassed him. He did like the beer they sent.

James started a column on food and entertaining in *Apartment Life* magazine. And in its April 1950 issue (same month he touched down in Paris), *Argosy* magazine published James's first "On the Fire" cooking column. *Argosy* had started publishing in the nineteenth century. It was the first pulp magazine, a mix of fantasy and true-crime narratives printed on cheap paper. In the 1940s, the format changed: semi-slick paper, and content tailored for men, with real-life adventure stories welded onto fiction. In 1948, *Argosy* had a new editor, thirty-four-year-old Jerry Mason, an alumnus of the Graduate School of Journalism at Columbia University.

Other men's magazines—namely *True* and *Esquire*—presented misogyny dressed as wolfish sexual conquest, with a focus on acquiring knowledge of food and drink as a means of seducing women. Even M. F. K. Fisher, in her "An Alphabet for Gourmets" (serialized in *Gourmet* in 1948 and 1949), wrote in "B is for Bachelors" that few unmarried men "under the age of seventy-nine will bother to produce a good meal unless it is for a pretty woman."

Though its target readership was blue collar, *Argosy* under Mason had a more refined sense of male motivation. It celebrated masculine accomplishment (hunting, fishing, camp cooking) as a virtue in its own right, not as a source of wiles for vanquishing women. James's "On the Fire" was a serious, straight-up cooking column, with a lack

of gimmicky framing about he-men cooks or the superior male epicurean sense. James wrote about making barbecue sauce and marinades;
grilling on skewers; cold broiled chicken for picnics and a green salad
tossed on the spot (don't forget your jar of homemade French dressing);
and corn "cooked within half an hour after picking," he'd write, roasted
in the husk over coals.

James's primary concession to heterosexual manhood would be his
byline. At Mason's insistence, in *Argosy* he'd be "Jim Beard." And "Jim
Beard" sounded a little like a guy who might tell a rich weasel like Earle
MacAusland to go fuck himself.

::::

Grete was an au pair when she met Sandy Watt. She'd come from
Denmark on the wave of migration that washed uprooted Europeans
and disaffected Americans into Paris after the war. Grete married Watt
and moved into his apartment, a cavernous suite overlooking the Seine
at 68 quai des Orfèvres on the Île de la Cité. On the ground floor was the
cluttered bookshop publishing house of Austrian refugees Martin and
Karl Flinker. It was a quick walk to the Palais de Justice and the police
headquarters that, hauled there in 1949 on a suspicion of theft, the expat
writer James Baldwin called "the great, gray Préfecture." When so many
cities were bomb-rutted and shattered, Paris after the war seemed an
island of calm and unbroken tradition. In fact, it was a nervous place,
desperately trying to make itself into a modern tourist capital.

As spring turned to summer in 1950, the book for which James
had an impressionistic vision at Maxim's began to take shape. Over
long lunches with wine in the Wattses' high-windowed rooms, gazing
at clouds whipped to soufflé heights drifting above the river and the
Pont Neuf, the trees and slate-roof blocks of the Left Bank, they made
rough sketches. The book would capture for the English-reading world
the depth and movement of postwar Paris, the excitement of food in a
place with a rooted culture refreshed by immigrants (Russians, Alge-
rians, Poles). Together they'd write sketches of sixty restaurants, rang-
ing from Maxim's to the grubbiest sawdust-floored bistros, with recipes

they'd flatter out of chefs and wheedle from rougher cooks. In the next six months, James would explore Paris in a way he'd been unable to do as a young man, using Watt's entrée to bistros and his own Sherry connections, including wine expert Alexis Lichine, Claude Terrail of La Tour d'Argent, and of course Vaudable, for grander research.

And at night, on his own, James would explore a different city.

: : :

PARIS AFTER THE WAR was a place where homosexuality was said to have been *"rasait les murs"*—literally, shaving the walls, creeping in shadows. After five years of German occupation, aided by French collaboration, the prewar openness to queer presence in certain bars and cafés and on the streets had mostly vanished. Like America under Truman and Eisenhower, France under De Gaulle adhered to strict gender roles as an act of patriotism, a display of moral strength in the ideological battle against the Soviets and Communism.

As De Gaulle's minister of cultural affairs, the novelist André Malraux would direct a massive scouring of Paris's great structures to make them clean for tourists, washing beautiful old patinas of grime from the sculpted reliefs on the Arc de Triomphe, even from the Gare du Nord. So, too, would French politicians scrub away things that smacked of prewar decadence. Though drag shows of French and North African queens persisted in Pigalle, it was a shadow of what had been. De Gaulle's wife, a family-values firebrand nicknamed Tante (Aunt) Yvonne, oversaw the removal of the city's *vespasiennes*, the circular metal stalls—semiopen street urinals—that harbored male cruising. Queer life in Paris went deeper underground.

In the 1950s, fashionable gay life centered on Saint-Germain-des-Prés on the Left Bank, where Jean-Paul Sartre and Simone de Beauvoir held court in two famous cafés, Flore and Les Deux Magots. *"Capitale du non-conformisme,"* the magazine *Futur* called the quarter in 1952: the capital of nonconformity. *"Le seul lieu de Paris où l'on peut se distraire selon ses goûts,"* *Futur* wrote, the only place in Paris where one can carry on according to their tastes.

"The art quarters of Paris house people of every kind and nationality," wrote the American radio host Osborne Putnam Stearns, in his 1952 guidebook with recipes, *Paris Is a Nice Dish*, "students, models, and a generous sprinkling of young Americans, many of them brilliant but erratic." From Thursday to Monday, the public baths of the Left Bank were jammed with university students, some of them Americans studying under the GI Bill of Rights, who lived in cheap *pensions* that lacked tubs. "It doesn't take long for even the serious student to lose his identity in that vitiating atmosphere," Stearns wrote, "because the odds against him are overwhelming, no matter how talented or earnest he may be."

James gravitated to Chope Danton, a Saint-Germain bistro with sawdust on the floors, a perennial throng of students from the nearby École de Médecine, carafes of Sancerre and Beaujolais on the tables, and solid bourgeois cooking. You could order chunky slabs of smoked ham warmed in cream sauce tinged pink with tomato paste, or *pauchoise*, a buttery stew of freshwater fish from Burgundy.

Most of all, James adored Brasserie Lipp, a fixture since 1871. Open until two a.m., it bustled with actors, university students, and the fashionable of Paris. Boys in blue jeans moved between Lipp and nearby Reine Blanche and Flore cafés. The crowd was neither obviously nor exclusively queer, but suggestively so.

James acquired a small circle of queer friends with whom he sometimes shaved the walls, or dined with, or with whom he visited Les Puces, the rambling weekend flea market at Porte de Clignancourt: Jan Barnes, an acquaintance from New York stationed in Paris for UNESCO; and André Quaintenne, who worked in publicity for the automaker Renault, which occupied an entire smokestack-covered island in the Seine in Paris's western suburbs.

James could wander alone in the early morning hours through the massive central market Les Halles, observing men: sex-starved farm boys arriving from the countryside along with the cabbages and leeks; rough-edged butchers and fishmongers and *fromagers*. As dawn approached, he'd remove to a nearby bistro, order an omelet or *choucroute garnie*, the sprawling Alsatian dish of sauerkraut baked with layers of cured and smoked pork and sausages, then return to the market to watch the buyers arrive. James was alert to the promise of eroded edges in the wee hours, the sexual charge in an exclusively male realm, the exaggerated performances of muscle and bravado followed by ambiguous glances.

Over the better part of the year he was wedded to *Fireside*, James's romantic life had wilted. Before he left New York in April, he'd met a Dutchman named Ate de Boer, a bar steward on transatlantic passenger ships for Holland America Line. De Boer was in his thirties. He had a lacquered swirl of light brown hair and surprisingly full lips set in a narrow face. He passed through New York occasionally, whenever his ship was docked. In Paris, James hoped to find a less fleeting connection.

In the spring of 1950, Horace Gibson, on vacation from his job at the Doubleday bookshop on Fifth Avenue, was making his first trip to Paris. Horace and James had met a decade earlier, when James was living with Jim Cullum near Washington Square; when Horace heard that James was in Paris, he sent him a note. James arranged an evening together at the Opéra Comique.

Horace spent his days sightseeing and his nights cruising for men, trolling the *vespasiennes* Tante Yvonne hadn't ripped out yet. He had a morning tryst in the Bois de Boulogne with a young priest in a long black cassock and nothing underneath. And with an introduction from another friend, the editor Bill Raney, Horace called on Alice B. Toklas at 5 rue Christine. In her salon stacked with Picassos and Matisses, they sipped tea and nibbled scones Toklas baked for the occasion.

James and Horace heard soprano Janine Micheau in Gustave Charpentier's verismo opera *Louise*, set in working-class Paris. Despite the presence in the audience of the seventy-six-year-old diva soprano Mary Garden, it was a less than magical performance—both preferred Grace Moore's version at the Met in 1943. Afterward, James took Horace to Brasserie Lipp, to see the mirrors and leafy old botanical wall tiles and electric chandeliers of filigreed brass. James ordered his seduction dish: *choucroute garnie à l'alsacienne*. It appeared on an enormous platter, a mound of hot sauerkraut melded with pork fat, smelling of juniper berries and smoked ham hock. It was piled with porky meats: lean bacon and half a dozen types of sausage. They drank cool pints of beer, Kronenbourg from Strasbourg.

Gibson found it delicious. He did his best to keep up with James but failed. They met once again over Brasserie Lipp's choucroute, the night before Gibson was to sail home on the *Liberté*. This time James ordered champagne and they drank to Gibson's last night in Paris, and to seeing each other again in New York.

Meanwhile Ate de Boer, whose passenger liner had docked at Le Havre, took the train to meet James, who'd sent a telegraph to Ate aboard ship, inviting him to look him up in Paris.

:::

JAMES TRAVELED HOME in the first week of November 1950, on an Air France flight with a son of the deposed shah of Iran and the socialist French cabinet minister Daniel Mayer. James had spent six months in Paris. The Sherry Wine and Spirits store had gone nowhere, thanks to the certainty of implacable French bureaucracy and James's inertia. James was determined, however, to see his Paris book take form.

From Paris, James had written to his friend Wendell Palmer, an editor who oversaw cookbooks in the New York office of the Boston publishing house Little, Brown and Company, with a brief proposal. It landed on the desk of Angus Cameron, a senior editor. Cameron thought the timing might be right for a Paris cookbook. French travel guides were selling, and James was a rising commodity—first-year sales numbers for *The Fireside Cook Book* were decent. Still, even with a million American tourists expected to flood Europe in 1951, there wasn't the market for a food-focused travel book. The book with the working title *Paris Cuisine* would have to appeal to buyers as a cookbook, not a city guide.

Sandy Watt wrote almost all sixty restaurant entries; as a journalist writing about the city's bistros for twenty years, the gig was baked into his bones. And since he was already friends with some of the owners, he was able to collect the bulk of the recipes. No surprise that James wrote the entries for his nighttime haunts in Saint-Germain-des-Prés (Chope

Danton and Brasserie Lipp) and for the food on Air France, the price of his flights. (He toured the airline's kitchens at Orly and adapted three recipes from the corporate chef, Monsieur Chemery, all to be cooked and sealed in vacuum containers, just like at an airline commissary.)

As 1951 arrived, James's focus was on the 158 recipes he and Watt (mostly Watt) had collected for the book. James's task: to translate, interpret, and test them for the American kitchen. His apartment at 36 West Twelfth Street was mostly useless, of course, what with counter space no bigger than a coffee-table top and dirty pans and dishes piling up in the bathtub. (He drew the curtain and blasted the shower to spray away grime, but the drain was always backing up, leaving the dishes to stand in greasy water.) Fortunately, Wendell Palmer, his editor, lived nearby with his boyfriend, thirty-three-year-old piano teacher Paul Burke-Mahony ("Burki" to James), to serve as tasters and depositaries of leftovers. Ann Seranne was a frequent guest for trials.

Still, some recipes were too involved, or needed too much space. Since Cheryl Crawford was spending most of her time in New York, overseeing rehearsals for *Paint Your Wagon* (opening at the Shubert in the fall), James moved into her kitchen at Eastham in New Canaan, as he had for *Fireside.* Ruth Norman, quietly seething that James had paid her nothing for work on that book—he didn't even acknowledge her assistance in print—stayed in the city with Cheryl. Isabel carried on with James's pieces for *Argosy, Apartment Life,* and the National Brewing Company journal.

James tested and wrote through the summer, working with a typist, Inman King, a music-teacher friend of Burki's. James made and perfected tripes à la Niçoise; puff paste and brioche; Brasserie Lipp's choucroute garnie; pieds de porc St. Menehould (pigs' feet poached, crumbed, and crisped under the broiler); even Pheasant Souvaroff, from that formative night at Maxim's, adapted with canned truffles and fresh chicken livers instead of foie gras. James included a Souvaroff variation with chicken instead of pheasant—Poularde Souvaroff—and with mushrooms instead of truffles, cautioning, "You will not get the same flavor." For a chocolate and hazelnut nougatine (actually a layered petit-four) from the bistro Chez l'Ami Louis, James had the chef and owner, Monsieur Antoine, air-ship samples to New York so he could taste them side-by-side with his adaptation and make adjustments.

Testing of the nearly 160 recipes for *Paris Cuisine* took seven months—about the same time it took James and Ruth to test more than 1,200 for *Fireside*. James had something extra to prove this time. He needed the recipes not just to work; he needed them to astound.

Making the recipes workable was harder than it seemed, since chefs' directions were almost always sketchy. And French ingredients were either not available in New York or tasted radically different.

Foie gras and truffles were available only as canned imports. American cream had a butterfat content adequate for sloshing into mugs of coffee, not turning pan reductions into silken sauces. Concentrating veal stock into demi-glace was practically its own métier in France. French butchers had their own ideas about how to take down a side of beef (grass-fed, not corn-plumped), and the chasm between a fat American duck and a lean French one seemed as wide as the Atlantic Ocean.

"The fresh butter has another taste," James would tell Jane Nickerson about trying to approximate Parisian ingredients in New York. "Vegetables and fruits, because they are grown in different soil and travel shorter distances, may be fuller flavored. The small, small peas the French so like are not offered in our markets." He knew these dishes at the source. The transformation that happened to them on another continent—the degree to which even nominally identical ingredients, carrots or salt or wheat flour, changed because of where and how they grew or formed—was a revelation to James. It was the beginning of the winemaker's notion of terroir extending to more than wines—indeed, to all the things the land produces in a defined region.

In later years, James would remark about how wrong it was for Americans to borrow French rules for the timing of meats, for instance. Authenticity was tricky; trying to duplicate another country's food in America was impossible. Wasn't it better to adapt a cuisine, as he'd begun to do in *Fireside* with French *cuisine bourgeoise*? To give it an American identity and make it something new?

: : :

THE PHONE SOUNDED in Horace Gibson's apartment in a graceful and decrepit old brick mansion at 21 Fifth Avenue, two blocks north of Washington Square. James was on the line. "I'm giving a birthday party tonight for a neighbor," he told Horace, "and it just occurred to me that you might like to join us."

It was the last day of January 1952, three months before Little, Brown would publish *Paris Cuisine* and more than a year since James and Horace faced each other across their second platter of choucroute at Brasserie Lipp, sealing with Champagne the promise of a future date. James's affair with Ate de Boer had cooled. They saw each other whenever Ate's ship docked in New York and he was bored enough to phone. With the call to Horace, James was excavating a flirtation from the past.

That night, Horace rang the street door at 36 West Twelfth, dashed up the stairs, and came to a stop. James was standing in the hall in front of his open door, poised to *faire la bise*, deliver a trio of Parisian greeting kisses on Horace's cheeks. In the apartment behind James, however, Gibson caught a flash of shapely bare legs. They belonged to the birthday boy, Paul Burke-Mahony—"Burki"—originally of Boston (and first cousin to the handsome congressman of that city, John F. Kennedy). He was wearing shorts, never mind that the temperature outside was below freezing.

Burki lived with his boyfriend, James's *Paris Cuisine* editor, Wendell Palmer, but, after James's dinner and the birthday cake Ann Seranne made, he left with Horace, not Wendell. James poured himself and Palmer another round of Cognac.

: : :

JAMES HAD NEVER SEEN a cookbook like the one in bound galleys before him. Of course, there were other Pacific Coast books. Lane Publishing, the people who put out *Sunset* magazine, pushed out titles for a regional audience with the frequency of Sears, Roebuck catalogs: what to do with abalone, Dungeness crabs, loquats, loganberries—things available in markets and from backyards only in states where the sun dipped below an ocean horizon. Then there was Genevieve Callahan, who left *Sunset* and wrote *The California Cook Book* of 1946. That book was nice. It was nothing like this.

Helen Brown's West Coast Cook Book, which Little, Brown would publish that spring, two months before *Paris Cuisine*, was unique. It featured historical research, by an author with a relaxed and confident expertise; a crisp, droll voice; and a zeal for eating. It had sensuousness and a polish that no fussy home-ec magazine editor could even get close to. Not *Sunset*'s editors. Not even Callahan.

Helen Brown's West Coast Cook Book, thought James as he pored over galleys Wendell Palmer delivered to his apartment, possessed style and a point of view. Like Elizabeth David, the English author who wrote of Mediterranean food as an expression of place, elevated above mere utility, Helen Evans Brown so completely understood. Browned scrambled eggs with avocado, Mexican roast loin of pork, and strawberries macerated in California Gamay wine: James had a wistful sense of kinship with this Mrs. Brown of Pasadena, California.

He wrote a jacket endorsement for the book, declaring himself a native son of the Northwest and therefore a natural ally of Helen Brown. He said he'd read her manuscript "with real delight and no little nostalgia."

By March 20, 1952, publication day for *Helen Brown's West Coast Cook Book*, Helen hadn't yet sent James a thank-you note for his kind blurb before a whole gushing letter from him arrived in Pasadena. He had to know everything about her.

::::

Paris Cuisine APPEARED in bookshops on May 15, 1952. Little, Brown hadn't skimped on design or production. Well-known illustrator Vladimir Bobri did the dust jacket illustration in modern cartoon style: an architectural dish bristling with garnishes threaded on *attelets* (ornamental metal skewers), a throwback to Carême, posed on a waiter's tray-stand draped with the *tricolore*, the French flag. Inside the book were more than a hundred Bobri drawings. James thought it was pretty, though with a price of five dollars (most cookbooks that size cost three), its sales were doomed. It didn't help that Little, Brown was terrible at marketing. By 1957, five years after its release, they'd managed to sell only a bit more than 8,600 copies; it was still $3,300 in the hole for production costs. James had received an advance and was entitled to royalties, though it didn't seem likely its sales numbers would generate any.

At the end of May, James presided over a book-release party in New York. Forty press and promotions people showed up at the Café Continental in the Barbizon-Plaza Hotel at Lexington and East Sixty-Third. Guests ate puff-paste turnovers filled with lobster à l'américaine, followed by roast chicken with cream and truffles à la Maxim's, both recipes from the book. Waiters kept glasses filled with Tavel rosé 1945.

A few days later, the *New York Times* published an interview with James by Jane Nickerson, "The Flavor of Paris." A month after that, the *Times* published a review of the book by Charlotte Turgeon. She liked it, though she thought James overestimated the shopping resources of the average American. "The transcription of the recipes is done with a masterly touch," she wrote, "but a bit of Paris still mists Mr. Beard's eye when he blithely suggests having the local butcher bone a chicken or duck or provide a piece of fresh pork skin."

The review annoyed Osborne Putnam Stearns, author of the competing *Paris Is a Nice Dish.* He sent Turgeon a five-page letter objecting to her praise for *Paris Cuisine.* Turgeon told James privately of Stearns's letter. "Such bitchery I cannot put up with," James complained to a friend. "Hell, life is too short."

Turgeon offered a capsule review of *Paris Is a Nice Dish* in her year-end cookbook roundup for the *Times.* She said it was full of "Osborne Stearn's [*sic*] rather naïve impressions, culinary and otherwise," which she found "in sharp contrast to James Beard's sophisticated and exciting tour through restaurants which he describes in *Paris Cuisine.*" It was nice to have friends at the *New York Times*, James thought. *The New Yorker* was still enemy territory.

In August, Sheila Hibben rendered her judgment of *Paris Cuisine*. "A very reliable, if uncommonly pompous, guide to Parisian restaurants," she wrote. She found the recipes accurate and easy to follow. It was everything else she hated. "It's not the authors' fault that they can't write and that their kitchen French is shaky." She compared the book unfavorably to a 1929 guide by Julian Street, *Where Paris Dines*. Though Street's book was filled with restaurants that no longer existed, Hibben still found it "full of the humor, easy erudition, and broad knowledge that *Paris Cuisine* so depressingly lacks."

It was an infuriating review, even more scaring than Hibben's roast of *Fireside* three years earlier. James knew that Jeanne Owen had a hand in it (both hands, judging by the number of knife cuts). That dig about the kitchen French: Who but Madame Jeanne would have noticed?

"Dear Sheila Hibben," James wrote sarcastically to a friend. "Such a display of personal malice I have seldom seen since she reviewed the *Fireside*. She must love me with a fiendish passion."

They could both rot in hell, along with Osborne Putnam Stearns and Earle MacAusland. James was proud of *Paris Cuisine*. There was nothing overtly autobiographical in it, yet it was his most personal book since *Fowl and Game Cookery*, eight years earlier; he'd lived every page. Besides, little did anyone—including Sandy Watt—realize James had assembled, at heart, an American book.

CHAPTER 10

PISSALADIÈRE AT THE HAMBURGER STAND

1952–1954

AMERICA IN 1952 was a nation more interested in the future than the past.

"Thanks to frozen foods and television," the editor of *Quick Frozen Foods* magazine told industry leaders at a conference in New York, "the family kitchen is on the way out. More and more the housewife is turning to frozen items, quickly and easily prepared, and eaten as the family sits around the set."

By 1954, Americans would buy four billion pounds of frozen food annually; five years later, it would creep to more than five billion. Ads for frozen haddock fillets, peas, chicken potpies, orange juice concentrate, TV dinners, lima beans, and peaches were everywhere. By the middle of the decade, companies were spending twenty-five billion dollars a year to advertise frozen foods. Appliance manufacturers hawked fridges with latest-feature freezer compartments into which a family could cram a hundred pounds of frosty packages.

The first frozen breaded fish sticks rolled off a Massachusetts production line in June 1953. A year later, more than sixty US companies were churning out nine million pounds of them annually, many destined for school cafeterias. Suddenly, per capita, Americans were eating more fish than ever before. The fishing industry surged; trawlers dumped indifferent hauls on the loading docks of manufacturers, who rendered this harvest of the nation's offshore waters into bland frozen rectangles. They spilled from conveyor belts in plants operating round the clock.

"The industry looks on the sticks as the biggest [thing] that has happened to it since Clarence Birdseye first began his quick-freezing experiments with fish in the Nineteen Twenties," wrote Jane Nickerson in the *New York Times*. From an eater's perspective, however, they were dreary. "The fact is," she said, "that frozen, boned fish lacks flavor."

Little, Brown's freshly appointed New York editor, Larned G. "Ned" Bradford, believed there might be a cookbook opportunity in this, in the small but increasingly vigorous gourmet publishing niche: a comprehensive cookbook devoted to the single subject of fish. Americans were eating more of it and nobody—including his wife, Pamela—knew a damn thing about how to cook it. There hadn't been anything definitive on the subject since Doubleday brought out Milo Miloradovich's *The Art of Fish Cookery* in 1949, and it was already out of print. America needed a sprawling, definitive work on the subject, and Ned Bradford believed James A. Beard, coauthor of Little, Brown's upcoming *Paris Cuisine*, could be just the fellow to write such a book. He struck Ned as a man of natural expertise.

He sent Wendell Palmer a memo: Let's have lunch with Beard and see if he'll do it. And no need to make it a rush job. Let him take a whole year to research and write it.

::::

"I THINK IT IS the most human bit of fish book yet to reel off the presses," James told a friend a year later, in February 1953, as he and Isabel finished the first draft. It had been a year of intensive research and recipe testing. James studied bulletins by the conservationist Rachel Carson, a series she wrote while working for the US Fish and Wildlife

Service in the 1940s, called *Food From the Sea: Fish and Shellfish from New England*. "They are worth adding to your collection for the information as well as the writing," he told a friend. "I'm afraid those days in Washington are gone when [they] will have someone like Carson to do a job like that." Dwight Eisenhower had just become thirty-fourth president of the United States. Republicans were talking about erasing what they saw as the humanistic excesses of the New Deal.

The research had put James in an elegiac frame of mind. So many US species had dwindled over the decades or were lost entirely, fished out or killed off by human practices, industry, or the expansion of cities. Likewise, so much American knowledge about cooking fish had died out, in just a generation or two. The possibility of so much pleasure had been erased. With so many families immersed in the culture of the fish stick and the TV tray, it was harder and harder to find an American under forty who didn't think cooking from scratch was either a cute exercise or old-fashioned drudgery.

"This rich land of ours is richer still because of the living things that swim or crawl in its waters," James wrote in the book's introduction. "In the seas and gulfs along our shores, in our innumerable lakes and ponds, and in our rivers and lesser streams are hundreds of different sorts of edible fish and shellfish. Yet I suppose that of this great variety the average American has cooked no more than three or four kinds." The story of the nation's fish was one of ruinous commercial exploitation and consumer ignorance, a tale of squandered delight on a continent once marked by ecstatic bounty. It filled James—about to turn fifty—with nostalgia, for both the vanished culture of America and his own youth.

Because fresh fish was a local commodity and Little, Brown wanted a book about fish from coast to coast, James had to remember the species he used to know. He used for the first time a phrase that a decade later would frame his most important book. "I am writing on taste memory," he wrote to fellow food writer Helen Evans Brown, "when I remember the sablefish and the dabs and such things and some of the other fish we had around Astoria and Gearhart."

More and more, James saw himself as the keeper of food knowledge

America had set aside in the name of industrial progress. More and more, he regarded his recollections as a kind of national seed bank of food memory.

It was about this time—the first weeks of 1953—that the publishing house of Rinehart and Company sent James galleys of a pending cookbook, part of a marketing initiative to generate industry buzz. *The Best I Ever Ate*, a collaboration by author June Platt and the writer Sophie Kerr, was a collage of food recollections. In each chapter, memories framed a far-ranging collection of recipes.

"The best bread I ever ate was in Spain," chapter six begins, "at the inn of Rivadeo on my way from Oviedo to Corunna." Platt and Kerr rambled on the subject of bread and vaguely breadlike things— from Portuguese bread and brioche to johnnycake, popovers, and pancakes—following tangents and indulging errant notions, showing off their wide experience and breadth of travel.

James loved it. "Stories and recipes and gaiety," was how he described it to a friend. "More and more I feel that the real future of the cookbook lies in that sort of book."

Besides stretching the form of the cookbook, *The Best I Ever Ate* pushed back against the dominance of home economics over American food culture. Platt and Kerr rejected frozen and canned foods, the consumerism that told cooks they needed to buy new appliances to cook well, and the nutritional science that characterized meals by their calories and fats, vitamins and carbohydrates. "The question the scientists have forgotten to ask," wrote Platt and Kerr, "—and so have many eaters—is: Does this taste good?"

James had come to believe that the ultimate arbiter of that question was his memory: All good food in the present bore an echo of James's past.

: : :

THE PORT OF LOS ANGELES at its southern tip was a vast cluster of fishing docks and canneries sprawled under a bleaching sun. The low horizon was craggy with the outlines of masts and palms, like an

Astoria that had drifted down the coastline and beached itself in the semitropics. James had stopped here in 1923 on the *Highland Heather*, en route via the Panama Canal to Southampton, England. He was back thirty years later, for research, to refresh his acquaintance with Pacific fish species and root around for inspiration.

Here at San Pedro now, he was a guest of the Mineghinos, an Italian-American family, owners of the Independent Fish Company. Frank Mineghino, the patriarch, wore a pinch-front fedora and work shirt. He reminded James of Delfino Antrosio, his mother's produce man, an object of teenage James's lust.

The Mineghinos had a lofty second-floor office with a view up and down the harbor, including a fully equipped kitchen with a vast round table at the center. Frank, his three teenage sons, and his brother-in-law enjoyed a large and leisurely daily lunch around that table, served midmorning (since they'd all started work before dawn). Friends and associates who stopped by the office stayed to eat.

James sat down with the family for octopus roasted with red wine and fennel seeds; sunfish braised with tomato; crisply fried rex sole; and sea bass steaks crusted with breadcrumbs and baked until browned on the outside, juicy within—all of it cooked by the Mineghinos. Every fish was caught or netted that morning. Also on the table: a platter of pasta, excellent bread, and plenty of red wine. James described the lunch for his column in *Argosy* magazine and collected two of the Mineghino recipes for his book. They reminded James how much he'd missed the West Coast, the closeness here between the table and things hauled out of the ocean.

James celebrated his fiftieth birthday twice, once on the actual day— May 5—at Eleanor Peters's rental mansion in LA's Hancock Park. As a boy in Portland, James knew Peters as Eleanor Hirsch, of the wealthy family that owned the Meier & Frank department store. Peters loved the stage, and after her divorce she became assistant manager of a Seattle theater, where she helped support the young dancers Robert Joffrey and Gerald Arpino. Every year, Peters brought her two sons to Los Angeles, to spend the summer surrounded by friends and the artists and performers for whom she acted as patron.

James's mother, Mary Elizabeth Jones, in an undated portrait probably from the mid-1880s, when she was governess for the Maxwells.

(Davies Studio; Fales Library and Special Collections, NYU)

In a christening gown, with his mother, 1904.

Studio portrait, about 1908.

At Gearhart Park, about 1908.

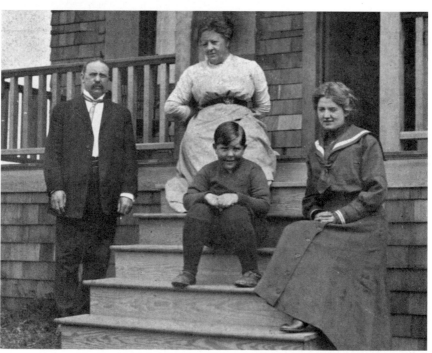

With his parents, John and Elizabeth, and his half-sister, Lucille,
on Salmon Street in Portland, about 1911.

In his second year at
Washington High School,
Portland, 1918.
*(Steffens-Golmer Studio, Oregon
Historical Society)*

The men of House I (plus Feathers the parrot, left), Reed College, Portland,
in April 1921, after James's exit; Professor Edmund Bechtold is
in the back row, second from right.

(Griffin Yearbook 1921, Reed College Archives)

Theatrical portrait, 1925.
(Edris Morrison Studio, Oregon Historical Society)

As the Bishop of
Broadminster in
the Portland Civic
Theatre's production
of *The Bishop
Misbehaves*, 1936.
(Oregon Historical Society)

Casting head shot, mid-1930s.
(Oregon Historical Society)

With Alexander "Sandy" Watt in France, 1951.
(Courtesy of Alastair Fiddes Watt)

The spring 1952 Sherry Wine and Spirits catalog imagined
James as a gluttonous medieval prelate. *(Sherry-Lehmann, Inc.)*

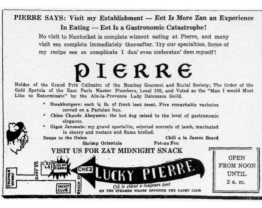

PIERRE SAYS: Visit my Establishment — Eet Is More Zan an Experience
In Eating — Eet Is a Gastronomic Catastrophe!

No visit to Nantucket is complete wizzout eating at Pierre, and many
visit ees complete immediately thereafter. Try our specialties. Some of
my recipe ees so complicate I don' even understan' dem myself!

PIERRE

Holder of the Grand Prix Culinaire of the Bombay Gourmet and Burial Society; The Order of the
Gold Spatula of the East Paris Master Plumbers, Local 102, and Voted as the "Man I would Most
Like to Exterminate" by the Aix-la-Provence Lady Delousers Guild.

* Steakburgers: each ¼ lb. of fresh lean meat. Five remarkable varieties
  served on a Parisian bun.
* Chien Chauds Aboyants: the hot dog raised to the level of gastronomic
  elegance.
* Gigot Javonais: my grand specialite, selected morsels of lamb, marinated
  in sherry and nectars and flame broiled.

Soupe to the Onion   Chili a la James Beard
            Shrimp Orientale   Pot-au Feu

VISIT US FOR ZAT MIDNIGHT SNACK

CHEZ **LUCKY PIERRE**
Où le client a toujours tort
ON THE STEAMER WHARF OPPOSITE THE YACHT CLUB

OPEN
FROM NOON
UNTIL
2 a. m.

Ad for Lucky Pierre restaurant, Nantucket, under James's reign—note the eclectic, high-low offerings—from *The Inquirer and Mirror* newspaper, July 1953.
(Nantucket Atheneum)

With Golda Weiss, a secretary for *Argosy* magazine, posing outside Lucky Pierre, Nantucket, 1953.
(Nathan Weiss, courtesy of the James Beard Foundation)

At a backyard party in Greenwich Village hosted by Associated Press food editor Cecily Brownstone in September 1953, with (from left) Wilma Lord Perkins, editor of the *Fannie Farmer Cookbook*; Brownstone; Tabasco publicist Martha Tupper; *New York Daily News* food editor Alice Peterson (partly visible); and Clementine Paddleford, columnist for the *New York Herald Tribune* and *Gourmet* magazine.

(Jack Sharin, courtesy of Jonathan Ned Katz; Fales Library and Special Collections, NYU)

At the Brownstone party with Lucille Shearwood, publicist for Taylor Wines, September 1953.

(Jack Sharin, courtesy of Jonathan Ned Katz; Fales Library and Special Collections, NYU)

John and Perdita Schaffner (with an unknown waiter) at the Brownstone party, September 1953.

(Jack Sharin, courtesy of Jonathan Ned Katz ; Fales Library and Special Collections, NYU)

Helen Evans Brown in her Pasadena kitchen, 1951.
(Serisawa Studio, courtesy of Greg Geyer)

JAMES BEARD and ANDRE SURMAIN

Are happy to announce
the opening of a

COOKING SEMINAR

meeting once a week
at 6:00 P.M.
from
October 8, 1956
to
November 19, 1956
at our offices and test kitchen
249 East 50th Street
New York City

For information and application please call
PLaza 5-3136

Postcard announcing the first Beard-Surmain
cooking class, 1956.
(Schaffner family)

JIM BEARD
has moved...

to 119 West 10ᵗʰ Street, New York 10, N.Y.
in the ♡ of Greenwich Village
and the phone is ORegon 5-4984

Postcard announcing James's move from an apartment at the eastern edge of Greenwich Village to a house on West Tenth Street, site of the James Beard Cooking School.
(Schaffner family)

Though Peters was six years younger than James, he looked to her as a kind of mentor, a source of unconditional support and understanding (including of his queerness). James made celery root rémoulade in Peters's kitchen; in the backyard adjacent to a golf course, he grilled shrimp, sausages, and steaks for a small gathering of LA friends near the pool.

The next day, he flew to Portland; the day after that, he arrived in Gearhart for his second birthday celebration. He had put out a call to old friends. There were cocktails at the beach bungalow (technically in Seaside) of his old interior designer friend Harvey Welch. They all moved on to Gin Ridge and dinner at the cottage of Mary Hamblet, who fried salmon cheeks in butter. James's sad and wonderful boyhood still lived here, in the place where everything was delicious.

: : :

MAYBE NANTUCKET WAS the model for Gearhart in the post–Narcissa Kinney boom age. The shake-covered and white-trimmed natatorium of James's childhood looked strikingly like the Steamship Authority terminal on Nantucket's wharf. The saltbox houses and wooden colonials he could see from the ferry looked like the summer mansions lined up along Gearhart's Ocean Avenue, above grass-flocked dunes. But this wasn't Oregon. James knew that Nantucket filled up with awful snobs, Bostonians and New Yorkers like Earle MacAusland, who kept a vacation house here.

Now James mingled with the mere mortals crowding the gangway of the Woods Hole ferry: women with scarves double-knotted against the wind, and men in flimsy cotton sweaters or pale suits. James had come to work as the manager of a summer hamburger stand with a dubious reputation and a salty name: Lucky Pierre.

The owners were Claude and Kathi Sperling. They lived on Manhattan's Upper West Side and spent summers on Nantucket. Kathi was an artist, a sculptor and ceramicist. She showed in New York galleries and exhibited under her maiden name, Kathi Urbach. Claude was a manufacturer's rep who launched a line of Kathi's work. James met them through Ruth Norman, herself a dedicated ceramicist. James and the Sperlings coined a joky name for their little trio over cocktails: The Bombay Gourmet and Burial Society. In 1952, James lent a handful of rustic, homey recipes (Lentil Casserole, Eggs Portugaise, Petite Marmite) to a brochure for Kathi's kitchenware line, bean pots and casseroles with Streamline Moderne silhouettes.

Early in 1953, the Sperlings had asked James to meet them for drinks. They made a proposition. They had an offer of travel for the summer, which meant being away from Nantucket. They ran Lucky Pierre, a slightly busted place on Steamship Wharf opposite the yacht club. Lucky Pierre was known to passersby as the place for an impulse bite, also to late-night drunks who needed the boost of coffee and a hot dog or a bowl of watery onion soup before navigating back to inns or rental cottages. Claude and Kathi had a droll sense of humor, and their little summer food stand poked at the conventions of fancy restaurants and the bad French of their menus.

The menu listed Chiens Chauds Aboyants (literally, "Hot Barking Dogs"), and Fevres [*sic*] Explosives ("Explosive Fevers"). In its margins were wiseass fake testimonials: one from Senator Joseph McCarthy ("I suspect their catsup"), the Vineyard Chamber of Commerce ("This ends Nantucket"), and Chef Boyardee ("A new low!"). "Lucky Pierre," of course, was the middleman in a three-way sex act, the versatile chap simultaneously giving and receiving pleasure. The Sperlings' logo pictured him as a leering sailor with a sneaky mustache and a leathery face, in a French navy cap topped with a scrotal pompon. Their motto was "*Où le client a toujours tort*" ("Where the customer is always wrong").

How would James like to run Lucky Pierre in their absence? The food was a little basic for the author of *Paris Cuisine*, but they liked James; he had the right sense of humor for their little loony bin, plus they'd put him up in Nantucket for the summer.

"Did I tell you," James wrote to his friend Helen Evans Brown, "I'm going to manage the maddest snack bar in the East for the summer? It is going to be fun but work." James called Lucky Pierre "a sex-mad Frenchman always in the middle." Besides, it would give him a chance to pick up New England seafood recipes for his fish book, at the source.

Three nights before he caught the train for Massachusetts, James was up at two a.m., writing to Helen. "It is one of those nights in New York when you drip and there is not a drop of air anywhere and everything seems still and hot and sticky. I am pouring with perspiration and following the midnight oil trying to catch up with myself before I leave on Monday afternoon. I almost decided not to go to Nantucket this summer but then felt that I would be foolish not to go. I am so anxious to find out surely some things which have been bothering me for a long time."

James had always fallen prey to depression, and deadline pressures made it worse. This year, he'd known the stress of his fish book on top of keeping Isabel fed with raw drafts of articles for *Apartment Life*, *Argosy*, the Sherry Wine and Spirits catalog, and the National Brewing Company journal. He'd produced a recipe booklet for Pernod; another for Adolph's Seasoned Tenderizer. In January, he landed a consulting deal with Edward Gottlieb and Associates, a public relations company for French Cognac producers. And he'd begun a promotional arrangement with Hamilton Metal Products, makers of a portable outdoor barbecue called the Skotch Grill. It had all taken its toll on James.

He feared he was wasting his time. Americans wanted supermarket foods: TV dinners and bagels from a can. In February, they asked him to come on the television game show *I've Got a Secret*. James pushed a teacart into the studio, in front of host Garry Moore and a panel of three. He set a plate of food before each of them and took a seat next to Moore. The panel would grill James to try to discover a secret about him. Before James had a chance to field even a single question, panelist Henry Morgan raised his head from his plate and let out a loud gasp.

"This is *octopus!*" he bellowed. The studio audience exploded in laughter. James had stewed it in his apartment that afternoon with red wine and basil, Mineghino style, and hauled it to the studio in a taxi. It was delicious, but most of America wasn't ready for octopus.

James had become disenchanted with food writing. He flirted with the idea of chucking it all to open a restaurant, the American equivalent of a sawdust-floored Paris bistro. A place that stayed open late and where one could dine alone, on one dish and a bottle of wine, from a menu that ambled between New Orleans prawns and a hamburger steak, and that featured carefully cooked vegetables and luscious pastries. A place that didn't judge its customers' appetites, only tried to satisfy them.

It wasn't until Warner LeRoy opened Maxwell's Plum in 1966 that you could find a truly eclectic restaurant in New York. Where you could order caviar and stuffed squab or a burger and chili, a place where unpretentious dishes made with fine ingredients coexisted with fancy ones. People on the West Coast took this high–low marriage for granted. In places like New Joe's in San Francisco, perfect osso bucco and risotto shared the menu with grilled liver and onions and a fabulous garlicky hamburger.

Lucky Pierre just might be James's chance to turn his ideas into practice; to show East Coast snobs what James believed to be the future of food and dining out, how it would leave snobbishness and pretension behind and focus on taking pleasure wherever one found it. James also hoped cooking would bring calm to his chaotic mind and allow him to clap the demons away. His mad trip to Gearhart the previous month had stirred thoughts of his parents' lives.

His mother's had been miserable, married to a man she hated, unable to live true to her real love, Stella—even to be close to her. For the first time in his life, James felt he could understand his father, to pity him—forgive him his separate life, finding happiness (love, he supposed) with a woman who loved him back. James always feared that growing up in a family where there was affection but never love had doomed him to a life of loneliness. That some people were simply born cursed, unable to be loved, and had to make their way without the company of others.

A memory returned: of being ten years old (the autumn after Jue Let disappeared) and finding a litter of kittens under the back stairs at Salmon Street, when the mother was off mousing somewhere. How James found a flour sack and stuffed the kittens in and took them to drown in a cistern filled with rainwater at the corner of the garden. How he heard their mewing as the sack lingered for a minute on the surface; felt the silence in his bones after it sank. He fished out the sack with a stick and buried the poor dead things in a shallow rut. He remembered thinking they were safe, that he'd kept them from a life of cold, fighting for mice in the larder, wailing from hunger or the cravings of heat. The mother cat, an enormous orange thing with fur like marmalade, seemed to know James had murdered her family. Forever after that, he'd notice her in the garden and feel she'd fixed him with the most terrifying gaze. Afterward, Elizabeth was furious that one of her flour sacks was missing.

Nantucket, he thought as he jostled with the crowd departing the Woods Hole ferry, might be the place where James could put old furies to rest.

::::

THOUGH SHE LIVED IN CALIFORNIA, Helen Evans Brown had a New York literary agent, John Schaffner. That summer, like every previous one, Schaffner and his wife, Perdita, were vacationing on Nantucket. In June 1953, Helen wrote to Schaffner that he should look up her friend, the food writer James Beard, on Steamship Wharf.

"I am certainly astonished to hear that he is running the eatery called Lucky Pierre's," Schaffner wrote to Helen, "because that is—unless I'm very much mistaken—nothing more than a hamburger and beer joint."

But after the Schaffners dropped in on James one afternoon, John had to admit in a letter to Helen how very mistaken he was. "I certainly must take back my harsh words about Lucky Pierre's," he wrote. "It is a simple sort of eatery but the food, as you can imagine, is pretty remarkable. When we were calling on him, Jim served us up pastry and coffee—and remarkably good coffee, too, I must say—and the little pie I chose from the tray was one made from a [Helen Evans Brown] recipe, a lemon cream tart." The Sperlings' joky hamburger stand was blossoming under James's touch.

James had assembled a scrappy crew for the summer. Before leaving New York, he'd put out the word and interviewed college boys from Columbia looking for summer work on the island. He inherited a few Lucky Pierre regulars, including a salty Beantown server, Marge Burns. And he brought on his own short-order cook, Irwin "Win" Chase, whose family owned a cottage on the island and who spent the rest of the year in a suburb of Boston.

James baked blueberry pies and hamburger buns. He experimented with different chowders; his favorite was Win Chase's, which called for some of the potatoes to be whizzed in the blender for smoothness and body. It contained no milk, only a garnish of sour cream. James turned fish heads, bones, and lobster shells into soups and bisques; since Lucky Pierre had only rudimentary kitchen equipment, he strained stocks through a thick layer of raw rice, his hack for a fine-mesh sieve. From the restaurant La Boule d'Or in *Paris Cuisine*, he made *Délice au Chocolat*, a dense, fudgy *gâteau* between cake and pudding, split and filled with praline buttercream, studded with almonds like a hedgehog's quills. He made chocolate rolls and sliced the pinwheel portions three fingers thick.

James made pizzas: brioche dough spread with fresh tomato sauce and lobster meat, dotted with butter and capped with grated Parmesan. He made pissaladières, thin tarts of cooked-down onions, anchovies, and black olives. He baked sourdough bread, topped burgers with green peppers and Mexican *salsa fria*, and made his own ketchup. He used Nantucket's sweet, delicate romaine for salads, and sourced linguiça, garlicky smoked pork sausage made by the local community of Portuguese fishermen. He served corn on the cob, grown nearby and picked just before dinner service. He bought summer-run salmon from Canada (since New England's rivers had been fished ruthlessly, local fish were commercially extinct), poached and served it with rémoulade and young island peas, a dish with echoes of summer feasts past. He wrote the day's menu on a chalkboard hung at Lucky Pierre's entrance. James's cooking was playful, ambitious, and spanned cuisines: a rough blueprint for what writers a quarter of a century later would dub New American.

It was magnificent.

"We are becoming known for our food," he wrote to Helen Brown's husband, Philip, "and the crowds swill in and slop themselves over the tables at all hours." He had, he said, "steady streams of old ladies for onion tarts and quiche Lorraine every day." He brought in Rudolph

Stanish, king of the French rolled omelet, for a two-week residency. A protégé of cooking teacher Dione Lucas, the dapper young Stanish was a fixture of parties on the Upper East Side, where with extraordinary dexterity he would make and plate technically perfect omelets before guests' eyes. "That boy is wonderful," James told Helen. "He turned out over two hundred last week in full view of the admiring audience at 2 dollars a piece plus salad and a roll. They clamor for him and pay him three dollars and fifty cents at night for a flaming soufflé omelet. . . . He came here for two weeks with us merely to have the restaurant experience and worked for little or nothing."

James was exhausting himself. "I have made about five or six chocolate rolls a day," he told Helen, "and all sorts of specialties and such and have been taken off my feet by the doctor and strapped up for overwork and being too much on the old pedals. So I only work twelve hours a day now instead of fourteen."

The work was taking its toll on his frame of mind.

The dairy farm supplying Lucky Pierre sent Claude Sperling an astronomical bill for all the cream and butter James was using. Claude confronted James in a letter; James was insulted that he would even bring it up. His food was bringing people joy, whether or not they were smart enough to realize it.

"The natives resent the off islanders so damned much," he reported to Helen. "We have had reports that we all take dope and have sex orgies in the middle of Lucky Pierre's all the time—then they come a snooping and find out they like it." All anyone had to do was try James's cooking; after that, he knew they'd love him.

He seethed constantly about Earle MacAusland. From Ann Seranne, his spy at *Gourmet*, James knew he was on the island, apparently avoiding Lucky Pierre. "I guess he's afraid I might put a drop or two of something or other into his chowder," James told Helen, "but I wouldn't—I'd give him an extra dollop of sour cream." A revenge fantasy dressed up as a dark joke—James's demons were back. They'd found him on the island.

He took sleeping pills and shoved a board under the mattress in his rented room, hoping to ease the pain in his back. He went to the cinema to try to distract himself. "I am so fed up with movies that I can't see straight," he told a friend. Summer was only half over, and James looked worn out. He'd lost seventy pounds, almost a quarter of his body weight. His trousers were always loose, even with a scoop-necked striped French sailors' shirt tucked in to anchor his waistband with bulk. He usually kept his hands in his pants pockets to keep them up. Finally, he threaded a length of rope through the belt loops, then cinched and tied it. Marge Burns, the server, thought he looked ridiculous and ran to a men's shop on Main Street to buy him a belt.

Marge scolded him. *Someone* needed to fuss over James, since he didn't seem the least bit interested in taking care of himself.

Though James would continue to harbor dreams of getting out of New York and running a little restaurant—maybe on the West Coast, or on the Eastern Shore of Maryland—Lucky Pierre left him disillusioned. Americans went out for chichi French food in fancy temples with waiters in tuxedos, or they stopped for hamburgers at roadside stands, but few seemed to understand the point of trying to bridge the two.

A month after James's return from Nantucket, American food took a decisive turn, and not in the direction of homemade hamburger buns or the pleasure of corn just picked from nearby farms in summer.

In October 1953, at the annual Newspaper Food Editors Conference in Chicago, C. A. Swanson and Sons of Omaha asked food writers from all over the country to sample a frozen product still in the testing stages.

"Packed on individual-portion, twelve-ounce plates of sturdy aluminum foil," wrote a *New York Times* correspondent at the conference, "the dinner consists of sliced turkey, stuffing, sweet potatoes, green peas and giblet gravy." It required no defrosting and was ready to serve after twenty minutes in a 450-degree Fahrenheit oven. The *Times* reporter called it "food for tasting and for thought."

Editors wouldn't have long to think about it.

Eight months later, the *New York Times* concluded that TV itself had revolutionized the way Americans ate, and that the Swanson frozen dinner was feeding a fundamental shift in the life of the nation.

"Television's influence is revising the family dinner," the *Times* reported. "Sales of the turkey dinner, after only five months in stores, have exceeded by 419 per cent the sales of Swanson's chicken pies in a similar period following introduction." Swanson was about to add a second entrée, a "TV Fried Chicken Dinner," a "complete repast on a throw-away aluminum tray." Even First Lady Mamie and President Eisenhower ate dinner in front of the television, on individual metal folding tables dubbed "TV trays." They were glued to the evening news: black-and-white images from the fighting in Korea and the blast-wind dust of A-bomb tests in the desert.

Far from signaling a break with the past, Swanson ads reassured Americans that what they were eating from those throwaway aluminum trays was familiar and comforting.

"An old-fashioned fried chicken dinner," a 1955 Swanson ad in *Life* magazine would read, "with fluffy mashed potatoes." In the new world of the TV tray and the no-fuss twenty-minute frozen supper, the language of nostalgia would move product. Whether that product would actually deliver on the promise of delight was a question the ad men didn't seem to be concerned with answering.

:::

THE PROJECT HAD BEGUN in September 1953, as soon as James got back from Nantucket. Sam Aaron, co-owner of Sherry Wine and Spirits, wanted to collaborate with James on a book about food and wine: how to cook with wine, how to buy and store it, how to know which bottle to serve with what. They started the project even before talking to publishers. Sam would put up the money, James would test recipes and begin writing.

Sam would write the wine chapters, sharing his thoughts about tasting and buying wine, and why Americans, like the French, should make it a daily companion to meals. James would focus on the simple, rustic French cooking he loved, dishes in which wine was an integral part. He persuaded Sam to send him to France for research. On September 22, 1953, James sailed from New York for Le Havre, to spend six weeks gathering material for the book. Ruth Norman went with him; it would be her first trip to France.

They planned to go to Bordeaux and the Médoc, to visit the wine importer Alexis Lichine at Château Lascombes, his recently acquired seventeenth-century estate. James and Ruth would explore the Dordogne before settling in Paris for a food editors' conference, including an event at the Ritz called Pillsbury Paris. The Minneapolis flour-milling company had sent a team of home economists to France for six months to test European pastry recipes with American flours. They would unveil the results to US home economists and food writers who'd come for the conference.

Grand French cooking had long been an obsession for American gourmets. Pillsbury was betting that, in years to come, even ordinary home cooks would want to master the art of French cuisine.

When he got back to New York in early November, James's thoughts weren't on fancy French cooking but rather on simple food. Even in rural France, the old ways were vanishing.

"Ideas for articles," he'd written in his datebook in France. "Workingmen's food in France:

- *Vendangeurs* [grape pickers]
- The man in the streets [with] his metal lunch pail[;] the one who buys hot potatoes and sausages—and bread
- Student snack bars
- Students and worker clubs
- Where are the appetites of yesterday?"

"Wine is for the people," he'd scribbled, "not for snobbery."

What James loved most about food in France wasn't any particular recipe but rather the pleasure French people in all walks of life took in what they ate, no matter how simple or cheap the food.

Getting Americans to do the same was a daunting task, when even the president of the United States ate dinner from a folding tray, in front of a television. And once you called food French, Americans wet themselves with thoughts of elegance, lusting after refinement that could only be expensive and imported, the way they lusted after a new-model Frigidaire.

Maybe the trick was not to call it French.

: : :

JOHN SCHAFFNER WAS now the literary agent for both James and Sam Aaron. Early in 1954, after weeks of peddling the wine book project, Schaffner finally had an interested publisher.

Permabooks was Doubleday's paperback division. Much like Pocket Books, which pioneered the magazine-channel distribution of cheap paperbound editions, Permabooks put out thirty-five-cent bargain titles: pop fiction, as well as handy guides on bartending, dieting, even astrology. The instructional angle on affordable wines and how to choose them was an easy fit, but James's recipes sounded rather elevated for Permabooks's newsstand customers. Freeman "Doc" Lewis, founding editor of Pocket Books, insisted on framing the Beard–Aaron collaboration as a book about thrift. He came up with a straightforward title: *How to Eat Better for Less Money*, which was pretty much a steal of the 1942 Gaynor Maddox wartime rationing book published by Dutton, *Eat Well for Less Money*.

By February, Schaffner had found a second publisher—Appleton-Century-Crofts—who agreed to buy the rights to a hardcover edition. The parties came to an agreement: Appleton-Century-Crofts would publish a hardbound edition first, in October 1954, followed by the Permabooks paperback edition in 1956. James and Sam would split the royalty payments, with James receiving two-thirds.

Even for James, who worked fast when motivated, *How to Eat Better for Less Money* came together at lightning speed. James and Isabel Callvert finished the recipes and text in five months. Naturally, James's borrowing, repurposing, and self-plagiarizing were all on display. Without acknowledging the source, the stuffed oxtail recipe came from *Paris Cuisine*. James did alter several of his earlier recipes, to simplify them or make them cheaper: pigs' feet St. Menehould and cassoulet from *Paris Cuisine*; Jeanne Owen's Poulet (changed to "Chicken") Vallée d'Auge from *Fireside*.

Though the physical book didn't cut much of a figure, *How to Eat Better for Less Money* offered a challenge to Americans to copy the French—not to be fancy but to build a home repertoire of simple, mostly thrifty dishes. James argued that good French home cooking was cheap but luxurious in effect. Making good meat stock regularly, for instance, was a way of wringing every bit of usefulness from bones and trimmings, and it yielded an always-available medium for good soups, sauces, and braises.

Appleton-Century-Crofts complained that some of the recipes strayed from American notions of strict economy. It's true that James's impulses tended toward exuberance. "He constantly had to cut back down to his original plan of action," Isabel told Schaffner, "and [be] reminded that he was writing on how to save money, not how to spend it in quantity."

James complained that the publisher wanted him to dumb down his recipes for some imagined audience of ignoramuses. "It is a challenge to me to have to do a book where I can't give everyone credit for having known that wine comes from grapes or that there is such a thing in the world as Kirsch or Cointreau," he bitched to a friend. "They want it to be for the folk who live three doors the other side of the Delta, Missouri stationhouse."

Yet in *How to Eat Better for Less Money,* James first articulated a point that ordinary American cooks found difficult to grasp in 1954: that a single humble ingredient, cooked with care, can stand up to the finest dish in the luxury canon.

"A much misunderstood word—gourmet," James wrote at the start of the book. "A boiled potato—a potato cooked to the point at which it bursts its tight skin and shows its snowy interior—can be gourmet food."

::::

LITTLE, BROWN PUBLISHED *James Beard's Fish Cookery* in October 1954, his second cookbook released that month. It was a large book:

a "giant haul" of recipes, according to the jacket copy, more than four hundred pages covering ninety species of fresh- and saltwater fish and shellfish, plus caviar, frog legs, snails, tortoises, turtles, terrapins.

Many were tangled in complicated identifications, with names varying by region. In the introduction, he thanked Helen Evans Brown for her information on West Coast fish, and Isabel for being "an invaluable aid in assembling material"—a shockingly tepid acknowledgment, considering Isabel was research manager, administrative director, editor, and collaborating writer. John Cosgrove, a friend in James's queer orbit in Greenwich Village, typed the manuscript. He went unacknowledged.

The book is a plea for readers to stretch themselves as shoppers and cooks, to trust their instincts and not rely on supermarkets. It resisted the currents of the day, which hoisted convenience and standardization above discovery and flavor.

"Like other kinds of food," James wrote, "most varieties of fish have their seasons—the particular times when they are in most abundant supply, at their best and cheapest. These seasons vary greatly from coast to coast and from fish to fish. Everything considered, the best authority on when to buy fresh fish is your own local fish dealer." Readers were supposed to search out local fishmongers and get to know them.

James Beard's Fish Cookery cemented its author's place as a singular figure in American food. His credentials were his biography; his authority rose from his vivid past in a place that preserved its regional tang.

Flashes of memoir keep the book from reading like a dry manual. James conjures the Columbia River fish runs he knew as a boy, his disdain for the lust of the throngs dragging smelt out of the water with anything at hand: burlap sacks, birdcages, old dresses. The baby's bathtub Elizabeth used for poaching salmon. Harry Hamblet frying oysters in butter. A carp he saw in France, so large it took two women to hoist it to the table on a plank. Margaret Jennings, a friend from long-ago Portland who added Scotch to a crab soup she meant to lace with sherry: a delicious accident.

In her *New York Times* review of the book, Charlotte Turgeon unveiled a new title for him. "Jim Beard is considered by most," she wrote, "to be the Dean of American Cookery." The capitalization made it seem official, like a proper title. James was now the gastronomical equivalent of the late William Dean Howells, the walrus-whiskered eminence known as the Dean of American Letters. James had become both an authority and a curious character, a serious man with lovable quirks—most notably his size. Who could accuse such a girthy man of not living to eat?

Little, Brown timed the book's release to the 1954 Newspaper Food Editors Conference in New York at the Waldorf-Astoria, at a luncheon sponsored by the National Fisheries Institute and the Shrimp Association of America. In the hotel's Perroquet Suite, its walls blazoned with parrots in a fantasy jungle, food writers and editors were served a bowl of James's Caribbean fish chowder garnished with shrimp and lobster. Maybe it was proof of how impressive *James Beard's Fish Cookery* was that Sheila Hibben, his severest and most powerful critic, declined to review it in *The New Yorker*.

James finally had his moment of adulation. And yet he wasn't satisfied. Writing was a hustle and a grind just to make enough to live on, and Lucky Pierre had shown him that translating his ideas into a restaurant was just as brutal. When the work was done, he had nothing left for himself. How would he ever meet someone? He was fifty-one. He'd never had a special friendship with a man that lasted more than a few months. Would he be alone for the rest of his life?

All he wanted to do was get away—from New York and deadlines, and more than anything from crippling loneliness, the depression that made him feel he was swimming in the rough, battling a current he couldn't push through.

CHAPTER II

AMERICAN CHEESE

1953–1954

HELEN EVANS BROWN HAD the jangly peasant style of some middle-aged permanent resident at a California arts colony. She liked loop ear-rings and handmade Mexican sandals, capri pants, and loose tunic tops of coarse-weave Japanese cotton. She wore a bracelet of silver charms—milagros—that made her wrist tinkle. She had bright, scrubbed skin usually free of makeup, and chestnut eyes that stretched to the outer edges of her face like Ava Gardner's. Helen's dark, wavy hair was short enough not to stray into her eyes whenever she lowered her head to work at the chunky wooden table her husband, Philip, built in their Pasadena kitchen, beneath a dangling welter of whisks, ladles, mesh strainers, and Chinese wire spiders.

She was born in Brooklyn in 1904. Her family then moved to Montreal, and as a young woman she spent two years at Yale, studying art. Afterward, she launched a catering business in New Haven with a friend, got married, moved to Long Island, and had two children, but the marriage ended in divorce. She met Philip S. Brown, an aspiring screenwriter. He was balding, with a thin face and a graphite-streak mustache like David Niven's. Philip's conversation was full of movie-patter wit.

In 1936, they married and moved to Southern California, where Philip found unsteady work in the rewrite and research departments at Warner Brothers and Universal Pictures. They bought an old craftsman bungalow on a double lot on Armada Drive in Pasadena. On the empty lot, they created a sunken garden and a brick patio. It had a screen of native oaks, and a canyon below, across which you could glimpse the Rose Bowl stadium.

Armada Drive was steep and wooded; during daylight, there was constant chatter from house finches, scrub-jays, and mourning doves. Helen planted a loquat tree and had another child. She cooked constantly, attuned to the bounty of California's fruits and vegetables, the riches of its Chinese and Mexican markets, and its wealth of wines and cheeses.

She filled the kitchen with old enamelware and new French sautoirs; cast-iron popover molds and tin Pullman pans; olive-wood spoons and spatulas, an antique spice rack and a copper fish poacher, bamboo steamers, earthenware *poêlons*—anything shapely or adventurous or that evoked some cuisine Helen was interested to learn. Philip, who presided over grilling on the patio, honed his skills with meat and charcoal.

The Browns loved old cookbooks. The house was beginning to fill with them, picked up at flea markets and auctions: Pierre Blot's *Hand-Book of Practical Cookery* from 1868, Urbain Dubois' *Nouvelle Cuisine Bourgeoise* from 1870, and stacks more, including rare early West Coast ones, charity cookbooks, and settlers' recipe manuscripts. Philip began dealing them on the side.

They found a circle of smart, creative friends with roots in the old Arroyo Seco bohemian collective of Northeast Los Angeles: small-press publishers, commercial artists, screenplay writers, Hollywood set designers. Drinking was a group hobby, and when Helen was cooking, with Philip grilling on the patio, it seemed there was no better food and ambiance in all of California.

In 1940, to supplement Philip's unsteady income and find an outlet for her passion for cooking, Helen began writing radio scripts and recipes for Robert Balzer, a local wine expert and champion of California vintners. Balzer inherited the family grocery business in Hollywood and turned it into a high-end emporium, where assistants to celebrities like Alfred Hitchcock and Marlene Dietrich regularly phoned for deliveries of Almaden White Grenache Rosé and Camembert. After a few years, Helen began writing Balzer's weekly advertising bulletin, which included recipes, and decorating the store's windows. She became food editor for a Los Angeles fashion and lifestyle magazine, *The Californian*, and authored a monthly column, "California Cooks." In 1948, the magazine collected her columns (plus twenty new recipes) in a book, also called *California Cooks*.

In the summer of 1949, Ned Bradford of Little, Brown wrote to Helen, whom he didn't know, on a hunch. He said he'd seen *California Cooks*, "which several of us here in Boston have now had a chance to look at, and which we all agree is just the sort of thing, in style and content, we would like to see in a larger, more comprehensive book that you might write." This was the seed that sprouted into *Helen Brown's West Coast Cook Book*.

James was the first outside of Little, Brown to recognize its brilliance, though he wasn't the last. M. F. K. Fisher lauded it; even Elizabeth David, never shy about rendering fierce judgments or calling out fools, expressed her admiration in *The Spectator*. It stood apart, she said, from the dreary recipes of American home economists, with their cake mixes and canned peas, their imbecilic shortcuts and ludicrously precise measurements for variable seasonings like ground black pepper.

Despite the praise of influential food writers, however, Helen's book was a flop.

Before Bradford first wrote to Helen, there had been internal debate at Little, Brown about the viability of a West Coast book for a national audience: cooks in Buffalo, Cincinnati, and Baltimore who couldn't find a kumquat or a tortilla or a geoduck even if they knew what such things looked like. And while Little, Brown was lousy at marketing cookbooks, at the elevated price of four dollars, Helen's book was an expensive curiosity, not a practical collection of recipes. Even for James, so much of the pleasure of *Helen Brown's West Coast Cook Book* was as a source of Pacific Coast nostalgia.

For Ward Ritchie, a Pasadena friend and craft printer, Helen wrote a pair of short, small-format recipe books with good design, six inches square. She did one in 1950 on chafing dish cooking, another a year later on patio cooking. By the summer of 1952—just about the time she received her first miserable royalty statement from Little, Brown—Helen knew she needed more than brilliance, small-press books, and a head whirling with ideas to make a living. She needed a partner, someone to help her build a national profile for selling books. Who better than James Beard? His books did well at Balzer's, especially *Fireside*—she told James it sold "like bananas in England." Privately, she told Ned Bradford she found *Fireside* "*too* darned attractive to ever become a kitchen bible. . . . The illustrations, though enchanting, are distracting."

Still, though: James's dust-jacket endorsement of the West Coast book had been a boost for Helen's credibility, nationally. Suppose their names somehow became linked?

: : :

SINCE NEARLY EVERY MAGAZINE editor and publishing house of any importance was in the Northeast, Helen needed an agent on the appropriate coast. In 1948, she became the first client of John V. Schaffner, of the Schaffner Literary Agency of New York City. His office was where he lived: 312 East Fifty-Third Street, an 1860s wood-frame townhouse, all creaky floors and knickerbocker charm.

Schaffner, thirty-five, had been a high school English teacher, a fiction editor at *Good Housekeeping* and *Collier's*, and finally the assistant to a literary agent in Boston, Frank Meador. Schaffner had the look of a boyish gentleman academic at an Ivy League school: a long, intelligent face and poindexter glasses; short hair gone prematurely white (making his age difficult to peg); a seersucker sense of ease and correctness.

Two years later, in 1950, he'd marry Perdita Macpherson, heir to an unconventional kind of literary royal family. Her blood mother was the Imagist poet H. D. (Hilda Doolittle); her adopted one was H. D.'s lover, the English novelist Annie Winifred Ellerman, known as Bryher—Schaffner called them Perdita's "mummies." H. D. and Bryher were close to Gertrude Stein and Alice B. Toklas, so when Perdita was a girl, she'd visit the famous couple annually at their country house in Bilignin, France, sixty miles east of Lyon. Basket—Stein and Toklas's adored succession of poodles, all with the same name—would be Perdita's summer companion. During the war, Perdita worked for the OSS in London.

Schaffner was nurturing and kind, a devoted husband and, eventually, father to four. He loved holidays and entertaining; he did most of the cooking. As an agent, he was old-fashioned, a confidant to his clients, going far beyond writing letters and forwarding royalty statements. He and Perdita had an understanding: Schaffner would lead a rich and rambunctious family life in plain sight, and a quiet gay one in private. Perdita had grown up in an unusual way, with iconoclastic parents in complicated romantic arrangements. She understood the need for partners to arrange their lives, at least privately, around certain truths, and perhaps yearned for a marriage that, given the social orthodoxy of the 1950s, looked simple only from the outside.

She and John kept separate bedrooms. Guests at the Schaffners' parties would include close male friends of John's, men who smelled of cologne and roughhoused with the growing brood of little Schaffners; men who celebrated Thanksgivings and birthdays with Perdita and the children. Schaffner kept late hours. After dinner with the family he'd ascend again to his office, composing letters into the Dictaphone for his assistant, Hubert Creekmore, to type in the morning. (A Mississippi-born poet related by marriage to Eudora Welty, Creekmore—likewise closeted—was Schaffner's lover.) Some nights, after the letters were done, Schaffner would go out to be with other queer men.

The summer when Schaffner and Perdita wandered into Lucky Pierre on Nantucket, to meet James, taste his coffee, and eat the lemon tart from one of Helen's recipes, it was no mere accident. Schaffner had been working with Helen for nearly five years. He very much wanted to meet James, to be his agent. Helen told him to look up James on Steamship Wharf.

One Sunday that August of 1953, James took a bus to Siasconset, the easternmost cluster of gray-weathered houses on the island, to take up the Schaffners' invitation for martinis in their summer rental. The three of them got along beautifully: stories of Helen, of Gertrude and Alice, and of Perdita's work in London during the war. Perdita didn't warm to everyone, but she liked James, who must have sensed at once the sort of arrangement the Schaffners had. And on a handshake, James acquired an agent and an important new confidant.

Afterward, Schaffner dashed off a note to Helen. "I'm only writing this to say that I want to thank you for letting me know about Jim. He promises to be a most entertaining friend."

:::

JAMES AND HELEN HAD much to talk about. In letters shuttled between New York and Pasadena, they spoke of recipes they were working on and the atrocities being perpetrated in the food pages of the national magazines (*House & Garden, Ladies' Home Journal*). James had been to a promotional lunch at which every dish featured bananas. It was nauseating. Helen was judging a recipe contest for *Western Family*, a magazine she'd begun writing for, and the entries were ghastly, straight from the home-economics school of cooking. "Your banana lunch sounds very much like the stuff Philip and I have been retching over for the last three weeks," she told James. The things home economists and the food industry were shoving into Americans' gullets were sad and disgusting, and nobody—certainly not magazine editors—had the fortitude to call it out.

Both despised *Gourmet*. James referred to it as "an esoteric sheet with no sense as regards food and drink." Helen found it smug and supercilious, with articles about "quaint and eccentric characters rather than cooking."

At forty-seven, Helen was struggling. She had stories in local magazines and her work for Balzer, but she wasn't breaking through nationally. Schaffner wasn't finding New York editors who liked her story pitches. Her mind spun with original ideas. Magazines wanted conventional service pieces that instructed housewives how to make dinner fast, with plenty of shortcuts calling for cans, mixes, and freezer fare.

She hated the heat and smogs that seized California every spring (which almost always arrived in February, sometimes earlier). Gut pains and canker sores were troubling her, and she was having paralyzing dizzy spells. The doctor couldn't figure out why.

Her second title for Little, Brown, released in the fall of 1952, was *Helen Brown's Holiday Cook Book*. M. F. K. Fisher, who'd last-minute bailed on contributing one for Helen's West Coast book, did the foreword. ("She believes passionately," Fisher wrote, "in the mystic importance of the feasting.") Besides recipes for obvious occasions such as Thanksgiving and Easter, Helen folded in as much eclecticism as mainstream publishing would allow, via recipes for Twelfth Night, Chinese New Year, Shrove Tuesday (Pancake Day, the eve of Ash Wednesday), Bastille Day, and the multiday Mexican Christmas celebration of Las Posadas. Los Angeles artist Harry O. Diamond, a friend of the Browns, contributed illustrations with mod personality and a playfully fluid sense of line. (Two years later, James would tap him to illustrate his fish book in a similar style.)

The holiday book sold just as poorly as the West Coast one. Helen's next proposal to Ned Bradford was for a book about cooking vegetables—in a decade of canned and frozen convenience, when the dearest aspiration for most Americans was a grilled T-bone, vegetables were an impossible sell.

"I have no doubt that she could write such a specialty book with unusual skill and imagination," Bradford told Schaffner, "but I can't help taking an extremely dim view of the sales potentialities of it. Vegetables are the least interesting item on the menu; in their cooked form at least I suspect they're the most marginal food for most people."

Helen's career was sputtering. "I don't know quite where to turn next to see if I can locate a publisher for you," Schaffner wrote. Her energy and originality somehow made publications suspicious. Besides, Little, Brown's sales numbers were making her an untouchable. Word from Boston was she was prickly and temperamental. Editors in New York thought of Helen as a regional author of limited appeal.

As Schaffner was scraping the lower reaches of the editor pool, he sent Helen's story pitches to Geraldine Rhoads of *Today's Family* magazine.

"In some respects," Rhoads noted with her rejection, "Helen Evans Brown has come to us with too many ideas."

: : :

AT THE END OF APRIL 1953, Schaffner received a long, giddy letter from Helen. James was in Pasadena for several days, making his first visit to Armada Drive.

"Jim Beard (James A., cook book author extraordinary) is out here and has spent a great deal of time with us. He is a nice guy—no typewriter cook, he—and I think we have both gained from the experience. I had an idea the other day and he thinks it's wonderful but it will be up to you to sell it if you think it has merit."

Their notion was to do a Beard–Brown collaboration in the form of an epistolary conversation, an ongoing discussion of food and cooking (with recipes), ricocheting between New York and California.

"The idea is that we have a cook's [sic] controversy by mail," Helen wrote, "and have the letters published in a series. We want, of course!!!, to sell it to some magazine that would pay very well. What do you think of this idea? And do you think we could retain publication rights and do a book of it afterwards?"

They'd plan to have friendly arguments—discuss dinner parties they'd mounted or were planning, cooking experiments that rose or sank—talking directly to one another (and the reader), and thereby eliminating the intervention of editors who dumbed down their work and erased their true voices. "A West Coaster transplanted to the East, he would have the European, Eastern male point of view," Helen explained to Schaffner. "I, an Easterner now wedded to the West would have the more informal outlook." Their cooks' controversy would be as original, personal, and opinionated as June Platt and Sophie Kerr's *The Best I Ever Ate*. It would have freshness and bite.

Though he'd been writing to Helen for a year, James and the Browns met for the first time one week before Helen sent her breathless letter to Schaffner. Their first dinner together was in the sunken patio on Armada Drive, with martinis followed by carnitas and chiles rellenos, recipes Helen had learned from Mexican cookbook author Elena Zelayeta. James felt he'd known the Browns forever. He and Helen were allies, mates in battle against a hostile field of editors and publishers.

"You and I know what we are doing," James told Helen, excoriating editors who grasped almost nothing about cooking for flavor. "We know the background—we can cook and we can produce—and then we are trampled over by a lot of phonies who can barely heat a frozen chicken pie without spoiling it."

They all got a tremendous kick out of one another, James and the Browns: liked to drink; loved to eat. In a week, they almost never stopped cooking. James felt he'd found family, the happy kind his birth had denied him. It felt right to be in Helen's kitchen, with its magical clutter and generosity of inspiration. His mother's had been as large and well equipped. But Helen's had an air of playfulness, the certainty of forgiveness if one messed up: a permeating grace.

Back home in New York, James was still feeling the glow. "I have returned here with my ideas in my head," he wrote to Helen. James was happier than he'd been since, well—since he could remember.

"The wonderful times we all had during the days I was there are something I shan't forget for a long time," he wrote. He longed to collaborate with Helen. "I am convinced that we should be and will be a team," he told her, "and if there is any chance of becoming tops in this field I think we can do it if we get a few breaks."

: : :

Two weeks into the new year of 1954, New York City became impassable. Ten inches of snow clogged the streets, stalling buses and slowing taxis to crawls on the major avenues. The temperature dipped to 15 degrees Fahrenheit. James's party seemed ruined.

He'd planned a dinner, elegant yet lively, in his cramped Twelfth Street place for acquaintances with important connections in Paris. The Formé-Becharats were friends of Henry de Vilmorin, the New York–based publicity man for Maxim's, and were members of the influential French gourmet society Club des Cents. The snow, however, stranded them on Long Island, after James had splurged: filet of beef, hothouse tomatoes (good ones, despite the season), cucumbers, and fresh peas.

To salvage his investment, he called his closest friends for backup. Cecily Brownstone, food editor of the Associated Press, trudged through the snow from her house on Jane Street. Helen McCully of *McCall's* magazine lugged over a fruitcake left from Christmas. Wendell Palmer, his old editor from *Paris Cuisine*, happened to be down from Boston, where he now lived. They ate onions belle aurore and got drunk on Italian wine, Pommard, and Champagne. Sam and Florence Aaron showed up late. So did James's neighbors, the couple Alvin Kerr and Peter Carhartt, along with friends they'd had to dinner at their apartment.

As everyone sipped liqueurs and coffee late into the night, James wedged open his hall door to keep from suffocating in the heat of so many bodies. When he awoke at six the next morning, he was alone: sunk in a chair, still with his clothes on and the lights blazing, dirty glasses scattered on every table, and the front door gaping. New York was a crowded and convivial place, but sooner or later friends scattered. James could never escape his feelings of loneliness for long.

The same depression he felt on Nantucket during his Lucky Pierre summer wouldn't let him go these past weeks. Blacking out in his chair provided a rare bit of rest. "I haven't slept enough lately to count," he wrote Helen Evans Brown. Six months after turning fifty, James was swallowed deeper into a kind of slow-creeping panic. He'd gained back all the weight he lost in Nantucket and then some. James was even finding it uncomfortable to move.

Money weighed on him; he grabbed at anything that looked like it might pay. He asked John Schaffner to pitch publishers of a French restaurant book, the *Guide Gastronomique de la France*, to hire him to do an English translation—they could pay him in francs. How about a collaboration with Ruth Norman on a travel guide for all of Europe outside the Iron Curtain? Schaffner dutifully wrote to publishing house after publishing house with James's pitches. Nobody bit.

It seemed there was no idea too kooky for James to entertain, as long as it promised money. Joseph Leon, a stage manager and sometime actor in Flushing, approached James with a scheme called Data-Guide:

twenty-five typewritten pages of cooking information and recipes shrunk down to fit on a single see-through plastic sheet. "They pay a royalty of 10 per cent on the wholesale price," he wrote to Helen, "which is about 3.7 cents each, and they sell for 69 cents, and they estimate each one to sell a million copies in the outlets they have. . . ." But James's Data-Guide sheet never materialized.

A publicity woman for Crosley freezers pitched James a story to try and sell to a magazine: a family hauls around an unplugged chest freezer packed with food for a fishing trip in the back of their Studebaker Conestoga station wagon (assuming there'd be electricity at their campsite, and the food wouldn't have thawed by the time they arrived). It was a ridiculous premise. Schaffner peddled it anyway—to *Esquire*, *Holiday*, the *Saturday Evening Post*, even *Argosy*. Nobody wanted it. (James scored a Crosley freezer for trying, though. He plugged it in next to the toilet, the only place in his apartment it would fit.)

"I am about to go into a nervous breakdown," he wrote to Helen. "Of that I am certain."

The Browns invited James to join them out West for a monthlong road trip in their Dodge Coronet convertible. Helen had long wanted to write a story on the wines and cheeses of the Western states. Philip and Helen would drive up to San Francisco to meet James. Together, they'd drive north to Oregon and Washington, over to Idaho and a corner of Wyoming, into Utah and south through Nevada, ending in Pasadena. Philip had worked out an intricate itinerary, with stops to see dozens of vintners and cheesemakers. They'd start the first week of April.

James hadn't seen Helen since she visited New York briefly the previous November. Though it would be a lightning trip, he'd be able to see old friends in Portland and Seattle and show Gearhart and Astoria to the Browns. James could keep up with his magazine commitments with Isabel via letters, using the portable typewriter Helen was bringing. He was better off clearing out of New York for a while. He needed to look at the Pacific and feel sand under his shoes.

"This is the last gasp," he wrote to Helen just before leaving. "I am pooped, bitched, bushed, buggered and completely at sea with ennui and bewilderment. But off we go."

And with any luck, and if they didn't drink too much gin at night after each day's ride, they'd be able to work on their book.

:::

AMERICAN COOKS IN THE EARLY 1950s were in the grip of frenzy. Shiny new grills and rotisserie gadgets, advertised like cars, loaded with the latest features, were everywhere. Outdoor equipment and appliance manufacturers rushed to market with portable backyard barbecues and plug-in kitchen roasters, meant to give Americans everywhere— even dwellers in tight city apartments—an approximate taste of grilled patio meat.

Postwar technology and American manufacturing prowess propelled infrared broilers such as the Cal Dek and the Broil-Quik. An Air Force officer, Brigadier General Harold A. Bartron, retired to Southern California in 1948 and spent his time in tactical study of a proprietary rotisserie with a self-balancing spit. He named it the Bartron Grill.

There was the Smokadero stove and Big Boy barbecue. There were enclosed vertical grills with radiant heat, hibachis from post-occupation Japan, and the Skotch Grill, a portable barbecue with a red tartan design that looked like an ice bucket.

In New York City, the high-end adventure outfitter Abercrombie and Fitch and the kitchen emporiums of big department stores did a bustling business in these new symbols of postwar meat consumption. There was even an Upper East Side shop solely dedicated to them, Smoke Cookery, Inc. on East Fiftieth Street. The only trouble was that many buyers of these shiny new grown-up toys had no clue how to cook in them.

For weeks in the spring of 1953, Helen tested electric broiler recipes, an assignment from Hildegarde Popper, food editor of *House & Garden* magazine, for a story called "Everyday Broils." A few broiler and rotisserie manufacturers sent their new models to Armada Drive for Helen to try.

"The subject turns out to be a huge one," Helen wrote Popper; she had enough material to break the story into two parts. "Jim Beard, of cook book fame, was here when my rotisserie arrived," she told Popper, "and he was a great help to me."

Word got around the New York editor pool. Suddenly, Helen and James seemed the ideal collaborators, storywise, to cover the new subject of grill and rotisserie cooking: West Coast and East, female and male, California suburban patio cook and Manhattan bachelor gourmet.

Meanwhile, cookbook publishing was surging. Doubleday became the first house to hire a fulltime editor, Clara Claasen, to fill its stable with cookery authors.

Schaffner took Claasen to lunch to discuss how he might be able to help. "She is very much interested in the idea of an outdoors cookbook," he wrote to Helen afterward. "This would combine barbecue, picnic, sandwich, campfire and every other aspect of outdoor eating." Schaffner and Claasen lunched again. James and Helen's "cooks' controversy" idea had run out of gas (Schaffner hated the idea anyway, especially after reading first drafts of a few Beard–Brown "letters"), so Schaffner managed to steer Claasen toward a different kind of collaboration for his two clients.

In November 1953, Helen flew to New York. She and Schaffner met with Claasen at the Doubleday offices. On a handshake, in the absence of James (who only the day before had returned from France on the *Queen Elizabeth*), they decided on a collaboration: an outdoor cookery book to be authored by Helen Evans Brown and James A. Beard.

Everyone was happy: Schaffner for nailing a deal for two clients at once; Claasen for bringing new talent to Doubleday. Helen was getting what she needed: a book with a major publisher. James was getting what he wanted: a reason to get even closer to Helen. Perhaps this was only the first in a long future of collaborations; they might one day even open a kitchen shop together and sell a line of their own jams and condiments. The possibilities were endless.

Claasen was eager to draw up a formal contract. All she needed from Helen and James was an outline.

: : :

UNDER THE GLOWING CABIN LIGHTS of a westbound red-eye flight on April 3, 1954, James found himself eerily alone. TWA's Super Constellation was an enormous propliner with seats for nearly a hundred passengers; that night, James was one of only four. He planned to rendezvous with the Browns in San Francisco later that week, but only after he took five days on his own in the city he'd loved as a boy. From there, the three of them would embark on a weeks-long research trip in the Browns' Coronet convertible, stopping at wineries and cheese factories throughout Northern California, Oregon, Washington, and Idaho. Helen needed to do research for a magazine article she'd long wanted to write. She and Philip had asked James to join them five months earlier, in December 1953.

Nearly a decade after the end of the war, San Francisco was a place of resuscitated glamour, with much of the shimmer and confidence James had known in the city of his youth, when he and Elizabeth would ride the trains of the Shasta Route south.

His plane landed in drizzling rain. For his first luncheon of the trip, James chose a place of old comfort: the dim, wood-paneled Fly Trap on Sutter Street. He wore a suit of windowpane-check tweed (the jacket button straining above his stomach, his thin bow tie slightly askew), eating cold, cracked Dungeness and sautéed sand dabs. The stationery in his room at the Palace had an engraving across the top, an illustration of pioneers trudging next to oxen pulling a Conestoga wagon. Above them floated an apparition: the hotel's neoclassical façade rising from the fog. "At the end of the trail," it read, "stands the Palace Hotel." James imagined himself the son of the pioneer he'd fancied his father to be. Was he now at the end of something or the beginning?

He spent his days and nights eating: A luncheon of poulet sauté with Dr. A. L. Van Meter of the San Francisco branch of the Wine and Food Society (they had met on the French wine junket in 1949); dinner at the Pacific Heights home of Frank Timberlake, vice president of Guittard Chocolate; a trip to San Jose to tour the Almaden Winery and meet its owner, Louis Benoist, over a marvelous lunch of pâté, asparagus mousseline, and an omelet. James dined at the Mark Hopkins with Bess Whitcomb, his abiding mentor from the old Portland Civic Theatre days—she lived in Berkeley now and taught drama at a small college. She wore her silver hair in a short crop; her gaze was warm and deep as ever.

Helen and Philip arrived on Sunday, and on Monday the tour began with a day trip. Philip drove the Coronet across the Golden Gate Bridge north to the Napa Valley, with Helen riding shotgun and James colonizing the bench seat in back. The afternoon temperature crested in the mid-seventies and the hills were still green from winter rain. Masses of yellow wild-mustard flowers filled the vineyards. They tasted at the big four—Inglenook, Beaulieu, Charles Krug, and Louis Martini—and lunched with a winery publicist on ravioli, chicken with mushrooms, and small, sweet spring peas. James kept a detailed record of their meals in his datebook. Elena Zelayeta, the San Francisco cookbook author and radio personality, cooked them enchiladas suizas and chiffon cake.

Next day they crossed the bridge again but swung west from Highway 101 to visit the farm town of Tomales, not much more than a main street of stores and a filling station. Among the rise of green hills dotted with cows, at the farm and creamery of Louis Bononci, James had his first taste of Teleme, a washed-rind cheese with a subtly elastic texture and milky tang. Within its thin crust dusted with rice flour, James recognized the richness and polish of an old French cheese, crafted in an American setting of rusted pickups and ranchers perched on stools at diner counters. It stirred his senses and revived his love for green meadows with the cool, damp feel of Pacific fog lurking somewhere off the coast.

Philip drove west to the shore of fingerlike Tomales Bay, where they lunched on abalone and a smorgasbord that included the local Jack cheese and even more Teleme.

The road stretched north along the coast: to Langlois, Oregon, with its green, tree-flocked hills converging in a shallow valley, where they stopped at Hans Hansen's experimental Star Ranch. Born in Denmark, Hansen spent decades making Cheddar. In 1939, with scientists at Iowa State University and Oregon State College, Hansen had begun experimenting with what would be known as Langlois Blue Vein Cheese, a homogenized cows'-milk blue inoculated with Roquefort mold spores.

(Production would eventually move to Iowa, where the cheese would be known as Maytag Blue.)

They hit Reedsport, Coquille, Coos Bay, Newport, Cloverdale, Bandon, and Tillamook. They stopped at cheese factories, candy shops, butchers' counters, produce stands, and markets. Already stuffed with suitcases, the Coronet's trunk became jammed with wine bottles and jars of honey and preserves; packets of sausage, dried fruit, nuts, and candy. The backseat around James filled up with bottles that rolled and clinked together on turns, with apples, tangerines, filberts, pears, and butcher-paper packets of sliced cured meat, smoked oysters, and hunks of Cheddar. The car had become a mad ark of food. James hauled anything regional and precious on board, as if later it would all prove to have been a myth if he didn't carry some away as proof that it existed.

In Tualatin, south of Portland, they dropped in on James's old friends from theater days, Mabelle and Ralph Jeffcott. To a crowd that included Mary Hamblet and her ailing mother, Grammie, Mabelle served baked shad and jellied salad, apple crisp, and the homemade graham bread—molasses-sweet and impossibly light—that was famous among her friends.

They lunched on fried razor clams and coleslaw at the Crab Broiler in Astoria and had martinis, kippered tuna, salmon cheeks, and Indian pudding at the Seaside cottage of James's beloved friend Harvey Welch.

In Gearhart, James trudged out to Strawberry Knoll, walked across the dunes and onto the beach. He regarded Tillamook Head, just as he did as a boy at the start of summers. He felt a weird convergence of past and present: the sting of sand whipping his face and the smell of charred driftwood lingering in the rock-circled dugout pits of ancient cookouts.

∶ ∶ ∶

FOR JAMES, the Northwest displayed a delightfully slouchy elegance he'd almost forgotten about in New York. It had taste without snobbery. At the Pancake House in Portland, they brunched on Swedish pancakes with glasses of buttermilk and French 75 cocktails—the sort of high–low mix he had aimed for at Lucky Pierre. Why did Easterners have so much trouble grasping the idea?

Before a meal of roast beef and Yorkshire pudding, they sipped a simple pheasant broth that, dolled up with half a dozen gaudy garnishes and called Consommé Louis-Philippe, would have been the jewel of Jack and Charlie's "21" in New York. Food here had honesty. It declared what it was. Like James, it was anti-"gourmet." Its purity was the ultimate elegance.

Thus far, James had fumbled at articulating a true American cooking. He'd taken rustic French dishes, called them by English names, and substituted American ingredients. There was something crude about such an approach. This trip had showed him American food made on French models—Gamay grapes and Roquefort spores and cheeses modeled on Camembert and Emmenthaler that tasted wonderful and were reaching for unique expressions, not just impersonating European originals. It had given James a clearer vision of American food taking root in the places it grew.

As a boy, he had glimpsed this with Chinese cooking, how a relative of the Kan family, a rural missionary, adapted her cooking to the ingredients at hand in the Oregon countryside. How her Chinese dishes took root there, blossomed into something new; how they became American.

They trekked to Seattle, where the Browns went to a hotel and James stayed with John Conway, his theater-director friend from the Carnegie Institute days. John's wife, Dorothy, was a photographer. She shot formal portraits of James and Helen in the Conways' kitchen—maybe Doubleday would use one as the author photo for the outdoor cookbook. They took an aerial tour of oyster beds and wandered Pike's Place Market.

Philip then steered the Coronet eastward across Washington, through the town of Cashmere in the foothills of the Cascades, where they stopped at a diner for cube steak, cottage cheese, and pie that James noted as "wonderful" in his datebook. In Idaho, at a place called Templin's Grill near Coeur d'Alene, they found excellent steak and hash browns. There was a Basque place along the way that made jellied beef sausage, and a diner in Idaho Falls with "fabulous" fried chicken and, as James scribbled in his daybook, "biscuits light as a feather." The fried hearts and giblets were so delicious they bought a five-pound sack to stuff in the hotel fridge and eat in the car next day for lunch.

The squat, industrial-looking Star Valley Swiss Cheese Factory in Thayne, Wyoming, with a backdrop of snow on the Wellsville Mountains, produced what James thought was the best Emmenthaler-style cheese he'd tasted outside of France, but this was American cheese. They had delicious planked steak and rhubarb tart in Salt Lake City, but bad fried chicken and awful pie in Winnemucca, Nevada, was the beginning of a sad coda to their journey.

Soon they were in Virginia City, home of Lucius Beebe—brilliant, bitchy, rich, alcoholic Lucius Beebe, dear friend to Jeanne Owen and the Browns and dismissive of James from the minute they met in New York City fifteen years back.

Lucius enjoyed the life of a magnifico in the nabob splendor of the Comstock Lode, among the graceful wooden neo-Renaissance mansions, peeling in the searing Nevada sun, built by nineteenth-century silver barons. His husband in all respects, save the marriage license and church wedding, was Chuck Clegg. Chuck was quarterback-handsome and courtly, in contrast to bloated, prickly Lucius. Helen and Philip were fond of them. They wanted to linger for a few days, which turned into four days of heavy drinking and blasting wit, much of it at James's expense.

"Drinks, Steaks, Drinks!" James wrote in his daybook. He disliked Virginia City, with its steep hills one couldn't climb without wheezing. One day, they all had a picnic on the scrubby flank of a hill, under a brutal sun. Chuck and Lucius brought a Victorian hamper filled with fine china plates, Austrian crystal, silver, and antique damask napkins. They ate cold boned leg of lamb and beans cooked with port. They lingered so long, over so many bottles of Champagne, that James's head became badly sunburned. Back at the motel, Philip, drunk, tried splashing James's head with gin, hoping it would bring cooling relief. Everyone cackled at his plight.

Finally, twenty-five days after they set out from San Francisco, Philip steered the Coronet home to Pasadena.

"The trip is one of the most happy and valuable memories of my life," he wrote to Schaffner from Pasadena. "I garnered a great deal of material, had a most nostalgic time in parts of the west most familiar to me and saw much I had never seen before. It was splendid, gastronomically speaking, to be able to see that there is hope in American cooking."

The best and most interesting food in America was inseparable from the landscapes that produced it. It was all right there, in country diners and small-town grocers' shops; in roadside dinner houses and bakeries. All you needed to do was look.

: : :

AFTER JAMES LEFT THE WEST, heading back to New York after a quick stopover in Chicago, Helen wrote to Schaffner. She fretted about James's state of mind.

"I suppose you might just as well know what a complex guy Jim is," she wrote. "Poor Jim—he is a lonely guy and an insecure one. Philip and I, talking about his craze for money, suddenly realized what it is. He knows he is not young and hasn't saved a cent. What's more he has no one to take care of him should he become ill. He's much too generous, too, and loves to live like a wealthy man."

He was, she told Schaffner, "one energetic[,] bright[,] sensitive[,] untidy, bossy man." His habits and working style drove her mad. Still, she and Philip loved him. "We . . . worry about him. Build up his ego when and if you can."

CHAPTER 12

WOO HIM WITH CALF'S HEAD

1954–1956

THE OUTDOOR BOOK with Helen seemed cursed. In January 1954, Clara Claasen told James and Helen she wanted the manuscript by the end of February, so Doubleday could publish it in time for the summer grilling season—she'd heard that Scribner's was planning to release a competing book in late spring.

But Doubleday hadn't even given them a contract. Before she could draft one and release the advance money, she'd need an outline.

Helen had never written a formal book outline, plus her mysterious ailments had flared up again: canker sores, gut pains, dizziness. By order of her doctor, she was taking phenobarbital, and as a result was finding it hard to focus. Instead, she made a rough list of things she thought they should cover and sent it to James.

By the end of January 1954, James had an outline. The title alone indicated his sprawling vision:

THE HELEN EVANS BROWN–JAMES A. BEARD GUIDE TO COOKING AND EATING OUT OF DOORS

The Complete Coverage of Picnics, Galley Cooking, The Manly Art of Barbecuing & The More Refined Art of Terrace and Patio Cookery.

James envisioned a book as big and comprehensive as *Fireside*, one that ranged from outdoor grill to indoor kitchen, from campfire skillet to garden-party chafing dish. It covered almost everything one could ever imagine eating outdoors: al fresco cocktail parties, "big garden crushes," he wrote, "with caterers and all the rest of the rented paraphernalia." He included travel cookery: snacks to pack for flights and car trips, "how to make a transcontinental trip a gourmetic experience instead of a series of diners and dirty spoons." He wanted a chapter with tips "to really romanticize eating in the wilds." There was a chapter on what he called Oriental cookery: "How to use the hibachi, make sukiyaki, teriyaki, satés, etc." He proposed a chapter on wine and drinks. And he hadn't given up on the idea of a cooks' controversy with Helen—discussions on the best ways to cook things, with digressions and lively disagreements, a back-and-forth that would show off their distinct personalities.

And despite the rigorous gender rules of the time, James's outline blurred the gender roles. His proposal for the chapter on "garden, terrace and patio cookery" didn't specify the cook's sex. "This is for the person who enjoys grilling in the out-of-doors," he wrote, "and who works in conjunction with the house." Elsewhere he sounded more circumspect, referencing "the man who wishes to show his prowess at the grill and range" and "the woman who likes to complement her husband's starring role." He raised a third possibility, too: "the man who likes to do everything." He neglected only the woman who'd also prefer to do everything, grilling the steaks *and* making the succotash to go with it.

He sent the outline to Helen. She vented her rage privately to Schaffner.

First, the book James proposed was too long. "Complete, yes," she wrote to her agent, "but not a [book that will take up a] blooming fifty foot shelf! . . . Why bring in the things that are cooked in the kitchen and just EATEN outdoors."

Second: "As for the managing [of] caterers," Helen wrote, "isn't that a bit. . . . . . ?" It was. Also the parts about romantic travel cooking and avoiding greasy spoons. James's ideas were precious.

Schooled in magazine food writing, Helen believed in a clear division of the sexes. She expected a firewall between men's cooking outdoors—building a backyard barbecue; manning the grill and rotisserie—and women's—planning the menu, making marinades and sauces, and preparing hors d'oeuvres and side dishes. James's outline was too big, too digressive, and too confusing about who should cook what.

"I don't get it," she told Schaffner.

James was merely warming up. "I think I have become pregnant with ideas suddenly," he told her. He proposed a campy new name in his next letter: *Balls, Picnics and Other Outdoor Pursuits.* "We can afford to be a little chichi in this book and to give them something new," James told Helen. "And shouldn't we call it *At Home Off the Range* just to be cute?—or would you prefer *doing it outdoors* in small letters as if it were by e. e. cummings; or would you like *Helen Evans Brown and James A. Beard [C]ook al [F]resco?* Sprinkle these with salt and pepper and add a little tarragon and then off to the races."

He wanted it to be carefree. Meanwhile, Helen just wanted to write a short, solidly useful book about grilling, to get it over with and move on.

Clara Claasen agreed that the book's focus should be limited: grilling and rotisserie cooking only, no chafing dishes or caterers, no airline snacks or romance of eating in the wilds, and no cooks' controversy. Claasen sought to keep the page count and production costs low. Instead of trying to rush it onto the market in mere months, Doubleday decided to publish in spring 1955. The manuscript was due in September 1954.

Buried in James and Helen's contract was a lousy advance, a miserable thousand dollars (just over nine thousand in 2019 dollars), split between them: half on signing, half when Doubleday accepted the finished manuscript. They'd get royalties on ten percent of sales. After Schaffner's commission, Helen and James each got $225 up front. James knew the Browns were hard up for cash; he offered to take $200 for the first payout and let Helen have $250. She could make it up to him on the second.

Collaborating on a manuscript was maddening.

In early May 1954, after his road trip with the Browns, James began a two-month stay in their rough attic guest room on Armada Drive. He'd hoped he and Helen could hammer the outdoor book into reasonable shape in three weeks, but so much else intervened. First they organized a sprawling Skotch Grill party for food media on the Browns' patio: a huge marble table with three of the red-plaid bucket grills for cooking shrimp and rumaki (chicken livers and water chestnuts wrapped with bacon), and for heating up morsels of carnitas, all on skewers. There was a punch bowl filled with martinis, and two Bartron Grills spit-roasting beef for sandwiches. General Bartron himself even showed up, toting a third grill.

Then James had to fly to Chicago for a lucrative one-day appearance representing Cognac. There were dinner parties: one at Eleanor Peters's house, another at the home of Judith Anderson, the lesbian character actor famous for playing Mrs. Danvers in Alfred Hitchcock's *Rebecca*. She served rumaki—the trendiest hors d'oeuvre of 1954—and coq au vin.

James and Helen went on *Mike Roy's Cooking Thing*, a CBS radio show broadcast to the nation from LA. They made several visits to Helen's favorite shop in Little Tokyo. James bought silk bow ties and a Japanese kimono-style short robe he wore on the sunken patio every morning, sipping jasmine tea and listening to the birds. Progress on the book was slow.

The way they worked couldn't have been less compatible. They tried testing recipes together, a grinding process. They tried writing by consensus, one of them at the typewriter while the other suggested sentences. When that didn't work, Helen proposed that James write first drafts; later she'd revise them and add her own thoughts. That proved just as difficult.

Schaffner received separate reports from both. Each complained privately about the other.

"Jim and I work very differently," Helen told Schaffner. "He bangs stuff out on the typewriter and never looks at it again so I am doing more condensing and rewriting than anything else. I am a polisher, which he doesn't believe in."

"The book is going slowly," James told Schaffner. "Confidentially, my dear John, Helen is quite upset—I think due to a physical condition and it is sometimes hard to get things accomplished. I have lost time. . . . Wish us well."

At the end of June 1954, eight weeks after they started work on the book, James prepared to return east. He rushed to finish up the last recipes. Friction had begun to grind away at his friendship with Helen, who seemed increasingly brittle. Meanwhile, James's lack of skill as a writer shocked Helen—she hadn't realized the extent to which Isabel rewrote his copy. And despite his having authored *Cook It Outdoors*, she was surprised by his lack of knowledge about grilling.

"Actually Philip knows much more about cooking over charcoal than does Jim," Helen told Schaffner. "But J is learning. J is doing most of the writing and frankly I think overdoing it. It's much too wordy and my job will be to rewrite it after he leaves. . . . That will be worse than doing the whole thing from scratch but it seems to be the best solution. Oh lord," she groaned, "why do I ever write another book?"

: : :

JAMES WAS SAYING YES to too many projects. In February 1954, he was finishing a small book for Jerry Mason, his old editor at *Argosy*. Mason had launched his own publishing company with Fred R. Sammis, Maco Magazine Corporation. The plan was to churn out cheap popular paperbacks with a retail price of seventy-five cents to sell in drugstores and supermarkets and on newsstands. (At the same time, a typical hardcover cookbook with good production values cost $3.95.) Mason also made a deal with Indianapolis-based publishing house Bobbs Merrill to produce hardback editions of all Maco soft covers.

Mason had enlisted James to write Maco's first title, a book on outdoor cookery. *Jim Beard's Complete Book of Barbecue & Rotisserie Cooking* appeared in May 1954: more than two hundred recipes on exactly the same subject as his planned Doubleday collaboration with Helen. James received a flat fee of $2,000 up front, with no royalties on future sales.

And though Schaffner raised this potential conflict of interest with Claasen, she didn't seem to mind. But then, Claasen was a strange and difficult editor. For weeks in her conversations with Schaffner, she seemed to think Helen's last name was "West," apparently having misread the title of *Helen Brown's West Coast Cook Book*. "You know," Schaffner noted with sarcasm in a letter to Helen, "Mrs. West, the author of the *Coast Cook Book*!"

It soon became obvious that Claasen had never edited a cookbook and knew little about food. Schaffner alternated between feeling sorry for her and thinking she was out of her mind.

"I won't go into any more details about what I have gone through with her lately or what she said to Jim," Schaffner told Helen, "but she certainly seems to be a mentally sick person." He found her emotionally exhausting.

Once back in New York, James worked to deliver the recipes he'd promised, but his passion for the outdoor book sputtered after Helen and Claasen bled the life out of most of his ideas.

He'd wanted to write an outdoor entertaining book that combined his panache, oversize personality, and adaptations of classic French recipes with Helen's contemporary tastes, her relaxed California style, and her wit. He'd envisioned a book with the high–low mix of foods he had unleashed at Lucky Pierre. Helen and Claasen, however, wanted a lean manual of helpful tips and technical information on cooking over charcoal. In essence, they were working on two different books. Instead of the marquee name that gave the collaboration credibility, James was starting to look like a liability.

"It is [Claasen's] idea that it was Jim's influence which led the book project astray in the beginning," Schaffner told Helen. "This seems a rather odd charge to level against the author of a column for *Argosy* magazine on cooking outdoors by men. But I must say for Clara that the evidence seems to be in her favor. Certainly, the material which has come in from Jim has been all for sauces and so on."

It was true. Helen nixed James's recipes for béchamel and mignonette sauces. She added back the béchamel after James complained; the mignonette stayed dead. James wanted to add desserts other than grilled fruit—the délice au chocolat he perfected at Lucky Pierre, for example. Helen and Claasen vetoed the idea.

Helen was frustrated—the job of finishing the manuscript was hers alone. Philip stepped in to test the recipe stragglers; he spit-roasted a whole albacore tuna and retested the rotisserie recipes to double-check timing and temperature. He edited Helen's copy, rewriting it where necessary, and typed the final manuscript.

James and Helen were contractually obligated to offer Doubleday their next books, whether solo or a second collaboration. James had soured on both possibilities. "What Doubleday—or rather Miss Claasen[—]gets out of me next," he told Helen, "is a book on how to sort garbage and use it for leftovers."

::: :::

IN AUGUST 1954, a month before Claasen would receive the finished manuscript for the outdoor collaboration, James's second title for Maco appeared. *Jim Beard's Complete Cookbook for Entertaining* contained nearly five hundred recipes. The cover showed a cartoony George Peter still-life in pink and pineapple yellow; the back had a photo of James shot by Josephine von Miklos, who caught him in a wicked laugh. The *Entertaining* book captured James's essence—authoritative yet alive to pleasure—with all the color and personality that were lacking from his labored collaboration with Helen.

James kept the book a secret from her.

In January 1955, Helen happened on a hardcover copy of the *Entertaining* book. As she flipped through its pages, she became furious. James had used some of the recipes that would appear in their collaboration—now titled *The Complete Book of Outdoor Cookery*—later that spring.

He had plagiarized the manuscript they had just finished, essentially stealing recipes from the book for which they were developed.

The recipe in *Entertaining* for Bacon and Egg Salad was identical to the one in their yet-to-appear Doubleday book. Shrimps Beard were word-for-word Shrimps Pierre (named for Lucky Pierre) in the *Outdoor* book. What's more, he lifted Escabêche de Pescado from *Helen Brown's West Coast Cook Book* without attribution. He gave a nod to Elena Zelayeta for some—though not all—of the recipes he borrowed from her. The closer Helen looked, the angrier and more appalled she became.

She wrote James a letter that hid her true fury. He was, after all, one of the most powerful people in food. And though they were friends, in 1955 it seemed unacceptable for a woman, especially an angry one, to challenge a man.

"To be perfectly honest I am a bit cross with you," she told James. "You have included stuff that is in our book and that I have been studiously avoiding using until it was published." She knew only too well his habit of plagiarizing himself and others. "I know that you won't resent it when I tell you, dear, that I really think you have repeated yourself too much in your last few books," she said. "That is why I think you ought to rest on your laurels for a while."

She unloaded her real outrage in a letter to Schaffner:

> He not only used innumerable of my <u>best</u> ideas without credit, he used some that I have NOT used anywhere because I wanted them fresh for the Doubleday book. He quotes from Elena, also without credit. (He apparently thinks that if he gives credit <u>once</u> that that is enough. It isn't.) He also repeats himself entirely too much. His last 3 or 4 books have many of the same recipes. People are going to say "the same old Beard stuff?" Truly I am worried . . . for him[,] and put out for others.

James apologized. He told her the Doubleday recipes found their way into the Maco book by accident. "When the mss was typed," he explained, "there were other sheets that got mixed up and around that weren't supposed to be in it." It was an obvious lie.

"Jim dear," she wrote back. "Your [*sic*] a sweet lamb not to be mad at me for balling you out. I did it only because I love you so much I didn't want you to make an awful mistake. Also maybe because I was a little jealous at your being smart enough to make so much money."

:::

DOUBLEDAY PUBLISHED *The Complete Book of Outdoor Cookery* on April 21, 1955, timed for the start of grilling season. It's a thin book, just under 250 pages, with no illustrations save some barbecue construction diagrams borrowed from *Argosy* and Virginia Plummer's stylish endpapers.

The book's central lesson was that meats cook best over charcoal kept low and steady. References to James and Helen's experiences are scarce. Instead, the book elevates outside experts: General Bartron; Jorge Ramirez, proprietor of the Acme Barbecue College in Alhambra, California; and Eagle Scout leader and camping expert Hugo Hammer. There's a dull, servicey, how-to quality to the writing. The style and tone echo Helen's magazine work, only without the usual brightness and clever turns of phrase. James's voice is silent, his typical opinions and anecdotes absent, and his manifest love for eating and pleasure nowhere to be found.

The collaboration both had pushed for yielded a dry book neither of them liked, a squandering of their personalities. Helen blamed Claasen. James and Helen would never collaborate on another book.

"You and I have never done one that is so dull to read," Helen told James a few months before publication day. "I am reading Alice B. Toklas which points out, more than ever, the lack of chit chat [*sic*] in ours." But chitchat was what James had wanted for the book from the start: Helen had said *no* as forcefully as Claasen did. Though James and Helen were still friends—still believed themselves allies against a food establishment deaf to original voices—the experience had drained the joy from their alliance.

The Complete Book of Outdoor Cookery was a commercial flop. The numbers for 1955 were bad; the ones in the first half of 1956 were worse. In August 1956, James opened his Doubleday royalty statement and was stunned. Nationally, only 292 copies had sold in the previous quarter. Doubleday didn't seem interested in trying to sell it.

"They didn't do a fucking thing about the book this year," he wrote to Helen. "I think it would be better to start a hamburger stand and make twenty thousand a year with it. It's murder!! That's what it surely is!!!!!!!!!!"

The truth is they'd produced a book so bland that nobody but serious outdoor-cooking hobbyists had a reason to pick it up.

Not since *Hors D'Oeuvre and Canapés*, his first, had James done a book in which he wasn't present. Of course, Doubleday and Claasen would show a lack of imagination, a narrow desire to cash in on the outdoor cooking frenzy while spending as little as possible on production. But Helen, he felt, had betrayed him. Despite his and Helen's shared disdain for home economists in cookbooks and magazine food, Helen had resisted all of James's attempts to write a book that put their personalities on display. Despite her original ideas, she still represented the dominant strain in American life, the suburban cook whose husband would man the coals while she assembled the rumaki and tossed the salad in the kitchen.

In August 1954, three weeks before their manuscript was due, James had urged Helen to scrap it. He wanted them to send the advance—such as it was—back to Doubleday and write the book they wanted to do. They'd find another publisher. Helen resisted.

Though James was one of the most famous food authorities in America, he knew he was above all a personality. And while there were many things about his life James couldn't let the public—and even some of his friends—see, he embodied a gourmet lifestyle that seemed new and thrilling in America. James was an American epicure devoted to pleasure at the table as an essential part of the good life. If he wanted to wheel out an exuberant homemade délice au chocolat as the perfectly wicked finish to a porterhouse broiled on a bed of molten blue cheese, well—it was an essential part of what made James fascinating.

Who cared if he didn't get the timing on rotisserie chickens exactly right? Even if Helen didn't, Jerry Mason at Maco surely saw what made James unforgettable.

:::

"SATURDAY I AM HAVING Ken Zwerlein [*sic*] from San Francisco," James wrote to Helen in 1954, months before their road trip. "[He] is one of the very chi-chi California bunch who will have only the greatest of everything."

James had got the name wrong. Ken Zwerin was a lawyer, a sort of satellite member of the San Francisco branch of the Wine and Food Society traveling to New York on business. He wrote to James, asking whether they could meet. An amateur gourmet, he cooked from *Fireside* and *Paris Cuisine*. He'd heard much about James.

Zwerin was born in San Francisco in 1911. As a youth, he studied to become a rabbi. In college, he switched to law and eventually became an attorney, though he delivered guest sermons at Reform congregations in San Francisco and elsewhere. In 1935, Zwerin took over his father's law practice, writing occasional essays on the subject of ethics in Reform Judaism. He had the blessings of success and a taste for luxury: an office downtown near the Palace Hotel, and an apartment in plush Pacific Heights, in a palazzo-style highrise building with a view of the Golden Gate Bridge.

The only wrinkle: Zwerin was queer.

Living openly would have cost him his law practice and standing in his congregation, so he kept his identity hidden. Behind the scenes, he joined one of the earliest gay rights groups in America, the Mattachine Society.

Mattachine formed in Los Angeles in 1950, when eight men, including Harry Hay, a Communist labor organizer and sometime actor, drafted a gay rights manifesto. It called for scizing cquality through direct political action. Except in the spring of 1953, at Mattachine's first national convention in LA, members voted to adopt a new, softer agenda. It called for an end to radical action in favor of a gradual move into the mainstream of society, an assimilationist strategy for achieving gay civil rights. It relied in part on the activism of influential homophiles—upstanding members of society (not gay themselves, presumably) who took an enlightened, tolerant view toward homosexuals.

Publicly, this was Zwerin's persona: a straight homophile lawyer who defended suspected homosexuals swept up in vice-squad raids and charged with vagrancy, a life-shattering conviction. Zwerin may have been motivated by conscience and conviction, but he wasn't purely altruistic. Few lawyers in the 1950s were interested in defending homosexuals. Accused men were desperate, willing to pay almost any fee a good lawyer demanded, especially one referred by Mattachine, as Zwerin was.

As a Jew, Zwerin was denied formal entry to the Wine and Food Society ("the holy of holies," James called it), though he did attend events as a guest and threw parties for members, no doubt hoping they'd drop their (unofficial) anti-Semitic covenant, at least in his case.

And so, James invited the visiting lawyer to dinner at his apartment, for a menu Zwerin requested, remarkably porky even for a Reform almost-rabbi: a Swiss onion tart with bacon, and choucroute garnie, the Brasserie Lipp recipe from *Paris Cuisine* (coincidentally, James's seduction dish). James invited "the boys": Alvin and Peter, Paul Bernard, Freddie Shrallow. The choucroute was superb; the Alsatian Riesling they drank with it was cool, liquefied gold.

While Zwerin may have been wooing James that night as a member of the Wine and Food Society, he was also courting him to become a supporter of Mattachine: a high-profile professional (closeted, as he was) to come out publicly as a homophile and endorse homosexual rights, as any dispassionate American of conscience would.

Six weeks later, in April 1954, Zwerin tried again. It was when James was in San Francisco, alone for a few days, waiting for the Browns to arrive in the Coronet for their infamous road trip. James and Zwerin met for dinner at Vince's Garden Restaurant in North Beach. A third man joined them.

Considering Zwerin's reputation as a gourmet, Vince's was a surprising choice. It was a so-so Italian joint, where a broiled steak came with an antipasto of salami and olives and a bowl of minestrone, and where the best bottle on the list was Beringer Burgundy. For privacy, however, it was perfect: deep, narrow, dark, and out of the way.

The third at the table that night was Elver Barker, a sweet, socially awkward young man with a long face and a high crown of blond hair. Barker was an ardent member of the editorial board of the San Francisco Mattachine Society. He had joined a year earlier, after being tossed from his job as an Oakland social worker when his supervisor deduced he was gay. Over calamari and zabaglione, the men talked.

Whatever Zwerin and Barker said to James about endorsing Mattachine and the homophile movement, it wasn't persuasive enough for him to become a public supporter and maybe, under a pen name, write something for the *Mattachine Review*. For the Dean of American Cookery, the risk at the other end of the calculation was too great.

: : :

PRACTICALLY EVERYONE IN James's intimate circle—the people he trusted, relaxed with, and thought of as family—was lesbian or gay.

There were Cheryl Crawford and Ruth Norman; also Ann Seranne and John Schaffner. Alvin Kerr and Peter Carhartt had been together since college, when both were aspiring playwrights and actors. Peter— heir to the Carhartt work-wear company—had a small part in a Broadway show once; later, he and Alvin wrote for *The Kate Smith Hour* on radio and did scripts for army training films during the war. Alvin worked with James at the Sherry wine store, and James and the boys were Greenwich Village neighbors. Likewise Freddie Shrallow, an interior decorator who lived in a large studio apartment in a townhouse on West Twelfth almost directly opposite James's.

Aleks Bird was a dancer in the ballet chorus for the 1944 revival of *The Merry Widow* at City Center, and he was in *Mexican Hayride*, a show with Cole Porter songs at the Winter Garden. He'd hung up his tights to write (try, anyway) about food and wine. Paul Bernard, married in all details but law to the artist Harry Marinsky, was James's regular theater companion for shows, including opera and ballet. Bernard worked in publicity. He stayed in the city during the week and on weekends joined Marinsky at their cottage in Connecticut, where Marinsky kept his studio. In 1957, James became good friends with Mateo Lettunich. He'd worked for the State Department in Berlin after the war as cultural affairs adviser, helping to rebuild the city's shattered theaters and concert halls. In New York, Lettunich wrote plays for NBC television.

And James's dearest friends who weren't queer—Sam and Florence Aaron, Cecily Brownstone, Helen McCully, and of course the Browns—were ones he could trust to know his heart, and a few of his secrets.

In 1954, someone new joined James's core of gay friends. At thirty-three, John Ferrone had a face reminiscent of busts of the young Augustus: large, soft eyes and a resolute expression, boyish yet fierce. He was from a small town in New Jersey, the fifth child of Italian immigrants. His father never learned much English, and Ferrone wasn't fluent in Italian, so his mother would translate: Ferrone grew up never having a direct conversation with his father. At nineteen, he left home to serve in World War II and had a brief stint on Guam. He went to college after the war, eventually landing at Stanford, studying creative writing with Wallace Stegner. In 1953, Ferrone moved to New York and met James's close friend Paul Bernard. Ferrone lived in a tiny third-floor walk-up on West Twelfth, doors from James's place. Bernard introduced them as neighbors.

Ferrone was working as a reader for Dell Books, a publisher of mass-market paperbacks, not respected among prestigious New York houses. He became an editor. Dell published inexpensive reprints of classic works; Ferrone's first assignment was persuading Noel Coward, who'd staged a recent comeback in Las Vegas, to let Dell publish a collection of his works: short plays, stories, lyrics. There was one song—"Mad About the Boy," from Coward's *Words and Music*—for which Ferrone couldn't find definitive lyrics, so he looked up Coward at his apartment in New York. He lay on his stomach on the carpet, scribbling in a notebook as the great man recited. The young editor had proved his meticulousness and gumption as well as his interest in older gay heroes.

Ferrone would go on to Harcourt, Brace and World, where he'd edit Eudora Welty, Anaïs Nin, and Alice Walker for its Harvest paperback imprint. He would also edit James, for Dell and other publishers, though they had become friends before that. Soon after Paul Bernard introduced them, Ferrone started dropping by James's for dinner, usually for dishes James was testing for his regular *House & Garden* features, the Doubleday outdoor book, or the one on entertaining for Maco. Eventually they cooked together, as often as three times a week when James was in town.

Like James, Ferrone was discreetly gay in his private life, closeted in his professional one. James trusted his closest friends not to violate the central rule of being queer in the brutal era after the war: that you never, ever publicly acknowledged being queer, or even hinted at it. No matter how flagrant the signs were, in any sphere but the private you didn't let on that you could interpret them. Caricatures of queens and fairies popped up in plays and movies, but you didn't as much as roll your eyes to a queer friend in public for fear of outing yourself—or them. For that you needed to be in a safe zone: a friend's apartment, or perhaps one of the few drinking establishments in the Village where, if you couldn't let your hair all the way down, you could tease out a few strands.

In 1958, James received a gift from his old friend Ken Zwerin: a year's subscription to the gay-rights magazine *ONE*. It was the monthly publication of the civil rights organization One Inc., based in Los Angeles. *ONE* launched its first issue in 1953, but the Post Office Department quickly deemed it obscene and refused to deliver it. In 1958, the US Supreme Court denied the Post Office its refusal. James's subscription started with the July issue, with a cover story on gay beaches. It wasn't the kind of thing one could leave lying around—ever. Even certain letters were risky.

James and his closest circle of friends had an unspoken agreement to protect the reputations of the others. It was, after all, how one survived.

:::

THE TRUTH IS THAT James had arrived in Mexico in July 1955 as a gigolo, a rich man's accessory. It gave James a laugh. Fate had destined

Elizabeth Beard's boy—all three hundred pounds of him, currently sweating into his best tan summer suit and feeling a second trickle of perspiration sluice down the back of his neck—to be a gigolo of the table. After all, it was nice to be wanted for *something*.

He had been flown down from New York, with a layover in New Orleans due to heavy rain. He was now in the back of a limousine in Ciudad de México belonging to Mr. Francis George Guth of New York—also of Andover, Massachusetts, and Spain, where he owned a castle.

Mexico City was a place too hot for anyone with sense to visit in July, except as the guest of a millionaire. James was grateful to be away from New York and his telephone and Helen's tortuously restrained letters of rage and recrimination. He'd been here before, not long ago in May, again as a guest of Guth and his wife, Barbara. James was here for only a week before he flew home and made a lunch of cold, crusty spit-roasted baby lamb and Basque piperade for Marilyn Monroe at Cheryl and Ruth's place in New Canaan. (She was so quiet and unassuming, really: just a terribly shy and thoughtful person.)

Guth was a little over thirty, born in Vienna. His parents had owned an enormous linoleum factory and left him a fortune. For being such a young man, Guth was well jowled. He had a small mouth that looked cruel, usually, though occasionally it struck James as passionate, attuned to pleasure, even sexy. His forehead was high and broad, under dark, rigorously barbered hair with a meticulous part. His jaguar eyes, which sometimes looked as though they were fixed on something in the distance, something he desired, were hard to look away from, and certainly to say *no* to.

Guth arrived in the US in 1940 to go to a rich boys' prep school and get out of Hitler's way. He settled in Andover and became a dedicated amateur gourmet. He gave tons of money to the New York Wine and Food Society, so of course Madame Owen and that crowd were all over him. And he was an investor, along with David Rockefeller, in Château Lascombes, Alexis Lichine's wine estate in Bordeaux (where James had visited in 1953). He traveled with the sole aim of tasting dishes he'd heard of and wanted to sample, and not just in Europe (though he always cited steak au poivre at Paul et Virginie in Paris as one of his personally defining dishes). Guth had sought out rock lobsters flamed with rum in Haiti and land crab asopao in Puerto Rico. He was fond of recalling a lunch in Havana of sautéed moro (stone) crabs finished with vintage Bacardi, which he enjoyed with beer.

Guth owned a regal old hacienda here in colonia San Ángel (not far from the studio of that artist who looked like a bulldog, Diego Rivera), with lawns and ancient trees and peacocks strutting behind a high wall. He'd brought James here to get his opinion, and to use him as a prop.

Guth also had opened a restaurant in Mexico City, a Continental steakhouse named Passy. It was at Amberes 10, a block from the deluxe Hotel El Presidente. James had seen it in May, just before the public unveiling. It had a patio and an open charcoal grill topped with sizzling T-bones and New York strips, the finest raised in the country. (One of Guth's hobbies was to prove that, contrary to the American prejudice, Mexican beef could be sensational.) "I've always wanted to have a place," Guth told local gossip columnist Pepe Romero, "where I could get what I wanted to eat at the time when I wanted to eat it."

Of course, Guth had servants to cook for him anytime, but he yearned to dine in a vanity restaurant to which he could invite businessmen, politicians, starlets . . . AND the most famous gourmet in America, now pulling up in Guth's limousine on a sweltering afternoon when even the peacocks squatting under the trees seemed stunned.

: : :

NEXT MORNING, Guth took James to the markets: Mercado Coyoacan and La Merced. That night, James was guest of honor at a dinner for thirty at the Passy restaurant, where the centerpiece was a grand baron of Sonoran beef, spit-roasted slowly on the patio. Waiters bearing bowls of colonial silver ladled béarnaise onto guests' plates. James did what he was brought here to do: He declared it marvelous, cooked to perfection, tricky for such a lean animal as this clearly was. Why, if he hadn't known better, he would have sworn he was eating beef from one of the fine French cattle of the Camargue.

On his May visit, he'd met an American, a bachelor like James, now living in Mexico City. Alan Taulbee was a former radio announcer turned PR man; his main client was the Mexican government, organizer of the annual road race on the Pan-American Highway, the *Carrera Panamericana*. (The 1955 event had recently been suspended, after eighty-three spectators were killed at the June motor rally in Le Mans, France.) Taulbee lived in the snug penthouse of the Hotel Prince on Calle Louis Moya. He had connections, locals and expats both, and moved in Mexico City's discreet but active gay circles. He took James to several Turkish baths, where one could find an old and lively male culture of socializing and sex, if one knew how to read and respect long-established codes.

One day, freed from his obligations with Guth, James met Taulbee at a restaurant to lunch on steak au poivre. Taulbee had invited a friend, someone he wanted James to meet. José Jorge Carlos de Jesús Palomino y Cañedo was lean-faced, aristocratic, and handsome. Jorge was forty-seven, a genealogist and man of culture, from a wealthy family in Guadalajara. His wife had left him three years earlier.

Close to four o'clock, after their long lunch, and slightly drunk, James, Jorge, and Taulbee went to the bullfights at the titanic Plaza Mexico ring, thundering with shouts and the stamping of feet and dueling trumpet bands. They watched lithe, youthful matadors in tight sequined and gold-embroidered *trajes*, with pink stockings and red-lined capes, make balletic passes in the leisurely sport of formal, ritualized slaughter, as fifty thousand spectators cried *"OLÉ!"* at the top of their lungs. They drank beer in their wooden box. They munched on peanuts electro-charged with chile and lime.

After the fights, Taulbee suggested they all have dinner. He chose a trendy restaurant: the Mauna Loa, a place like Trader Vic's in San Francisco, with Polynesian décor and Chinese food. James thought everything tasted atrocious, though after a day of being partially, functionally inebriated, they all got well and fully blitzed on rum drinks.

And actually, James realized next morning, waking with a hangover to regard the colonial sumptuousness of his bedroom at the Guth hacienda, just being in the presence of Jorge made him feel a little drunk. James had never met anyone quite like him.

Two days later, again free of Guth, James spent an afternoon and an evening with his new friend. Jorge loved to drink, to go out and stay out late—at bars, nightclubs, and crowded house parties where all the guests were men. He displayed sharp intelligence, at least until he got good and ripped. And what he said about his family history and the numerous cuisines of Mexico, so vast as to be practically unknowable by one person in a single lifetime, was fascinating.

Jorge had lent James his grandmother's handwritten cookbook; Guth was translating it. James was ecstatic. He wrote to Helen. He described the Palomino y Cañedo family (without naming them) as one of Mexico's most distinguished. "These are family recipes from before the Empire and are fabulous," he told her. "I shall have them all and we shall see what we can do with some of them. . . . It is fabulous and wonderful reading."

James had been so drowned in work and obligation, so exhausted and depressed, he hadn't allowed himself to fall in love with anyone. His fling with Ate de Boer felt as though it had ended ages ago. Since then, James had been ill and become so fat. He'd come to believe no one would want to spend time with him. Mexico, with its baths full of married men who came to be with and touch other men and never speak of it; even the way men on the street dressed to be looked at, adored like young matadors; and of course Jorge, who embodied a long, proud history: All this gave James hope that a fascinating world of understanding *did* exist, if only quietly. Here was comfort that, in a bathhouse on a sequestered block in Mexico City smelling of tortillas and detergent, where sticky jacaranda blossoms carpeted the street in purple, there were men who'd never heard of him or seen his picture but knew exactly who he was.

As much as James had come to Mexico to be Francis Guth's gourmet-for-hire, he'd come to be anonymous—to lose himself temporarily before he had to go home, feel it all roaring back, and sense the gray chasm opening again.

Taulbee and James made the winding, perilous, six-hour trip to Acapulco, Taulbee driving and dodging dogs, cattle, and boulders on the roadway. They spent four days looking at the Pacific, eating carnitas, tamales, and avocado soup, drinking in hotel bars, and watching boys dive from the heights of La Quebrada. Back in Mexico City, James went to the baths again before flying home to New York, with a layover in Los Angeles.

The original plan had been for the Browns to drive their Coronet convertible from Pasadena to Mexico City, pick up James, and all drive home together, stopping to explore as they went—a Mexican version of their northwestern road trip of 1954. They needed to talk about writing another book together, or at least having a proposal to offer Doubleday, as stipulated in their contract, despite the fiasco of the outdoor book. Helen, however, killed the idea of the Mexico trip.

"It is definitely off," she told Schaffner. "We are broke, [Philip] can't get away at that time and everyone, including my doctor says 'NO.' It's too hot this time of year." She worried about James surviving an arduous car journey. "The trip back in all that heat might kill Jim." James was annoyed, but it was probably better this way. Bitterness over how the book turned out still lingered, as did Helen's fury about his betrayal and dishonesty. Best not to spend weeks together confined to the brocade upholstery of a car rolling through a foreign country.

Yes, James used people, even (perhaps especially) the friends most loyal to him. But he considered what he gave them in return as part of the transaction. He was always generous with the Browns, forever talking up Helen to anyone in New York who'd listen, constantly angling for opportunities for her. What was taking credit for a few recipes here and there against that?

Less than two months later, in September, James saw Jorge again—at the small apartment Jorge kept on East Fifty-Seventh in Manhattan. They dined that night at Johnny Johnston's Charcoal Room, a swank steakhouse on Second Avenue and East Forty-Fifth.

They saw each other again four months later, in January 1956, this time in Paris. James had sailed for Genoa in December; he was taking a six-week vacation through Florence, Nice, Aix-en-Provence, Bordeaux (where he'd be installed as a Commandeur de Bontemps de Médoc, thanks to Sam Aaron), Paris, and London. He spent three days with Jorge in Paris. They dined together five times, once at Maxim's, where James arranged a romantic menu, simple and lush, for two: foie gras frais, poularde aux Champagne, and a dessert of pears.

"Worth the price," he noted in his datebook, and underlined it heavily.

: : :

FELIX'S RESTAURANT AT 154 West Thirteenth Street in the Village was a bit of a hole, but at least it was dark and stayed open late. You walked slightly down to the door on the ground floor of a brownstone, past the host stand and into the bar, which seemed windowless because the heavy front curtains were always closed. If James stretched out both his arms, they'd probably take up half the width of the place; no more than twenty people could drink in there. Through a dark curtain at the far end was the restaurant, big enough for maybe seventy. Though it was close (cozy if you were optimistic, or were happy-drunk or in love), and you never went when New York was the least bit muggy, you felt enveloped—or, to be accurate, protected. Because Felix's was one of those peculiar places in the Village where, if you were a gentleman who behaved yourself, you could entertain another gentleman without the owner, Felice De Gregorio, or his son Felix Jr., tossing your mink coat and your bonnet at you and telling you to get out.

Somewhere back in time, Felice had sung with the Chicago Opera Company and the San Carlo Opera Company (so they said, though James was dubious), and perhaps he'd learned to be tolerant of the boys. But the clientele, or the mugginess, or the stubborn reek of the drains wasn't why Felix's was a hole. That was due, as James knew better than anyone, to the food.

You could get fish or frog legs Provençale, and dinner came with spaghetti or ravioli, bean soup, and salad (Clementine Paddleford had called it "middle price, middle good," and that about summed it up). The gimmick was that every so often somebody stood up or walked to the center of the room to sing an aria: maybe Ralph, the baritone waiter who'd been there forever; maybe one of the customers, a boy who'd had the right number of drinks; maybe Felice himself, for a few lines of "Vesti la giubba" from *Pagliacci*. On that night in April 1956, the food didn't matter. Because that night James, who had come to Felix's to escape, ran into some friends. At their table was a forty-two-year-old architect's draftsman with the firm Harrison & Abramovitz. He was an Italian with a quiet manner, kind eyes, a soft accent, and a delicious dimpled chin that looked sculpted from marzipan. They introduced him as Gino.

Gino Pasquale Cofacci was born in 1914 in Bologna, to Benedetta Camastro Cofacci and her husband, Davide. While Gino was still a boy, the family (now including a girl, Elena) moved to Rome. The Cofaccis grew close to their neighbors, an Austrian family named Taussig. The father, Stefan, was a professor of geography; eventually he landed a job at Cornell University in Ithaca, New York. In 1939, at age twenty-five, and with Stefan Taussig and his wife as hosts and sponsors, Gino immigrated to the United States to enroll at Cornell, in the School of Architecture. America instituted the draft in October 1940, and in July 1941, five months before Pearl Harbor, Gino was inducted.

If he had been born in Japan, Gino would have been discharged and interned to a relocation camp when war was declared. As an Italian alien, he was able to keep serving. By 1942, because of his drafting skills, Gino was named Technician Fourth Grade and carried the rank of sergeant. He was part of an engineers' outfit, designing airstrips and airfields in the Pacific, working one beat behind advance units as they opened new fronts: across the north coast of New Guinea, through Indonesia, and to the Philippines, always prone to attack. Gino received an honorable discharge in July 1945 and returned to Ithaca to pick up his studies. He became a Gargoyle (a member of Cornell's architectural society), and in 1948, at age thirty-four, received his bachelor's degree.

In James's gaze, Gino was a gorgeous individual from the kind of fascinating foreign places James found ripe with escape and understanding. He was odd and funny, this Gino, alternately shy and almost shockingly frank, blurting out observations and opinions in a way other people didn't, socially. The bad spaghetti and overcooked fish and tortured singing receded into a barely noticeable periphery. The next night, James had Gino to dinner at his apartment.

Three days later, he had Gino over again, this time for Saturday lunch. James invited John Ferrone to join them for the spread: a few cold hors d'oeuvres followed by tête de veau, a boned and poached calf's head served with vinaigrette. Afterward no dessert, only cheese.

James took care with the calf's head, preparing it the way Sandy Watt's butcher in Paris told James to do it: meat and tongue served first, then the more delicate brains as a separate course. And the vinaigrette, instead of shocking with a jolt of acidity, had to be soft, herbaceous, and capery in a way that underlined rather than erased. Gino was such a strange and gentle person, one who seemed to wear thought and emotion on his skin; James sensed that subtlety would not be lost on him.

They all three lingered, drinking wine, until the afternoon shifted almost imperceptibly into the first hints of evening. After Ferrone left, James twisted the blinds closed and they moved to his bed; with fine draftsman's hands, Gino traced everything on James body, not shying or pulling away.

James was captivated; probably (and for the first time), he was in love.

PART FOUR

CHAPTER 13

PERDITA BAKES A LAYER CAKE

1956–1959

At the end of 1955, Frank Schoonmaker had asked James to be his collaborator on a monumental book about wine. Schoonmaker, born in 1905 in South Dakota, was one of the world's best-known authorities on wine. Soon after Prohibition ended, he opened an import business in New York City, promoting winemakers rather than shippers, and authored *The Complete Wine Book* for Simon and Schuster. By 1940, he'd begun selling American wines, lifting their status. It was Schoonmaker who convinced California winemakers to abandon the European regional designations they'd been using and instead give their wines names that combined location with the dominant grape varietal: "Livermore Chardonnay" instead of "California Chablis," for instance, or "Fountain Grove Sonoma Pinot Noir" instead of "California Burgundy." Schoonmaker's polished writing for *The New Yorker*, *Gourmet*, and *Holiday* educated a generation about wine. He was an architect of American wine culture.

Reaching out to James to be his collaborator was a mark of respect.

James recognized it as an honor. "I have always admired Frank and feel that he has done more for California wines than anyone," he told Helen.

In 1956, as spring arrived, James and Schoonmaker were under contract with Random House to deliver a large book: how to buy and appreciate wine, how to cook with it, and which wine to pair with what. They had a deadline of July 1, 1957, and received an advance of one thousand dollars each. They'd need time and freedom from distractions to write it, so Schoonmaker decided that Spain would be perfect for knuckling down. He had been sent there during the war as a spy for the US Office of Strategic Services (OSS), predecessor of the CIA. Now he owned a house at the north end of the Costa Brava, a hundred miles up the shore from Barcelona, in Palamós. It was once a quiet fishing village, but the government of Francisco Franco, Spain's dictator—eager for tourist cash—decreed that Palamós would become the Mediterranean's newest international beach resort. Hotels were rising.

Schoonmaker and his wife, Marina, would rent a nearby villa for James. He and Schoonmaker could spend the summer banging out an outline and typing stacks of draft pages, four thousand miles from their editors and persistent telephones in New York. Somehow, James had a bad feeling about all of this: the trip, the book. He'd heard Schoonmaker had originally planned to write it with Jeanne Owen. Maybe James said *yes* to Schoonmaker because he was flattered to be asked, or because John Schaffner told him he should do it, or because he wanted to feel he'd surpassed Jeanne. Yet James found himself numb to the work.

Slated to sail at the beginning of June, James canceled at the last minute. He flew to Madrid three weeks later and arrived in Palamós on July 6. What was he supposed to do in Spain for two months without Gino?

: : :

PALAMÓS WAS PICTURESQUE ENOUGH. Wine grapes grew in clearings on the scrubby hills within sight of the ocean. Once the fisher-

men were through for the day, rows of sardine boats covered the fine
sand beaches. The town was overrun with French and British tourists,
however, joined by budget-conscious Americans looking for a cheaper
stretch of the Mediterranean to splash in than the swanky waves lap-
ping the Côte d'Azur. Together, they ensured that local restaurants
would be touristic and dull.

"I am not the person to settle down to a routine of a beach resort
in Europe any more," James wrote to Schaffner. "It seems to have
charm and grace and drive, but the food is not good and the cooking
is not good and I really would prefer being somewhere else to put it
quite honestly."

The Schoonmakers weren't getting along. "Marina is a boring bitch
and fights with Frank constantly," James reported to his agent. "It is
really difficult. If I had a car or something for escape or if Gino came
here for vacation it would be a different thing." They were making little progress on the book. Schoonmaker's gout had flared up. He spent
hours in bed every day.

"Marina came over here to vent her spleen because Frank is in bed,"
James wrote Helen, "and two hours of her extreme bitchiness drove me
to drink and Miltown." (James had started taking the tranquilizer—
its chemical name was meprobamate—earlier that year for anxiety and
depression.) God only knows why he'd agreed to come to Palamós.

He was annoyed at Schaffner for prodding him. "As you remember,"
James wrote, "I did not really want to come over this summer—and
I was right. I am sure that there will be no major work done on this
project until [Frank and I] are separated again." He asked Schaffner
to send him a telegram in care of Frank and Marina with some bogus
explanation for why James needed to be back in New York by the third
week of August. "This will be the official out."

Spain did have mitigating charms. His little villa came with a housekeeper who cooked, Mercedes Figueras. She was small and slight, with
dark eyes and a soulful look, like a face in a Coptic portrait. Some mornings James met her early at the market. He watched her make tortillas
de patatas (thick potato omelets), the Catalan garlic mayonnaise called

allioli, and paella. One day he told his agent, "We have just finished a magnificent lunch of Mercedes['] version of a paella, superb and delicate in its mixture of flavors and seasonings."

And the men of Palamós were beyond words. "I wish you could visit here," he wrote to Schaffner, "and see the quality of the fisherboys—something really classic and indescribable. I feel that Franco has chosen the right people for the right jobs."

: : :

WITH SCHOONMAKER LAID UP and in misery, James escaped to Barcelona on a crowded train. He checked in at the Ritz. He went to Bel y Cía, the esteemed clothier on Paseo de Gracia, where a tailor measured him for shirts with subtle pastel stripes, a suit, and a camel's hair coat, to be made and sent to New York. He met a friend from Houston, Jack Raglin, who worked in public affairs for Conoco. They dined late at Los Caracoles in the Gothic Quarter ("the slums," as James described it to Schaffner) on fresh sardines and chicken, next to the front wall of doors that folded back to let diners feel part of the sidewalk. James found it enthralling: the food, and the easy way Catalans carried on in public; the narrow streets and medieval buildings. And he had an eye for the hustlers, their poses and swagger; the aura of unrepressed sexuality.

"You sit on the street and are cruised by everything in the world," he told Schaffner, "and there are all sorts of hawkers and photographers and practically everything in the world which makes for color. Even Tennessee Williams cruising the cripples like mad."

The Random House advance was boring a hole in James's pocket. He shopped for antiques. "I have seen a sofa I want so badly here," he wrote to Schaffner, "that I am almost ready to hock my soul—I know I can't make that much from my body." It was Catalan, eighteenth century. "I look like an old king of Spain—I hope I have the sex right[—] when I'm sitting on it[. . . .]" In fact, it made him feel like a glorious old queen.

Even though exile in Palamós was agony for James, money gave him

ways to find the charm of living. Especially when he thought of returning home to Gino, whose letters had been wonderful.

James felt effervescent. "I find myself more and more attracted by
this person," he told Schaffner. "Overwhelmingly so, in fact. I shall
have to see what comes out of it all when I get back. But it is surely
completely enthralling to me at this point."

Still, even for a man temporarily at ease with the world, being queer
brought fear and anxiety. Near the end of James's time in Spain, a friend
came to stay in his villa. Robert Tyler Lee was an art director and set
designer working for CBS television in Los Angeles (he'd received an
Emmy nomination the previous year for his work on *Shower of Stars*).
James met Lee and his live-in boyfriend, Robert Checchi (also a set
decorator and designer), through Eleanor Peters. Lee planned to spend
a week with James in Spain before flying to Cuba, where Checchi was
working on interior designs for the Havana Hilton, then in the planning stage.

When Lee got to James's villa, he was distraught: Six weeks had
passed since he last heard from Checchi. Had he been picked up on
the street for loitering? Entrapped at a bar where queers were known to
gather by President Batista's goons and locked in a Cuban prison? Lee
couldn't ask Checchi's employer without raising suspicions, or revealing
outright that he was homosexual, thus getting him fired.

James asked his agent to make discreet inquiries. "I fell upon the
idea of asking you to make a call and find out what you can," James
told Schaffner. "It will be a great favor to me—but then it seems you
are always doing me favors." Lee reached out to Schaffner, too, plead-
ing for help. "I hope he isn't in such a position of job or such that [he's]
embarrassed to write. . . . Please remember that he is quiet, full of pride
and dignity," Lee wrote. So much complicated delicacy was needed to
navigate a queer life.

Schaffner wired Lee to tell him Checchi was fine, merely unable
to write, and phoning from Cuba was out of the question. Soon, Lee
would be on his way to Havana for a reunion, and James, just three
months after meeting Gino, was already trying to figure out how they
could live together. Discreetly.

Schoonmaker rallied in time to rough out parts of the Random House project before James needed to return to New York. It was to be a book of menus, organized by season and occasion, with appropriate wines. There were other cookbooks that mentioned the seasons, but none took the seasonality of dishes as an organizing theme. "It is going to be revolutionary in some ways," James told his agent. But there was a hell of a lot more to do.

A month after he got home, James rented the empty apartment on the first floor of his building at 36 West Twelfth. Gino could have the bedroom in the new unit, while James would use the rest as his office, keeping his bedroom—officially—in the existing unit upstairs. For anyone who didn't know that they slept together, they'd seem like roommates.

Introducing Gino to Helen by letter, James described him as "an architect and rather a swell guy."

Gino filled both apartments with houseplants and worked, despite James's naturally sloppy habits, to keep things clean and tidy. Gino's mind demanded order and precision; it thrived on detail. When Isabel asked him for help translating recipes from the Italian original of Ada Boni's *Il Talismano della Felicità*, Gino took on the assignment like a grad student. He researched unfamiliar Italian dialects so he could understand the regional ingredient names Boni used. He spent hours at the New York Public Library on Forty-Second Street, poring over Italian dictionaries and researching the peninsula's edible frogs and songbirds before reporting back to Isabel.

Gino was capable of infinite patience, yet in social situations he seemed unable to buffer his opinions with politeness or observe the usual conventions. If after-dinner lingerers in the living room on Twelfth Street bored him, he'd say so aloud before retreating to his bedroom. Some of those closest to James, including John Ferrone, thought Gino unworthy of their friend. More and more, they treated Gino not as someone at the center of James's emotional life but as his irritating roommate. Everyone seemed happier after Gino had gone to bed.

: : :

ANDRÉ SURMAIN HAD the grace, carnality, and alabaster whiteness of a young satyr sculpted by Praxiteles. He was born André Sussman in Cairo in 1920. His parents founded Aziza Cosmetics and distilled perfumes using Cognac as a base. André grew up in Paris and served in the French army before fleeing to New York in 1940. He served the American war effort as an operative in the Office of Strategic Services (OSS) and was sent back to Europe, parachuting into France six weeks before D-day. He changed his name to Surmain to hide that he was Jewish, in case he fell into German hands.

In the early 1950s, Surmain was working in New York with Serge Obolensky, his old OSS colleague, in public relations. In 1953, when James was chasing research and recipes for his fish book, he met André and Obolensky, PR men for New Bedford scallops. André had been running a catering company for first-class in-flight meals out of his brownstone on East Fiftieth Street, first for Varig, the Brazilian national airline, loading stacked trays into his turquoise VW bus and driving out to Idlewild Airport with his Greek chef. In time, Surmain converted an old barn near Idlewild into a commissary. He called his company Epicure Kitchens. Besides Varig, he produced in-flight meals for the Mexican airline Aeronave, eventually renamed Aeroméxico.

Surmain started a gourmet club, Les Ambassadeurs du Bien Manger, and ferried a dozen or so members out to his Idlewild barn for opulent French dinners. He was ambitious and arrogant, sexy in a way that combined savageness and femininity, and a womanizer. James would remember this young man of looks and drive. He might be useful. But it was Surmain's wife, Nancy, who first stoked James's entrepreneurial fires.

Born Nancy Wormser into a comfortable Scarsdale family, she was creative, stylish, and had flair. She married André in 1953 and oversaw the conversion of his four-story East Fiftieth Street brownstone into a rambling home. She opened a fashionable boutique on East Fifty-Second and named it Chauncey's; it had a small but chic selection of gourmet items, including caviar and foie gras in cans. One day when James was visiting Chauncey's in early spring 1955, Nancy asked whether he'd consider teaching a cooking class in the shop.

Soon Nancy, André, James, and Ruth Norman were talking about starting a cooking school. Cookbook author Helen Worth had one, and she was acid tongued and awful, in James's opinion. Dione Lucas had a famous school on the Upper West Side, run out of her apartment in the Dakota. "If Dione," James asked Helen Evans Brown, "why not us[,] who are honest[?]"

At the end of November 1955, James and André decided to make a variety of pricey, elegant pâtés to sell at Chauncey's, in time for holiday parties. With James's name and recipes and André's marketing skill, the pâté pop-up was a sensation. They even charmed the skeptical Sheila Hibben of *The New Yorker*, James's old nemesis. "Mrs. Hibben is now begging André and Nancy with my aid to do soups," James wrote to Helen in Pasadena. "She is determined that we are going to be the epicurean shop of New York."

By spring 1956, as James and his new partners were planning a cooking school located in the Surmains' brownstone, he was partnering with them in other ways. Together, they worked out a publicity campaign for O'Quin's Charcoal Sauce, a tomatoey condiment husky with liquid smoke. They did a luncheon, including jellied eggs with O'Quin's sauce, for food editors. Nancy assembled swag baskets containing a gingham tablecloth and napkins, hen figurines, bottles of O'Quin's, and the company's sham story, spelled out in André's longhand, about its having been around since before the American Revolution.

Schaffner and Helen thought James was squandering his reputation on endorsements of questionable products; they marveled at the sheer number of his commitments. He seemed only too eager to piss away his time on Skotch Grills and O'Quin's Charcoal Sauce. "He divides himself into many fragments," Schaffner mused to Helen, "and it must be an exhausting experience and in many cases unrewarding, emotionally as well as financially."

Helen wrote back: "I . . . wish he would decide what he wants of life, and do it."

James's pursuit of piddling jobs was partly that: a restless search for what he wanted from life. Perhaps he'd find one that stuck, something that would bring bring him happiness. His commitments were piling up: the long recipe inserts, called "cook books," for *House & Garden*; his Corkscrew columns on wine for the same magazine (all the result of patient editing by Isabel Callvert, who went uncredited); stories for *Collier's* on beans and picnics, collaborations with Helen, who did most of the work and all of the seething about it; the book he'd begun with Schoonmaker. There was something unfulfilling about each of them, yet each was something he couldn't chuck.

He began to open distance between himself and the *gourmet* label he once sought. In a late 1955 interview for P.S. from Paris, humorist Art Buchwald's syndicated column, James blasted the very word by which he was known: *gourmet*. James felt that *epicure* was a better, more honest label, because *gourmet* had become such a cliché. In fact, it was a not-very-subtle jab at the Wine and Food Society of New York and Jeanne Owen, its self-styled "gourmette." James said he didn't consider large gourmet societies to be serious organizations. "The gourmet vintage 1956 wants sauces and elaborate dishes," James told Buchwald. "Some of them are so bollixed up he doesn't know what in the devil he's eating. The epicure wants to preserve the simple dishes. To him scrambled eggs can be a work of art." America was churning out food snobs by the thousands. James told Buchwald he'd started his own club, the Society for the Suppression of the Word Gourmet in America—a joke with a serious shadow.

Ever since he was a boy, when Elizabeth took him to adult parties and had him shock and delight the room by airing precocious judgments, James had craved the attention that came from flexing surprising opinions.

Buchwald asked him to name the ten best restaurants in the country. James's list was mostly conventional (Le Pavillon, "21," and Quo Vadis in New York; Jack's in San Francisco; the London Chop House in Detroit) but with a populist twist: the Pancake House in Portland, where the scrambled eggs were artistry and James would always just be lovable old Jimmy.

: : :

THE COOKING SEMINAR was coming together. James and André were now a public relations and promotions company for food. They called it André Surmain Associates (James appeared on the masthead as "consultant"). There was so much space in the Surmains' house on East Fiftieth that James planned to move his office there, his books and files. "We shall have a test kitchen and room for the lessons," James told Helen, "room for photography and enough office space for anything we want." Classes were scheduled to start in the first week of October 1956: four lessons, once a week, with ten students in each. Because of James's name, they were filling up by word of mouth alone, including food editors and magazine people: two each from *Life* magazine and the *New York Times*.

They were to be hands-on classes; afterward, they'd all sit together at the dining table, eat and drink wine, and discuss what they'd cooked— an echo of André's gourmet dinner club in the Idlewild barn. James and Ruth Norman worked out an intricate syllabus of high-level dishes, as laid out for Helen:

> We are giving a complete menu with variations. For instance
> one will have a Canape Marquise for a tidbit, a spinach and
> cheese soufflé for the hors d'oeuvre, three different kinds
> of duck with accompaniments, a vegetable and for dessert
> another type of soufflé—such as the lemon one with no flour
> or a regular ginger one. In this way the soufflé question,
> the duck question, the vegetables styling will all be covered
> with one lesson. In another we shall have for instance turkey,
> capon and goose with various stuffings. We expect to work
> it so that everyone works every different station in the course
> of work. Then when one sits at dinner it becomes a seminar.

In September, they sent postcards to everyone they knew. It showed a cartoon James, in chef's toque and long apron sheathing his enormous bulk, carrying a steaming roast goose on a platter. "JAMES BEARD and ANDRE SURMAIN are happy to announce the opening of a

COOKING SEMINAR meeting once a week . . . at our offices and test kitchen, 249 East 50th Street, New York City."

They began with forty paid students and invited a few members of the media to attend for free. At the last minute, James and Ruth simplified the first session, to make it friendlier for novices: an hors d'oeuvre spread, chicken three ways, corn bread, salad, a layer cake. "Not exciting but the right thing for a beginning class," James explained to Helen. "For some reason I am looking forward to the classes because of the fact I am such a ham I guess."

One of the students for that first session was Perdita Schaffner, who almost never cooked. "You will be fascinated to hear that the James Beard–Surmain cooking school is a terrific success so far," John Schaffner reported to Helen. "It is particularly so for one Perdita Schaffner, who made her first layer cake on her first lesson, along with learning five hundred other things."

The day after the class was Schaffner's birthday. Perdita asked James whether she could buy the cake she made, to take home to her husband. The cake, glorious with candles and a beaming Perdita to present it, was beautiful and delicious. James's restlessness, his false starts and frustrations, melted away when he was teaching. He'd found his stage, the spotlight he'd been seeking for thirty years. He'd become the master of ceremonies for a complex orchestrated performance that felt easy and natural. A show that made everyone happy.

"I think the class is going to do wonderful things for Perdita," Schaffner told Helen, "and Jim's method of teaching is apparently so sympathetic and disarming that all of her fears and lack of self-confidence have vanished quite away. I know she is looking forward with all of the eagerness of a child to a party toward the next lesson. I do think this is quite wonderful, don't you?"

CHAPTER 14

CORONATION CHICKEN

:: :   :: :

1957–1960

JAMES THOUGHT OF Alice B. Toklas as a dear but distant mentor, an eccentric lesbian auntie. *The Alice B. Toklas Cook Book* was an inspiration to him in 1954. The recipes flowed through the text in Alice's book, not unlike the way Mozart made his arias further the drama in *The Marriage of Figaro*, not just stand apart as pretty adjuncts—recipes *were* the story. He admired Alice for resisting the manipulations and conventionalizing of home-economist book editors, or ones like Clara Claasen, who insisted that the outdoor book be useful at the expense of voice and personality, humor and gaiety. Alice was the architect of the narrative cookbook.

James met her in 1955, when he paid a visit to 5 rue Christine, where Alice lived with Gertrude Stein, dead since 1946. James's companion was Henry McNulty, an American based in Paris, public relations man for French Cognac and Champagne producers; he was forty-two, a Princetonian, and during the war a foreign correspondent for United Press. He knew Miss Toklas, knew she'd be delighted to meet the author of *The Fireside Cook Book* and *Paris Cuisine*. James had arrived in Paris only the previous day, but that night he cooked for McNulty and his wife, Bettina, in their apartment with a kitchen the size of a closet; he had trouble even turning around in it.

James cooked choucroute with truffle sausage and duck. When it was done and plattered, he half-buried two splits of Champagne, standing up, in the mounds of hot sauerkraut. When he popped the corks, they gushed like fountains, wine sluicing into the dish and bathing the meats. It was James at his most performative: the three-hundred-pound sybarite and showman whom a Paris apartment could barely contain, exuberantly in love with life.

The next day, he met the gentle, brittle-looking Alice. She wore the clothes she always did at home (beige blouse, wool skirt, thick stockings, rustic sandals), her face birdlike beneath the famous bangs. "She is really a darling," James reported to Schaffner. "And living in the midst of all those Picassos and Braques and [Francis] Rose[s] and all the other things with all of the Memories of Gertrude around in that flat it is one of the wonderful and fabulous pictures of the twentieth century."

Alice told James she was a fan of his work; also of Helen's West Coast cookbook. It floored him. He told her she should publish in magazines, and that his agent, John Schaffner, would be happy to place her articles. "She has one now on Champagne with wonderful stories and fabulous recipes which I think should go into *McCall's*—or even the *Atlantic*," James wrote to Schaffner afterward. "I hope you won't skin me alive for doing this." But Schaffner was thrilled to have such an illustrious new client.

Two years later, again in Paris, James proposed that he and the McNultys drive Alice outside the city for an old-fashioned Sunday picnic. They would each contribute something.

It was unseasonably cold for May. They picked her up in the McNultys' car and drove an hour southwest to Montfort-l'Amaury, above the Rambouillet Forest, a village set in low hills. They found an expanse of pasture with small stands of apple trees, spaced widely apart, and laid down a canvas tarp (there were cow pats and the grass was damp), followed by blankets and pillows excavated from the car's boot. There was a view of stone ruins of a tenth-century castle, also a slate-roofed turret in the house where Maurice Ravel had lived. Alice was all in black: her beloved Pierre Balmain coat and a hat of lacquered straw bristling with short ostrich plumes, like a flattened feather duster. She insisted on sitting with her back to the scenery. "I never face the view," she said. "It takes my mind off eating."

James had gone to Hédiard and the markets on the rue Cler that morning; as recalled later, he brought "a fine duckling pâté en croute, bread, and a jambonneau. The last was one of the delicious little ends of the ham that the French cook and cover in crumbs, and which are very flavorful." Bettina had made a salad and stuffed eggs; Henry brought two magnums of Champagne packed in ice. Alice brought a roasted chicken James described as "crispy brown, not overcooked, still slightly warm, and deliciously juicy." He'd never tasted a better one.

When it suddenly started to rain, they pulled up the tarp and sheltered under it, and everyone laughed. James had charmed one of his heroes, the woman he adored for having written *The Alice B. Toklas Cook Book*, a work of narrative genius and personality. James had now surpassed his idol. He was not only the best-known food expert in America, but a beloved character, a man whose face, physical presence, and voice in magazines and books belonged to the nation. In 1958, Clare Boothe Luce, President Eisenhower's ambassador to Italy (the first American woman to hold such a high diplomatic post), hired James for private cooking lessons in New York. Even in elite circles, James had become iconic.

At the sixteenth annual Newspaper Food Editors Conference in Chicago in 1958, organizers acknowledged him as one of the nation's leading cookbook authors. That same year, Craig Claiborne, newly anointed food editor of the *New York Times*, wrote of James as a culinary master, not just of the United States but a gastronome of "international repute."

In February 1959, James traveled to Europe for a series of junkets and promotional events. Writing from Brown's Hotel in London, he told Alice B. Toklas he'd be in Paris soon and would love to see her. To Alice, Brown's seemed majestic—how fitting that he was there. This was James's moment: He was the prince of gastronomes, poised at universal fame.

: : :

ON A TUESDAY NIGHT in March 1955, at the drunken end of a dinner at Café Chambord on Third Avenue and East Fiftieth Street, James shook the hand of Frank E. Taylor and agreed to write the biggest, most comprehensive book of his life. Taylor was editor-in-chief of Dell Books. He was charming and flamboyant and spent lavishly. Dinner that night at Chambord, which Taylor sprang for, and which included Taylor, his wife Nan, James, and John Ferrone, then an editor at Dell, cost $110. It was astronomical. James was impressed. Taylor was not some cheapskate Clara Claasen, rationing paper clips. The book advance would be $3,000—half on signing, the rest on delivery. And it would be published in paperback first, followed by a hardcover edition—a reversal of the standard rollout. Taylor could almost guarantee that the book would sell. The royalty checks would not be paltry.

James said yes before anyone asked the question: What type of cookbook would it be? Taylor was at a loss. Nan said she didn't think there'd been a good comprehensive cookbook since the last revision of *Fannie Farmer* in 1945 (she didn't count *The Joy of Cooking*, a book, she said, that always left her cold). *Fannie*—originally *The Boston Cooking-School Cook Book*, first published in 1896 and reissued and revised about two dozen times since—was a favorite of James's, too (he also preferred it to *Joy*). A modern *Fannie* it would be. By the time they'd drained the last bottle of *Bourgogne rouge*, they had a working title: *James Beard's Basic Cook Book*.

: : :

THE JAMES BEARD COOKBOOK was released in April 1959 as a Dell Laurel Edition paperback (cost: seventy-five cents), four years after the shockingly expensive dinner at Chambord and almost two years after James and Isabel delivered the manuscript. Isabel and her husband, Ron, had pushed back on James. James had agreed to split the advance with Isabel, but this time, unlike what happened with *James Beard's Fish Cookery* and *How to Eat Better for Less Money*, Isabel would get a coauthor line on the title page, though not on the cover: "In Collaboration with Isabel E. Callvert."

The book, which was practical and sprawling, left James cold. It was mildly revolutionary, he supposed. Its prime rule, "Buy good food, and buy often," challenged the supermarket ethos of 1959. James decried mixes and frozen foods; advised readers to try to find a poultry farmer who'd deliver fresh eggs to their front doors. Still, *The James Beard Cookbook* had a paltry number of what James called "the narrative type of recipe," the "rather chatty style" he preferred. Isabel let stand a few touches of Beardian memoir: Braised Beef, Bordeaux Fashion, which he ate "with the local pickers during grape harvest time" at Alexis Lichine's chateau (though he didn't mention that); also Polynesian Stuffed Leg of Lamb, which he'd watched Restaurant Associates chef Albert Stockli throw together on the fly.

Besides those, the book was what the title promised: basic. It even described how to boil water, an echo of Mary Lincoln's *Mrs. Lincoln's Boston Cook Book* of 1884, *Fannie*'s precursor. James made it facetious enough for sophisticated readers to know he was making fun of kitchen bibles, and simple enough to enlighten the innocent.

Ironically, the cover was James's most personal to date. In a photo by George Lazarnick, James, in a polka-dot bow tie, a striped bib apron, and one of his custom-made shirts from Bel y Cía in Barcelona, poses with an octagonal platter of choucroute garnie. Under a pouf of curly parsley, a ruffle of pink ham slices covers a mound of sauerkraut and browned slabs of pork rib roast, all framed with two kinds of glistening sausage.

Dell Books had doubts about the photo. An author portrait on a cookbook cover was rare, but James was an extraordinary author, and a paperback first release was unorthodox. It was more the dish he was flaunting that Dell feared might hurt sales. For a nation focused on TV dinners and dieting, choucroute was rustic and porky. The image of a fifty-five-year-old James, however, with his extravagant double chin, open-mouthed grin revealing an eager tongue, eyes nearly disappearing into skin folds and smile creases, looked porcine. James owned his indulgence. Seen by a nation that scrambled to buy the latest fad diet book, James's obvious love of eating was an argument for pleasure. It was an irresistible cover.

The first reports from Dell were astonishing; *The James Beard Cookbook* was looking like it would be a smash seller. "We are definitely in the best seller class and outselling *Anatomy of a Murder*," James reported to Isabel, referencing the 1959 Dell edition of Robert Traver's best-selling novel, released the same month, "and seem to be the freak of the publishing world at this point." It was selling out at newsstands, supermarkets, and bookstores around the country. "Please God let it continue to grow," he told Isabel, "so that we can make some dough out of this horrible thing."

It had a positive reception. Craig Claiborne's enthusiastic review in the *New York Times* focused on James. "There is not a gastronomic cliché in the book," he wrote, "and the principal reason undoubtedly is that Mr. Beard is not an armchair cookbook author. He is a kitchen wizard." The book's cover further popularized James's status as the nation's affable, avuncular, and gluttonous authority on food and entertaining.

Within the first year, *The James Beard Cookbook* sold 150,000 copies in paperback. (Dutton would publish the first hardcover edition in October 1961.) The paperback did outsell Dell's *Anatomy of a Murder*, though only in New York. *Publishers Weekly* reported that, as a result of Claiborne's review, "The [*New York*] *Times* woman's page department had so many inquiries that it had to shut off its telephones."

In a way, *The James Beard Cookbook* is a refinement of *Fireside*. It's a better and more useful recipe compendium, an improved kitchen bible. Helen Evans Brown was right: *Fireside*'s showy production, the Provensen illustrations and culinary quotations, make it hard to cook from. In contrast, Dell herded James into a cheap, utilitarian package, with minimal illustrations and simple design. Comprehensive kitchen bibles were the best-selling cookbooks in America. Despite the rash of niche cookbooks on the market throughout the 1950s, the average American wanted one definitive source for recipes and cooking information, instructions on making everything from Boiled Celery to Coquilles St. Jacques. Even the chapters in *The James Beard Cookbook* appear alphabetically, by subject—starting with Appetizers and ending with Vegetables and Legumes—so a cook in a hurry wouldn't even need to check the index, any idiot could find his way. Yet James was bored with recipe bibles.

The James Beard Cookbook had proved to be meteoric. "Everyone seems stunned at the [Dell] office that it has had the success so quickly," he told Helen. It wasn't that he didn't love the royalty checks. It was that, once again, the great narrative food book he'd always hoped to write had evaded him. Perhaps he would insist, next time, on writing a book about his memories of food, to hell with what publishers said they wanted. He believed the future of cookbooks lay in authors relating stories about their lives—though of course in James's case, the details would have to be selective.

:::

ON THE GRAY AND SLUSHY last day of 1959, James threw his fifth party of the month.

It was the second of two holiday bashes he was contractually required to host for Edward Gottlieb and Associates, the American PR firm for French Cognac and Champagne. Today's shindig was for a new Gottlieb client, Puerto Rican rum. The guests were food editors and writers. The venue was James's still-new classroom kitchen, in the house in Greenwich Village to which he and Gino had moved in September.

The house at 119 West Tenth Street was a simple, squat, three-story brick townhouse with a basement. It sat midblock between the twin hubbubs of Sixth and Greenwich Avenues, a few doors up from the Patchin Place gate and across from the towering old brick-and-limestone Jefferson Market Courthouse, now abandoned to pigeons. Next to that was the New York Women's House of Detention, a twelve-floor art deco monolith, imperious and brutal. It housed convicted sex workers, political radicals, and other female transgressives. James's second-floor front salon looked obliquely across at the barred windows of inmates' cells. It's why the house was cheap.

"Living across from the jail is most enlightening," he told Helen. "I never knew how many people screamed up at their friends and families—very dramatic—they have cops to chase them away most of the time."

James was pleased with the house, and happy, finally, to be in the heart of Greenwich Village—he traced a heart on the address-change postcard he mailed to friends and associates. It was probably only a matter of time before the city razed the lovely old courthouse and threw up some hideous apartment block. The modern world committed savage acts daily against the past.

President John Kennedy was preparing to move into the White House; the next decade would no doubt be a rush job to the future. James's new house would stand as a kind of witness to the past, crammed—like one of Elizabeth's old curio cabinets—with his beloved antique dishes, his French and English kitchen knickknacks.

The ground floor of 119 West Tenth was rented as office space to Sutter's, a French patisserie owned by a Greek immigrant who'd adopted the name "Edison Sutter." The bakery itself was three doors down, at the corner of Greenwich Street. James loved the shop's crisp plain cookies, made with real butter in a nation mad about margarine—even Eleanor Roosevelt had appeared in a recent television commercial for the stuff.

James and Gino occupied two floors of the house. The second story had a salon and a kitchen classroom that, while moderate in size, could accommodate twelve students. The third floor had a small suite for Gino and a bed-sitting room that officially belonged to James, though it served as the couple's private living room. There were two bathrooms and a basement with a backup freezer-fridge, plus shelves for storing foods that manufacturers were sending by the case—corn syrup, dried coconut, canned soups—hoping James would slip the names of their products into an article. As sales of *The James Beard Cookbook* continued to rise, the descent onto the West Tenth house of free products—what James called "all manner of junk"—felt like an avalanche.

The kitchen classroom doubled as James's recipe lab. It was unlike anything ever devised for a home-based cooking school.

At its center was a big custom worktable in the shape of a squared-off U, topped with vermillion Formica. Three electric cooktops and built-in wooden chopping blocks for students were arrayed on the surface. James called it his grand piano. During classes he stood in the center, with the students ranged around the table, facing him. It was James's stage.

Since the first class with André Surmain, James's teaching had been a platform for performance. Now at last he had the perfect stage—one where he was both orchestra conductor and soloist. His virtuoso moment came during the lesson on soufflés, when he held a copper bowl of stiffly beaten egg whites above his bald head and turned it upside down, as students gasped or said, "Aahh!" The mass stayed in the bowl—a demonstration of how stiff proper soufflé whites should be, made riveting through showmanship.

Custom-made Formica covers edged in rosewood fit the grand piano's surface to hide its burners and cutting boards and transform it into a buffet, as it was for today's rum party.

Agnes Crowther White, James's old friend from Portland theater days, found the house. White's husband was a real estate broker, she an interior decorator. James had given her carte blanche. The wallpapers she chose were bold evocations of the past.

Paper for the living room, hallway, and stairs suggested an etching of a papal arbor from the Renaissance, a mighty trellis with sumptuous leaves and fruit. For the kitchen, White designed a wallpaper of three-foot-tall pineapples from a botanical illustration, a 1746 engraving from Abbé Prévost's *Histoire Générale des Voyages*. The fruit was lush and spiky, hoisted like an imperial standard above a burst of spiny leaves. The scale was operatic, the feeling carnal.

The kitchen had a second wallpaper, a checkerboard pattern in tangy shades of green that covered the wall of windows overlooking West Tenth Street. Shirred café curtains of pink French toile only half-obscured the eccentric view of the women's prison and the abandoned courthouse.

For the rum party, James had placed his antique seven-armed Italian candelabra at a corner of the buffet. It cast a theatrical glow on his English majolica jardinières and Wedgwood strawberry plates, the Minton tureen with sides like a woven basket and a molded heap of dead game on the lid. He'd brought in ferns and ivy to give the rooms the feel of a conservatory in a Victorian country house. He'd stuffed his vintage copper lavabo, hung on the checkerboard wall between the windows, with breads, fruit, and a taxidermied pheasant in full plumage. Christmas balls dangled from his "girls," his pair of six-foot-high, eighteenth-century terra-cotta figures of Terpsichoria Nectambrosia, the so-called tenth muse, the spirit of gastronomy.

James's hors d'oeuvre tidbits were tangerine sections marinated in rum and rosemary, and avocado balls glistening with rum-spiked vinaigrette. An apricot-and-rum–glazed ham bristled with French silver *attelets* (antique garnish picks). He served grog—hot spiced Puerto Rican rum—and smoky Russian tea.

James wore a black shirt under his suit jacket and one of the Thai silk bow ties the Browns had sent from Pasadena as a Christmas present. He spotted one of the guests, fellow cookbook author and home-based culinary teacher Helen Worth, arrive and immediately duck upstairs to inspect the rooms. She returned to the kitchen and asked for a drink. "That's nerve," James later remarked to Helen Evans Brown.

His house was the buzz of New York's food world. Helen McCully talked about doing a big photo spread in *House & Garden*. Craig Claiborne had been at a previous housewarming bash, one of two that James threw. The next day in the *New York Times*, he declared James Beard's new house and classroom "handsomely styled and spacious." It was all grist for the enrollment mill.

James's house was a conundrum. On one hand, it was public space, a house with a classroom at its core, and a theater set for James's official persona as bachelor epicure. At the same time, it was private space of a critically sensitive nature for 1959, a queer nest in Greenwich Village. Then again, James and Gino's real home existed not so much as physical quarters but as a floating temporal one. They found intimacy at times when the eyes of the world were closed, late at night or shortly after dawn, hours when the public James was offstage.

In his New Year's letter to Pasadena, James confessed to Helen his desire to take off at the end of 1960. He wanted to go to London for a few months, possibly also Mallorca and the south of France.

"If I do this I shall write a memoir cookbook which is the [thing] I have wanted to do for about a year or so," he told her. "I have a lot of good food stuff around and a hell of a lot of memories at this point which I feel could make a good deal of fun. My mother's story and the Hamblet story and my father's deft fingers in the kitchen and Let the old chef and my first introduction into Chinese and French cookery and my war experiences and experiences since then all seem to me to have good material for a book that might see me through about six or eight months."

James was fifty-six. He was proud of his fish book, and of *Paris Cuisine* and *Fireside*. He'd yet to write a book that expressed all his experiences, though, and convictions about food and eating.

"Yes," Helen wrote back, "I think it is time you did your memoirs. A good long thoughtful book with you, not Isobel [*sic*], coming through. And I think you should go away to do it, or you will be constantly interrupted."

She was right. The new house was a constant swirl of people and ringing phones. It was clear to James that he and Gino needed a housekeeper.

:::

In December 1959, James interviewed two candidates for the job of housekeeper, a unique position of a rather sensitive nature. Neither applicant seemed right.

Nancy Surmain had someone to send him, a person she employed to help out for parties; someone especially good at arranging flowers. James assumed it was a woman. When Clayton Triplette knocked on the door one night as a class was wrapping up, James felt mild shock.

Clay was thirty-two. He had a slight frame, a soft manner, and skin the color of ripened caramel. His legs were lost in baggy, pleated suit pants that revealed only a few inches of shoe; a crisp shirt collar and a precisely knotted tie were signs of his fastidiousness. He worked sometimes for Nancy Surmain, yes—he'd met her through Judith Garden, who owned a flower shop on East Fifty-Seventh known for unusual arrangements with branches and other things, in unusual vessels. Clay used to help out there. Joan Crawford (Mrs. Alfred Steele, recently widowed) was a client of Judith's—that's how Clay met her. In fact, he'd worked at Miss Crawford's penthouse at Seventieth Street and Fifth just that afternoon. He also spent a few mornings a week at Craig Claiborne's apartment, cleaning and straightening: another job Nancy had helped him get.

Clay was born in Buffalo. Anyone who saw him, Clay said, took him for black, but it was more complicated than that. On his father's side, he was black and Iroquois; on his mother's, Irish and Polish. His mother and his Iroquois grandmother were both fine cooks, he said, so if James needed an extra hand, Clay could help out with cooking sometimes. In fact, his mother had a restaurant.

Clay always said his mother was something else, her way with fried chicken, and she always made biscuits. After church, he said, he and his siblings would have to change their clothes and help out—peeling potatoes, for example. He'd learned to cook that way.

James asked him whether he did any other kind of work. Clay gave him a look and said, "Do you want me to tell you?" James replied that he did.

Clay revealed he sometimes appeared on stage, performing a striptease—strictly tasteful—at some of the nightclubs downtown. Female impersonation, they called it at places like Club 82 and Moroccan Village. The customers were often folks from out of town, or men who brought their wives to gawk at the "ladies."

"You're not!" James said. He was amazed that Clay would admit it to a stranger considering him for a job. But of course, Clay needed only the briefest glance at James to read the score. He took in the kitchen's pineapple wallpaper, its regal bottles of Guerlain Impériale eau de cologne, repurposed to hold olive oil and vinegars.

"My mother says it's honest money," Clay said. "She always tells me, 'You show what you got to get what you want.'"

James asked for Clay's stage name. Politely, he declined to say.

"If I told you," he said, "you would know who I am. I was famous at the age of twenty-two."

Within that carefully correct suit and tie, Clay had fire. He hadn't stayed in Buffalo a second longer than he had to, taking the bus to New York City the very next day after turning eighteen. Since then he'd seen some things—especially in the nightclubs. He had promised the universe that the only way he'd return to Buffalo was in a pine box. It was obvious to James that Clay would keep secrets, and he was nobody's fool.

He took him on for a week, as a trial. After that, James asked Clay to stay on as his full-time housekeeper and manager.

Clay lived in a room on the Lower East Side. He'd get to James and Gino's house in the Village every morning by six or six-thirty, begin to organize the kitchen for recipe testing or classes, make James's toast and tea. He knew to have it ready when he heard James winding down his early morning gossip calls upstairs.

Soon, James was calling Clay "Babes."

"Smells good, Babes," he'd call down on a morning Clay was cooking bacon for breakfast.

As a treat sometimes, Clay would make his mother's fried chicken for lunch. He soaked the pieces overnight in buttermilk, then took them out and tossed them in a paper sack filled with flour seasoned with a teaspoon of ground cinnamon and a little salt. He fried the shaggy pieces in bacon grease, sometimes with additional chicken or goose fat if any happened to be languishing in the fridge.

James said he'd never tasted finer. It was the cinnamon, neither too little or too much, hovering somewhere beyond detection.

:::

IN APRIL 1960, James sailed without Gino on the SS *United States*, bound for the UK. He paused in London before flying to Zürich for meetings with Nestlé. James had been consulting at the company's US headquarters in White Plains, north of New York City, to help develop a line of fancy sauces in jars. From Switzerland, James flew to Venice before sailing on the Adriatica Line's MS *San Marco*: a ten-day tour of the Dalmatian coast, the Greek islands, and Istanbul, ending in Marseille. From there, he'd take a train to Barcelona, then on to Paris before returning to Zürich for the flight home. On the ship out of New York, James took time to think about what he wanted from his cluttered whirl of a life.

Zürich was beautiful, "a strangely exhilarating city," he wrote to Schaffner. Queer men were everywhere. They seemed to let their guard down in public so much more fearlessly than men in New York. "Certainly it is blessed with more of the brotherhood than any city I know in Europe," James told his agent, "and such ravishing chapters as they look to be!"

Clementine Paddleford of the *Herald Tribune* met up with him there. Together they toured the storybook-tidy Maggi bouillon-cube factory in Kemptthal, outside Zürich, with its brick smokestack and steep-roofed buildings amid groves of trees.

He missed Gino—five weeks was an eternity away. "Give Gino a call," he wrote to Isabel, "and have dinner with him some night if you feel like it." Still, James dreaded going back to New York. "I really have had it," he wrote to Helen. "I'm sick of the rounds of New York and I'm sick of the people. It's endless and crazy and not worth it."

Aboard the *San Marco*, James described to Helen both the peace and his feelings of isolation. "I loved this trip and for the first time in ages have been completely away form everything and have been rested and perhaps relaxed." And yet, after his meetings with Nestlé ended, he didn't really have a purpose.

"I find I don't want to go home," he told Helen. "I am trying to figure where I'm going and what is going to happen next. I am certain I am not achieving much . . . and am not being excited by the things I do. . . . I am so rushed I have nothing of myself any more."

He still had a sex life with Gino, but their early intimacy had gone. "[He] gets increasingly busy and although we have a delightful understanding it is not a companionship where things are shared."

James knew dozens of people, but there was nothing more to say when talk of food, opera, or the theater ended. "There is really no one in New York with whom I can have a fine close talk. . . . I'm really terribly alone and terribly *distrait* [moody] about the next years, or the next year to be completely honest."

He observed his fifty-seventh birthday in Istanbul. He rose early and went to Topkapi Palace; later he stopped at a little place for lunch: tarama, stuffed vine leaves, and tender kibbeh with rice pilaf. The previous day, he'd walked to the Grand Bazaar, and the physical exertion took its toll on his body. "Very tired for 57 years!" he wrote in his datebook. His health had begun to worry him. It had been a year since his doctor diagnosed an irregularity in James's heart, the same condition his mother had suffered, and he'd spent the intervening time trying to eat a little less. He was trying to take it easy. He took Miltowns during the day and sleeping pills at night. He'd lost enough weight to make his dinner jacket fit again. He thought more and more about the past.

Before James left New York, he and Isabel wrapped up work on a book for Jerry Mason's Ridge Press: an outdoor cooking compendium, *James Beard's Treasury of Outdoor Cooking*. The manuscript was done and delivered, but at the last minute Mason decided the book needed a chapter on picnics: recipes plus an introduction. In his room at the Gritti Palace Hotel in Venice, James first wrote out a list of recipes, then—in the loose, rambling way he usually typed out his thoughts for Isabel's editing—the introduction.

"I think my first picnic memory was a thriller," he wrote. "We were invited by the Hamblets to go out in a great touring car."

He then typed up four pages of picnic memories: his boxed lunches on the train's observation car to Gearhart; birthday parties and treks to Tillamook Head. They were of no use to Mason, who instead wrote a fictionalized version of James's picnics on the beach. "The ladies brought salads, or desserts, or cuts of meat to be cooked. The men toted the hampers and buckets and camp chairs; they gathered the wood and built and tended the fire." *The Treasury of Outdoor Cooking* was a fantasy. It was a joke.

The illustrations were a jumble of original artwork, museum reproductions, and photographs from British-born John Stewart featuring bizarre styling: a lacquered roast suckling pig with a dazed expression, wedged into the branches of a tree; a small table for two planted in a forest glade, in front of a half-blurred naked woman, running as if being hunted.

In the *New York Times*, Craig Claiborne called James "an imposing culinary angel," but he flayed the book for its arty excesses and coffee-table grandeur. "Better suited to the parlor than to the barbecue pit," he wrote. "It would be a pity to soil it with charcoal dust."

Furious that Mason had murdered his manuscript and made him look ridiculous, James refused to promote the book in any way. Outrage was just the goad James needed. He resolved, finally, to write his memoir cookbook.

He wrote to Helen. "I think you are right that I should take a year and finish off the thing I want to do. . . . I think I may go to Venice or Istanbul and live for three or four months. . . . I must do this to get close to me again. I don't think I've met myself in the passage for a hell of a long time."

CHAPTER 15

"MORE CAKES, MORE TASTES"

1961–1964

IN JANUARY 1961, James sent John Schaffner a slapdash outline for his memoir. It was an impressionistic heap of thoughts and recollections.

1. An analysis of good eating as against fancy eating. . . .
2. My mother and her fabulous food—what her old Chinese cook learned from her—she from him—her professional ability in management—her holiday preparations—winter storage—incredible picnics—preserving ideas. Our beach living and the wonderful raw materials available to us. Recipes, naturally, with nice little bits and pieces of anecdotal prose, I trust.

Above all, it needed to be amusing.

"My feeling," James wrote, "is that the book should be completely uninhibited without being bitter."

James was due in Houston for a series of cooking demos for Cognac. He asked Schaffner to write the book proposal for him, based on his jottings. "Make notes," James told him, "then either dictate a letter to Pat or send it back to me for editing."

Pat was Alfred A. Knopf Jr., son of the fearsome Alfred A. Sr. and Blanche Knopf. In 1959, Pat left his parents' publishing house, and with Simon Michael Bessie and Hiram Haydn launched an imprint of his own, called Atheneum. As 1960 wore on, Pat Knopf and his partners were building Atheneum's author list. Meanwhile, sales of Dell's *James Beard Cookbook* were exploding. Pat was keen to add James to his list.

In the first week of 1961, Knopf met James and Schaffner for lunch, to talk over possible books. James talked about the memoir he wanted to write. He even had the title: *James Beard's Delights and Prejudices*. He and Knopf shook hands. All Atheneum needed to draw up a contract was a book outline.

A week after James sent Schaffner his jumble of notes, Schaffner had a proper proposal for James to review. It began:

SUGGESTIONS FOR A BOOK
to be entitled
JAMES BEARD'S DELIGHTS AND PREJUDICES
by James A. Beard

The book would open with a description of one of James's memorable luncheons in France, perhaps Auberge du Père Bise in the Haute-Savoie, or Fernand Point's La Pyramide in Vienne, and go on about restaurants in general. "I could branch out in various directions," wrote Schaffner-as-James, "allowing myself latitude in time so that I could skip about between past and present to provide anecdotes from my own experiences to bolster my arguments."

It was to be a book of essays sparked by reminiscences. They would ignore linear time, bouncing from past to present and back again, the way one does in conversation. There would need to be recipes.

"While I do not conceive of this as a cookbook primarily," Schaffner/ James wrote, "a generous index of the recipes would assure the reader that he could easily use it as such."

James made three changes to Schaffner's draft. He crossed out a reference to his work "as representative for the Cognac interests"; he added the word *much* to amplify the "colorful material" he'd gathered from students in his cooking school. For the chapter on James's mother, Schaffner had written, "I would here give many recipes which I had from her and from her cook and there are of course many happy reminiscences of my childhood which could be included."

James scratched out the word *happy*.

: : :

"I NOW HAVE AN OFFER from Pat Knopf," James told Helen. "It is just the kind of book I've wanted to do for ages[,] with plenty of narrative attached and what recipe came from where and . . . why I like it." He hoped to take two or three months in Europe to rough out the manuscript. Travel almost always revealed to James who he was.

At the end of February 1961, James signed the contract. The manuscript was due on January 1, 1962. He had asked for a $5,000 advance, but that would have necessitated approval from Pat Knopf's partners, and Knopf was worried they might turn down a book so unusual in scope: not a straightforward cookbook, a standard essay collection, or a formal autobiography. Instead, Knopf gave him $3,500, payable in seven monthly installments—essentially an allowance. James would be able to afford to go to Switzerland to write.

In May, a week after his fifty-eighth birthday, James sailed alone aboard the SS *United States*, with his typewriter. He would go to Paris and Lausanne, then Venice and Vienna, with detours to Paris, London, and Bordeaux.

In June, James arrived in Lausanne. He had a room at the Hotel Central-Bellevue, with its fine old façade of balconies and shutters, cavernous belle-époque brasserie facing the street, and terrace restaurant at the rear, on the shore of Lake Geneva. From the terrace, he could see the lake recede in the east through a progression of mountains like ivory layers in a Chinese puzzle ball.

"I'm getting some work done," he reported to Helen. "Yesterday I worked solidly for six hours. Looking over the lake and having no distractions is a fairly good idea." The day after arriving in Lausanne, he met up with Alexis Lambelet, a man who worked for Nestlé. They went to the Saturday market that sprouted under awnings in the streets. "Peasanty and fabulous," James noted in his datebook. His mind was open to the past. "Last Saturday we went to the market and had a whirl," he reported to Helen. "There were tiny new potatoes such as mother insisted having all her life." He returned to Alexis's apartment on the rue du Simplon, across from the train station, and cooked them with sausages for lunch.

In the six weeks James stayed in Lausanne, he saw Alexis often, usually for lunch or dinner at his apartment. They went to the ballet. When James wasn't at Alexis's, he often took his meals at the Grand Chêne, an antique brasserie in the Lausanne Palace Hotel. Fancy Swiss cooking had proved disappointing. James preferred simple food: the Grand Chêne's braised pigs' feet with Madeira, or grilled kidneys.

Like Portland and the Oregon coast, Lausanne had a setting both rugged and refined, a place with the perennial feeling of a frontier. At the small Saturday market in Lausanne's Old City, farmers set out marble-size potatoes and kohlrabi the color of jade, cherries so freshly picked they had a dazzling gloss. Fruits, vegetables, and flowers spilled from crates and bins set on steep sidewalks. A little square on the hill above was where butchers and *charcutiers*, cheese vendors and fishmongers set up. No American city had anything like it. Here was a weekly outdoor food market flowing into the life of an urban center.

In Lausanne, James felt as though he'd slipped into an archetype of the past, where crystalline air sharpened the colors and smells. He moved through a landscape of memory, wiped of the loneliness and emotional ambivalence of his actual childhood. He thought of the characters in his life—his father, Jue Let, Harry Hamblet, and especially Elizabeth—in a new way, as the symbols of an American past gone extinct through forgetting. Gearhart and Salmon Street would serve as the sets for his grand fable of reconstruction.

"I have done about sixty pages of manuscript—and extra size pages so far," James told Schaffner in early June 1961. "I have not reread any of it. All I know is that some of it flows like water and some is difficult."

James feared that Isabel wouldn't be up to the task of this book. James needed the right editor to prune and graft his mess of tightly spaced typed legal-size pages into the brilliant book he was so eager to author.

By November, Pat Knopf was demanding to see part of the manuscript that was supposed to be due just two months later, on New Year's Day of 1962. Knopf had wanted to publish *Delights and Prejudices* in time for the 1962 Christmas shopping season. Schaffner begged for an extended deadline.

"It depresses me no end," Knopf told Schaffner. "I don't see how we're in any position <u>not</u> to extend the deadline . . . but please consider my incipient ulcers."

What could Knopf do? James's name now had national reach—and something almost unheard-of for cookbook authors: the upper hand over a publisher. Knopf gave James a three-month extension, until March 15, 1962, though he doubted he'd see the manuscript then.

:::

THE WORLD JAMES HAD KNOWN was dying fast. The previous July, he'd eaten again at the place he once considered the best French restaurant in the world: the late Fernand Point's three–Michelin-star La Pyramide, south of Lyon. Point had died in 1955, but his widow, Mado, kept the restaurant going as a tribute. James found it mediocre and moribund. The old garnitures were gone; the foie gras mousse en brioche and the terrine en croûte were both flabby; everything seemed overworked. It was all rather sad, James reported to Helen, this holding on to dead classics. Paris was as lovely as ever, but the food he loved was all but gone. "The good restaurants are becoming fewer and fewer," he told Helen. "It is shocking what the Coca Cola age has done to the world!"

That October, Judith Jones, an editor at Knopf who worked mostly with translators of French authors, phoned up West Tenth Street. To her surprise, James answered. "I have a remarkable manuscript," Jones said, "and you've got to look at it." She described a book Knopf was about to publish, a sort of detailed translation of classic French cuisine for the American home cook: the inflexible rules, plus the ingredients an American cook was allowed to substitute for French ones.

"He seemed intrigued," Jones later recalled, "saying he would love to see a copy, and hoped he could help." It was by two French women, Louisette Bertholle and Simone Beck, and one energetic American, Julia Child, and it had a magisterial title: *Mastering the Art of French Cooking*. James had heard of Bertholle and Beck (everyone called her Simca)—in 1952, the same year as *Paris Cuisine*, they were coauthors with James's friend Helmut Ripperger of a sixty-three-page spiral-bound recipe booklet called *What's Cooking in France*. The publisher noted up front that the recipes had been culled from a future, more comprehensive work—no doubt this was it. James had never heard of Mrs. Child. Jones sent the manuscript to West Tenth.

Two days later, James called Jones. "He just devoured it," she recalled. "And he said why it was remarkable."

The French book *was* wonderful, he told Helen, "until they get into the chicken and meat department and then I think it falls flat on its face." French rules be damned. "The idea of cooking a piece of American boiled beef for four hours is insane. Paula [Peck] did a *pot au feu* for twelve people the other night and the beef cooked 1½ hours and was perfection." Cooking a filet to 136 degrees Fahrenheit and expecting it to turn out rare? Absurd. And all the chicken recipes were overcooked. "Otherwise it is a great book," he told Helen. "Nothing new or startling, but a good basic French cookery book."

James told Jones he wished he'd written *Mastering the Art*. Was he merely being affable? Jones knew there was a vast difference between James and Julia. "He had a different mindset," Jones would say of James. "He wasn't Julia." Like June Platt, Julia was fussy and inflexible when it came to recipes. James cooked by feel. He was at his best improvising—tasting and adding bits of this and that.

James said he'd do what he could to promote *Mastering*. He asked what Judith was planning. She seemed unsure about what to do. "I've never done a cookbook like this before," she said. The essential thing, James said, was to get the authors to New York. He'd organize a party. He'd present them to everyone who mattered.

Julia was already in the United States; Simca arrived a few weeks later. (Bertholle remained in France.) James invited Julia and Simca to drop in at West Tenth Street to observe one of his classes.

"Welcome, ladies," James addressed them in front of his students. "You have written a wonderful book."

James began to demonstrate a cheese soufflé. As usual, he folded the beaten egg whites into the base with his bare hands. "That's the only good way to fold in the whites," he announced. "You've got to feel it with your fingers."

Simca was horrified—this was not how it was done in France, where anything but a spatula and the proper flick of the wrist was unthinkable. Julia was unfazed.

James empathized with Julia—they were both, in their particular way, oddballs. A year later, in 1962, he took Julia to the Culinary Institute in New Haven to speak to the students. No one had heard Julia speak on television yet—*The French Chef* would debut almost a year later. When the culinary students heard her high, breathy diction, several of them snickered. James knew how it felt to be what they called *curious*.

James asked Dione Lucas to host the party for Simca and Julia at one of her restaurants, The Egg Basket, near Bloomingdale's at Lexington and Fifty-Ninth. "Jim personally invited what was then a very small nucleus of food and wine people and magazine editors," Jones recalled. The party, a sit-down dinner for thirty, teetered on the brink of disaster. Both Henry Sell of *Harper's* and Poppy Cannon said they'd come. "Dinner was held a half hour for them," James reported to Helen. "They never showed!" Craig Claiborne declined to attend, but Clementine Paddleford, June Platt, the wine importer Julius Wile, and *Vogue's* Marya Mannes all showed up. Also Julia's friend Avis DeVoto, and William Koshland of Knopf, but neither Alfred Sr. nor Blanche Knopf.

Jeanne Owen was there. ("The look she gave me," James said, "would have killed a weaker person.") Her presence upset Lucas, who had a migraine—"so she said," James noted in a catty aside (it was rumored that she drank). Lucas cooked sole with white wine sauce. Julia and Simca did braised shoulder of lamb, then came Lucas's salad and what

James called the worst Bavarian cream he'd ever eaten. "Dione told me she had never done such a terrible one!" he reported to Helen. Wile pressed James to get up and say a few words about the Bollinger '55 Champagne they were drinking; James told him to get Owen to do it. She begged off. Too shy, she said.

"Shy—shit," James fumed to Helen. "She never had a shy bone in her body. She would have laid someone in the streets if he couldn't have made it up to her room in her prime!"

The next day, James took Simca and Julia and Paul Child to The Four Seasons for lunch, for a tasting of dishes for the winter menu. They met Joe Baum and Albert Stockli. They ate Cheddar soup, barbecued pork loin, and individual coffee soufflés, and drank wines from California and High Tor, a vineyard forty miles north of New York City and a mile west of the Hudson. Whether or not *Mastering the Art of French Cooking* was to be a big hit, James found he adored Simca and the Childs (even Paul, whose personality took some time to come to life). Claiborne's major opus, *The New York Times Cook Book* was also just out, and Craig had gotten a sweet deal—all the rights were his. In just three months, nearly thirty thousand copies had sold. Claiborne was going to be rich. Some people had all the luck.

The more James existed in his own past that winter, as he tested hundreds of recipes for *Delights and Prejudices*, the more the world seemed to be hurtling toward a future he didn't recognize. His book would be about the deepest part of himself—his past—and yet there was so much that would have to stay hidden. But what if he could express the past not as a series of events but as a history of the things he'd tasted?

Not long after the launch party for *Mastering the Art*, Pat Knopf was irritated—it had been a month since Schaffner answered his last letter, about giving James until mid-March to deliver the manuscript of *Delights and Prejudices*. "I wonder if some of Jim's bad habits aren't rubbing off on you," Knopf wrote. Schaffner begged for more time. "There might not be much point in pressing Jim for a March deadline, since for all the times I have known him I have observed that while he always eventually meets his commitments, he has to do so in his own time and his own way." And this book was different. "This is a work that he cannot knock out to order," Schaffner said, "as he would do with a cookbook."

Meanwhile, James had some news for Helen. "John Ferrone is doing the book with me and we are beginning to get somewhere," James wrote. "John senses the idea of the thing at once and I feel confident that it is going to take shape from now on. That is[,] if the phone ever stops."

:::

THOUGH HE WAS TWENTY YEARS younger than James, Ferrone was still part of a generation of homosexuals who were careful about what they admitted about their lives, and to whom. To be exposed as queer would destroy your career and your reputation, and of course leave you vulnerable to arrest. Most lesbians and gays who lived in the Village lived with fear. They lived behind walls of discretion, but even there they parceled their lives into separate boxes.

A 1963 front-page exposé in the *New York Times* aimed to shock readers with the revelation that homosexuals were starting to seep from a depraved underground into the ordinary life of the city. "The city's most sensitive open secret—," metropolitan reporter Robert Doty wrote, "the presence of what is probably the greatest homosexual population in the world and its increasing openness—has become the subject of growing concern of psychiatrists, religious leaders and the police."

"In Greenwich Village," Doty reported, "a center for the bohemians of the homosexual world, one real estate management concern estimated that about one-fourth of the 245 apartments in its West Village buildings were rented by homosexuals."

And yet, like James, a queer could insulate his private box with others like him. "A New York homosexual," Doty explained, "if he chooses an occupation in which his clique is predominant, can shape for himself a life lived almost exclusively in an inverted world from which the rough, unsympathetic edges of straight society can be almost totally excluded." The challenge for James was being a public person: to bear his new fame as the Dean of American Gastronomy and the face of the popular *James Beard Cookbook*, holding a platter of choucroute garnie on the cover—in addition to making at least a dozen appearances a month and keeping his emotional center in the inverted world.

It was John Schaffner, at the end of 1961, when *Delights and Prejudices* was nothing but a mess of badly typed pages, single-spaced on thin, crackly onionskin paper—"just a clump of patches of writing"—who thought of asking Ferrone to do battle with it.

In Ferrone, James would find the ideal accomplice: an editor who did major sculptural work on James's copy (and occasional ghostwriting) and who had as much at stake as James did in keeping secrets. Ferrone was cautious by nature. He feared that James, before meeting Gino, took risks (he pursued men a bit too openly, and was indiscreet). Ferrone would use his discretion to help James craft *Delights and Prejudices* into a memoir "uninhibited without being bitter," as James's original prospectus promised—one that elided James's feelings of ambivalence and depression, emphatically erased his loves, and expressed all emotion in relation to eating. He pulled pages from the top of James's stack. "Ah," he said, "this would make a nice ending." The onionskin paper James used for typing made editorial marks impossible. Ferrone would have to retype everything. As James told Helen, Ferrone *had* sensed the idea of the thing.

Ferrone understood that what James had pounded out on his portable typewriter in Lausanne wasn't a typical memoir but rather a fable, a kind of bildungsroman, the story of a character's artistic and psychological growth. Only James's was a narrative about his burgeoning awareness of taste as a force that anchored him in the world. James's favorite bildungsroman, one of the novels he loved best, was Willa Cather's *The Song of the Lark*, featuring a young woman—Thea Kronborg—who, convinced of her own genius, leaves a dusty town in Colorado to become a great opera singer in Chicago, and eventually New York.

:::

"As I told Jim over the phone," Pat Knopf wrote to Schaffner in March 1962, "those two chapters are miraculous." John Ferrone had shaped James's thoughts into the first two chapters of *Delights and Prej-*

udices: his family's history, his mother's boardinghouse, her stormy relationship with Jue Let, and the memory of the feel of cold chicken jelly on James's throat. "They're beautifully done, full of marvelous material, and if they begin to represent what the rest of the book will contain, I could only be happier if the entire manuscript had come in December." All Knopf wanted was for James to turn it into a real memoir: to note the dates when everything happened—"the placement of the exact years," he wrote.

James and Ferrone added three or so date markers to the first chapters, most of them vague. Then, in April, before James departed for a monthlong tour of Asia and the Middle East, they delivered the manuscript to Atheneum. Knopf had objections. James's original proposal had listed chapters devoted to his school, on his experiences doing cooking demos across the country, and on wine, but they were missing from the book on his desk. Besides, Knopf complained, the latter part of the book, in which James shared his thoughts on the proper way to barbecue, and the best way to throw a party, strayed from the memoir angle of the book's beginning. They were, Knopf said, "involving themselves too much in advice and too little in reminiscence." What he was looking for was the kind of charming memento Atheneum was getting ready to publish in fall 1963: *The Margaret Rudkin Pepperidge Farm Cookbook*.

That book was to be Rudkin's sweet and conventionally nostalgic account of growing up in late-Victorian New York City, before adapting to country life on a Connecticut farm, from which she launched her famous commercial bakery. Children's book illustrator Erik Blegvad would decorate it lavishly, with whimsical sketches: an old stone grain mill, cats in a rambling country kitchen, pilgrims arriving to the first Thanksgiving, and plush loaves of white bread. It was a fake, really, a shameless plug for the Pepperidge Farm Company stuffed into a gingham frock and tied with ribbon. It was reminiscence with one purpose: to sell a brand. James and Ferrone had delivered to Atheneum a subtle bildungsroman about discovering taste.

James, writing to Schaffner from the Peninsula Hotel in Hong Kong, was furious. "I certainly feel that he has a book," James wrote, "and if he doesn't like it we can peddle it somewhere and give him another." He might consider adding *one* more chapter, "but I'm not going to make it the Complete Biography of James A. Beard."

Schaffner again tried to placate Atheneum. "Your objection is, I know, that he has skimped on the life of James A. Beard," he wrote Knopf. "His reply is that he was not writing an autobiography but a series of reminiscent essays about his experiences in his chosen field." Schaffner suggested the compromise James had floated: an added chapter or perhaps several new passages inserted into existing ones. If Knopf didn't like it, James would have no choice but to pull the manuscript, return the advance, and look for another publisher.

Knopf stood firm.

"Pat Knopf insists on more and more material for the book," he reported to Helen, "but he offers more money, so I am thinking it over. . . . He will not give it up and says he will publish it as is if I insist, but begs for one or more chapters."

James relented. "Going to extend the book about three chapters," he told Helen. "It won't be out now till spring of 64 or fall of same year. I don't care—I'll get another trip out of it this way."

: : :

LOU BARCARÈS WAS a long, low house—an old Provençal country house, or *mas*—of thick stone and a tile roof, with a stable at one end and seven acres of farmland. It lay just outside the town of Saint-Rémy-de-Provence, twelve miles from Avignon and fifty-five miles from Marseille. It was here, in early May 1963, that James came to finish *Delights and Prejudices*. He found the *mas* through friends, Bill and Donna Fifield, who lived nearby. Lou Barcarès's *propriétaire* was Yvonne Baudin. She lived onsite in her own quarters with her eighty-six-year-old mother and twenty-year-old son. James's apartment had two bedrooms and a tiny kitchen with an ancient gas stove.

James had begun *Delights* two years earlier in Lausanne, with a view across Lake Geneva to the French Alps. Now he was in this old Provençal *mas* looking onto Les Alpilles, a chain of low limestone mountains—

bleached and rounded, worn by the mistral—with patchy stands of pine at their feet. There was a gravel terrace where James could grill, ringed with a rock wall where lizards scrambled when you passed. The air in June smelled like sun on lavender, *serpolet* (wild thyme), and scrubby weeds. James tried to capture the essence of the scent by steeping lavender flowers in alcohol, but it was poor cologne. It was as if James had lost the ability, or maybe just his appetite, for the distilling experience. "I go struggling on blindly," he wrote to Schaffner.

His struggle with *Delights and Prejudices*, his immersion in a past that sometimes seemed too heavy to resurrect, had left James raw. His life in New York—the classes, his consulting for Le Bec Fin in Philadelphia, and regular deadlines for *House & Garden* and others—had made James's life more reckless and chaotic than ever. His relationship with Gino had changed: Increasingly, their lives ran on parallel tracks. In December 1963, James's emotional paralysis worsened. "My mood is becoming more and more depressed," he'd confessed to Helen, "and I don't even want to live much any more. And I suppose I'm just getting into an emotional bath of some kind—but I sure don't give a shit."

Finishing *Delights* in a place without a telephone was one reason for this trip. Another was simply to get away.

Yet James had worked diligently since arriving. On Saint-Rémy's weekly market day, he rose early and walked to the Place de la République for asparagus, tiny potatoes, and strawberries. As always, food was James's restorative.

He found dark-crusted levain, rice from the Camargue, and green-gold olive oil from a mill near Les Baux. He bought white and rosé wines in refillable ceramic-topped liter bottles from a maker in the Alpilles, a Monsieur Pol. Madame Baudin and her son raised free-range chickens that delivered eggs with yolks of a rich orange color; they grew tomatoes, peas, and garlic, still green and mild in June. "Ate like a nut five pieces of garlic bread!" James recorded in his datebook, meaning he smeared five slices of levain with moist green young garlic from Madame's garden and devoured them for supper with hunks of tomato and sausage.

On his portable typewriter, James banged out a rough draft on eating in Provence for *House & Garden*. He mailed it to Isabel and began another draft on English food. He wrote the extra pages for *Delights*.

By the middle of his second week at Lou Barcarès, James's typewriter ceased clacking. "I think I have finished the book," he recorded in his datebook. The next day, he was certain he had. "Sonnez la trompette!" he wrote—sound the trumpet! "*Weeeeet!*" He celebrated by going to Arles and enjoying a lunch of roast fowl and a Gigondas 1959 he noted was superb. James saw the Fifields and went to a party at the house of Jean de Beucken, who'd written a new biography of Cézanne.

And yet it was a summer of disappointments. He found three-Michelin-star La Baumanière overrated. "The gigot is beautiful and good but not three stars," he noted in his datebook. He cooked a pot-au-feu but found the local beef lacking. "Our meat is much better for it really," he jotted. "The marbling is best to keep it juicy."

At the last minute, William Templeton Veach, James's American expat friend who lived on an old farmhouse estate in the Loire valley, decided he couldn't come south after all. It was the same with Elizabeth David. In May, she suffered a breakdown, James told Schaffner, "and was sent to the hospital for two weeks and then made to stay in bed for another fortnight." (In fact, David had suffered a cerebral hemorrhage, probably brought on by stress. "She does a great deal of overworking," James noted to his agent, "and getting upset with editors—this is her great downfall.")

James had so wanted David to visit him in this part of Provence, a landscape she knew well. "However," he told Schaffner, "there has been so much change in some things I am afraid she might have been saddened." Even here, supermarkets and factory-made baguettes were obliterating the past, remaking the world in shiny plastic.

Ferrone then arrived, to finish *Delights*. "John seems to feel that we have found the additional material for the book and has cut some and let some remain," James reported to Schaffner. "I hope to God Pat is satisfied this time for I think we have given him all that should go into that particular book—and more!" And then they thrashed out material for James's next book for Dell.

: : :

DELIGHTS AND PREJUDICES is a book about James finding his authority in the world, his artistry and sense of mission. James shaped memory to serve the narrative. Gearhart and the garden at Salmon Street
became romantic sources of the world's immanent beauty and wisdom.
Taste is the revelation of a delight that exists within things: Dungeness crab, oysters, butter, huckleberries, corn, strawberries, peas, all in
a perfect state. They all had spiritual force for James, one only he—with
his gift of taste memory—could feel.

Before, James had used the term *taste memory* to mean simple
recall—the thing, like hearing a song on the radio and being trans-
ported to the past, or overcome with feelings you'd put away: nostalgia charged with emotion, like the zap of electrical current from a
faulty cord. ("For an art as transitory as gastronomy," he wrote in his
appreciation of M. F. K. Fisher in her 1954 omnibus *The Art of Eating*,
"there can be no record except for a keen taste memory and the printed
word.") But in *Delights and Prejudices*, taste memory takes on the status
of a rare gift.

"The ability to recall a taste sensation, which I think of as 'taste
memory,' " James wrote in *Delights and Prejudices*, "is a God-given talent, akin to perfect pitch, which makes your life richer if you possess
it. If you aren't born with it, you can never seem to acquire it." And he
says that growing up on food that had no particular feeling attached
to it is crucial for being able to taste properly. "Not all taste memory
is accurate," James writes. "Many people think of Mom's apple pie or
Grandmother's dumplings as delicacies that cannot be equaled today.
These memories are associated with happy times, and to the untrained
palate the pie or the dumplings seemed delicious."

But since James grew up largely a stranger to happiness, at least at
the table, "I think I developed an accurate taste memory early in my
life. I was not sentimentally attached to the cooking of any one person
at home, and we ate in restaurants a good deal." It's a sad revelation, the
opposite of nostalgic platitudes in books such as Margaret Rudkin's.

There, learning to make biscuits or a chocolate layer cake is an act of intergenerational bonding, if not love, as a grandmother reveals her precious secrets to a child.

Years later, Ferrone would write that, "For Beard, food was autobiography." No wonder Pat Knopf was frustrated with the manuscript for omitting the usual elements of memoir: It isn't one. The beginning of *Delights and Prejudices* was like an orchestra tuning up before a majestic overture. "When Proust recollected the precise taste sensation of the little scalloped *Madeleine* cakes served at tea by his aunt," the text goes, "it led him into his monumental remembrance of things past. When I recollect the taste sensations of my childhood, they lead me to more cakes, more tastes: the great razor clams, the succulent Dungeness crab, the salmon, crawfish, mussels and trout of the Oregon coast; the black bottom pie served in a famous Portland restaurant; the Welsh rabbit of our Chinese cook, the white asparagus my mother canned, and the array of good dishes prepared by the two of them in that most memorable of kitchens." In *Remembrance of Things Past*, the narrator's taste of *Madeleine* crumbled into tea reminds him of an act: his aunt Léonie, on Sunday mornings when he went into her room to say good morning, giving the boy a taste of tea-soaked cake. It was a treat, a kind of benediction—an act of love. For James, remembered tastes conjured not acts of human connection but a seemingly endless chain of other tastes.

With Ferrone's literary help, James built a myth of himself as a man so focused on eating that nothing else mattered. So many of the actual people in his life—like Gino, or Ferrone, or any of the half-dozen of his closest friends—would have to be stripped out, beyond the inverted world of open secrets the Robert Doty article revealed. It was easier to paint himself as a single man intent on solitary conquests of food.

For the dust jacket of *Delights and Prejudices*, illustrator Earl Thollander painted an image so apt it became an indelible rendering of James. The setting is the beach at Seaside, with a view to the waves and tree-covered Tillamook Head. We see James from behind, seated alone at a table on the sand. It's been laid with a white cloth. James is holding open a menu and ordering from a white-jacketed waiter without even making eye contact. The sheer volume of space and the landscape dwarf James. You imagine him enduring a lavish and lengthy meal with only the scenery for company. There is no one in James's life to share his moment of rapture.

CHAPTER 16

COLD SICILIAN ROULADE
WITH THE MASTER

1964–1969

HELEN EVANS BROWN was declining fast. For more than a decade, she had suffered from things her doctor had trouble finding causes for: bouts of dizziness, gastrointestinal ravages, canker sores. She worked hard and rarely took a break. It was stress, Dr. Maurer would say. She needed to learn how to take it easy.

In 1964, as Helen turned sixty, her maladies were intensifying. That spring, she and Philip went to Europe for a long-delayed grand tour, plus Helen's daughter from her first marriage, Oakley, had moved to West Germany with her husband, Charles "Joe" Goodner, a physician assigned to a US military hospital. The Browns were starting in Paris before moving on to Spain and Italy, where they all planned to meet up in Rome before traveling together to Germany.

James was busy organizing cooking demonstrations for the 1964 New York World's Fair. He hoped to be in St. Tropez when the Browns were in France; he suggested they rendezvous there. In February, he had a health scare of his own: heart palpitations, resulting in a stay at

Doctors Hospital on the Upper East Side. His doctor put him on digitalis and forbade unnecessary travel. St. Tropez was out.

In Santander, Spain, not long after the Browns' trip began, Helen suddenly crumpled, her whole body inexplicably weak. At their hotel, she had difficulty raising her head from the pillow. Reached by phone, Goodner surmised hypokalemia (low potassium). He recommended feeding Helen rich chicken broth—the hotel's chef made a concentrated one from an entire chicken. It worked. Helen rallied enough to fly to West Germany to see Oakley and Goodner but had a relapse en route. She nearly died in the military hospital. Eventually, she was cleared to fly to Los Angeles, where she spent weeks in the hospital before feeling strong enough to return to Armada Drive.

"Certainly after all the months in the hospital," James wrote to her, "you must feel to just look out in your garden is almost enough to make a whole day."

But after a mild recovery, Helen worsened. Her heart weakened dangerously. James, who had gone to France after all, wrote her in August from Lou Barcarès, on an evening when the electricity happened to fail. "I understand the feeling when your legs get so tired and seem to give out," he wrote her. As usual, he described the meals he'd been having and told her he thought the French food writer Robert Courtine was a son of a bitch. He said he had to sign off so he could finish some editing work for the Dell book before the sun set.

"Lights are still out and it's getting dark," he told her, "so I'll send you love and kisses."

Helen died that December. She was sixty. At her request, there was no funeral.

In grief, James was silent. But then, even before she died, James had insulated himself from his feelings for Helen. Sooner or later, James distanced himself from all of his closest relationships, as if he were doing his friends a favor, cutting them out before they could see just what an unworthy thing he was.

: : :

JAMES BEARD'S MENUS FOR ENTERTAINING had been one long fight with Dell and its editor, Ross Claiborne, but by June 1965, James's thirteenth book was all wrapped up—including the name. "I must say," Schaffner wrote to James, "I am disappointed in the title they have put on the book, as I think more people are interested in the cookbook aspect than in menu-planning." James didn't seem to care.

Dell would publish *Menus* under its Delacorte Press imprint later that fall, but in June, more than six months after delivering *Delights and Prejudices*, James still felt drained. Getting *Menus* together had all been rather a chore, even though he'd only done the recipes and menus— and those he built on the skeleton of the aborted Schoonmaker collaboration. John Ferrone had done most of the writing for *Menus*, from scratch, without James's customary stack of onionskin pages. He had a fine ear for James's voice—but then, James's voice was a Ferrone creation, starting with *The James Beard Cookbook*, which he edited from Isabel's manuscript, and ending with his own extensive cut, paste, and rewrite job on James's chaotic drafts for *Delights*.

But a messier fight was brewing: what to pay Ferrone. His freelance moonlighting had always been acts of friendship, partly, but James had come to expect more and more from Ferrone, as he had from Isabel. For ghost-authoring *Menus*, James had given him $1,000 as a down payment (James's advance was $5,000), with an indefinite hold on talk about sharing royalties. But Schaffner didn't expect many of those to accrue for this book, especially after a pretty sizable advance. They'd agreed Ferrone would not get a credit in the book, and because of that, he expected to see a bigger cut of the advance. James would have to work something out.

Menus for Entertaining is a book of practical recipes and party tips, set in the colorful mastic of James's official persona, which by now had idiosyncrasies and an adorable aspect. Most of the book's color photos show James in a tuxedo, grinning, amid his ornate *objets* in the house on West Tenth Street: slicing a ham in front of the copper lavabo, on a table packed with breadsticks and Minton crockery; decanting wine before a candle in his teaching kitchen. One of his six-foot terra-cotta "girls" stands guard over a large unmolded Bavarian cream dotted with candied violets, the table set with vermeil plates and glass Victorian wine rinsers.

James's recipes stand in simple relief to the arcane grandeur of the visuals. They're rustic and seasonal: oxtail ragout, anchovies with radishes, sliced tomatoes with basil, parsleyed new potatoes—the kind of things that would appear nine years later in Richard Olney's *Simple French Food*. Even the ferocious Nika Hazelton purred her approval. "Like almost all great food," she wrote in the *New York Times*, "[it] is simple, that is, concerned with the native goodness of the ingredients and no spurious disguises."

A year after *Delights and Prejudices* painted James as a man with shadows, *Menus for Entertaining* showed him as a rather strange but harmless bachelor uncle, obsessed with food and antiques. Even in the text, in the introduction to "Dinners to Prepare in Advance," Ferrone has us see James as an eccentric, a kind of lovable oddball. "I have a predilection," the section begins, "for rising early, and when I am preparing for a dinner party, I enjoy rising at 5:00 or 5:30 and going straight from the bath to the kitchen. I call this 'cooking in the nude.' It is so cool and quiet in the early hours and before midmorning one can have a whole dinner ready except for the final bits of cooking and the garnishing." The contrast between photos of the tuxedo-clad James, all jowls, a chin indistinguishable from his neck, and smiles, with the mental picture of a naked James, prepping ceviche in the morning stillness of his kitchen, is strange. But age and bachelorhood had made James sexless, in any popular reckoning. He was a eunuch, the soft, fleshy, and affable majordomo of the women's quarters, with a peccadillo for naturism.

James's asexuality would become a hook. In December 1965, Screen Gems took out a full-page ad in *Variety* to flog James's new daily television program, *The James Beard Show*. An enormous closeup of James's face takes up most of the page. Its lines are blurred, as if James were looking through shower glass fogged with steam. He doesn't smile; his eyebrows arch. His expression is critical and demanding—he's hard to please and impossible to fool. Below is a small, full-body image: James in one of his graphic bib aprons, arms akimbo, hands clutching a wooden tossing fork and spoon, in front of a table bearing a bowl of salad. The headline reads LADIES' MAN—it's a pun, since James's show is for a daytime audience of housewives. But the joke carries a charge, since nothing about the supercilious man in the picture suggests any particular feeling for women.

In 1968, Time-Life Books paid James $250 to affix his signature to a letter it had written in his name soliciting subscribers to its Foods of the World book series. (James had been a consultant for the first volume, released that same year: *American Cooking.*) "Dear Reader," it began, "It's been said of me that I write about food the way some men write about women. Perhaps. But is there another way? Unless I can convey my love of well-prepared food to the reader (or TV viewer), why should she (or, increasingly, he) love it—or want to cook it?" The implication was clear: James's only lust was for food.

James did like to cook naked in hot weather—he liked being nude generally, when it was muggy, but it could be more than that. "It is past midnight," he once wrote to Helen, "and I should be putting the body to rest in a decent way. It's hot and I'm sitting at the desk in the nude tearing off these little lines."

James had built his public life around concealment. The act of revealing even a partial picture of his personal history, as he'd done in *Delights and Prejudices*, gave him an urge to reveal more. Describing his nakedness was a trial unburdening, a flag James waved. Would he still be lovable if everyone glimpsed the truth of who he was?

: : :

IN 1965, James signed a contract with Little, Brown to write a cook-book on food from the South of France, called *Flavor of Provence.* It would be inspired by his time at Lou Barcarès, Madame Baudin's farm-house near Saint-Rémy. He needed to return there to do research. And something miraculous had happened since the end of 1964—his relationship with Gino had flowered again. James wanted to show him the Provence he'd fallen in love with.

James left for Paris. Gino would start his vacation from Harrison

& Abramovitz later in the spring. He and James would meet in Nice at the end of May and travel together to Saint-Rémy, then on to Barcelona and Lisbon, and finally to London en route home. It would be their first time traveling together in Europe.

James met Gino at the airport in Nice. The next day, they traveled to Cannes and hired a car to navigate the nine miles north to Brama-fam, Simone Beck and Jean Fischbacher's property outside Plascassier, where they had a lovely three-story stone house. Julia and Paul Child were staying at Bramafam—they had plans to build a place of their own on Simca and Jean's property. Well, good for the Childs. TV and the book deal combined had made Julia practically rich—and anyway she'd have Paul's government pension to help grease the skids. They all had lunch together on Simca's terrace.

"The trip has been a marvel to me," James wrote to Schaffner. "I have had rest and relaxation for the first time in years."

James and Gino traveled to Avignon and Nîmes and spent a night at Lou Barcarès, to see Madame Baudin. James sent a picture postcard to the Schaffners: two handsome, leather-faced cowboys of the Camargue on horseback. "Gino decides he prefers the Riviera to Provence," he wrote, "but I'm still loyal! It has been three weeks of great and delicious activity—and I'm sure I feel better for it."

They walked the streets of Barcelona like tourists. "Showed Gino his first Gaudí," James recorded in his datebook. Amid the clutter and exuberant tiles of the restaurant Los Caracoles, they shared langoustine (James: "marvelous"), sole, and wild strawberries. They flew to Lisbon, where they met Ruth Norman and Cheryl Crawford, shopped for old tinware, and ate wonderful seafood salad, pasta al percebes (gooseneck barnacles), and fresh raspberries. In London, James saw Elizabeth David. She took him to a warehouse to look at stock for a kitchen shop she planned to open. He took Gino to a supper party at the restaurant Prunier. Gino seemed better in social situations. He was almost affable.

In October 1965, a month after he and Gino returned to New York, James had a momentous talk with Ned Bradford of Little, Brown.

James had been working as a consultant for Little, Brown, giving advice about what cookbooks to publish. He'd convinced Bradford to publish Bill Veach's *A Bon Vivant's Cookbook*, the last book for Veach's collaborator, Helen Evans Brown, before she died. The book tanked. James had also persuaded Bradford to substantially revise *The Fannie Farmer Cookbook*, to which Little, Brown held the rights. That year, the Boston publishing house brought out the eleventh edition of *Fannie Farmer*, revised—completely modernized, really, like a Victorian house gutted and redone with shag carpet and a wet bar—by Wilma Lord Perkins (Fannie Merritt Farmer's niece by marriage), who'd been overseeing smaller updates to *Fannie* since 1929. It gave Bradford a taste for something monumental from James. Over drinks, before James departed for the West Coast on a book tour for *Menus*, they agreed that James would write the greatest book of his career: a Stonehenge for the ages.

It would be a kind of mapping of all of James's thoughts and experiences at the table, as sweeping as *Fannie* but with the flavor of James's life and travels—no one in the world had a mind as encyclopedic as his when it came to food. Bradford's understanding of it was fuzzy yet definite. It was to be a book that would mark the apex of James's career. Schaffner called it simply "the comprehensive James Beard cookbook." James figured maybe he'd think it through enough by February to be able to sign a contract. By December, Schaffner called the still-amorphous project James's "big ultimate book." Ned Bradford had begun to call it James's "really comprehensive cookbook."

By then, it had eclipsed all plans for James's French books. Without telling James, Paris-based journalist and author Naomi Barry, borrowed some of the research she'd done for *Cuisine of France*—a planned collaboration with James on French chefs and their favorite recipes—to include in her column in *Gourmet*. It was poetic justice, considering James's history of undermining his collaborators—and it gave him an excuse for walking away from the book, research for which had proved to be a grind.

As for the other, Schaffner suggested that James could incorporate that material in "the major James Beard book," and rip up the contract for *Flavor of Provence*. Bradford agreed, and in March 1966, James signed a contract for his major opus, "to put down at last the essence—nay, the quintessence," Schaffner wrote, "of all his accumulated knowledge into one great big James Beard book." It came with a check for $7,500, the first half of an advance so large only Julia Child could expect anything like it.

:::

"I'M HUNGRY!" James delivered his line suddenly, in a deep roar, and it electrified the class.

In late winter 1966, the writer John Skow, on assignment from the *Saturday Evening Post*, shadowed James. He observed him at a wine tasting at The Four Seasons, paid a visit to West Tenth Street one morning for an interview, and sat in on a class of the James Beard Cooking School. James's classes had captured the imagination of Manhattan's professional class: male business executives who dabbled in cooking as a relaxing hobby away from the boardroom, and their wives, under pressure to host dinner parties for their husbands' clients. Saying you'd learned the fondue Orientale or strawberry sorbet recipe from one of those expensive classes at Jim Beard's down in the Village gave your dinner party a sense of sparkle, rich and worldly.

Since the untimely death in January 1966 of Henri Soulé, owner of Le Pavillon and La Côte Basque, "many knowledgeable restaurateurs," Skow wrote, looked to James as the nation's ranking food expert and as a personality with wide appeal. In a decade of teaching, James had honed his classes until they wheeled along like immersive theater. His roar—"I'm hungry!"—was the dramatic catalyst: the gunshot in Act I that marked the real start of the play. Nobody but James could pull that off.

The course ran for six evenings and cost $135 (adjusted for inflation, that's the equivalent of about $1,000 today). "Eight or ten people, about half of them men, had gathered in Beard's living room the night I visited the class," Skow wrote. James would time his appearance for maximum effect. Skow catalogued the students, all of them affluent enough to afford the steep tuition: two export-import men, a CBS executive, a husband and wife who'd driven in from Connecticut, "and a woman who was a consultant to one of the big food corporations." As they waited for James, they donned the aprons they'd been asked to bring. "It says something about the national uneasiness toward fine cooking," Skow wrote, "that one man put on one of those Father's Day aprons that say EAT AT YOUR OWN RISK."

James walked downstairs into the salon in a green-striped butcher's apron over his dress shirt and bow tie and, with crisp authority, took charge. "The pupils listened," Skow wrote, "in attitudes of respect seldom seen in these days of student protest." James described the dishes they'd cook that night and took questions. Yes, one could buy a good copper omelet pan at a shop he knew in the Village. ("The students," Skow said, yelped in excitement.") The dinner they'd sit down to after the class, James pointed out—the dishes they'd cook in the class— would probably be cold by the time they got to them. Then he stated with conviction that almost everything in the world of food is actually better cold. The students diligently took notes. Who could argue with James Beard?

"The chatter hushed," Skow wrote, "and the class moved soberly into Beard's kitchen. Modern kitchens often resemble operating rooms, but this one is pleasantly old-fashioned, with a minimum of plastic and porcelain." James stood along the long wall, with the pineapple wallpaper like a stage backdrop. He was demonstrating how to make Sicilian-style veal roulade, a drop-dead first course for dinner parties on the Upper East Side.

With his enormous hands, James showed how to flatten a scaloppine with a brass meat pounder and handed it to a student to take over. He demonstrated how to lay out the slices in an overlapping geometry of pale-pink flesh, eventually forming "an elaborate jelly roll" of veal, salami, mortadella, and prosciutto, to be wrapped around hardboiled eggs laid end-to-end down the center. "Then Beard held a piece of thinly sliced, larded sausage to the light as if it were a page of incunabula," Skow observed, and then it happened: "Deep diagonal furrows appeared above his eyebrows as he looked slyly from one student to another and said, in a voice that echoed up from the cargo-carrying recesses of his hull, 'I'm hungry.'"

He supervised the students as they rolled the meat into a huge cigar shape. It was missing one last layer before it could be placed carefully in an enormous sauté pan and seared. "Dr-r-r-r-ape it in bacon," James bellowed, like Lear shouting at storm clouds on the heath. A lesson in omelet-making followed, with each student stationed around the grand piano at one of the electric burners, trying to get the hang of rolling and plating. After that came a twenty-minute intermission—everyone was back in the salon, sipping Americano cocktails. James called it a teaching device. "Students, who think of cooking as frantic and messy," he told Skow, "see that it can be leisurely and civilized."

Ruth Norman took over for the second act, a seafood stew *méditerranée*, with clams, lobster, and shrimp, but James was still in charge. "That will serve twelve," Ruth said. Almost as though they'd rehearsed it, James interjected a correction: "I should say six or eight." None of that rationing cherrystones for the guests: James was large and magnificent, and unafraid of pleasure or excess. Indeed, Skow noticed at The Four Seasons wine tasting how James's physical size seemed to put people at ease. "In a way that is hard to analyze but easy to detect," Skow wrote, "the size of the man makes people feel good."

His bigness and exuberance gave James authority, Skow wrote, "and since he is an expert showman, it strikes in exactly the way he wants it to. He is fat, for instance, but fat in a way that makes thin people wistful. Most cooks are fatty, which is not the same thing; they are puffed and pounded from a lifelong battle with cream sauce. Beard's great body is that of the rare athlete who is exactly sized for his specialty. He has a thick, powerful neck and small, pointed ears. He looks like a wrestler who has begun to melt, or a genie who has started to solidify."

The class that night ended with eating food that was, just as James predicted, cold: the Sicilian roulade, seafood stew *méditerranée*, a salad, and a flaming *baba au rhum*, with everyone seated around the marble-topped table in the salon. There were glasses of a delightful white wine Skow failed to get the name of. Sessions at the James Beard Cooking School had seemed shockingly expensive, but after an evening of food, drinks, and being up close at a demonstration of James's learning and flair, "the price," Skow wrote, "seemed very small."

The *Times* article felt like vindication for James, at a moment when his depression had returned. *Delights and Prejudices* was so far a commercial flop, but the Skow story was a boost. "Too bad it didn't make the cover as they originally planned," James wrote. Still, he was happy. Schaffner enlisted Alvin Kerr to help round up copies from newsstands on the Upper East Side to keep for James. They found only three.

: : :

THAT THERE WERE so many men in James's classes echoed a shift in the cultural life of the United States: Turning out the perfect rolled omelet had become a power leisure activity for executives. (James would tell *Business Week* in 1970 that the audience for his classes was "the great army of people who cook as a creative pursuit, just as there are people who paint on their days off.") Six months before John Skow spent his evening on West Tenth Street, Nika Hazelton had noted the change in the *New York Times*. "Today," she wrote, "the average man's wish to be called a gourmet belongs with our quest for civilized living." For Hazelton, this new passion marked the neutering of the American male.

"I don't know why healthy, able-bodied men should want so badly to fix small, delicious morsels," she wrote. "Is gourmet cooking a form of transvestitism nowadays, part of the same compulsion that makes women wear pants, since society still frowns on men in skirts, though not in aprons?" With an arch flourish, Hazelton gestured at New York's open secret: That the city's gourmet male establishment—James, Claiborne, the concert-pianist-turned-cooking-teacher Michael Field, who clung to a marriage of convenience—was a ring of fairies. Once the students of the James Beard Cooking School departed for the evening, and there were no reporters to entertain, Hazelton knew that the man at the very top of New York's gourmet bachelor brotherhood behaved in ways that would have revolted readers of the *Saturday Evening Post*.

Once after a class on West Tenth, James shared an unexpected confidence with a student. Alfred Rosenthal had revealed he was president of a company that produced needlecraft kits: open-weave canvas printed with a pattern, packaged with the yarns needed to embroider it.

After class one night, James took Rosenthal aside and told him he had a secret. When the other students were gone, James led him upstairs to his bed-sitting room, where James had his collection: more than a dozen pillows James had designed and stitched himself. Most of the designs were bouquets of flowers, copied from magazine photographs. James confessed that he liked to do needlepoint on trains. It relaxed him. Rosenthal was astounded. He pledged to keep James in blank canvas and needlepoint yarns for the rest of his life.

Over the years, Rosenthal would take many classes from James. He never saw more than a couple of embroidered pillows scattered around the public salon off the kitchen. Meanwhile, just one floor up, a private world bloomed.

:::

THE TASK WAS MONUMENTAL and had no boundaries: to put down in writing everything James knew about food for the Little, Brown book. A tape recorder—that was the thing. James could free himself from typing (his fingers never fit that well on keyboards anyway, and lately it had become worse). He'd have Dick Tiernan transcribe his daily talk.

Ned Bradford, too, was struggling with the idea of capturing James's mind on the page. He had Little, Brown's art director, Martha Lehtola, reach out to Earl Thollander, the artist Atheneum used for *Delights and Prejudices*, to see whether he would work directly with James. "We are very excited at the prospect of publishing an elegant and elaborate cookbook by James Beard," Lehtola wrote. But it was all so far in the future, this enormous, amorphous cookbook.

In July 1966, James flew to London to work on the book. He was staying in a rented flat in a Victorian red-brick-and-stucco row house at 25 De Vere Gardens, near Kensington Palace. He'd been writing to an old friend in Portland, sixty-four-year-old Cathrine "Katie" Laughton. Until recently, she had been the author of the Mary Cullen's Cottage column in the *Oregon Journal* and of a 1946 book *Mary Cullen's Northwest Cook Book*. They had an idea. "It seems now," he wrote to Schaffner, "that the book is going to be a tome of American cookery with the various foreign backgrounds. As I see it now, it will cover material no one has done in one volume and with perhaps English, French and Spanish derivatives included should be a rather fascinating tome." He and Laughton had been brainstorming. "[We] have a good deal of it already in hand outline wise."

James's comprehensive cookbook would be historical, then: a kind of family tree of American food, with the roots traced back to Europe. History weighed on James in London. He was sleeping on a street of ghosts (Henry James once lived across the street from James's flat, and Browning died in the house next door). He went to the Royal Opera House in Covent Garden to hear Schoenberg's 12-tone *Moses and Aaron*. "What a marvelous production," James reported to Schaffner, "and how many nude bodies writhing and reeling."

The burning bush and the pillar of fire might have been stylized props, but the Israelites' orgy scene around the golden calf, with staging that called for "a naked youth," "four naked virgins," and a river of fake blood, looked convincing enough—certainly the bare asses. In the libretto, Moses calls God *"einziger, ewiger, allgegenwärtiger, unsichtbarer, und unvorstellbarer"* ("unique, eternal, omnipresent, imperceptible, and unrepresentable"). It could have been a description of James, as he looked back on the history of his life in food, unsure how to capture it, confused about where to start. Thank heaven Katie Laughton would impose order. But James wasn't feeling particularly eternal. It had been an exhausting summer, one with a depressing revelation: *Delights and Prejudices*, James's greatest book, was a commercial failure.

"I only wish I wrote popular cookbooks instead of *Delights and Prejudices*," James wrote Schaffner from Philip Brown's house in Pasadena—Helen's house. "Maybe someday!" In late September, back from London, James was on the road again, this time to the West Coast for book promotions and paid appearances. He wrote to Schaffner on Helen's old stationery, after crossing out her name on the letterhead: an apt remembrance. James had traveled more than five thousand miles, from London to California, only to find more ghosts.

"Isn't it a shame that *D and P* doesn't sell?" James was in Surf Pines on the Oregon coast, near Gearhart. He was staying at the beach cottage of an old friend, the interior decorator Harvey Welch, and his romantic partner, the architect Halsey Jones, who designed the cottage. "I realize, though, that it never had the right chance. People who read it buy another copy usually. The reports on it are fabulous. It just died aborning I guess."

Mary Hamblet had come to the beach, and James's gay Portland friends, "all of the fraternity." John Ferrone had flown west to visit. They all drove south along the coast to the wide beach at Neahkahnie, with its brooding view of the ocean. They had a picnic on the sand, but something was different for James. "I can feel age for the first time in my life," he told Schaffner.

Surf Pines was a gated community of low-rise houses with gray clapboard siding the color of washed-up driftwood, bleached by sun. Inside, Harvey and Halsey had given the place a quality of Nordic quiet: pale wood paneling and bleached floors, and furniture covered in varying blues, like indigos caught at different stages of fading. Tall windows looked out at the Pacific across a deep mat of beach grass, the shiny strands tossed by wind. To the south, you could see Tillamook Head, low and gray, floating on mist.

Harvey's grumpy little Yorkie, Fergus, patrolled the deck outside, yapping at seabirds. Always a man of restrained good taste, Harvey wore a shirt with an open collar under a tweed jacket; Mary wore a shift dress in a sober fabric, with her short, white, tightly waved hair shrouded in a scarf tied at the chin. They ate simply. James, in a shirt of olive-colored plaid, with a green bow tie, presided over lunch: a salad of butter lettuce and tomatoes, cold cracked Dungeness crab, thick and shiny homemade mayonnaise, and chilled bottles of Muscadet. He was home, yet his mind was restless.

He had bought a camera to take snapshots of the house for Gino. One morning, three younger men, friends of Harvey's from the antiques trade in Portland, drove out to spend the day. They laid out towels on the deck beyond the sliding-glass doors off the dining room and changed into bathing suits to bask in the sun. The sandy blond wore a tight red suit, the dark-haired boys wore almost matching white trunks with racing stripes down the side. They exuded sex. Ferrone lolled on the bench that ringed the deck, in long pants and a long-sleeved shirt, observing from behind sunglasses.

Surreptitiously, James snapped a few pictures through the window— souvenirs, to show Freddie and Alvin back home. But there was a new yearning in him. He felt tired—he looked pale and old when he caught his face in the glass—but time wasn't stopping for James. Everything was changing. Boys were freer now, more open than his and Harvey's generation could have ever imagined. They'd all had to walk a thin line, his generation. With his wealthy clients in Portland, Harvey was always polite, always correct in mixed company, never slipping into queeniness. But these boys sunning: They looked like they didn't give a damn what anyone thought.

:::

In May 1967, after James turned sixty-four, he intended to tackle the comprehensive American book with the vigor of a kid. He'd come to Provence, one of his favorite places in the world, to work. He was in Plascassier again, this time staying at Julia and Paul Child's new house on Simca's property, called La Pitchoune ("La *Peeech*," Julia called it— "The Little Thing"). His collaborator Katie Laughton and her new husband, Philip Hindley, had rented a place about two and a half miles away—a cottage on the property of an English couple. Here on Julia and Paul's stone terrace, under a gnarled old olive tree, looking across a kind of canyon at hills speckled with white villas, James knew he could really get something done.

"I'm fairly happy with the way the book has started off," James reported to Schaffner. "For some unknown reason we started on lamb and I have been going through that meat like a fool. . . . Our darling little butcher in the village has really very nice things at this point . . . and I find I don't have to tear down to Cannes or Nice when I want especially nice things." Good thing, because the road to Cannes had become impossibly choked, as more and more tourists prowled the area.

Once a week, James and Julia went to the enormous Carrefour

supermarket—dubbed *hypermarché*—in Nice. It took up a whole city block and had underground parking, complete with food vendors. "You wheel your little truck into the elevator and into the lower garage for your car and there are rotisseries going and lunch counters and everything but a pool!" A gallon of Johnnie Walker Scotch cost fifteen dollars—cheaper than in New York.

British writer Sybille Bedford was La Pitchoune's neighbor, along with her American wife (also a writer), Eda Lord. Julia was trying to arrange an evening for them to come to dinner. "Sadly," James wrote, "Elizabeth David and Renée Fedden arrived here the hour before we did and left so that we missed them completely. Liz is broken hearted as I am." James would try to get her to come to New York.

All through May, James worked on the lamb and veal chapters, while Katie took on cakes and cookies. "She has an endless collection from her years on the paper," James told Schaffner, "and she has done nothing else since we arrived." Katie's husband, previously managing editor of the *San Francisco Examiner*, helped out by editing the fresh drafts. The weather in Provence was freezing for May, and James's leg swelled and throbbed. He walked with a cane. The book began to grind.

As impossible as the task seemed, he had to persevere. This book could vindicate James's whole career—Julia and Paul had told him it would be the most important thing he'd ever done. It could get him back on TV, as *Mastering the Art of French Cooking* had done for Julia, and TV, combined with books, was where the money just rolled to you.

"It will consolidate your position as <u>the</u> American food authority," Schaffner assured him.

When spring at last arrived—"glorious sun and air filled with the perfume of roses," he told Schaffner—James's optimism soared. He now realized it was merely life in New York that was making him feel low. "I'm quite sure, to tell you the truth, that certain people really gave me a true inferiority last winter and spring and that when I found myself released again, over here, I felt the determination to finish off and get things done. I can hardly bear the idea of getting back to New York again and cringe at the idea of having to spend too much time there."

Only the day before, James had convinced himself to keep on with the book. "It is going to be long and I shall probably never get it done as I want it for it couldn't take that much room. But it is exhaustive and I think interesting. At any event it has to be done and I know that now no matter what anyone says."

James's depression usually eased during travel. La Pitchoune was a lovely place of self-imposed exile. "I sit upon my little shelf with the remote world so far away that I am startled [to] think only of the world where I am," he wrote to Schaffner one evening.

"I keep making a dachshund with a bushy tail out of the trees across the valley and make patterns of the lights of Grasse at night and love the solitude when I have it."

PART FIVE

CHAPTER 17

SHATTERED GLASS AND SCHNECKENOODLES

1967–1972

Word of James's epic American cookbook pinged around New York's editorial offices. Geraldine Rhoads, the new editor-in-chief of *Woman's Day* magazine, told Schaffner what she thought the title should be: *ALL THERE IS TO KNOW ABOUT FOOD* by James A. Beard. The promise of the ultimate compendium from the man who had *lived* American food in the twentieth century was thrilling.

But would cooks in the United States, still deeply enchanted with French and Continental cuisines, even want it? In 1967, Americans were enthusiastically trying recipes for blanquette de veau and gâteau Reine de Saba, still propping open the stained pages of *Mastering the Art of French Cooking.* James and Katie were working out plain American roast leg of lamb and Lazy Daisy Cake. "I have moments of wondering if anyone will care if there is an American book or not," James wrote to Schaffner from Provence, where—ironically—James was suffocating in French food.

That summer, Julia and Simca worked on the long-awaited follow-up to *Mastering the Art of French Cooking.* (Louisette Bertholle, coauthor of the first volume, had long been out of the picture.) They'd hoped it would take two years, but things were grinding on. Judith Jones, their editor at Knopf, had insisted they come up with a foolproof baguette for American kitchens, and it wasn't going well. Julia and Paul had gone through hundreds of pounds of American flour. The perfect French loaf still eluded them. "Simca has enough energy for ten persons," James told Schaffner, "and is on the run all day and half the night." He, in fact, felt more of a connection to Julia: "She is such a dear person and so understanding—for she has her own little problems . . . and the same struggles I have."

Schaffner urged James to look up another client of his, a neighbor in the vicinity of Plascassier, a forty-four-year-old American who wrote about wine and food (in French) for the magazine *Cuisine et Vins de France.* Richard Olney yearned to write a *real* French cookbook for Americans. He'd found *Mastering the Art of French Cooking* simply ridiculous, fussy and inauthentic and lacking the true spirit of France. Simon and Schuster told Schaffner they were interested. Surely James would have run into Richard by now, since he was a good friend of Sybille Bedford and Eda Lord, La Pitchoune's neighbors. And because of course Richard, too, was queer.

But James had met Olney before, briefly. It was in Paris in 1961, at a reception of an international food society. Richard was there with the editors of *Cuisine et Vins.* The party was crawling with Americans, though the only one Richard would remember was James, who was impossible for an aspiring food writer not to notice—not least because James had the power to open so many doors in New York.

:::

JOHN FERRONE ARRIVED in Plascassier in July 1967. James pleaded with him to help turn the chaotic pile of badly typed and scrawled-on manuscript pages of the American project into a book, just as he'd done with *Delights and Prejudices.* He'd pay him $5,000 and put off for later any talk of shared royalties. Ferrone said yes. It would likely take them another year to finish—perhaps they could return to Provence in the spring of 1968 to wrap things up, to hell with Little, Brown's schedule. "Ned is just going to have to wait for it," James told Schaffner.

In August, James traveled to Stockholm. "I'm in love!" he told Schaffner. "No not that—but this country. It is the most refreshing and enchanting place I've found in years. . . . The coolth and the breezes do nice things for my soul. I guess maybe that's what I've been needing for quite a while—that soul of mine gets well worn." He'd given the partial manuscript for the American book to Ruth Norman, his last visitor of the summer in Plascassier. He asked her to deliver it to Ferrone in New York. "I know it needs to be done over well but I trust it's good."

James visited Oslo, then went on to Berne to meet Gino. They rented a car and drove to Lausanne—the Hotel Central-Bellevue and the room where James had written the first draft of *Delights and Prejudices*. He wanted to look out again over Lake Geneva, to anchor himself in it. The world seemed to twirl so fast these days.

In May 1968, as James turned sixty-five and the American book was still far from being done, his depression returned. He felt it as a persistent numbness, impossible to shake.

"I take a very dim view of the . . . book and feel that it is never going to be finished," he wrote to Schaffner from Pasadena; he was doing a series of cooking demos with Philip Brown in L.A. "It was the greatest mistake I ever did to take it on, of this I am certain. It has no idea in my mind and so far I feel it is nothing—absolutely nothing. I still may just pay back the royalty bit by bit for I can't see it at all and have no feeling of its form or content whatsoever. It is a colossal bore to me at this time."

His impulse was to run, again to exile himself, this time someplace even the ghosts couldn't find him. "What I should do had I the money to do it with," he told Schaffner, "is to get away for three to four months and do nothing but think—and that in a place where I've never been before and get collected instead of going along completely fagged all the time and without a thought in my head."

Schaffner tried to rally him. "It seems to me that anything you have to say about any aspect of American food is going to be of value and will have your own unique knowledge and the effect of your personality to give it color and flavor." Schaffner told James he didn't see how he could fail to produce anything but a significant book. Plus, he said, it might even get James back on TV, maybe make him as rich as Julia.

"The climax of all your previous triumphs," Schaffner said, "and [it] should, like Julia's, lead you on to a successful television career. . . . You have within that magnificent cranium of yours all the knowledge, plus the wit and charm, for expressing it gracefully and attractively, which so many of your rivals and counterparts lack."

James didn't escape to someplace he'd never been. He returned instead to Harvey Welch and Halsey Jones's softly blue-gray house in Surf Pines, with its spectacular view across mounded beach grass to Tillamook Head. "Coming here to Gearhart has been the best thing in the world for me," he told Schaffner. James felt like another person, and wholly himself. "It's amazing to think in this age that you can come back to some things you knew sixty years ago and still find the Indian paintbrush and the tons of wild strawberries and broom in the same spots and the beach as peaceful as it still is. And the deer walk out on the road and watch us with little fear. And I'm sure people still lose their virginity on Strawberry Knoll as most of us did and still ride horses up the beach."

By June 1970, the book he'd begun four years earlier and was still incomplete had a title: *James Beard's American Cookbook*, or else *The American Cookbook by James A. Beard*. When it came to the nation's food, James had earned equal billing.

: : :

ON THE MUGGY NIGHT of June 28, 1969, a Saturday, James saw an old friend in New York: Lloyd Rigler of the Adolph's Meat Tenderizer Company, visiting from Los Angeles. They met for dinner and spoke of business and opera. Earlier that morning, a rebellion had erupted in Greenwich Village, not a three-minute walk from James's house. At 1:20 a.m., eight members of the New York Police Department launched

what they no doubt thought would be a routine raid on a low-life mafi-
oso bar where queers clustered like roaches. At the Stonewall Inn at 53
Christopher Street, the cops scoured the interior with searing lights.
They rounded up the two hundred patrons: standard procedure. Outside, they released all except the bar's employees and the crowd's most
extravagant queens.

The chaos that followed blurred everyone's recollection of events.
Marsha P. Johnson was among the drag queens and trans women who
hurried to the scene in the first surge of protest, and who whipped purse
and pocket change at the cops and screamed. The police ran back to the
bar and barricaded themselves. Someone tossed a rock from the street,
smashing a second-floor window above the bar's entrance. The shouts
and sirens, the screams and broken glass, the chants from the chorus-
girl kick line when police tried to clear the street—James and Gino
would have heard it all.

James had known bars like the one at the Hotel Astor, and of course
Felix's, where queers were tolerated if they followed the rules. And
everybody knew that there were seedy trade bars near Times Square
where you could get rolled by blackmailers. Even in Paris, on the Left
Bank, the straight old *patronne* turned a blind eye to the boys being
picked up in her establishment. But a bar where queers *demanded*
accommodation, as if it were a right: James had glimpsed them long
ago, as a young man in London, and in Paris long before the war. Mys-
tery and romance curtained off the very idea of those places. Imagine
being part of a generation—this generation of 1969—that wore queerness not as something to regret but as a badge of pride; a generation
that could flaunt rules of conduct that had been built up forever. It was
outrageous. It was terrifying.

Agitators continued to mass in Sheridan Square all the next day and
into a second night of revolt; the shouts continued until about four on
Sunday morning. Protests went on for another two days, and then grad-
ually diminished, but on Wednesday, when the *Village Voice* landed on
newsstands with an incendiary report on the uprising it referred to as
"fag follies," boys and girls and drag queens massed outside the paper's
offices and threatened to burn it down.

What happened on Christopher Street that week left marks as defining and indelible as a keloid burn scar. The revolt launched the popular queer civil rights movement like a Saturn V rocket, to flare in the atmosphere above the United States and Western Europe and linger like the dark spots on a retina. That week in 1969 changed forever the life of Greenwich Village, along with the comfortable, older, professional, closeted homosexuals like James and his friends.

They were men, mostly, who had built lives of equilibrium in the West Village. They had their brunches and dinner parties, and the last thing they needed was a lot of black and Latino kids—also drag queens and dirty rebellious types—taking the A train down from Harlem and the Bronx and starting trouble that would attract even more police. Queer men and women of James's generation in the Village had everything to lose and weren't convinced they had anything to gain. In October 1969, the month the Stonewall Inn shut down, *Time* magazine ran a cover story called "The Homosexual in America." "Their new militancy makes other citizens edgy," *Time* wrote, "and it can be shrill."

Suddenly, to be fully gay meant coming out of the closet to seize your rights and take your place among a diverse citizenry, with no shame or fear. "Encouraged by the national climate of openness about sex of all kinds and the spirit of protest," *Time* wrote, "male and female inverts have been organizing to claim civil rights for themselves as an aggrieved minority."

But shame and fear were not things people of James's generation could fling away so easily, like pennies at cops. James had become a master at inventing myths about himself: He needed to. "We are . . . a people who walk in darkness," wrote Donn Teal (under the pseudonym Ronald Forsythe) four months before Stonewall, in an anguished plea in the *New York Times* for works of art—even groundbreaking ones, like Mart Crowley's play *The Boys in the Band*, which opened in April 1968 Off Broadway—to depict queers as anything but desperate or tragic. "We must create our own happiness in and of ourselves," Teal wrote. "It has not been prepared for us, we cannot seek it out among the classics. And among the great modern creations, we still look in vain for the *happy ending.*"

Dell took risks with *The James Beard Cookbook*, released in April 1959 as a cheap paperback splashed with a George Lazarnick cover portrait—some Dell editors worried that the platter of choucroute garnie d'alsacienne, a pork and sauerkraut dish, looked gross and fatty.
(Penguin Random House LLC)

Portrait of Clayton Triplette (artist unknown) in 1959, the year he started working for James.
(Courtesy of the James Beard Foundation)

With Julia Child in the backyard of 119 West Tenth Street;
photo by Julia's husband, Paul, May 1964.
*(Photograph by Paul Child. © Schlesinger Library, Radcliffe Institute,
Harvard University. ID W584789-1)*

In the kitchen at 119 West Tenth Street, with the famous pineapple
wallpaper; photo by Paul Child, May 1964.
*(Photograph by Paul Child. © Schlesinger Library, Radcliffe Institute,
Harvard University. ID W584788-5)*

Recipe comic drawn by Alfred Andriola (a Greenwich Village bachelor, like James), best known for the syndicated strip *Kerry Drake*, 1966.

(The Cartoonist Cookbook [Hobbs, Dorman & Company])

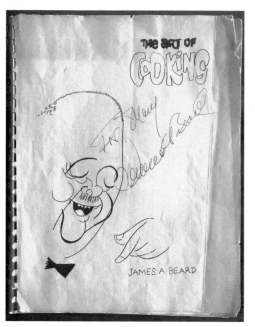

Class recipe handout featuring a caricature in the style of Al Hirschfeld for a 1967 cooking demonstration in Hartford, Connecticut; the Mary of the inscription is unknown.

With Richard Olney at Bramafam, Simone Beck's farmhouse in Plascassier, France, 1974.

(Courtesy of Judith Olney)

Release party for *Beard on Food*, Trattoria da Alfredo, New York, November 1974; Simone Beck is to the right of James; Richard Olney is seated on the floor, center, next to Carl Jerome, in the light-colored suit; John Ferrone is standing, third from right; José Wilson (in the sleeveless dress) is behind James's right shoulder.

(Dan Wynn, © Elizabeth Wynn, courtesy of the James Beard Foundation)

Leaving the *Beard on Food* party, New York, November 1974.

(Dan Wynn, © Elizabeth Wynn, courtesy of the James Beard Foundation)

Presiding over a cooking class in San Francisco in the late 1970s, with Marion Cunningham. *(Bob Sibilia,* Contra Costa Times; *courtesy of Chad Sibilia)*

With Sam Aaron of Sherry Wine and Spirits, 1978.

Sporting a gift box lid as
a party hat, 1979.
(Courtesy of Clark Wolf)

Evaluating wine
outside The Four
Seasons restaurant in
New York, with the
Seagram Building as
backdrop, 1980.
*(Eugene Cook, courtesy of
Claudia d'Allesandro)*

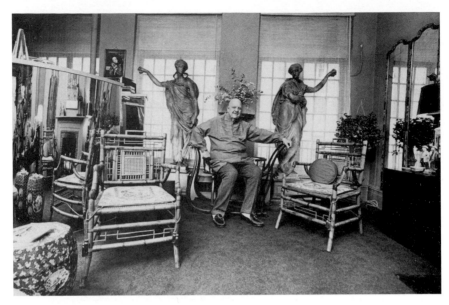

In the sitting room at 167 West Twelfth Street, New York, 1983.
(Dan Wynn, © Elizabeth Wynn, courtesy of the James Beard Foundation)

In Chinese changshan and Velcro slippers, at the entrance to his mirror-ceilinged sleeping alcove at 167 West Twelfth Street, 1984.
(Dan Wynn, © Elizabeth Wynn, courtesy of the James Beard Foundation)

At sixty-six, with his neighborhood, and the world, changed literally overnight, James was terrified of coming out, of shaking off the fiction of perpetual bachelorhood. When Stonewall was raided, he and Lloyd Rigler were just two discreet, opera-loving gentlemen out for an evening in Manhattan. Yes, life had not been prepared for men and women of James's generation; they had to make it themselves, out of nothing but talent, cunning, and will, however they could. Who cared whether everyone important in New York knew he was gay? James was a national celebrity, the Dean of American Cookery, and yet he was a pariah. (As *Time* pointed out, "63% of the nation considered homosexuals 'harmful to American life.'") Maybe there were subtler ways of coming out than shouting in Sheridan Square. Maybe there was a longer, less exposed road to the happy ending.

In 1971, an aspiring young chef from a wealthy family in Lima, Peru, appeared at West Tenth Street to introduce himself. Felipe Rojas-Lombardi was twenty-six and beautiful (a "Peruvian Adonis," purred Richard Olney), with dark, soft eyes and a look of perpetual sweetness. He'd been in New York since he was eighteen, and despite his gentleness, it was clear Felipe had ambition. He'd brought a man he introduced as his business manager, a forty-year-old former B-movie actor from Hollywood, Tim Johnson. Johnson had chefs' jackets custom made for Felipe, tailored to show off his slim physique and cut low at the neck to expose a sexy tangle of chest hair. It was clear to James that Johnson and Felipe were lovers. Such a degree of obviousness, James knew, was dangerous: a career killer.

James took Felipe under his wing, as an assistant for cooking demos. Somebody had to explain to these kids, to show them how to protect themselves.

: : :

LITTLE, BROWN PUBLISHED *James Beard's American Cookery* in May 1972, an unsettling month at home and abroad. America's war in Vietnam thrashed with bloodier force, after the United States and South Vietnam walked out of the Paris Peace Talks when the North refused further concessions. President Richard Nixon ordered the mining of harbors in the North and a searing new aerial bombing called Operation Linebacker. "The bastards have never been bombed like they're going to be bombed this time," Nixon told National Security Adviser Henry Kissinger. That month, the Watergate burglars broke into the Democratic National Committee's offices in Washington, DC, and slipped wiretaps into phones. And in Rome, a Hungarian-born geologist, Laszlo Toth, slipped a rock hammer into St. Peter's Basilica and struck fifteen blows to the left forearm of the figure of the Virgin in Michelangelo's monumental *Pietà*, while shouting, "I am Jesus Christ, risen from the dead!" He left a wrack of fear and shattered marble.

Large and substantial and printed on stock that glowed with the delicate amber tone of true Jersey cream, *James Beard's American Cookery* was more than a cookbook. It was bedtime reading for Americans who found comfort in its implicit celebration of traditional values. Even as James argued that a distinct American cuisine existed, he was also delivering a lament for the destruction of so many of the nation's once-pristine natural resources, and the degrading of its native foods. The book was an 875-page elegy for America.

Little, Brown gave *American Cookery* the tea-stained look of an heirloom, with archival-looking type and Earl Thollander's sketches of antique kitchenware, based on items in the Oakland Museum of California and his wife's collection of thrift-store finds. Even the jacket illustration of a harvest still life in mod 1970s earth tones, beneath a log cabin with a smoking chimney, spoke of American folk charm. In fact, it was the art of a true primitive, Little, Brown editor and amateur artist Mary Purcell.

But just as *Delights and Prejudices* isn't quite autobiography, *American Cookery* isn't quite a historical survey of cooking in the United States. Rather it's James's proposition—which he argues with the force of personality—that America possesses something analogous to France's *cuisine bourgeoise*: a genre of humble everyday cooking that aims for simplicity, honors flavor over dubious thrift, and achieves perfection using fine ingredients. Its focus is primarily on the contributions of America's European immigrants.

The creators of that tradition were mostly women writing for other women. In his dedication in *American Cookery*, James calls the authors of the nation's food traditions "my favorite great ladies of the American kitchen." He lists seven: Philadelphia's Eliza Leslie, author of ten pre–Civil War cookbooks; Mrs. T. J. Crowen of New York, who wrote *Mrs. Crowen's American Ladies Cookery Book* of 1847; the prolific Sarah Tyson Rorer, who produced recipe books in the second half of the nineteenth century; Fannie Merritt Farmer, whose *The Boston Cooking-School Cook Book* first appeared in 1896; Irma Rombauer of *The Joy of Cooking*; James's dear, departed Helen Evans Brown; and June Platt, whose 1953 culinary memoir *The Best I Ever Ate* helped inspire *Delights and Prejudices*.

That roster implied that James's focus in the more than eight hundred pages that followed would be a kind of mechanical conjuring of the past, like the talked-about new Animatronic spectacle at Walt Disney World in Florida, called The Hall of Presidents, which made life-size mannequins of John Quincy Adams and Abe Lincoln lurch and click and come to life. Instead, the book was a script (the word James used to describe it) made up of recipes and cooking techniques that traced his life in food. And because James had been the face of food in the United States for a generation, his fingerprints on it automatically made a dish American.

If anyone had the misconception that *American Cookery* was a historical cookbook, all they'd have to do is turn the page from the introduction to find the chapter "Cocktail Food," with variations on the same dips, cheese logs, and chilled poached shrimp James had been including in his books for decades. There are antique recipes and quaint regional ones in *American Cookery*—Blushing Bunny and Tyler Pie—but they serve mostly as accessories or points of departure, like Elizabeth David's textual descriptions of evocative recipes in *Mediterranean Food*, and Helen's pungent and charming historical dishes in *Helen Brown's West Coast Cook Book* and *The Virginia City Cook Book*: as inspiration, authenticity markers, and conjurers of mood.

Eleanor Lowenstein of the Corner Book Shop on Fourth Avenue near East Eleventh lent James countless antiquarian cookbooks and advised him on research. But James had other sources besides dusty books for the more than fifteen hundred recipes that ended up in *American Cookery*. Katie Laughton (Cathrine Laughton Hindley), his first collaborator for the book, provided many of the baking recipes: Eier Kringel, Lebkuchen, Gingerbread Men, Chocolate Potato Cake, Old-Fashioned Six-Layer Cake, Lazy Daisy Cake, and on and on. Many were copied exactly or showed up with slight tweaks from Laughton's 1946 *Mary Cullen's Northwest Cook Book*, published by the Portland daily *Oregon Journal* (most tweaks involved upping the amounts of butter, which in 1946 was still being rationed).

Ever stingy with acknowledgments, James failed to note the sources of specific recipes, although he did thank Laughton on the acknowledgments page for "testing and research" and for being "a most satisfactory consultant." Many of the European baking recipes—such as Génoise—he took from *The Art of Fine Baking*, by his late protégé Paula Peck (he even credited Peck for her Melting Tea Cake). Likewise, he failed to acknowledge the source of the Snickerdoodles on page 705, which he requested from France in a letter to Robert Stevenson of Chillingsworth Inn on Cape Cod. But James was gracious to an old enemy. Not only did he name the recipe on page 792 Jeanne Owen's Corn Bread, he called her "a brilliant cook and stalwart disciple of good living." Well, the book *was* James's grand reflection on food that had meant something to him over the long span of his life. He made sure he'd go down in history as magnanimous.

James's instincts in assembling his sources were right. Many of Katie Laughton's recipes had started out as reader submissions to the *Oregon Journal*. She had tested and refined them, but they still held on to their Western folk charm and preserved on their roots the soil of the place where James had been a child. They expressed something about James. Same with Peck's more elegant recipes, which spoke of Paris and Vienna and the places where he had sought escape as an adult.

The recipes in *American Cookery* appear like snapshots pried from the pages of old scrapbook albums, made to serve as pixels in a blown-up portrait of James. There's Elizabeth's cream of tomato soup and Harry Hamblet's fried oysters, recipes from Eleanor Hirsch, whose family owned the Meier & Frank department store James knew as a boy, the Portland Women's Exchange, and he even quotes a recipe for spiced salmon from Amanda Reed, whose husband, Simeon, is the namesake of Reed College. There's Mabelle Jeffcott, Mary Hamblet, and Helen Evans Brown (James even credits her in two of the five recipes he's slipped in), plus Elena Zelayeta, Cecily Brownstone, and Julia Child's sister-in-law Freddie.

He borrows without credit from Louis P. De Gouy's *The Gold Cook Book*, Imogene Wolcott's *The Yankee Cook Book*, and Marjorie Mosser's *Good Maine Food*, and slips in recipes from his own books: *Cook It Outdoors, How to Eat Better for Less Money,* and *The Complete Book of Outdoor Cookery.* He credits recipes from the Coach House in New York, the Palace in San Francisco, and Betty Groff's Pennsylvania farmhouse restaurant.

Woven into *American Cookery* is a kind of secret record of twentieth-century gay migration to cities from across the country and beyond its shores. Slaw with Egg Dressing traveled from Iowa to Los Angeles along with Bob Balzer, the queer wine writer and high-end grocer. Lemon Cake Pudding was an old recipe Frank Hearne (Emil Kashouty's partner) brought to New York after fleeing family in Texas. Lebanese American Emil lent James a handful of his mother's Middle Eastern recipes: Lentil Soup with Chard and Lemon (*Adas bi Haamud*) and Kibbeh Naye. James chronicled dishes queer exiles kept alive.

Maybe the most surprising thing about *American Cookery* is that James's vision of an American *cuisine bourgeoise* is, at heart, French. Take away the colonial curios and Victorian knickknacks and the book represents the ripening of a message James began to articulate in 1949 with *The Fireside Cook Book*: that an American cuisine is possible by grafting native ingredients onto simple French methods.

An extraordinary number of recipes in *American Cookery* are straight-up French, with sometimes weak arguments about why they should be considered naturalized, from onion soup ("believed to be typically French, but it was brought to this country a century and a half ago") and ratatouille ("came from Provence in '40s . . . few dishes have gained such popularity in the United States"). But it's really more the structure of many recipes, the underlying techniques and reliance on butter, cream, vinaigrette, stocks and court bouillon, browning, and reduction that reveals the French heart of *American Cookery*. And that's because James regarded France as the place where people ate beautifully because each ingredient was perfect in its own way.

"There is something about the very air of France that makes gourmets out of us all," James wrote in a draft for a 1955 article about eating around the world. "Perhaps it is an aroma, imperceptible and omnipresent, covering the whole land—the fragrant steam of poule-au-pot being cooked in ten million kitchens, the scent of baking bread in the boulangeries of ten thousand villages, the bouquet of thirty million bottles of wine being opened every day." France was the model, the quintessential place of delight in eating and drinking.

The idea of French cooking in America was moving away from fancy recipes to focus on a certain approach to cooking, a dedication to quality and simple techniques. American cooks needed to learn that lesson—to apply the things we found in our markets according to French principles and find luxury in plainness.

American Cookery was always supposed to contain James's accrued food wisdom. It's there, just behind Blushing Bunny. For nearly a quarter of a century, at a time of unprecedented change and upheaval in American life, James had been a constant. For some Americans, deeply unsettled by what seemed to be a dismantling of the nation they knew—seeing riots and rebellions, and new calls for civil rights and equality play out on the evening news—the idea of a unifying food identity was welcome comfort.

:::

JAMES'S FRIENDS SENT private notes of praise. "I spent most of last night thumbing through your magnum opus," Pat Knopf scribbled, "and it is magnificent." Elizabeth David sounded a measured hurrah: "For certain it will be a very great seller, and a great classic." Julia Child was effusive: "A stupendous achievement. . . . It looks and reads like the definitive Jim. How did you ever do it! Salutations on a real block buster." She drew hearts and a cupid's arrow on her letter in red felt-tip pen. M. F. K. Fisher thought it marvelous, though its length made the physical book rather heavy to pick up and hard to hold. "You have definitely proved your point," she wrote, "that there is an American cookery. And you have done it with such deftness!"

Others were critical—in public.

In 1971, a burned-out Craig Claiborne stepped down as the *New York Times* food editor and chief restaurant critic. His replacement was Raymond Sokolov, an arts writer and ex–Paris correspondent for *Newsweek*. At a time when everything in America seemed to be changing so fast, Claiborne seemed stale, if not reactionary. Sokolov brought from Paris a new whiff of the counterculture.

He was only thirty-one when a review copy of *James Beard's American Cookery* landed on his desk. Instead of treating it like the long-awaited masterwork by the eminent Dean of American Cookery, he reviewed it alongside two other Americana-themed cookbooks: Atheneum's *Home Made,* by Sandra Oddo, and a ninety-five-cent Popular Library paperback, *Edith Bunker's All in the Family Cookbook*, a tie-in with the CBS Saturday-night sitcom that launched in 1971—a marketing novelty, ghostwritten by a guy who did *Playbill* write-ups for Broadway shows. Sokolov's joint review was the equivalent of reviewing Leonard Bernstein's *Mass* alongside the 1971–72 season of *The Brady Bunch*. They were roughly contemporaneous, but pounding them to fit the same story would say less about the works and more about the reviewer's will to wield a hammer.

That was especially true since *Edith Bunker's All in the Family Cookbook* appeared a whole year before the other books: the mail clerk didn't just happen to drop all three into Sokolov's in-basket on the same day. He made a point of dredging up Edith Bunker to stand next to James, a severe act of putting him in his place. For the first time in his career, and for the biggest book he'd ever done, the *New York Times* treated him like just another cookbook author, a man out of touch with the times, who didn't grasp the complexity of food in the United States.

Oddo was a New York City journalist who moved upstate to live simply, amid woods and pastures. She revived American recipes from just after the Civil War and adapted them only minimally. In the searing and pessimistic year of 1972, Oddo found solace in the barely modified formulas of what looked, if you turned away from the TV evening news, like halcyon renewal. Her book, *Home Made*, was countercultural in the way that a crazed and patina-covered stoneware preserving crock was a radical substitute for Corning Ware. The book's cover called it "An alternative to super-market living . . . Recipes from the nineteenth century, rescued, reinterpreted, and commented upon." Sokolov loved it.

"[Oddo] thinks . . . that the way our self-reliant forefathers cooked had a special, down-to-earth genius to it," he wrote. "And she deplores what America has contributed to the art of the kitchen in this century." Thus, James and his work would represent everything bad about twentieth-century American food.

It was foolish to try to define anything as diverse and sprawling as American cooking. "America is not a homogeneous nation state like France," Sokolov wrote. "And American cooking . . . is a federation of recipes that has grown up with local roots." Ironically, James agreed. In the introduction to *American Cookery*, he calls his book "simply a record of good eating in this country with some of its lore," in spite of what he acknowledged were American food's "grotesqueries." *American Cookery* was what James said it would be in his earliest conversations with Ned Bradford: a record of everything he knew about food.

Julia Child's confidante Avis DeVoto clipped the *Times* review and sent it to La Pitchoune. Julia was furious.

"A rather quick note while our garlic soup is on the boil," she wrote to James. "That little snip—it's like a gnat buzzing around the head of Zeus. Seems to me that little chap is getting a bit beyond himself."

Even Sokolov, privately, seemed to bow before the commanding Dean of American Cookery. "I am a long and great admirer of you and your work," he told James in a letter sometime after the *Times* review appeared, "and . . . whatever I may have written was done in the spirit of a zealous acolyte."

To readers old enough to remember a time before the dumbing down of eating in America—the soggy, paper-wrapped fast-food hamburgers, antiseptic supermarket aisles, synthetic whipped dessert top-ping, and frozen dinners in flimsy foil trays—James became a kind of national hero. Many wrote to thank him for keeping alive the memory of foods and recipes they feared had gone extinct.

A native of northern Michigan, Avis DeVoto wrote to applaud his inclusion of Cornish pasties, the kind British miners had brought to the upper Midwest. "You've got the recipe right," she told him—and Avis was hard to impress. *American Cookery* offered the balm of nostalgia and something more: hope for a future American food that remembered what was good about the past.

"Dear Mr. Beard," wrote sixty-nine-year-old Benson Eschenbach, a retired California architect who'd grown up in Pennsylvania. "I am an old man, and the eloquent testimony of *American Cookery* evoked childhood memories of a time almost forgotten—of bacon sweet and smoked, and Smithfield hams and Pennsylvania scrapple, called ponhaus—of cream, heavy cream in shiny tinned farm milk pails that wrinkled in thick, yellow folds." He enclosed a recipe for his mother's schneckenoodle cookies, a variation on snickerdoodles.

"I'm sure your files are replete with old recipes handed down thru the family for years and years," Eschenbach wrote, "but try it."

James had become the repository for the nation's mostly forgotten recipes, as if, staunch amid the flying wrack of shattering worlds, he'd preserved an endangered legacy, keeping it alive for a generation too busy waging revolution to know they'd someday want it.

CHAPTER 18

SALMON QUICHE À LA CARL

1972–1976

CARL JEROME WAS twenty-three and a faggot. Not politely or apologetically homosexual, not ambivalently gay, not ashamed or embarrassed, and not particularly interested in hearing what you had to say about it. Maybe you bookmarked the Bible passages condemning sodomy to use as talking points, rehearsed your disapproval, vaunted your doubts, professed your "tolerance," as long as men didn't act like girls or flame in the streets. That was your hang-up. Carl really didn't give a damn, which, honestly, would come to rather frighten James. And it would turn him on.

Carl had eyes like the mirror glaze on top of a bittersweet chocolate gâteau. He was bearded and hunky without being a muscle queen. Through the Oxford dress shirt Carl had donned before venturing to West Tenth Street to meet the Dean of American Cookery, James could sense the furriness of Carl's chest. You'd also see the same blue jeans he wore to brunch at the Eagle or a night at the Mineshaft, because Carl wasn't giving those up for anything. He'd worked for the right to flaunt them.

Carl was raised in the South. He was Jewish, a Yankee born in Brooklyn, and queer—in 1960s South Carolina, those were three strikes that had you out, and could literally get you knocked out cold on some sidewalk. Carl grew up learning how to carve protected spaces for himself, and he knew when to punch to defend them. But even the best fighter eventually gets tired. After college, where he studied sociology and psychology, he knew he had to escape, to move to New York City for an authentic existence in the capital of gay liberation.

Carl arrived in Manhattan at the start of summer 1972, looking for a job. He tried driving a taxi; it wasn't his scene. Food was the only thing Carl was really into. He tried cooking in restaurants but lasted only a few months (the adrenaline rush terrified him). A friend, Annemarie Huste, had been Jackie Onassis's private chef, until she blabbed to Weight Watchers about the ex–Mrs. Kennedy's diet and got herself fired. Jackie wanted her back. Annemarie declined. Instead, she recommended Carl, who'd taken a cooking course that summer and learned to make a few French dishes Jackie happened to love. The job paid $150 a week.

After lunch at Jackie's Fifth Avenue apartment on day three of Carl's tenure, the forty-three-year-old former first lady praised his cooking, especially his coeur à la crème, which she declared the lightest she'd ever had. But the next day she fired him. He asked too many personal questions, she said (he swore later that he'd asked none). After that, Carl spread a little dirt around for *Washington Post* syndicated columnist Maxine Cheshire. He told her Jackie's silver serving trays were pathetic, and her glasses were just that: glass, not crystal. He described the scandalous state of the kitchen, creeping with roaches, dry goods flecked with weevils.

Details of the family's shabby circumstances rippled through the many dailies that ran Cheshire's column. The lesson? No one should mess with Carl. He'd survived being gay in the South and besides, a liberated faggot did not go out like that, at the whim of a rich lady, without making some noise. It put him back where he'd started, though. Carl needed a job.

The thing to do, he decided, was try to work for a famous cook who could put him on the map. Julia, he knew, lived all the way up in Cambridge, so he wrote a beseeching letter to Craig Claiborne. Claiborne didn't answer. Carl then read that the James Beard Cooking School was ten blocks from his place in the Village. He looked in the telephone book and voilà: James A. Beard. He rang and the great man came on the line. James told him to stop by the house and they'd talk. It felt like a job interview, only Carl didn't know what the job was.

Carl looked nervous, James noted, and overwhelmed: by the house, by James's cologne, which Carl asked about, and James said it was from a London shop, Floris. They talked for twenty minutes—Carl was looking to get into food and wondered whether Mr. Beard had any suggestions. James knew this scenario: young and inexperienced person dazzled to meet the famous James Beard, who would give them a few platitudes about making it in the business before telling them to seek out a culinary school. Perhaps Mommy and Daddy could send them to the École Hôtelière in Lausanne? But Carl seemed different from the others.

James gave him a tour, pointing out the operatic wallpaper with the pineapples and the leaves that looked like flesh. James explained that pineapples were symbols of hospitality, with the frisson he'd put on that word, for the right guest, as a hint that maybe Carl could stick around and they could get to know each other. Carl didn't seem to notice—or, if he did, he didn't flinch. After he left, for days James couldn't stop thinking about Carl. So he called the number he'd scribbled on a notepad and asked him to come work for him. Clay, who'd been listening, gave James a look. James said Oh, now Babes, they'd find *something* for the young man to do.

On his first day, Carl opened mail. And since he'd been a cab driver, he became James's official driver—although James didn't own a car, and there were always taxis and hired limos and friends to provide rides uptown to Quo Vadis or the Met Opera.

At the end of his first day, after there was no more mail to open or answer and the telephone had slowed and Clay didn't need him to haul anything else down to the basement, Carl told James he was leaving and that he'd see him the following morning. James was seated on a couch.

James asked Carl if he could kiss him good-bye. Maybe he went too far, after Carl bent down, aiming for his lips instead of the cheek Carl offered, forcing Carl's mouth open to slip his tongue inside. Carl was a young man who could take care of himself, James thought. From the way Carl pulled back, James saw that he'd startled him. Carl hurried from the house, down the stairs and into the street. Another look from Clay.

Let's see if he comes back, James's shrug said, and next day he did. This time, though, when Carl said goodnight, James noticed he was standing eight feet away.

: : :

A NEW CLASS CYCLE was starting, and it was part of Carl's job, now that he was an adjunct of James's household, to observe it, standing by, ready to fetch any forgotten thing. José (pronounced *Josie*) Wilson, ex–food editor for *House & Garden*, was James's assistant for the classes, taking the place of Ruth Norman and the late Paula Peck.

The class was appalling. James was distant and removed, literally and figuratively. No longer did he stand at the center of his classroom grand piano, giving his students close instruction. After the cooking lesson, when everyone sat down to eat, James and José sat off by themselves, sequestered in the kitchen while the students ate in the salon. A dozen people had paid a stiff fee for a class with the Dean of American Cookery, and he was only peripherally there.

The next day, James asked Carl what he thought of the class. Carl said it was terrible. He didn't think the students learned anything. James's teaching was poor, and when the lesson was over, James and José should have eaten with the students, not at their own table in the kitchen.

Carl was a bulldog. James saw his ambition; he asked Carl to assist with the classes. At the next class, James took his new assistant's advice. He stood in the center of the U-shaped counter. Later he sat with the students.

Though James hadn't realized it, it's what he'd been looking for: a new identity for the school, new energy and vitality, a youthfulness and focus James hadn't felt in some time. Even before Carl reached his six-month anniversary as assistant at the James Beard Cooking School, James named him director. José faded from the classes.

James had good reason to want to inject fresh blood into the school. By 1971, the number of home-based cooking schools in New York City had surged. Would-be students could choose from dozens of classes. You could learn basic Chinese cooking in Grace Chu's apartment on the Upper West Side; in a modern kitchen upstairs from the Oriental Country Store on Mott Street in Chinatown, you could learn to make the recipes Virginia Lee had picked up recently in Taiwan and Hong Kong; you could master regional Northern Italian cooking in Marcella Hazan's kitchen on West Fifty-Fifth Street; immerse yourself in the cuisines of Mexico with Diana Kennedy (advanced instruction in tamales and mole Poblano was extra); learn French cooking in Lydie Marshall's renovated brownstone in the West Village; and take private lessons of your choice at the Upper East Side home of Helen Worth, whose shtick was technique, what she called her "reasons-behind-the-recipes" method.

The most stylish classes were in the Upper East Side apartment of Perla Meyers. With minimal makeup, an unfussy hairstyle, and a penchant for wide slacks that flared to the hems, Meyers captured the mood of health-conscious Manhattan in 1973. She was born in Vienna and had lived in France, Spain, and West Germany. She spent summers in Europe, as an unpaid *stagiaire* in a different multistarred restaurant every year. In her cooking school, which she called the International Kitchen, she talked about cooking with the seasons, about shopping for produce just harvested or growing your own, about cooking with a light touch: no heavy sauces to mask the deliciousness of ingredients in their pristine state.

James, of course, had been writing about buying from farms and market stalls and European "peasant food" for years, but Perla Meyers provided a generational shift. Instead of advice and opinion from an old man with jowls and a body that represented excess, Meyers delivered a gospel of fresh, seasonal cooking with an implied connection to health and vigor and looking amazing, living close to the garden not as a hippie but as a young, stylish New Yorker equally at home in Paris or Milan.

James's fussy antique crockery, wallpapers, and copper lavabo mounted on the wall seemed fuddy-duddy. He still had Carl—James's "able co-star," in the words of newspaper cooking columnists Carolyn Flournoy and Marilee Harter. They noticed James's "black-haired, bearded young associate." Carl looked good in a showy striped dress shirt with the sleeves folded back to midforearm and a second button at the collar left undone so you saw the patch of chest fur: seductive yet professional. Carl's hands garnishing a platter of Lamb Marrakesh for a class were sexy, and so was Carl's backstory —his experiences as a cook, Flournoy and Harter reported, ". . . in the kitchens of the world's 'beautiful people,' " which must have meant his four infamous days with Jackie and Ari Onassis.

And Carl was smart and capable, with a "computer bank mind . . . quite literally a walking encyclopedia of culinary lore." James lusted after Carl, yes, but was clear-eyed enough to see the charm his new director exerted on students.

José knew far more than Carl did about food and cooking. She was a talented editor, a good writer—like Isabel and Ferrone before her, she knew how to conjure the timbre of James's voice to the typed manuscript page. In 1970, she revised and updated *How to Eat Better for Less Money* for Simon and Schuster, who'd acquired it and thought to capitalize on the US recession that had begun in 1969. It was selling. And while José had a wicked sense of humor, she didn't exactly show charisma with students. At a time when Perla Meyers and Graham Kerr were stars, Carl swept the dust away from the bric-a-brac. James at sixty-ninc lacked the energy and stamina to refresh the classes alone.

Rehabbing the classes was a crucial task. In 1972, James told a writer for *Life* magazine that he had a waiting list of five hundred—an outrageous boast even for James, and a lie. There was no waiting list. Even if his classes had lost some of their luster, James was still a master of spinning shiny magic.

: : :

HOW ELECTRIC and yet how wearying it was to exist in James Beard's household. Carl took it all in, every tip and shortcut of the master's, noting every life lesson and showman's trick. He studied how to taste and season and trust his senses, and he filed away all the gossip about the writers and editors and PR people he should never trust. James taught Carl how to fake it "on stage," how to turn a disaster into a demo that got the housewives clapping. James mentored Carl in how to roll into Houston, Cleveland, or Rochester and in ten minutes locate a source for the veal scallops and fresh tarragon that the lazy and incompetent local organizer had failed to find.

Yet James was demanding—constantly, with practically no letup—for twelve or fourteen hours a day. James left Carl no time to have a social life, certainly not a boyfriend. James knew that what he had to offer someone like Carl was a priceless apprenticeship, and James had known from the beginning that Carl had the kind of ambition to make him want to stay—at least for the time being. For anyone who wanted to open a food business or write for the magazines, James's friendship was crucial. James was grooming his successor, his chosen heir.

And James was hopelessly in love with Carl. Some of James's closest friends thought James was dangerously in love with Carl. Mary Hamblet, who spoke to James by telephone every Sunday from Portland, knew her old friend was perilously close to losing his judgment, the discretion he'd worked so hard at keeping aloft these many years. She wrote to tell James he was being a fool. Judith Jones called James to tell him his obvious infatuation was unbecoming, as well as dangerous to his public image. It seemed that everyone hated Carl. They gossiped and clucked. They resented his closeness to James. It was throwing everything out of equilibrium, James's careful balance of private and public.

Carl would get to the house early every day, not long after Clay. James, of course, was an early riser. He often had insomnia and would be bored after making his early calls and eager to get to work. Usually, he would be having breakfast alone; early on, when Carl first started, James would have breakfast with Gino, but then that stopped. James had never really been in love with breakfast anyway.

Carl would get to work sifting papers, opening mail and answering queries, or testing recipes. In 1974, when Little, Brown proposed a revision to *James Beard's Fish Cookery*, James went through a copy of the

1954 original with a red felt-tip pen, crossing out recipes that seemed dated and ones he knew didn't quite work and weren't worth the time to rehab. Carl had to retest several of the recipes—sometimes three a day to keep up with the publisher's schedule. Some recipes had to be adapted for the popular new food processors; many others needed to be retimed according to a Canadian method James had recently discovered (ten minutes of cooking for every inch of thickness). Others—like boiled lobster—had been wrong to begin with. When *American Cookery* came out, Avis DeVoto told James that she and Julia were convinced that the time he'd given for cooking lobsters was shockingly insufficient ("lobsters are so damn expensive that an undercooked one is a real tragedy"). The salmon pie needed to be redeveloped as salmon quiche and there needed to be a footnote about the imminent extinction of the grotto sculpin. The list went on and on.

Carl would cook lunch for anyone who was in the house: James, Clay, and José at the beginning, though later it included Emily Gilder, the office secretary, and of course Gino—he was always somewhere in the rafters now that he'd quit architecture.

Sometimes Clay would cook, since the phone seemed to ring constantly, and in the afternoon there was a lot of paperwork—more letters, doing the planning and logistics for upcoming demos on the road. Dinner was usually out, at the Coach House or Trattoria da Alfredo. James expected Carl to join him. They might go to The Four Seasons, where Tom Margittai and Paul Kovi would lavish them with food, perhaps even a new dish the Swiss-born chef, Seppi Renggli, was developing. They opened bottles for James. A stream of people James knew came by to chat. The meals dribbled on for hours.

There was no structure to the daily schedule. Every hour followed James's lead, his decision about what to do next. The long, looping days ran on constant orders from James about what to take on next, which critical thing needed attention pronto and which could wait—or maybe stop the thing you started and do this other thing first. There was no filing system. James had baskets where he'd drop papers, many different baskets scattered around his shelves, with no visible sense of order. But if Carl needed to find something—a letter or a recipe or a contract—

somehow James knew which basket Carl should search. Carl tried to impose an organizing system; it died being born. James did not want organization, or an end to the chaos and his own relevance.

If things got a little quiet, James would say, "I'm bored, let's go downstairs and make a recipe for the column," and Carl would have to follow him to the kitchen and roll up his sleeves. Setting up cooking demos in halls and department stores and suburban-mall cookware boutiques was a physical grind (there was no way James could have managed on his own) yet exhilarating. And the travel was amazing. Carl flew to London and to Venice to make appearances, sitting in first class, with the overflow of attention settling on Carl.

Stewardesses brought drinks and food in never-ending succession. The pilots would come back to pay genial respects and make sure the crew was taking good care of him. The actor Van Johnson, who found himself on a flight with James, asked how he could get into one of his cooking classes. James laughed his twinkly laugh and said the classes were so booked up maybe Johnson would have luck next year, or the year after that. Then he sent Johnson a drink. Less august passengers might approach James nervously and tell him that their wives had *just* made his recipe for roast beef or salmon loaf or raisin pie. Then they'd ask whether he wouldn't mind signing a plane-ticket envelope or a cocktail napkin just so she'd believe her husband had *actually* been on an airplane with the great James Beard and wasn't just pulling her leg.

Wouldn't mind? Wouldn't *mind?* What a laugh, Carl thought. Absolutely hysterical. Because being asked to sign something—to sign anything—had become James's purpose. He was always looking for the next younger man to help and perhaps pursue—hoping to conquer him emotionally, which Carl had resisted.

But James had not made peace with having to keep his distance from Carl. He still held out hope that something more intense than the constancy of a business companion was possible. In 1974, they went to Miami together to stage demos for the opening of Burt Wolf's Good Cooking School in Burdines department store at the Dadeland Mall, a setup graced with palmettos and light. In the hotel, in James's room,

James was seated on the bed, wearing one of the white cotton robes he liked. Carl was talking, distracted, not looking at James.

James undid the tie of his robe and opened it, and he was naked underneath. James went on talking, in the exact same tone he'd used when the robe was closed. He went on casually, calmly talking about some detail of the next day's class, leaving it up to Carl to decide whether or not to accept this passive offer of a diversion and get closer to the master.

But Carl decided to look away, and James discreetly folded the flaps of his robe back across his midsection. Neither said a word about it later.

CHAPTER 19

LATE RASPBERRIES
FOR CHRISTMAS

∴ ∴ ——————————————————————— ∴ ∴

1972–1978

IN THE MIDDLE OF THE twentieth century, the Stanford Court Apartments was a place unfamiliar to genteel citizens of San Francisco. This was despite its privileged site at the corner of Powell and California, up which cable cars ascended on whirring machinery sunk into the street, while the flat, dinging sound of the cars' bells clanged at the intersection. The residence hotel was on a flank of Nob Hill, though by reputation firmly in the Tenderloin, a district respectable people thought of in part as a refuge for no-goods, libertines, and queers.

That changed in 1972, when, after a $17 million remodel, the Stanford Court reopened as a hotel for affluent visitors to San Francisco. The new owners modeled it after a fine hotel in Switzerland, an alternative to large American chains like Hilton and Sheraton that felt factory-assembled; the staff-to-guest ratio was almost one-to-one. The Stanford Court's motto was "For people who understand the subtle differences." Newspaper profiles presented James Nassikas, its part-owner and president, as the most creative hotelier since César Ritz. He'd made sure the Stanford Court's carpets were wool, the plants and flowers live and lush. Bona fide Empire and Italian provincial antiques filled the lobby and guest rooms, including grand armoires for hiding vulgar-looking televisions (plus an additional TV in every bathroom, for guests who preferred to linger on the john and not miss a guest on *The Phil Donahue Show* or a minute of *The Waltons*). Every room had at least two phones, heated towel racks, soaps with botanical perfumes. All that in addition to elegant white cotton robes—they cost the hotel an astounding ninety dollars each—for guests who liked to shed their clothes yet not feel naked.

Above all, the Stanford Court was a hotel that honored guests' every request and enshrined their privacy. The staff studied their customers, placed crimson Cattleya orchids or single-malt Scotch in their suite if a guest liked them; stocked Comtesse chocolates from the Godiva boutique in New York or iced Caspian Sea beluga to attend their arrival. Guests were free to pursue delicate affairs or satisfy sexual urges without worry—the hotel provided extreme discretion, enabling appetites and shielding from scrutiny. It never revealed its guest lists, the names of the dignitaries, royalty, corporate executives, and film stars who stayed there. The security staff ejected reporters who tried to scope out arrivals.

Nassikas, who was in charge of food and beverage, opened a standalone restaurant in the hotel, Fournou's Ovens. Its centerpiece was a hearth and a bank of six wood-burning ovens with elaborate Victorian iron doors, set in a wall of baroque Portuguese azulejo tiles. The restaurant had its own entrance to the street, and its own telephone number separate from the hotel. Nassikas designed Fournou's Ovens to compete with any high-end restaurant in San Francisco.

Restaurants in European hotels were elevated; in the United States, they were either serviceable coffee shops or expensive traps serving Continental-food clichés. The Stanford Court revived the city's legacy of French glamour with its coffee shop, Café Potpourri, which recreated the tea shop from the old City of Paris department store, then being demolished.

In July 1972, not long after the hotel debuted, James received a letter from the Stanford Court's general manager, Michael Kay. Chet Rhodes of San Francisco's Convention and Visitors Bureau had told Kay that James would be in the city that fall, and Kay had taken the liberty of entering a reservation for James.

All of this (including, perhaps, the invisible legacy of the basement apartments in the Stanford Court's previous iteration) was perfect for James.

Much about San Francisco, actually, was perfect for James.

: : :

IN THE FIRST WEEK OF 1973, AN ITEM RAN IN *THE OREGONIAN*:

> In a Christmas note from James Beard, word is that he
> is finally going to do two master classes in cooking this
> spring—in Oregon. "The classes will be one week each, and
> each entirely different, with different menus and dishes.
> As with all my classes, they will be participation and lim-
> ited to 15 people each. Students may be men or women,
> and we plan to cook in the morning and have lunch." He's
> been asked so many times to do something like this on the
> coast, that it is entirely possible the sessions may be over-
> subscribed. . . . The teaching will take place at Seaside
> High School, with some field trips to restaurants, perhaps
> some berry-picking expeditions or clamming or picnics on
> the docket.

By June 1973, James looked defeated by age; he was a month past seventy. His eyes were sunk in deep hollows, surrounded by ruched layers of papery skin. There was a pensive set to his lips, under his pale gray bristly mustache. A fold in his neck rested on his Thai silk bow tie with orange and red stripes, set slightly askew. He was still James, of course; still telling anecdotes in the bland Seaside High School Home Economics kitchen and growling at his assistants. There was a sense of ennui about him here, though, from his perch on a high stool, wearing an apron in bright checks—orange, red, and pink, also of Thai silk—that didn't quite suggest cheer.

For the first daytime session, on crêpes, there were sixteen students. They'd come from Portland, Seattle, San Francisco, even New York. During the three-week summer classes—each week would have a new crop of sixteen students—the kitchen was organized into five stations centered in the classroom's cubicles, each with a range and sink and color-coded bowls and utensils. Three students would work together at each (one team had four), tackling a different dish in the daily five-course lunch menu. "I hope no one came expecting to lose weight," James said, to predictable twitters from the students. Marian Greenough, Seaside High's home-ec teacher, fluttered around the room, finding utensils that had gone missing, washing stray bowls and knives. In New York, Clay had packed up a dozen big crates of utensils for the class: pots, pans, knives, small appliances.

Opened in 1963, Seaside High School was a low, flat-roofed, ranch-style structure. The home-ec kitchen had a bank of large aluminum-frame windows set high in the wall, gazing at the sky; outside was a small courtyard with a garden. The school lay a mile and a half south of James's childhood cottage in Gearhart. It perched on the edge of the estuary at the mouth of the Necanicum River. You could walk out the kitchen's back door, through the courtyard and a parking strip, stand on the muddy beach, and look out on Tillamook Head rising above a strip of cypresses in the middle distance.

An obscure high school on a quiet estuary was a strange place for the Dean of American Cookery to haul his omelet pans and cleavers, his whisks and potato ricers, but James had a practiced retort for anyone who puzzled over it.

"Everyone was giving classes in Venice and Florence, Italy," he'd say, "so I thought it would be nice to do it in Seaside, Oregon—it's a wonderful place, with lots of good seafood, fruits and vegetables. I thought it would be an amusing idea." James had spent his career being iconoclastic, decrying gourmets and chichi cookery and snobs, but this was different. James was still popular, in fact legendary, but he wasn't exciting. That summer, Richard Olney would conduct a series of cooking lessons in Avignon, France; Perla Meyers was teaching a series called "Peasant Cooking: A Return to Freshness" from her garden in Connecticut, emphasizing fruits and vegetables. These were exciting, even sexy. James was slowing. He was circling home.

James prowled the class, ambling, checking on the students— middle-aged, mostly, more women than men, with nervous excitement for the first session. He caught Antoinette Hatfield trying to bury her thick, leathery crêpe in the trash. Someone had turned the heat up under a pan of mushroom duxelles and walked away. "Who turned this burner up high?" James growled. Another team's Benedictine soufflé was a bust—they'd forgotten to whip the egg whites to soft peaks before beating in the sugar. "You'll just have to do it over," he said firmly, with a quiver of exasperation. Behind him, Felipe Rojas-Lombardi, James's protégé and sometime class assistant in New York, smiled at the students, flashed his dark eyes with the long lashes, whispered, "We'll do it together this time," to Team Soufflé, whose members looked as deflated as their whites.

In a week, Felipe would be off to France to assist Olney in his Avignon classes. José Wilson, James's editorial assistant and ghostwriter, would arrive to take his place.

From his stool, James called out platitudes, polished over years of use in his New York classes. "There are only about fourteen basic recipes," he called out, in his clipped voice of professorial authority. "Everything else is a variation on one of them." And, "Cooking is very simple if you boil it down." He looked around the room, mugging to underline his well-worn gag. No one seemed to get the pun.

The classes spun along, though, a tribute to the resourcefulness and stamina of the team around James: Felipe and José, and especially Carl Gohs, a food writer based in Portland who'd helped test the bread book, who sourced the unsalted butter, heavy cream, seafood, meats, and produce for two five-to-eight-course meals, twice a day, for twenty people.

After three hours on the first day, the long table covered in vinyl tablecloths in the home-ec kitchen was covered in dishes for lunch: a many-layered crêpe cake spread with mushroom duxelles; rolled crêpes filled with crabmeat and drenched in curry sauce; baked Italian crêpes stuffed with sausage and ricotta; a chocolate crêpe cake; Crêpes Directoire (baked bananas folded into crêpes, doused with kirsch and ignited). The well-oiled machine of the James Beard Cooking School was still clicking and grinding.

:::

ONE OF THE STUDENTS in that first class was a fifty-one-year-old woman from California, amazed that she'd even made it to Seaside. Marion Cunningham was tall with blond, gray-streaked hair bunched back in a ponytail, a look of uncultivated glamour. She had wide eyes and high, lovely cheekbones that made obliques when she smiled. She had a sunny, freshly scrubbed look—rather like Doris Day, only lankier and more elegant.

She'd grown up in a working-class family in Glendale, east of Griffith Park in Los Angeles, the daughter of an Italian mother and an Irish father. She married a lawyer and they settled in LA. While her husband was at work, Marion would check out cookbooks from the public library, James's books in particular (*Fireside* was her favorite). After a while, her husband landed a job with a firm in Oakland. They bought a house east of there, in Walnut Creek, at the edge of a state park. Fruit and nut trees clustered on the property. From the dining room, there was a view out to Mount Diablo, which shifted dramatically with the seasons, from vivid green in winter to pale gold in summer. Horses and cattle roamed the valleys below. The Cunninghams had two children and kept horses. The marriage was difficult. Marion began to drink.

She'd always been agoraphobic; it was one her many phobias. She sometimes felt pursued by demons. She dreaded crossing bridges, fearing she'd lose control. Elevators terrified her.

Wine helped her feel better. She drank discreetly but from need, a medicating impulse. Eventually, she made herself stop. She read AA books and pamphlets but never attended a meeting. She learned the Twelve Steps and cleared her own path to sobriety.

In the late 1960s, her passion became cooking classes. She'd drive to San Francisco and take classes from Lonnie Kuhn, Joyce Goldstein, Mary Risley, Josephine Araldo. She attended for the knowledge she'd gain, yes, but largely for the social aspect, the ability to be with friends and meet strangers in the context of food. It eased her agoraphobia.

In 1973, a friend of Marion's, Betsy Pipe-Myer, read about James's classes starting in Seaside that June and urged Marion to go with her. Despite her phobia about flying, Marion said yes. The lure of taking a class from James—the master, her idol for so long—made her take a deep breath and buy the ticket. When it was time to board, she panicked. As Marion cried, her son told her that if she didn't get on the plane, she'd never go anywhere; she'd never do anything or be anybody. She boarded. It would be her first time leaving California.

She stayed in Seaside for two weeks, participating in two weeklong cycles. It was all just fun, she said. James was down to earth, not snobbish. There was a summer camp feel to it, a bonding and closeness with the other students. Always gregarious, Marion found the extreme sociability of the classes transforming. Before she left, she told James she'd be back the next year, and she said if he happened to need another assistant she'd be thrilled to volunteer. Everything—the classes and the camaraderie, the beach town—it was magical.

Marion saw food as a social imperative. Home cooking and sharing meals around the family table were essential to her view of the world, and they were imperiled. She never particularly cared for French food; Julia Child's books didn't interest her much, not the way James's American vernacular of home cooking spoke to her. The shared meals around the table during the Seaside classes, the cooperative and communal feeling, made a strong impression on her. She longed for a nation of shared tables and homemade meals.

By the time she returned to Walnut Creek, James had already written to her. There might be an opportunity to teach some classes in San Francisco soon, at Fournou's Ovens at the Stanford Court Hotel. It sounded like it might prove great fun, if she might be interested in helping with that.

Marion was finding life—perhaps her purpose—in cooking, for

advocating a way of eating communally that she felt was important. From outside, James was an odd teacher for this vision of families coming together around the table (clearly he was gay), yet he was able to gather up strangers—students from so many various places—and conjure a sense of fellowship around food.

For James, Marion had an oddball quality he recognized, someone marginalized by circumstances and whatever demons assailed her. She was the furthest from Greenwich Village queer, this suburban mother, but he nevertheless felt a rapport, the sense of Marion being a fellow traveler, as they said. He saw the fun in her.

She'd have to stop being so nice, of course. He could certainly teach her that.

As she waited for the Stanford Court classes to come together, Marion wrote to James in her signature pink Flair felt-tip pen. She was teaching classes on her own, in her small home kitchen and a nearby community center. She approached teaching with discipline, as a calling.

"I try new restaurants all the time, it's interesting and very useful information to pass on to my students. If I'm not eating, cooking or reading about food I'm shopping or sleeping[,] James—I feel I've received a gift to have a subject that has fulfilled these years so pleasantly. I am looking forward to your spring coming and helping you in your classes any way that is useful." Marion had joined the world.

::::

JIM NASSIKAS HAD proposed the cooking classes at Stanford Court when James first stayed there, in 1972. They started nearly three years later, in April 1975. James and Carl Jerome offered two weeklong sessions, each limited to a dozen students: one five-class session for beginners, the other an advanced seminar. The price for each was a rather astronomical $250. Two lunches and a dinner were included in the price. Marion Cunningham and Lonnie Kuhn assisted James and Carl; Chuck Williams (Williams-Sonoma took reservations and handled ticketing) was on hand, too.

James and Carl also taught two stand-alone Saturday classes ($50 each)—one on breads, the other on basic skills, for men only.

At the start of the first session, James gave his speech about abhorring snobbery, never mind that the students—ten women and two men—were well off enough to afford the fee. "We're not here to learn some special kind of cooking," he told them. "Instead, we are to become the arbiters of 'good cooking,' " pronouncing it as if he were putting quotes around it. "Everything that is good to eat." James wore a plaid shirt open at the neck, with voluminous sleeves; he wore his black, thick-framed eyeglasses. He looked vigorous. Eclecticism was on the rise, James told the students, standing before the extravagant tiled hearth. "Look at the new boys coming along, Paul Bocuse and others like him. They are taking food and cooking ideas from everywhere for their great restaurants." He described dragging Pierre Troisgros recently to the Coach House in New York. The French chef went crazy, James said, for corn sticks. Corn sticks! The world was opening up. Inspiration was all around. All that was needed was to trust your appetites.

Carl, wearing a windowpane-check dress shirt with rolled sleeves, was brisk and efficient. He showed the class how to bone ducks for ballotines, stuffed with forcemeat of ground ham and pork belly and roasted. He then demonstrated how to make boeuf à la ficelle, a rump roast suspended from string lashed to a wooden spoon set across a stockpot's mouth, and poached.

There was something in the air of San Francisco that made James feel invigorated.

Of course, James had a circle of gay friends in San Francisco, like some West Coast shadow of his Greenwich Village circle back when New York life was less complicated and ponderously byzantine and fewer people were traipsing through his house. There was Chet Rhodes, head of the San Francisco Visitors' Bureau. Also Gerald Asher, the wine writer, who lived in a large and gracious old apartment high up in a Spanish rococo building atop Russian Hill. It had panoramic views of the bay out to the Golden Gate.

There were Chuck Williams of Williams-Sonoma and Mike Sharp, his partner. They lived in a converted "earthquake cabin," a little clapboard shack built in Golden Gate Park after the 1906 catastrophe and eventually hauled up Nob Hill by some enterprising homesteader. It was a doll's house, all trim and lovely: beamed ceilings, everything painted pure white, walled with cookbooks and shelves of plates and French clay daubières and bean pots. Mike had been an antiques dealer when he met Chuck, and he stayed in the business. He collected old English oak furniture and Staffordshire ware on trips abroad as props for the kitchen store. Eventually Mike opened his own antiques shop on Sutter Street, four doors down from Williams-Sonoma, where he sold grand French objects to wealthy people and their designers. Mike furnished the earthquake cabin with smaller, more curious, and expressive pieces.

Chuck and Mike would host little dinner parties for James and his small San Francisco queer circle, maybe a New England boiled dinner, chicken and dumplings, or oyster stew.

One night in 1972, Gerald Asher took James to a quirky little eight-month-old place he'd discovered in Berkeley, dubbed Chez Panisse after a character in an old French movie trilogy. It was in a creaky 1900 wood-frame house with potted ferns and a few posters, and had mismatched china and silver, and almost all the staff looked like college kids. James would return every time he came to San Francisco. He gave it his highest praise in his 1974 roundup of the best and most interesting restaurants he had visited that year, this co-op venture of young people, the way they cooked French food, both classic and bourgeois dishes, with an exuberance that made up for the lack of finesse.

The lead owner, Alice Waters, a friend of Marion Cunningham, arrived at the Stanford Court after James's class one day, joining the usual throng of young chefs and other people who showed up to sit around Fournou's to chat: a woman who said she was writing a detailed book about Chinese cooking, Barbara Tropp; Patricia Unterman; Shirley Sarvis. He met the chef of Chez Panisse, Jeremiah Tower, at a party Marion threw for James in San Francisco. Tower was gorgeous, tall, with curly bronze-colored hair and cheeks that looked ruddy from sailing or something. He had presence and an intriguing kind of arrogance. He was someone James wanted to see again.

: : :

J AMES ALWAYS OCCUPIED the same digs at the Stanford Court: a two-bedroom corner suite on the fifth floor. One set of windows looked north to Pacific Heights, toward the mansions and elegant old high-rises. The other set looked east to the bay, the low-luster gray steel towers of the bridge, and the far hills of Oakland. After classes, James would hold an impromptu salon for friends. Jim Nassikas made sure to stock James's suite with an abundance of whatever he desired: bowls of mangoes the year when his doctor recommended a diet of them; raspberries (James's favorite) delivered to his room early one Christmas when James was there for the holiday. The raspberry season had been exceptionally late that year. James ate a large bowl of them with cream, looking out at the quiet city and the distant boats on the bay.

San Francisco was a place of sexual liberation, queer and otherwise. For James, it held out the possibility of sex, in part because of the hotel's discretion, but also for the privacy he enjoyed away from the fishbowl of home, where Clay and Gino were always watching and listening.

Here, James felt freer to ogle boys, this new generation, like Carl and even bolder, unafraid of presenting as queer in public, any time of day or night—even the clerks in shops and men on the street.

Almost from the first day Chuck Williams opened his store on Sutter Street in San Francisco, he sold kitchenware items by mail. In the 1960s, he sent out mailers featuring line drawings of the products by Mike Sharp. In 1972, Williams-Sonoma sent out its first formal catalog. The orders were filled in the dingy basement underneath Mike's antiques shop. By 1975, the first year of James's classes at Fournou's Ovens, Williams-Sonoma's holiday-catalog business was surging (especially for the bay-leaf wreath, introduced the previous year—a runaway smash).

In November 1975, James returned to San Francisco to rest up at the Stanford Court after a grueling five-month schedule that included classes in Seaside as well as in Venice's Gritti Palace Hotel. One day, James visited Mike Sharp at his shop. Mike took him below to see the bustling catalog operation, down the L-shaped wooden stairs to the dim basement lined with shelves of merchandise, where twenty or twenty-five young men (except for Ginny, who'd been there longest)—every one of them gay—were working to fill orders.

Chris Lenwell was one of them. A friend of Chris's, Mark, had a boyfriend who was a clerk at Williams-Sonoma. Mark recruited the seasonal catalog crew: queers in their twenties, like Chris, who spent their nights at discos like the Frisco Club and the Rendezvous and bars like The Stud, then worked temp jobs during the day to pay for partying and rent, in that order.

James showed up in the brick-walled basement every day of that trip, navigating the five wooden stairs down to the landing, where he'd slowly lower himself to sit. He'd observe the frenzy of boys with feathered hair parted in the middle, some with beards, in snug-ass flared jeans and flannel shirts and the odd tight-fitting faux–football jersey.

He made them laugh, telling them stories of queer life. To Chris, James seemed naïve, sitting there alone; he just wanted to entertain the boys, and in return get to look at them. James told them about the time in 1940 when he saw Laurence Olivier in *Romeo and Juliet* on Broadway at the 51st Street Theatre, and the audience was full of gay men stunned by Olivier's beauty. "There wasn't a dry seat in the house," James told them. Chuck and Mike were much more reserved gays, careful about not letting on about the truth of their relationship. James was more open, less cautious in San Francisco.

The catalog crew gave campy nicknames to people who descended to the basement, the names taken from Williams-Sonoma products. They called marketing director Wade Bentsen Corn Dolly, after a decorative wheat weaving. James was the Rolling Mincer, sharp cutting wheels at the end of a handle. They wobbled, the way James did when he came downstairs. And "mincer," well: That was just slang for "old fairy."

Had he known about his nickname, James would have laughed. San Francisco made him jubilant. Not least because of Louie.

: : :

IN 1975, Louis Worden was twenty-five and working on the front desk at the Stanford Court. He was muscled and solid, but there was gentleness in Louie's demeanor, a thoughtfulness, almost a feeling of tranquility. He was on the desk when James arrived in late April to conduct his first classes, with Carl Jerome and Jim Nassikas and the whole posse that always seemed to coalesce around James. James was three times Louie's age. Still, Louie was taken with him: James was funny and charming. Louie felt a tinge of recognition.

Louie had been at the Stanford Court practically since it opened, in 1972. He was working for a temp agency, in accounting, and was assigned to the hotel in that capacity. When that ended, the hotel offered him a full-time job at the desk.

The desk could be a grind. If any guest at the Stanford Court wanted to bitch about anything, it was almost always the desk clerk who got the earful; occasionally a guest would get Louie so mad he'd have to check himself from throwing a punch. Also, there were never any tips on the desk, so the pay was shitty. When a bellman spot opened up, Louie took it. The guests generally liked bellmen. They'd ask for tips on where to go, or ask a bellman to make a reservation, or ask if he could run out and pick up something up for them. If it were convenient (if a manager said *yes*), Louie would do it. Whenever James arrived, Louie would make sure to be on, ready to muscle his many bags and boxes upstairs.

Looking back later, Louie could see that James had flirted with him across the front desk the first time they met. (Louie wasn't the kind of kid to think anybody would want to flirt with him.) Louie thought James was just very, very nice, not condescending like a lot of the other guests.

On James's seventy-fifth birthday, in May 1978, Alice Waters gave a small dinner party for James at Chez Panisse, and James asked Louie to join them. Carl Jerome had a rental car, so it was the three of them plus Marion Cunningham at dinner, and Alice sat at their table. (Marion was always buzzing about Alice's brilliance.) James was ecstatic that night, over the cold poached snapper and bay shrimps, fettucine Alfredo, and porterhouse steak grilled on mesquite charcoal and served with housemade bread and garlic butter. He introduced Louie to the chef, Jeremiah Tower. Louie was overwhelmed by the whole experience. He hadn't been out to eat that much in his life and he was living pretty much paycheck-to-paycheck, basically just making rent on his apartment in the Mission. Another time, James asked Louie to go with him to a dinner party at Jim Nassikas's house in Marin County, where Danny Kaye (a real gourmet) was one of the guests.

The thing is, nothing at the Stanford Court happened without Nassikas knowing about it and giving permission for it. James's legs were really bad then: purplish and painful from the edema resulting from his heart struggles. He had to have his ankles and calves wrapped in bandages every morning and stuffed into compression socks; at night, it all had to come off before he could go to bed. Soon, Nassikas gave permission for Louie to come in early in the morning to help James, to wrap his legs after his bath. Likewise at night, when dinner was over and the last guest had left James's suite, Louie would knock and it would be just the two of them, talking, while Louie unwrapped James. They were moments of real connection.

Louie was in a bad situation with a man—it had gone on for years and would continue years longer. They talked about relationships. James recommended self-help books, including M. Scott Peck's *The Road Less Traveled*, about distinguishing dependency from love, open marriage, and the imperative of self-actualization. They talked about Gino; James told Louie they lived in separate apartments. They connected in their loneliness, James and Louie. James was charming and needy. He didn't need Cattleyas or raspberries or the feel of genuine wool under his feet at the Stanford Court. He needed intimacy, even the smallest flicker.

One night at Fournou's Ovens, the winemaker Dick Graff (owner of Chalone Vineyard) introduced James to a young man he was seeing. Michael Butusov worked as a busser at the Hayes Street Grill. His passion was pastry and he had worked as an apprentice for Jim Dodge, pastry chef at the Stanford Court. Butusov looked like a model from a men-of-the-Ivy-League spread in *GQ* magazine: lustrous hair capping a square forehead, full lips, a resolute jaw, and a gaze that seemed right for staring down a lacrosse opponent.

James told the young man to come see him in his suite one afternoon after class; they'd talk about baking. When Butusov arrived, James was in a chair, wearing his Stanford Court robe, purplish calves and ankles visible. James's assistant left. Butusov asked James about New York, whether he thought it might be worth moving there and apprenticing himself to a well-known pastry chef—and if so, which one.

James saw Butusov look out at the bay, remark on the lack of smog that day, how it was possible to see all the way to Mount Diablo. James opened his robe; he was naked underneath. James was not aroused; he merely made himself available to the young man. He watched Butusov turn his head and notice, saw his startled look, and watched him look away again out the window. Butusov's face was red; he began talking quickly: some nonsense about apprenticeships. James closed his robe.

The boy had to learn how the world worked—the truth that need was what kept it grinding.

CHAPTER 20

RAISIN BREAD REDEMPTION

1971–1981

In 1971, Judith Jones, the feared and admired editor at Alfred A. Knopf, committed herself to shaping James Beard into something he was not, at least not exactly.

In December 1961, when James had escorted Julia Child and Simone Beck and *Mastering the Art of French Cooking* into the small and bloodthirsty world of New York food—gave Julia and Simca his protection and his blessing—Judith felt a debt of gratitude to James. Like her authors that year, Judith had held no sway in New York food before *Mastering* took off. Judith had disdained the world of cookbooks and magazines. Even after the clamor for Julia and Simca's book, Judith didn't like to think of herself as so lowly a thing as a cookbook editor. She was a literary editor who, between manuscripts by John Updike, lent her time to cookbooks she believed could be extraordinary.

The women who worked as food editors of the big magazines—*House Beautiful* and *McCall's* and *House & Garden*—Judith had contempt for them. The recipes were uninteresting, all those ghastly mixes and cans and pathetic waxed boxes of frozen vegetables: They made

Judith shudder. Could anyone imagine buying them? They were home-ec people, these magazine women. And really, Judith thought, they surely hated food: the beauty and sensuousness of fine ingredients, cooked patiently. They were all secretly out to push Campbell's this and General Mills that, with recipes those companies promoted to sell their products—printed on cartons of instant mashed potatoes and the like. The horrible home-ec women of American magazine publishing were only out to make a buck. And the cookbooks they wrote: Judith liked to call them "box-top books."

Still, Judith needed those women to promote her authors. For that, she had James. He'd been so sweet with Julia and Simca, and so jealous of them, poor man.

She pitied James a little, and of course it made her want to laugh, the ridiculousness of pitching products like that portable Skotch Grill, rather than just showing American women how to cook, the way Julia did so beautifully. The Skotch Bucket! But Jim connected with readers. Judith felt he was nowhere near Julia's level, of course, but he did have knowledge and authority; he knew what was good, and, like Evan— Judith's husband—James believed in American food, its bounty and variety, the diversity of its regional character. Judith had seen this at one of James's classes, his way of getting women to put aside their fears of making a soufflé or roasting a chicken. He connected—with women as well as with men. Judith wanted to bring men into the kitchen, and of course into the constituency of cookbook buyers. If the highest goal of a cookbook was to teach technique, Jim Beard had an uncanny ability to make even complicated things look like such fun. Judith wanted him to write a bread cookbook for her.

As the 1970s dawned, bread—wholesome, dark, and peasanty, peb-bled with seeds and wheat berries, the antithesis of factory-extruded Wonder loaves—had become a movement. In February 1970, Blooming-dale's on Third Avenue unveiled the Bread Basket, a boutique selling more than a hundred types from nine artisan bakers: brioche and Bau-ernbrot, Hungarian potato bread, Russian pumpernickel, and ring-shaped Italian *pana con ciccolo*, flavored with lard and pork cracklings. Bread's allure stretched far beyond the Upper East Side of Manhattan.

MAGICAL MYSTERIES OF MAKING BREAD, ran the headline for a 1971 *Chicago Tribune* story on the counterculture phenomenon of *The Tassajara Bread Book* by Edward Espe Brown, a Zen monk in California.

"Currently there's a revival in home bread baking," Mary Daniels wrote for the *Tribune* story. "Lots of folks are tired of the bland beige pillows stuffed with airy cotton that is sold on supermarket shelves. Deep in their brains are mouth-watering atavistic memories of something much better . . . heavy, crusty, crunchy, chewy, dark, coarse, satisfying rectangles made of stoneground whole grains."

Shambhala, a hippie publisher in Berkeley nobody had ever heard of, struck gold with *Tassajara*. Judith knew that a *real* publisher in New York, if it got its bread cookbook just right, could easily outdo a bunch of counterculture kids—probably unwashed—in California. The New York Times book division was rushing to get a bread-and-soup cookbook on store shelves, but they'd make a mess of it. Knopf could win the bread book game, especially with a byline from James Beard, the master of teaching difficult things. Besides, who else but James had atavistic memories stretching so far into the bread-scented mist of an idyllic past?

Over a few months, starting at the end of 1970, when James was still working on *American Cookery*, Judith invited James to an informal series of monthly lunches. By early March 1971, they had a letter of agreement for the *Bread Cookbook*, Judith's working title. James would deliver the manuscript on October 1, 1972 (a tentative date), with publication in fall 1973, and release of the $7,500 advance only when James could show he was well underway with the manuscript. Separately, James arranged to pay John Ferrone twenty percent of the advance to be his editor and uncredited cowriter.

"I hope you will tell Jim how delighted I am to be getting a book from him at long last," Judith wrote to John Schaffner. "Everyone I mention it to gets so excited that they can't wait to get it in their hands."

Knopf's preliminary fact sheet for what came to be titled *Beard on Bread* revealed Judith's hopes to create the definitive American bread book. "The craze for bread-making is sweeping the country," it explained. "Everyone is doing it, 6-year-old kids, hippies, business tycoons, restless housewives. This is a book addressed to all types, and Beard is a name they'll reckon with."

The final manuscript—one hundred recipes, for everything from basic loaves to donuts, griddlecakes, and pita—reflected Judith's talent for shaping James's image. In *Beard on Bread*, Judith took James's persona from *Delights and Prejudices* and *American Cookery*, a man blessed with a long memory stretching to a golden age in the nation's food life. Hippies in their twenties may have started the craft bread revolution, reviving old recipes and home baking methods, but in Judith's molding of James, he was a survivor of those blessed olden times, the elder of American foodways, who bridged generations.

Instead of using photographs of James, she hired an illustrator, Karl Stuecklen, to depict him on the dust jacket not as aged, tired, and puffy (all of which he was) but instead as lithe and dynamic. Stuecklen's cover portrait shows James's face as lean and masculine, with an unwrinkled head that doesn't so much reflect light as beam energy. He's dressed in a rolled-sleeve shirt of commanding, optimistic yellow, under a single-strap butcher's apron suggestive of male power. The kitchen around him thrums like a workshop: a bowl of rising dough atop a stockpot billowing like a steam engine, amid a battery of tools and vessels.

Schaffner disliked the way Judith wasn't just an editor but became de facto literary manager for her authors, shaping their images along with their voices—she was usurping that role from Schaffner. But Schaffner feared her power, as James did, and was careful not to challenge her directly. As soon as he received his advance copy of *Beard on Bread*, he sent a timid critique. "I have to say I don't like the jacket," he told her, "but I have never liked drawings of Jim because they always tend to come out caricatures. True, this one makes him seem a kindly sort and I'm sure his admirers across the land will not complain."

Stuecklen also did the book's amber line drawings that illustrated the process: how to stir, knead, and shape dough. For those drawings, James wasn't the model; Judith had a photographer capture a woman demonstrating those hand techniques, in a studio. In Stuecklen's finished drawings, those hands have Jamesian plumpness and flair.

In a way, those drawings symbolize Judith's genius for creating mythic commodities of her authors—because, just like the hands that Stuecklen drew, the recipes didn't exactly belong to James. Though by the time *Beard on Bread* hit bookshops, Judith Jones made sure they had the stamp of no one else.

::::

JAMES SPENT THREE WEEKS in Norway in June 1972, a guest of the Export Council and the National Tourist Office. Gino, still smarting from his spring apprenticeship with Richard Olney, met him in Oslo. (Coincidentally, Norway had decriminalized male-to-male sex two months earlier.) James and Gino walked the open-air folk museum at Bygdøy and the fish market at Bergen; sailed up a fjord and visited a flat-bread factory—the Flatbrødfabrikken Ideal—in Hamar. At a farm on the Drammensveien Road outside Oslo, they watched Elizabeth Oven-stad bake a batch of her twice-weekly loaves, rich with wheat kernels, rye and whole-meal flour, and milk.

At the end of June, Gino returned to New York. James flew to Nice. He burrowed in at La Pitchoune with Julia and Paul Child, ostensibly to work. A columnist for *The Oregonian*'s *Northwest* magazine and a friend of James's from Portland, Carl Gohs, arrived to help with the manuscript. When he wasn't at the typewriter, Gohs scoured boulange-ries for typical Provençal breads to set before James.

Yet Scandinavian breads, not French ones, were the core of the hundred recipes in *Beard on Bread*. They give the book a wholesome iden-tity, cozy and rugged like a Norwegian sweater. If the hippie breads in *Tassajara* gave a nod to the brown-rice macrobiotic sensibility of Japan, the loaves in *Beard on Bread* had a footing in Europe, though in brood-ing landscapes far north of the typical American tourist zone.

Other recipes in the book are uncredited adaptations from James's stash of paperback Pillsbury Bake-Off books. James's Dill-Seed Bread, for one, is all but identical to the winner of the 1960 Bake-Off, Dilly Cas-serole Bread, by Leona Schnuelle of Crab Orchard, Nebraska. Alas, James didn't mention the hapless Leona. Pita and lamb-topped Lebanese flat-bread were uncredited contributions from James's friend Emil Kashouty.

James's recipe for Mother's Raisin Bread added a second layer of deception. In an early draft of the recipe headnote, James wrote: "I grew up on this particular bread and had it toasted and fresh and often on picnics and for tea on Sunday. Sometimes tiny currants and bits of shaved citron were substituted for the raisins but either seems elegant to me. This was my mother's creation after she had been unsuccessful in getting the Palace Hotel to give here [*sic*] their recipe—and this on [*sic*] turned out to be almost better."

While it's true that Elizabeth made currant bread, the recipe in *Beard on Bread* is based on a Pillsbury one for white bread enriched with powdered milk. James enhanced it with a swirl of raisin filling (golden sultanas plumped with sherry or Cognac—the booze was a late-draft enhancement—with mace and orange zest to stand in for candied citron). Though the reader might believe it was a recipe straight from Elizabeth's handwritten recipe book, in fact it was only a simulation of a bread James remembered from Salmon Street.

James cited his sources for some recipes: the flatbread factory in Hamar, Elizabeth Ovenstad, and the Norwegian Government School for Domestic Science Teachers; also Clay Triplette (corn sticks), Helen Evans Brown (Corn Chili Bread), Carl Gohs (potato and zucchini breads), his old friend Alvin Kerr (Zephyr Rolls), and Myrtle Allen, owner of the Ballymaloe Inn of East Cork, Ireland (although Allen's brown bread recipe is from a 1944 book James doesn't cite, Doris Grant's *Your Daily Bread*).

James aimed one of *Beard on Bread*'s most egregious slights at Craig Claiborne, with whom James was cordial in public, though privately they hated each other. "This . . . appeared in the columns of the *New York Times* several years ago," James wrote in the headnote to Sourdough Rye, without mentioning that Claiborne introduced it; likewise Finnish Sour Rye. Both appeared in a 1968 *Times* feature. Claiborne was nearly as guilty as James in failing to acknowledge his sources, writing that "generous readers" (whom he didn't name) had contributed the recipes.

Judith prodded James to add at least a vague note about the sourdough rye's source. "JB," she wrote in her editor's pencil, "will you give credit to <u>Times</u>?" In a way, though, attribution didn't matter.

Ever since *Hors D'Oeuvre and Canapés*—his first book—curation was James's mode of authorship. His great talent was his knack for making a widely scattered collection of recipes seem authentically his. James's work made up a canon of American food, almost as though it were crowd sourced. Erasing the authorship of others fit two of James's mythologies. One was personal. It had to do with James's encyclopedic knowledge and experience of food—for James to cite all of his sources would have challenged the narrative of his vastness.

The other was cultural: his conviction that building an American cuisine was a collective effort, a group project of readers who mailed recipes to the *New York Times*, women and men who entered Pillsbury Bake-Offs, and home cooks like Emil Kashouty, a Lebanese American who'd moved to New York City to find enough breathing space to live a cautiously queer life in private. James's plagiarism was inexcusable. It also gave James's books a Whitmanic quality, a democratic eclecticism, and a sweeping sense of the American character.

In James's lifetime, by far the most popular American cookbooks were compendiums such as *Better Homes and Gardens New Cook Book* and *Betty Crocker's Picture Cook Book*, the work of teams of uncredited recipe developers, writers, and editors. James did something similar, in a way, only under his own name and mythic persona. James's fans were certain he embodied the nation's food life. To James, that seemed like reason enough to commandeer a few recipes. And if it involved a little lying, either actively or by omission, well: James's life always had been a continuous performance of concealment and dissembling.

: : :

ON A SPRING DAY IN 1971, a letter arrived at the office of Reed College's alumni bulletin. It was from Ellen Mandleberg, an enterprising publicity agent at Atheneum Books in New York. Atheneum was about to publish a new book by James, "with the assistance," according to the title page (though the cover showed James's name alone), of Gino P. Cofacci. It was a small book without recipes, directed at Americans crowding onto budget flights to Europe—a glossary, basically, of dishes appearing on menus in France and Italy, with a guide to wine. Atheneum hoped that sales at airport bookshops and newsstands would be brisk.

Mandleberg had been reading James Beard's author questionnaire (used internally for marketing purposes), in which James mentioned he'd gone to Reed. Mandleberg wrote to the alumni bulletin's editor:

> World-renowned culinary authority James Beard, who is an alumnus of Reed College, has written a new book, HOW TO EAT (AND DRINK) YOUR WAY THROUGH A FRENCH (OR ITALIAN) MENU, which Atheneum is publishing on June 21. Since Mr. Beard is a Reed alumnus, we think you will be interested in seeing his new book. Unfortunately Mr. Beard has not indicated the year he was awarded his B.A. from Reed, but we imagine it was some-time around 1924.

The letter caused a stir. James Beard, a Reedie! Why had no one at the college ever talked about it? Alarms went off in the fundraising office: One of the leading food personalities in America—willing, pre-sumably, to lend his valuable name to benefits, if not make a donation of his own—was one of theirs! Over forty-some years, in countless inter-views, James had never mentioned Reed; didn't mention it in *Delights and Prejudices* or in any of his autobiographical notes for his syndicated newspaper column or magazine pieces. This was huge news.

Someone looked up James's official record and reported it to Flor-ence Lehman, the alumni director, who was also in charge of fund-raising. "James Andrew [*sic*] x 24," the note to Lehman read. 'Wash. H.S. Dropped in Jan. for deficiency in scholarship." Lehman called him in New York; she spoke with Emily Gilder, James's secretary. Lehman noted his address, how he talked with his old friend Mary Hamblet every Sunday afternoon, and was very busy; how he had suffered a heart attack recently but hadn't slowed his schedule.

After word got out, James received a few letters from old classmates. In April 1972, one Reed alum who wrote him, Gladys Chambers, reported back to Lehman on what James had told her of his months at

Reed: how he lived in House I, a farmhouse across Woodstock Road, in a single room; how his close hallmates in the house were Herman Kenin, Max Gordon, and "Mr. Bechtold of the faculty."

In 1973, the Oregon Historical Society discovered James. Its director, Thomas Vaughan, asked James to write the foreword to a reprint of *The Web-Foot Cook Book* by the women of the San Grael Society of Portland's First Presbyterian Church, originally published in 1885. Through Vaughan, James met Morris Galen, a Portland attorney who also happened to be a member of Reed's board of trustees. They met in Gearhart—actually in Surf Pines, the development just north of it, where James was renting a house. Galen (Morrie) and his wife, Evelyn, owned a weekend house there. James connected with them and hired Morrie as his personal attorney. In a way, it was as if Reed at its highest tier—the board of trustees—was taking James back, forgiving him his great shame.

Though he'd been a student there less than six months, James had always felt that Reed fit him—its democratic ideals and scorn for chi-chi; the grandeur of its solitary spruces and the introspection inspired by its greenness and distance from the city. Decades before, scandal and fear had caused his exile; Reed had seemed blocked to him forever. How he would dream that he walked its pathways and entered through the pointed Gothic doorway of the chapel. He had always loved Reed, had always been devoted to it in his heart, maybe even his soul, though James didn't believe in the existence of souls. Reed was his first escape from home, the place where he'd pushed aside the paralyzing weight of his family and found a freedom and agility he'd only ever known at the beach.

In 1974, James surprised organizers by replying *yes* to the invitation for the class of 1924 reunion party. Maybe it was time to put his shame to rest. What had he been guilty of, really? He was the victim of politics, nothing more. Carl Jerome was a daily example of what a life of no shame looked like. In Miami the previous year, at the end of a long day, he had asked Carl where he was going. A gay bar, Carl said, and James asked if he could go along—he, James, for whom the gay bar had long been a place of potential calamity, of raids and exposure: a place to avoid. That night, he got up the will to overcome.

The place was empty (it was early). They sat at the bar, drinking beer from bottles. The two bartenders kept glancing over and murmuring.

The one who'd served them approached again. "Aren't you James Beard?"

Cautiously, James answered that he was.

"Cool," the bartender said. "Uh . . . do you want a glass for your beer?"

James kept swigging from the bottle.

:::

THOUGH JAMES STILL ADORED IT, the West Tenth Street house was now too small. Every weekday it filled up with people: Clay and Carl; his secretary Emily Gilder and Betty Ward, who managed his travel and demonstration schedule. Plus so many who dropped by: Felipe Rojas-Lombardi, John Clancy, and Barbara Kafka; Helen McCully and Cecily Brownstone; not to mention anyone he knew visiting from the West Coast or Dallas or any one of a dozen places. There were young men like Carl who'd write or call cold, asking for advice about professional culinary schools or about getting a job in cooking. James might tell them to come by and they'd talk, if he got a hunch about them. Journalists lobbied to schedule time for profile interviews.

The ringing phone cut through every conversation. One or more typewriters clacked and dinged from morning to early evening. James had taken to doing all his writing by talking into his Sony tape recorder, often at five in the morning on Sundays, when there was enough of a lull in the life of the house to give him time to think.

And then, of course, there was Gino. Since leaving architecture, his bent for precision, his patience, and his need for order and controllable processes had led him to baking. He declared himself a pastry chef. He'd perfected the dacquoise, a delicate layer cake with (in Gino's version) crisp layers of hazelnut meringue and a coffee crème au beurre, a meringue buttercream. He cut out a precisely shaped stencil for decorating the top with powdered sugar in an architectural design.

James had been making dacquoises since the 1950s; in 1959, his friend and protégé, John Clancy, who'd just launched a small catering business in New York, sold them (along with cassoulet) for holiday parties.

Gino had perfected his dacquoise for James's dinner parties, which he, Gino, usually did not attend. Eventually, James persuaded a couple of restaurateur friends in the Village—Leon Lianides of the Coach House, Alfredo Viazzi of Alfredo's Trattoria—to add Gino's dacquoise to their menus. (Nobody found it easy to say *no* to James Beard.) Gino also made a rich, almost flourless chocolate cake for his pair of wholesale customers. He made no more than a few per week. To meet his self-imposed high standards, each cake took time.

Gino was finding new confidence in pastry, and it spilled over into how he felt about himself. His face had aged into rugged voluptuousness. His lips seemed fuller, his dimpled chin fleshier. He was nearing sixty and felt handsome still, though he fretted over his creeping baldness. Eventually, James assented to Gino's follicular unit grafts (they had a joint checking account, so it wasn't as though Gino needed a bag of cash to move ahead), plugs that created a new, lower hairline, drawn as meticulously across his forehead as Gino wanted. It boosted his confidence even more. He wanted to stay presentable for James, and for other men. In the crevices of James's hectic life, early in the morning, before the first phone call to Cecily or Tom Margittai, they had an intimacy no one but Clay could witness.

They'd stopped being physical, at least in a sexual way. Still, Gino tended to James's body. He helped him dress and undress, wrap and unwrap his legs, pull up and peel off his compression stockings: to express his devotedness to James's body, the abiding joy of having found each other in middle age, two men no one else had wanted, who understood loneliness and depression. They'd long ago stopped being exclusive with each other. James's need for intimate endorsement was too strong, and Gino had spent so much time away from James, during James's long and frequent stays abroad. Things were different now. Gino felt desirable again, and his dacquoises convinced him he was finally doing vital work. So many of the people James would have tramping through the house would not—*could* not—understand that. Gino needed space, order, and quiet to do his work.

Gino wanted a new house, one with a larger apartment for himself, and his very own kitchen for baking and assembling cakes. It was essential that they move.

::: :::

THE BRICK FAÇADE OF 167 West Twelfth Street had been tweaked so much over the decades that it appeared quasi-institutional: a grand first story of large multipaned windows with two stories of insignificant brick townhouse above. James and Gino's block of West Tenth was smaller scale, more truly villagelike, despite the proximity of Sixth Avenue and the grime-and-disinfectant aura of the women's prison. The western nub of West Twelfth was treeless and exposed, somehow vulnerable to the traffic strafing Seventh Avenue.

It had been an apartment building for some years when James bought it in 1973, though from 1922 to 1945 the street floors held the offices of the Co-Operative League of America, a progressive organization that provided education about worker co-ops and the dangers of predator capitalism. In fact, the league's founders had had the entrance floor redone in 1922 in Colonial Revival style—hence the Mount Vernon lower windows, the porte cochere–scale lantern above the front door. In a way, it was perfect for James's vanity. As America was gearing up for its bicentennial year (1976), James was the George Washington of the soufflé and the chicken casserole.

The third floor had a large enough apartment for Gino; they could rent out the fourth-floor apartment. James would have his teaching kitchen on the half-subterranean ground floor, between the small dining room in front and the large backyard. The second floor would have the living room and the cookbook library, with James's office against the back wall, above the garden, and his bed would be in a little alcove overlooking the street, above the front door. The tight-switchback staircase was nearly impossible for James to navigate. At least Gino was happy. In the spring of 1974, they officially christened the place, but it needed decorating help, something to give it Jamesian style and scale.

Somewhere at the end of 1975, a man who'd been in James's Seaside cooking classes rang up. Jerry Lamb—a friend of Mary Hamblet—was sweet, funny, and queer. He had a busy interior design business in Portland, with clients in Manhattan and Washington, DC. Lamb said, "I'm here in New York." James told him to stop by for dinner.

Lamb grabbed a cab and went down to the house. They had dinner. Over a glass or two in the library, James said, "If I turned you loose, what would you do with this house?"

Lamb spun a few ideas. James told him to have at it.

He reupholstered the furniture, brought in fabrics, chose wallpapers from James's large collection. For the library walls, James asked for Chinese red; Lamb custom-mixed a darkish tomato soup color. The kitchen crouched in a dark, airless corner. To liven it up, Lamb proposed the world-map wallpaper he had used for his own bathroom in Portland—to underscore James's status as a man of the world, he said. James yielded.

Lamb lined the walls and ceiling of James's bed alcove with mirrors. James was moving ever more slowly by then; sometimes he liked to lie in bed when there were guests, and he could see them reflected in the living room as they talked. Lamb mirrored every surface in the bathroom. He designed Gino's minimalist apartment, including his private pastry kitchen with cupboards of dark walnut and Italian wall tiles glazed with a watercolor effect in umber and cream.

Eventually they expanded the house. Gino drew up plans to smash through the house's rear wall and glass in part of the backyard to form a conservatory dining room, twenty-five feet square and twenty-five feet high. Gino designed a steel staircase and had it fabricated—no more squeezing up and down the tortuous front stairs. James also needed a roomier bath. Lamb suggested siting it on the eight-foot-wide balcony above the greenhouse, open to the sky and the wash of light from the backyard. The nozzles were behind a folding screen, so James could have privacy.

When the greenhouse became the dining room, the office moved to the front of the house, off the kitchen. James had a contemporary Knoll table with a black marble top; McGuire chairs of heavy rattan with rawhide bindings. He designed a huge sideboard with racks for displaying

James's majolica, which spread beyond it onto the walls and the surface of every credenza and side table. It was a beautiful mausoleum.

Lying in bed in his mirrored alcove after everyone had gone, the telephone next to him having ceased ringing for the day, James had time and space to think. He could see his chest with its scars from a quarter century of hospital procedures and take comfort: Someday, maybe soon, everything would be gone. That included everything he'd ever collected, the antiques and mementos. They'd be sold, or carried off surreptitiously by the hangers-on, anyone desperate enough for grifted glory. It would be the final delicious absurdity—only Helen Evans Brown, his past and forever kindred outsider in the world of food, would have truly appreciated it.

One evening in November 1981, James Villas, the food and wine editor for *Town & Country*, stopped by 167 West Twelfth to accompany James to dinner. James had phoned him earlier: "Kiddo," he said, "what are you up to?" Villas was queer. Even at forty-three, he possessed perennial golden-boy handsomeness, a North Carolina soft drawl, English tailoring, and country-club social ease. He and James talked opera, food of course, and gossip. James adored giving him hugs. Sometimes Villas accompanied James and Gino to the Coach House. They'd sit at adjacent tables, James and Gino facing each other at one, Villas at the other. Gino would sit silent while James and Villas spoke of Wagner and country hams.

On that November night, James and Villas dined *à deux* on the Upper East Side at the Post House, a new steakhouse with a manly roughrider edge. James drank his usual (Glenlivet; his celebrity doctor, Denny Cox, had forbidden him wine) and they ate what seemed like the entire menu: a veal chop sweating abundant pinkish juice and black-crust rib steak, rare inside, along with hash browns, creamed spinach, and onion rings; crab cakes and steamed lobsters; black and white chocolate mousses and a lemon tart. After dinner, James, somewhat tipsy, sang a few lines of *Tristan* at the table. Earlier, Villas had told him about Rounds, a hot new gay club on Fifty-Third Street, instantly notorious for the model looks of its high-class hustlers, where Tennessee Williams and closeted Wall Street executives—the descendants of Jim Cullum—entertained with iced bottles of vodka and Champagne.

"Kiddo," James said, as they rose to leave and the maître d' sent someone scurrying for their coats, "what about that place with those boys? Any chance we can stop by there?" They kept their hired driver waiting outside Rounds while, inside, they were led to a banquette. James ordered Scotch—in their tailored jackets, he and Villas looked flush with cash. A pair of handsome working boys sat down on either side of James. He bought them drinks. Villas asked whether they'd ever heard of James Beard and they shrugged and shook their heads. James bought more drinks.

When Richard Sax, the thirty-two-year-old food editor of *Food & Wine* magazine, walked into Rounds that night, he spotted Villas with the Dean of American Cookery, holding court on a banquette, flanked by hustlers. Sax approached, dropped to one knee, and, in a gesture of hammy obeisance, leaned over to kiss James's cocktail ring, as though he'd been granted an audience with the pope.

Sax said, "Jim, are you aware that back there on that banquette is Vladimir Horowitz?"

Villas inched his way to the rear of the club, returned, and reported it was true; the great Horowitz was likewise surrounded by pretty young men. James howled. So much of the public face of American culture, the books and records and TV programs that moved the nation's housewives, salesmen, secretaries, and bank-branch executives was shaped by those compelled to live behind walls, nursing half-open secrets. Survival depended on the willingness of everybody else to keep silence. There were things that nobody who lived outside the walls ever needed to know.

Barbara Kafka had come close to breaching James's wall in 1978, when she got him to say into her tape recorder—for a series of interviews on which she hoped to base a book of memoirs—that it was time to come clean about being gay. (Barbara, whom James mentored as he would a daughter, had a knack for making him open up.) But he'd made no promise to let her publish a transcript of the recording—at least while he was alive.

For years, Judith Jones had been urging James to write a second volume of his memoirs, to pick up in the mid-1960s, where *Delights and Prejudices* ended. She'd call it *Menus and Memories*. From time to time, Judith would send a writer she liked—Mary Goodbody and Irene Sax—to see whether they could get James to open up about the past, but those efforts went nowhere.

James's sexuality was never part of the memoir Judith had in mind. At Knopf, James's reputation with conservative, churchgoing cookbook buyers in Des Moines would be safe. Judith saw James's value as a repository of cooking knowledge, a great teacher able to calm the apprehensive masses in their kitchens. His future books for Knopf would mostly be a repackaging of existing recipes and essays. His syndicated newspaper columns became 1974's *Beard on Food*; his *Gourmet* stories bloomed again as 1977's *James Beard's Theory and Practice of Good Cooking*. For the latter, James hired Nick Malgieri, a twenty-seven-year-old pastry chef who'd worked in France with Richard Olney, to go through stacks of old *Gourmet* magazines, tear out every article James had ever written, and paste them into a binder. The only original thing in *Theory and Practice* was an appendix—the Concordance, a detailed ingredient glossary.

How better to peddle James to the churchgoing women of America than with the ecclesiastical word *Concordance*?

∷ ∷

On May 16, 1976, James received a kind of closure from the institution that in so many ways had shaped his life. Morrie Galen, his attorney and a member of Reed College's board of trustees, had put James's name into the college's candidate pool for honorary degrees. And so, on a cool, overcast Sunday, on the lawn facing Eliot Hall, James, dressed in an enormous black doctoral gown and square academic cap, stood and wept as President Paul Bragdon conferred on him a Doctor of Humane Letters degree. (I. F. Stone, the progressive journalist and author, received an honorary degree that day along with James.)

In his remarks, Bragdon hailed James as a person "whose impact on society can truly be said to have been a force for the improvement of the quality of human life." Bragdon lauded *American Cookery* as more than a collection of recipes, but rather "the definitive work on the evolution of American food." And though he got the title wrong—he called it *Delights and Pleasures*—Bragdon cited *Delights and Prejudices* as a book that, in its evocation of a golden age of Portland food, "might well serve as an inspiration and model for the rehabilitation of the city's restaurants and markets."

Three weeks later, back in San Francisco, in his suite at the Stanford Court, James suffered a serious heart attack. He lay in a bed at Pacific Presbyterian Medical Center in Pacific Heights, his well-scarred chest planted with electrodes, his loose, slack-skinned body existing precariously under a lattice of wires. His weight had tipped above three hundred pounds; his doctor had put him on an apocalyptic diet of six hundred salt-free calories a day. Marion Cunningham left his side only when she had to, when visiting hours were over.

Carl showed up at the hospital to tell James he was resigning as director of the James Beard Cooking School. He was clearing out, flying to London to be with a man he'd met the previous spring. It was during a stopover, en route with James to Venice for a teaching stint at the Gritti Palace Hotel. That night, Carl had slipped out of the hotel to unwind at a gay bar; he hooked up with someone. They'd secretly kept in touch.

To James, Carl's announcement felt like two knives to the chest: losing his assistant at his moment of greatest physical and emotional need and losing Carl to another man.

But what could Carl do? In four years, James's control over him had never relaxed—Carl was desperate to flee. Hadn't he endured everything, knowing that a moment like this was inevitable? Being on call twenty-four hours a day, shouldering the twin demands of travel and public appearances with a man whose body was failing. And then there was the constant weight of James's need, expressed as lust (though in truth it was psychosexual), beamed across an unbridgeable gulf. This was the moment Carl had waited for—his opening to escape. He hoped to leverage all he'd learned to start his own career as an author and a teacher, speaking in his own voice.

It crushed James.

"Go have a good life," he told Carl with bitterness. It was the end.

Not really, though. Weeks later, James and Carl began a correspondence across the Atlantic, via messages spoken onto a single cassette tape that each would record over and return. They shared observations on food and daily life in London and New York, nothing deep. James didn't want paper letters, nothing that could be stuffed into a drawer and discovered later. In Seaside, James would talk to Carl on a pay phone, secretly, to avoid the disapproval of friends.

James had come close to dying in San Francisco. After that, Morrie Galen advised him to write his will—especially since James had no obvious heirs, and his book rights and royalties, spread across decades and several handshake agreements, were complicated.

When it came time to draw up the will, James seemed to draw a blank. He knew he wanted Gino to keep his apartment on the third floor, for as long as Gino lived. And he'd need a monthly cash stipend. Clay should get some cash. Apart from that, James wanted everything to go: the house to be sold (with the stipulation that Gino would stay), James's things to be auctioned off. He'd already sent his papers to the University of Wyoming. (The American Heritage Center there had hoped to establish a major US culinary archive, though after the effort failed, James's papers would be returned east, to New York University.)

Morrie told him he would have to decide who would inherit the money after everything was sold; who would inherit the rights to the books, and receive royalties after Gino's death.

James couldn't say. He'd always lived in the present, never thought far into the future. Thinking about his will was no different. Should he leave his estate to a charity or a nonprofit? Which one?

Well, Morrie said, of course there was always Reed College. James could certainly name his alma mater as beneficiary. James shrugged. He agreed.

In August 1976, Morrie arrived in New York with the completed will. James signed it, witnessed by his secretary, Emily Gilder, and her husband, and Morrie filed it. Just like that, the institution that had been a prime architect of shame and fear for James was in line to become the ultimate guardian of all he'd achieved. In a twist of harsh and delicious irony, Reed would become heirs of a food career James stumbled onto after failing at everything else, following the forced expulsion that bled his confidence.

"I don't want a monument when I die," he told Jerry Lamb one day, as they sat in the greenhouse on West Twelfth Street, gazing toward the birch trees and the fountain and the large stone sculpture of James's head, floating above the bluestone terrace. He didn't want a tomb or a plaque or a memorial. He wanted his ashes scattered in the surf off Gearhart Beach, to become part of the sand tumbling ashore, like the delicate green and blue glass floats he conjured at the end of *Delights and Prejudices*. They were designed to keep fishing nets aloft in the water, but some always broke loose. They rode the currents for nearly five thousand miles, so far from their original purpose that when they got to Oregon, it seemed they only ever existed to bob free.

MISS LEWIS'S BISCUITS
FOR THE DEAD

1985

FOR WEEKS IN THE SPRING OF 1985, the promised event had the momentum of a Lincoln sedan rolling at maximum cruise. In the days leading up to it, the food pages of the *New York Times* guaranteed something historic would unfold in Rockefeller Plaza, a glittering black-tie gala on a scale that was rare even for New York, a seat harder to score than *A Chorus Line* or *Cats*. Foodies of the Upper East Side, the ones who jammed the reservation phone lines of Union Square Café and Arizona 206, scrambled for tickets.

Fourteen of the nation's chefs, rock stars all, would cook in one place to show off the bold flavors and cocky brilliance of the new generation of restaurants they'd built. At the very height of the "Reagan renaissance" of American power and glamour, the nation's food would be crowned best in the world, and these chefs—from Wolfgang Puck in Los Angeles to Paul Prudhomme in New Orleans—its masters. In a way, the Citymeals-on-Wheels gala of June 3, 1985, was a ceremony of succession.

Technically, the gala was a tribute to the late James Beard, dead nearly five months. James—the Dean of American Gastronomy (an upgrade from "Cookery," his epithet of thirty years)—was part of the previous generation of American food masters. Along with Julia Child and Craig Claiborne—both still very much alive—James was the ultimate amateur cook, dedicated to home cooking. The new generation of American culinary authorities were chefs, each exciting and glamorous in ways James, Julia, and Claiborne never were.

At first, organizers of the annual Citymeals fundraiser had designed it as an eighty-second birthday party for James. With *New York* magazine's Gael Greene, James was one of the founders of the nonprofit that delivered weekend and holiday meals to homebound elders. Though age and illness had slowed James, his image (the bald head, massive size, and jowly smile) was an enduring icon in American food, recognizable everywhere from advertising, magazine articles, and books. He was the wise and jolly old bachelor uncle of the American kitchen, the nation's gourmet guru. The man who taught a nation how to make bread and pasta; how to pulse-chop onions in that new Cuisinart he'd advised Americans to buy. The man who taught a couple of generations how to throw a party; to master Thanksgiving with confidence and just enough style.

But on January 23, just weeks into the new year of 1985, when the ice was still thick on Wollman Rink in Central Park and the snowbanks in front of James's Greenwich Village townhouse hadn't yet turned to slush, the old man died at New York Hospital, in a room looking out to the great tidal estuary known as the East River.

As word of James's death spread, the fundraiser's planners huddled. Soon, Greene and chefs Larry Forgione and Jonathan Waxman announced a revised plan. The gala would still be a party for the beloved old man, but instead it would be a tribute, a celebration of his life, a public sanctification of New American cooking—James's legacy—in the capital of ceviche, baby lamb chops, and Mumm Champagne, and at the same time an emperor's funeral.

The morning before the gala, the *Times* ran head shots of four of the chefs, all cooking in Rockefeller Plaza. Waxman, of Jams in New York, had the shaggy, virile look of a bust of the Emperor Hadrian. Bald, bearded Forgione, of An American Place in Brooklyn, had the composure of a Union general; flyaway-haired Jimmy Schmidt of Detroit's London Chop House flashed the hellion glint of Bo from *The Dukes of Hazzard*. And Puck, Austrian maestro of Spago and Chinois in California, posed with fleshy, sensuous lips and a white neck scarf, the ends tweaked to signal impishness. They were the seductive young lions of American food.

Guests who descended the stairs to lower Rockefeller Plaza the next night found a dazzling spectacle. Jeremiah Tower, from Stars in San Francisco, had set up a massive shellfish bar around a ziggurat of ice luminous with gold light. Jeremiah, pugnacious and charming, had maneuvered his way to a prime location.

The crowd was New York at its most bombastically trendy: men with feathered hair and Tom Selleck brush mustaches, in tuxes and wing collars; women in bouffant-shoulder gowns, with stiffly sprayed down-dos in an Ivana Trump shade of pale gold. They clutched glasses of Chardonnay and Pinot Noir, nibbling Waxman's red pepper pancakes, Prudhomme's seven-steak gumbo, and Alice Waters's baby vegetables flown in from Chino Ranch in California.

They devoured Mark Miller's cinnamon pork loin with ancho chile preserves, Forgione's salmon cheek skewers, and Bradley Ogden's blue corn cakes with caviar. They went back for seconds of Schmidt's white chocolate ice cream with passion fruit and macadamias. It was a coming together of culinary genres recently christened by the food press: New Southwest, New Southern, New American, California Cuisine. At almost every station, red and yellow bell peppers, balsamic vinegar, and fresh ginger—1985's sexiest ingredients—starred in at least one dish, sometimes more.

Only one of the fourteen chefs, Edna Lewis—her white hair pulled tight, in a somber print and gracefully dangling earrings, a touch of muted opulence—seemed to grasp that the evening was a memorial for the deceased. From a subprime location near the back of the plaza, Lewis dished up baked Virginia country ham, buttermilk biscuits, and strawberry jam, three things James had loved when he was alive. In the shadow of such spectacle—the gilded ice temple and zigzags of ginger-balsamic reduction on the tasting plates—Miss Lewis's offering was easy to miss. The only thing easier to miss, perhaps, was James Beard. "The present lionization of American chefs," Jeff Weinstein, food critic for the *Village Voice*, wrote after the gala "doesn't democratize American food the way Beard enabled." Nobody but alt-weekly readers seemed to care.

On a night of brash new luster, big personalities, and the glamour of restaurants from around the country, the departed Dean had become a fussy old ghost, a figure from a time that was almost hard to remember.

On the cover of the evening's program, a Milton Glaser portrait showed James's face as an eerie collage of marbled endpapers, a specter formed of discarded books. The face had a ghoulish pattern, like a cluster of flexed wings in mother-of-pearl tones above a bow tie of red kimono fabric. The small, hooded eyes, scraggly mustache, neck wattle, and rutted forehead all seemed to be melting.

James's body had been rendered into ashes only months earlier, scattered on the beach at Gearhart by his oldest friends, Mary Hamblet and Harvey Welch. James was a wax figure already melting, the lines becoming less and less distinct.

:::

JAMES HADN'T WANTED any of this adulation. He loved being famous—loved seeing his name on a marquee—but he hated being old and feeble. He was used to hospitals. For the last thirty years of his life, he'd been admitted at least once a year for one crisis or another, all of them having to do with his heart and circulatory system. Lately, his breakdowns had become more critical.

In May 1983, for James's eightieth birthday, Jim Nassikas threw a huge bash at the Stanford Court in San Francisco. Table decorations included bowls of bread dough slowly rising throughout dinner, and stiff mounds of egg whites whipped for soufflés—both emblems of James's teaching, of the ways he'd elevated knowledge of technique in

American cooking. After that, James seemed reluctant to wade into big public celebrations.

Despite James's desire to fade from view, however, Tom Margittai organized a New York party in the Hunting Room of the Four Seasons. The list of invitees included old friends of James's as well as distinguished guests, including New York socialite Brooke Astor, choreographer Agnes de Mille, and singer and civil rights activist Marian Anderson. Margittai packed the menu with James's American favorites: roast country ham, potato salad, lamb stew, Clay's recipe for baked macaroni and cheese. Margittai had raised donations from ten of James's most important friends, including Joe Baum and Sam Aaron. They commissioned Arbit Blatas, the Lithuanian émigré artist, husband of opera diva Regina Resnik, to paint James's portrait.

At the party, James stood up to speak. He was crying. "I think I have onions in my eyes," he told the guests, and everyone clapped and laughed or said, "Awww." But when Margittai unveiled the portrait, James was horrified. It was a dark rendering. Blatas had painted James to look old and feeble, a figure half-consumed by shadows—an accurate depiction, though not a flattering one.

James smiled and nodded stiffly as the luncheon guests applauded. Privately, the portrait horrified him. As the party wound down and guests said good-bye to James, shook his hand or kissed him, he whispered to Margittai that he despised the portrait, that he'd be damned if he'd allow that hideous thing into his house.

It stayed at the Four Seasons.

In January 1985, days before he died, James told Margittai he was tired of living, that he just wanted to turn his face to the wall and leave.

In 1984, a plagiarism scandal had badly affected James. One of his protégés, Richard Nelson, had written *Richard Nelson's American Cooking*, which lifted thirty-nine recipes, nearly word for word, from Richard Olney's *Simple French Food*. James had written the book's foreword. He told the press he hadn't even read Nelson's text, and he claimed Nelson had plagiarized some of his—James's—recipes as well. To save face, however, James had sacrificed his protégé. Everyone in the food world knew of James's habit of borrowing others' recipes. Olney suspected

Nelson found his way to the recipes through James, to whom Olney had sent unbound galleys of *Simple French Food* so that he could write the foreword. To avoid a trial, Nelson's publisher, Atheneum, paid Olney an undisclosed settlement—rumor had it that the figure was enormous. James had been tarnished.

In the New Year of 1985, James told Tom Margittai that when he died, he didn't want a memorial service or celebration; that he wished only to vanish. Marion Cunningham already knew that, when the time came, she'd need to fly from California to clear out and destroy any last incriminating papers in the house—anything gay, an indiscreet letter he might have overlooked and failed to destroy himself—a stray magazine, something to trouble his legacy or embarrass his friends.

Clay knew he'd have to gather up all James's thousands of objects— the majolica, the knives and chairs and books—and sell everything James hadn't already promised to Reed College. To see it all drift away at auction; to disperse into the atmosphere like fly ash.

Margittai dropped in at West Twelfth Street one afternoon, in the first days of 1985. James's phlebitis-swollen ankles were captured in white compression socks. His feet were in what had to be the biggest black felt and Velcro-strapped shoes ever made, lying on pillows Barbara Kafka had set on porcelain drum stools, one for each foot. An enormous ice-blue Chinese changshan shrouded his torso; his pants were pink and green checks.

James was tired, and yet in the lamplight he looked almost young to Margittai. It wasn't even four, and already the darkness of New York winter was settling in the corners of the room. The massive pair of glazed terra-cotta statues James had hauled back from France a generation earlier, each with an arm stretched out gracefully from fine folds of her robe—his girls, the Terpsichore twins—flanked him like guardians of a troubled spirit.

James had become bitter. He crossed out in red felt-tip pen Isabel Callvert's name on the title page of *The James Beard Cookbook* on the shelf upstairs in his library. He told an interviewer he thought Philip Brown had been the real genius behind Helen's cookbooks.

Gino was seeing younger men. Irene Sax, the writer Judith Jones assigned to James to write *Beard on Pasta*—the book that would be his last—spent weeks at the house on West Twelfth in 1980, recording recipes as James and his new assistant cooked corn macaroni and crab ravioli. Sometimes, as Irene sat in the kitchen near the doorway to the front stairs and foyer, Gino would accompany some young man to the door, guys who'd obviously spent the night in Gino's apartment. One morning, James looked up at Gino's departing guest—an unshaven man in his late twenties—shook his head, and growled a single word, a commentary on the youth of Gino's conquest of the night before: "*Veal.*"

James Beard, Inc. was still churning at full speed, even though the master had slowed. He had a new assistant, Richard Nimmo—Carl's replacement. Richard was bald, with a mustache and a gentle spirit. Queer, of course. Richard was quiet, especially when he drank, which he did every day. A bottle of vodka in Richard's general vicinity disappeared fast. His duties included assisting Gino with the dacquoises, though eventually another aspiring food writer, Robert Carmack, relieved Richard of that.

Jackie Mallorca, a woman in San Francisco who'd been the force behind the Williams-Sonoma catalogs, was doing James's syndicated column now, after José Wilson took her own life in 1980. Richard helped with the column and radio scripts, the pleas to show up for demos at department stores and fundraisers, the book galleys and endorsements that had to be okayed, the requests by magazines to name the best new restaurants or to pass along a favorite trick for carving Easter lamb. And yet how lonely James's world remained, despite the cheerful clutter of chinoiserie and majolica tchotchkes, the hanging ferns in the high windows, the mishmash of Minton fish plates, Victorian wine rinsers, and pitchers shaped like ears of corn.

For all of Jerry Lamb's decorating, James disliked 167 West Twelfth Street; it had always been too cramped and too dark. James relished the thought of it being sold after he made his final curtain call on this life that had played for far too long, though he took comfort in knowing that Gino would be safe upstairs. Gino had glimpsed more of James's heart than anyone still alive—beautiful, maddening Gino. He'd lived through the best and worst of James. Perhaps only Clay knew more about where James had hidden almost all the bones from the skeletons of his past.

On January 8, for what would prove James's final journey to the hospital, the ambulance men strapped him onto the stretcher. They made him wait until another attendant arrived from Saint Luke's across the street: It would take three of them to carry him down the atrium stairs. In the minutes they waited, James held Clay's hand and said, "This is the last time, Babes. I know I'm not ever coming back." He looked at Clay and said, "Nobody would believe it if they knew," because he understood that Babes had seen a lot, but still he didn't grasp it all.

And Clay said, "I know, Mr. Beard, I know. They just wouldn't believe it."

There was so much that nobody knew.

ACKNOWLEDGMENTS

To WRITE A BIOGRAPHY is to plead with ghosts to move in so you can study them; it's only later that you discover what stubborn houseguests the dead can be. So first I want to thank my husband, Perry Lucina, for his patience with the greedy shadows who demanded most of my time and nearly all my focus. My love to Perry, also, for serving as chief researcher and supporter of this book, acting as road manager during our summer of sifting through archives in New York City, and for embarking on this journey—same as all the others we've taken—with an appetite for wonder and a taste for change.

How do I begin to describe my gratitude to my onetime *Lucky Peach* editors Chris Ying and Peter Meehan? I can't repay the debt I owe them for prodding along "America, Your Food Is So Gay," my 2013 essay that contained the kernel of this biography, just as I can't stop mourning the food magazine that nurtured writers and artists like no other.

Thanks likewise to Lukas Volger and Steve Viksjo, founders of the queer food magazine *Jarry*, for tracing the outlines of a world that James drew first in invisible ink. They invited me into the very first issue, and we found a community.

To my agents, Steve Troha and Dado Derviskadic of Folio Literary Management, for all the times they had a surer sense of my voice than self-doubt allowed me to hear. To my editor, Melanie Tortoroli, who trusted where the manuscript took me. Also to Maria Guarnaschelli and John Glusman, likewise in the Norton family, who thought I might have something to say; and to Will Scarlett, associate director of publicity at Norton, whose excitement for this book has never cooled.

Thanks to those who knew James and who dredged up anecdotes

and memories: Peter Aaron, Gerald Asher, Ariane Batterberry, Hilary Baum, Ronald Bricke, Robert Carmack, Billy Cross, Jim Dodge, Morris Galen, Mary Goodbody, Dan Greenburg, Madhur Jaffrey, Matt Kramer, Jerry Lamb, Chris Lenwell, Alec Lobrano, Nick Malgieri, Cornelius O'Donnell, Judith Olney, Madeline Poley, Ruth Reichl, Claudia Roden, Irene Sax, Raymond Sokolov, Caroline Stuart, Jeremiah Tower, Patricia Unterman, Alice Waters, Golda Weiss, Michael Whiteman, Clark Wolf, and Louis Worden. I'm grateful to Carl Jerome for his kindness and generosity, and especially his openness. The same to John P. Carroll, who invited me to sit at his table in San Francisco for long talks and Jue Let's tea cake.

And to those, sadly, who shared what they knew of James but passed away before this book could take form: John Bennett, in his memorabilia-crammed home in Oklahoma City; Charles "Joe" Goodner; James Villas; and especially Tom Margittai, who took me to lunch at Zuni Café in San Francisco and charged me with making my biography a good one—a challenge, as I understood it, to capture James in all his complexity.

To those who cast light on James and his world by remembering friends, parents, or other relatives who knew him: Renée Davis, Nicole Duplaix, Jonathan Ned Katz, Jim Mellgren, Elizabeth Randal, Mike Rhode, Lumi Sava, Tim Schaffner, Jill Stanford, and Alastair Watt.

To the historians and scholars who were generous with their time and their knowledge: Víctor M. Macías-González of the University of Wisconsin–La Crosse; Jacqueline Peterson-Loomis of the Portland Chinatown Museum; Charles Kaiser, gay historian of New York City; Thomas A. Guglielmo of George Washington University; Giovanni Dall'Orto and Gerard Koskovich, specialists in European LGBTQ history; Joanna Black of the GLBT Historical Society in San Francisco; and Rachel Hope Cleves. A huge thanks to Sara B. Franklin, author of a forthcoming Judith Jones biography, for generously sharing selected transcripts.

I'm grateful to David Kamp, author of *The United States of Arugula,* and Robert Clark, who wrote the last Beard biography, for moral support and other gracious gestures; likewise to Mitchell Davis and

Diane Harris Brown of the James Beard Foundation. I could not have researched this book without the help of Marvin J. Taylor and Nicholas Martin of NYU's Fales Library and Special Collections, and their 2017 summer crew of pages, who delivered box after box of archival materials with cheerful efficiency. At Reed College, my thanks to Gay Walker (now retired), Dena Hutto, and Kevin Myers. To Tom McCutchon of Columbia University's Rare Book and Manuscript Library, and to Kansas State University's David Allen, Jane E. Schillie, and Andrew Le.

Scott Daniels of the Oregon Historical Society was helpful and accommodating. So was Jeff Roberts, principal at Seaside High School in Oregon, who gave me a tour of the home-economics classroom where James taught in the 1970s.

This book would have been impossible to write without the support of Kathleen Squires and Beth Federici, makers of the 2017 documentary *America's First Foodie: The Incredible Life of James Beard.* Thanks also to Bonnie Slotnick of Bonnie Slotnick Cookbooks in Manhattan's East Village, who lent me vintage materials, and Matt Sartwell of Kitchen Arts & Letters on the Upper East Side, who helped me connect with a source.

Love to my group-chat friends Nik Sharma and Mayukh Sen—the Cecily Brownstone and Ann Seranne to my James, though on screens, rather than early morning telephone calls—for the daily round of industry gossip, career advice, media critiques, and Tears of Joy emoji. And to friend and fellow writer Sarah Henry, forced to endure the saga of this book's coalescence in real time.

Finally, I could not write at all without the mentorship of my mother, Barbara, who taught me how to love books and who still feeds our shared hunger for words, characters, and stories. Nor without the love and support of my late father, Walter, who was proud of me when I feared nobody could be, a lesson in showing compassion, even to those who happen to be less than perfect—ghosts included.

NOTES

MOST PRIMARY-SOURCE MATERIALS come from four places: the James Beard Papers at the Fales Library at New York University; the Lilly Library at Indiana University Bloomington, where most of James's letters to Helen Evans Brown are archived; the John Schaffner Papers at Columbia University in New York (also the source of Helen Evans Brown's fascinating and voluminous letters to Schaffner); and the James Beard Archives at the Oregon Historical Society in Portland, site of Isabel Callvert's papers, including drafts of books and articles that show her edits. Other important research documents include James's datebooks at NYU, covering 1953 to 1977, with some gaps in the later years; other datebooks from the 1970s are at the Oregon Historical Society. James's scrawl isn't easy to decipher, but his datebooks are a direct chronicle of what he ate, drank, saw, and thought, in a life too often mythologized.

ABBREVIATIONS

JBF   James Beard Foundation's private archives

JBI   John Birdsall Interview, unpublished transcript

JBP   James Beard Papers, The Fales Library and Special Collections, New York University

JSP   John Schaffner Papers, Rare Book and Manuscript Libraries, Columbia University

JWI   Judith Weinraub Interview, *Voices from the Food Revolution: People Who Changed the Way Americans Eat*, The Fales Library and Special Collections, New York University

KSI   Kathleen Squires Interview, unpublished transcript

LL   Beard Manuscripts, The Lilly Library, Indiana University, Bloomington

OHS   Oregon Historical Society

Reed   Richard Nelson Papers and James Beard Collection, Special Collections and Archives, Reed College

SBFI   Sara B. Franklin Interview, unpublished transcripts

PREFACE

ix   **"In the beginning":** Gael Greene, "The Father of Us All," *New York*, June 3, 1985.

xi   **"America, Your Food Is So Gay":** John Birdsall, "America, Your Food Is So Gay," *Lucky Peach*, Issue 8: Gender, Summer 2013.

xii   **"His entire life was gay":** JBI with Carl Jerome, February 16, 2017.

xii   **"it was a part":** Marion Cunningham, quoted by John P. Carroll, JBI Session #1, November 26, 2017.

xiv   **"To find traces":** Avram Finkelstein, curator's statement, "Found: Queerness as Archaeology," Leslie-Lohman Museum, New York, June 7–September 10, 2017.

xiv   **"Even if we knew":** Jean-Yves Tadié, *Marcel Proust: A Life*, translated by Euan Cameron (Viking, 2000), p. xviii.

CHAPTER 1: THE SWADDLED HAM

3   **Warrenton. Columbia Beach. Carnahan:** *Morning Oregonian*, advertisement for the Clatsop Beach Line of the Spokane, Portland, and Seattle Railroad, July 28, 1922.

3   **three times a year:** James Beard, "A James Beard Memoir," in *The James Beard Celebration Cookbook*, James Beard Foundation, ed. Barbara Kafka, p. 33.

4   **father rarely joined:** James Beard, *Delights and Prejudices*, p. 205.

4   **on the deck of the observation car:** Ibid., p. 207.

5   **Elizabeth took him to hear:** Heidi Waleson, "Beard on Opera," *Opera News*, July 1983.

5   **sticky homemade marshmallows:** James Beard, *James Beard's American Cookery*, p. 828. "I remember a friend of my mother's who made extraordinary chocolates, marshmallows—very fashionable then—and wonderful nougat, redolent with the flavor of nuts and sometimes fruits."

5   **the cooked ham:** Beard, *Delights and Prejudices*, p. 206.

5   **still-new Hawthorne Bridge:** "December 19, 1910: Hawthorne Bridge Opens," City of Portland Archives, 1902 to 1952, https://www.portlandoregon.gov/archives/article/284517.

6   **blue serge suit:** Beard, *Celebration Cookbook*, p. 24.

6   **At 8:15 their train:** "The Road Schedules Change," *Morning Oregonian*, September 10, 1907.

7   **Beard family cook:** Beard, *Delights and Prejudices*, p. 34. "After [Let] returned to the country of his birth, when I was about ten, I never again tasted a teacake with as much character."

7   **He knew it all:** James Beard, "Picnicking Can Be a Gourmet's Delight," in *James Beard's Simple Foods*, pp. 151–52. "I adored that trip, and I knew every inch of the landscape, the river, and the towns and landmarks."

7   **Next was Rainier:** Beard, *Delights and Prejudices*, p. 207. "[T]he first stop of any importance was Rainier on the river." According to train schedules, St. Helens was the first stop; Rainier was second (though James's assessment of Rainier as the first stop of importance is no doubt correct).

8   **larking about:** "Summer Heat Drives Crowds to Seashore," *Sunday Oregonian*, August 8, 1909.

8 **the Daddy Train:** Greg Gordon, "Astoria and Columbia River Railroad," *The Oregon Encyclopedia*, OHS, https://oregonencyclopedia.org/articles/astoria_and_columbia_ river_railroad. "Special weekend service was known as the 'Daddy Train,' as businessmen could leave Portland on Saturday, spend the weekend with their families vacationing on the coast, and be back at work on Monday morning."

9 **He almost relished:** Beard, *Delights and Prejudices*, p. 207.

9 **butter-and-marmalade sandwiches:** James Beard, S.S. *San Marco*, to Isabel Callvert, undated [1960], OHS. "I remember sitting on the observation platform of the train to Gearhart and having a little box of marmalade sandwiches and a hardboiled egg and some fruit and cookies to while away the hours till lunch on arrival at Gearhart."

9 **bitter-orange marmalade:** James Beard, "Marmalade, Bittersweet Treat," in *The Armchair James Beard*, ed. John Ferrone, p. 154. "To those of us who were brought up with some British background, the epitome of marmalade is the dark, tart kind made from Seville oranges, which have a bitter tang like that of wild oranges."

9 **a cruel husband:** Beard, *Celebration Cookbook*, p. 24. "Mrs. Harris was a very independent woman who was married to a bastard."

9 **pasture's edge of Oregon City:** US Bureau of the Census, "Grace M. Harris," 1910 United States Federal Census. Grace M. (age thirty-eight) and Charles B. Harris (age forty-seven) are described as living in "Abernathy, Clackamas, Oregon."

10 **a low trestle bridge:** Historical photographs ("Seaside Train Crossing Young's Bay, 1912"; "Astoria Municipal Docks, 1918"; "Columbia River Jetty, 1910"), "Astoria and Columbia River Railroad," *The Oregon Encyclopedia*, OHS, https://oregonencyclopedia.org/articles/ astoria_and_columbia_river_railroad/#.XX_BSiV7ndR.

10 **Astoria, city of salmon!:** Beard, *American Cookery*, p. 119. "I can remember when Astoria at the mouth of the Columbia was the center of the salmon industry, a city on piers, with canneries and nets and fishing boats strung along the waterfront as far as the eye could see."

10 **spitting range of any train:** Historical photograph (undated), "View of the Train Trestle Where the Train for Several Miles on the Way to Astoria," in "Astoria," PdxHistory.com, http://www.pdxhistory.com/html/astoria.html.

10 **Finnish and Norwegian gillnetters:** Historical photograph, undated (1904–1910), "Erik Erickson, Alfred Erickson, Astoria, Oregon, Gillnetters," in "Columbia River Gillnetters," *HistoricFishing*, https://historicfishing.smugmug.com/History/Columbia-River-Gillnetters2/i -xNWkvCR.

11 **whirl of its sawmills:** Various historical photographs, "Astoria," PdxHistory.com, http:// www.pdxhistory.com/html/astoria.html.

12 **Harry Hamblet:** Beard, *Delights and Prejudices*, pp. 208–9. "Harry Hamblet was the most thoroughly generous and outgoing man I think I ever knew."

12 **Peter Grant:** Beard, *Delights and Prejudices*, p. 217. "[Peter Grant was] in the cannery business and commuted all summer between Gearhart and the plant in Astoria."

12 **forming a shallow V:** Historical photograph (undated), "Boarding the Train at Gearhart Depot," "Gearhart by the Sea," PdxHistory.com, http://www.pdxhistory.com/html/ gearhart.html.

12 **as if she were:** Beard, *Delights and Prejudices*, p. 208. "When she stepped from the train, it was like the arrival of a celebrated prima donna."

12 **Mary Garden:** James Beard, quoted in Heidi Waleson, "Beard on Opera," *Opera News*, July 1983. "[Garden] was a perpetual flame wherever she was. . . . She had . . . that great quality of always being in front of everybody else." My description of a specific photo of Garden descending at the Gare du Nord is fanciful.

13 **John Tyberg:** James Beard, *Delights and Prejudices*, p. 208. According to Ancestry.com, Tyberg was manager of the Gearhart Garage in 1917.

13 **boxed-lunch picnic:** Beard, *Delights and Prejudices*, p. 250. "Mother packed the sandwiches in individual baskets for each family group and put name tags on them. . . ."

13 **beach breakfast of hotcakes:** Beard, *Delights and Prejudices*, pp. 243–44.

13 **had to write early:** Helen Knopf, quoted in Evan Jones, *Epicurean Delight: The Life and Times of James Beard*, p. 15. "[Mrs. Beard] would only take as many reservations as she chose to handle—no overbooking."

14 **in the Beard cottage:** Knopf, quoted in Jones, *Epicurean Delight*, pp. 15–16.

14 **pedestrian boardwalk:** Michelle, "Days Gone By in Gearhart," *Shell's Cottage*, June 1, 2016, https://shellscottage.com/days-gone-by-in-gearhart/.

14 **Clatsop Indians trudged along:** City of Gearhart Historic Landmarks Commission, *Gearhart, Oregon, Historic Context Statement*, second edition (revised), September 1999, pp. 13–14.

14 **camass roots and razor clams:** Koler/Morrison Preservation and Planning Consultants, *A Survey and Inventory of Historic Resources, City of Seaside, Oregon*, 1987, p. 9.

14 **called to them for salmon:** City of Gearhart, *Historic Context Statement*, p. 16. "[A] seasonal fishing community, or string of communities, existed along the elevated eastern bank of the Neacoxie from well north of the present [Gearhart] city limits all the way to Little Beach."

14 **sacred fish:** Koler/Morrison, *Historic Resources*, p. 9. "[The] Clatsops believed the salmon to be a divine gift from the wolf-spirit Talapus who created the great fish to save their people from extinction at a legendary time of near disaster."

14 **tomorrow morning by five:** Beard, *Delights and Prejudices*, p. 211.

14 **washed-up skate carcasses:** James A. Beard, *James Beard's Fish Cookery*, p. 200. "Abundant on both coasts, the skate is regarded by most people as something odd and uneatable that floats in on the tide. Children are fascinated by them, and dogs like to roll on top of them, apparently preferring them to any other type of dead fish. . . ."

15 **studiously pastoral cottages:** City of Gearhart, *Historic Context Statement*, p. 19. "[T]he houses that sprang up in Gearhart had at least one thing in common: they were all 'beach cottages' . . . Gearhart was a place of magic and fantasy, and the cottage needed to reflect that. . . ."

15 **worshipful pursuit of leisure:** Ibid.

15 **Philip Gearhart:** City of Gearhart, *Historic Context Statement*, p. 15.

16 **bought up acre after acre:** City of Gearhart, *Historic Context Statement*, p. 16.

16 **Narcissa oversaw the platting:** City of Gearhart, *Historic Context Statement*, p. 17.

16 **no alcoholic beverage:** "[Narcissa Kinney's] great heart was stirred to its very depths by the wrongs inflicted upon defenseless women and children by the liquor traffic . . . so she threw her whole soul into the battle for prohibition." *Portrait and Biographical Record of Western Oregon*, Chapman Publishing Company, Chicago, 1904, p. 121.

16 **Chautauqua Literary and Scientific Circle:** Andrew C. Rieser, *The Chautauqua Moment: Protestants, Progressives, and the Culture of Modern Liberalism* (Columbia University Press, 2003), pp. 54–57.

16 **In its prime:** Michelle, "Days Gone By," *Shell's Cottage*, June 1, 2016, https://shellscottage .com/days-gone-by-in-gearhart/.

16 **Lewis and Clark Centennial:** Heather Arndt Anderson, *Portland: A Food Biography*, pp. 101–2.

17 **Kruse was a German:** George Painter, *The Vice Clique: Portland's Great Sex Scandal*, p. 218.

17 **field of undulating green:** James Beard, quoted in John Minahan, introduction to *James Beard's Simple Foods*, pp. xviii–xix. "[T]here in the beach house, it was sort of an idyllic existence, because we were in the center of a big meadow near the ocean."

17 **tongue-and-groove fir:** James Beard, "A James Beard Memoir," in *The James Beard Celebration Cookbook*, James Beard Foundation, ed. Barbara Kafka, pp. 32–33. "I have more of a fondness for the beach than I do for that house. It was quite a small house. It was shingle tongue and groove fir and natural finish. It was never painted inside. It was always natural wood."

17 **real estate office:** US Bureau of the Census, "Harry Hamblet," 1910 United States Federal Census. Harry (age forty-two) was described as being in the real estate business. In 1895,

Hamblet purchased a cigar store in Astoria, to annex for his business next door [*Morning Astorian*, February 7, 1895].

18 **The stove itself was tiny:** Beard, "Tools of My Trade" (1973), in *The Armchair James Beard*, p. 11. "In my early years at the beach in Oregon, I cooked on a small woodstove that could hardly hold one big pan and required an intricate regulation of heat."

18 **They would write:** Beard, *Delights and Prejudices*, p. 208.

18 **rash of fires and vandalism:** City of Gearhart, *Historic Context Statement*, p. 23.

18 **the Louvre's men-only:** Anderson, *Portland: A Food Biography*, pp. 181–82.

18 **would take James to dine:** Beard, *Delights and Prejudices*, pp. 174–75. "Mother was out of her mind to take me there in the first place."

18 **to rezone Gearhart:** City of Gearhart, *Historic Context Statement*, p. 21.

19 **Gin Ridge:** Since it lay just west of Narcissa Kinney's legal dry zone, Ocean Avenue (along with Kruse's hotel) was booze-friendly territory.

19 **Summers became a whirl:** "Bathing and Excursions Are Diversions at Coast Resorts," *Sunday Oregonian*, August 19, 1906.

19 **mugged for portraits:** Various historical souvenir portraits, undated (1916–1919), "Seaside Museum Historical Beach Photos," Seaside Historical Society Museum, https://www.seasideoregonmuseum.com/Historical/beach.html.

19 **porch like a colonnade:** Historical photograph, undated (1910?), Fred H. Kiser, "Grand Hotel at Gearhart, Oregon," OHS.

19 **to take charge:** Marion Kingery, quoted in Jones, *Epicurean Delight*, p. 15. "[W]e'd usually meet at the old coastal hotel where Mrs. Beard often supervised the preparation of dinner."

21 **slurry of English mustard powder:** James Beard, "Happy Hamming," in *James Beard's Simple Foods*, p. 122. "In that hamper there was sure to be a delicious cooked ham, simply glazed with mustard, crumbs, and a bit of brown sugar. We would have two good meals from it. . . ."

22 **Chinese ginger jars:** Beard, *Celebration Cookbook*, p. 25. ". . . [G]inger in jars—those beautiful jars that people buy in antique shops now, the blue-green ones and the sort of drab gray ones, and some of them had beautiful patterns on them. You'd have those to use for everything. You'd take them to the beach and use them for flowers."

23 **"grandest and most pleasing prospects":** William Clark, entry for January 8, 1805 [1806], *Journals of the Lewis and Clark Expedition*, University of Nebraska Press, https://lewisandclarkjournals.unl.edu/item/lc.jrn.1806-01-08. "We set out early and proceeded to the top of the mountain . . . which is much the highest part and that part faceing [*sic*] the sea is open, from this point I beheld the grandest and most pleasing prospects which my eyes ever surveyed, in my frount [*sic*] a boundless ocean. . . ."

23 **freedom enough to dawdle:** Beard, quoted in Minahan, introduction to *James Beard's Simple Foods*, p. xix.

23 **pick huckleberries:** Beard, *Delights and Prejudices*, p. 232.

23 **troll the Necanicum River:** Beard, *Fish Cookery*, p. 349. "As a young boy, I often fished for crawfish in the Necanicum River in Oregon, using a piece of liver on a string."

CHAPTER 2: MANGOES IN PANAMA

24 **The baby arrived:** This is an imagined scene. The details of James's birth are unknown, though he surely would have been born at home, at a time in America when doctors had taken the place of midwives.

24 **thirteen pounds!:** Beard to Helen Evans Brown, June 3, 1955, LL. "[The lobsters] weighed exactly thirteen pounds (just what I weighed when I was born)."

25 **Let's Welsh rabbits and apple charlottes:** Beard, *Delights and Prejudices*, p. 18. "Another famous dish of Let's was his welsh rabbit." Beard, *Delights and Prejudices*, p. 143.

25 **Episcopal prayer book:** Later in life, in letters, James Beard quoted from *The Pocket*

Prayer Book, Second Edition, The Philanthropic Society (St. George's Fields, London, 1807), suggesting he had been familiar with it as a boy.

25 **BORN:** Birth notices, *Morning Oregonian*, May 6, 1903.

25 **January 7, 1861:** Obituary for Mrs. John A. Beard, *Oregonian*, August 17, 1940.

25 **near Westbury, in Wiltshire . . . . Charlotte and Joseph Jones:** "The Prangley Family of Corsley, Wiltshire, England," http://freepages.rootsweb.com/~rykbrown/genealogy/prangley_world_database.htm. This genealogy might offer clues about the Jones family of Wiltshire, except, though it shows a Frederick Jones (possibly James's Uncle Fred, born in 1880), it fails to mention a Mary Elizabeth Jones, born in 1861.

25 **Mary Elizabeth Jones:** Obituary for Mrs. John A. Beard, *Oregonian*, August 17, 1940.

26 **white chalk horse:** Michael Randall, *Westbury in Old Photographs* (Alan Sutton, 1988), p. 93.

26 **Hawarden Castle:** James Beard, "A James Beard Memoir," in *The James Beard Celebration Cookbook*, James Beard Foundation, ed. Barbara Kafka, p. 16. "My grandfather was a superintendent, first of Mr. Gladstone's estate."

26 **cottages of Irish workers:** Ibid.

27 **her aunt Clara:** Beard, *Celebration Cookbook*, pp. 16–17.

27 **British Holiness Movement:** Ibid.

27 **a woman visiting London:** Beard, *Celebration Cookbook*, p. 17.

28 **confusion, a rush:** These details are from a contemporary account by Robert Louis Stevenson, "Traveling on an Emigrant Train, 1879," in *The Amateur Emigrant*.

28 **landed her first position:** Beard, *Celebration Cookbook*, p. 17.

29 **Chinese truck farms:** *Dreams of the West: A History of the Chinese in Oregon 1850–1950* (Ooligan Press/Chinese Consolidated Benevolent Association, 2007), pp. 70–71.

29 **a death in the family:** Beard, *Celebration Cookbook*, p. 17.

29 **the Maxwells:** Ibid.

30 **returned to London:** Beard, *Celebration Cookbook*, p. 18.

30 **Lizzie H. Curtis:** *Langley's San Francisco Directory for the Year Commencing April 1886*, p. 386. "Curtis Lizzie H. Mrs., r. [residence] 1037 Post."

30 **her stylish boardinghouses:** *San Francisco Chronicle*, August 7, 1883. "Parties desirous of obtaining an elegant home without the care pertaining thereto can do so by applying to Mrs. Curtis of 1037 Post street, who proposes renting one of the best-appointed and most elegantly furnished private houses in the city; it is situated on Sutter street, east of Larkin, and will be devoted to the comfort of a few couples, who will have the use of drawing, billiard and smoking-rooms; stable attached."

30 **live in San Francisco:** In both *Delights and Prejudices* (p. 11) and *The James Beard Celebration Cookbook* (p. 18), James suggests that Elizabeth went to work for Mrs. Curtis at her Portland boardinghouse. City directories don't show Mrs. Curtis in Portland until 1892, however, and since the rough timeline James offers has his mother in the boardinghouse starting in 1886 or 1887, I contend that in fact Elizabeth worked at the Curtis properties in San Francisco. A residency there would also explain Elizabeth's familiarity with the city in later years, when young James accompanied her there.

30 **"Superior table":** *San Francisco Chronicle*, May 2, 1889; "excellent board": *San Francisco Chronicle*, October 12, 1884.

31 **Stella Chase Ainsworth:** *Oakland Daily Evening Tribune*, May 22, 1886.

31 **Salmon P. Chase:** "Amusements," *San Francisco Examiner*, December 6, 1887.

31 **invited her to New York:** "Gossip," *Oakland Daily Evening Tribune*, June 4, 1888.

31 **Pacific Mail steamship *Granada*:** Pacific Mail Steamship Co. notice, *San Francisco Chronicle*, July 13, 1888.

31 **Aspinwall . . . on the Caribbean:** "From Aspinwall to Panama," *New York Times*, April 4, 1885.

32 **his mother's sexuality:** James strongly suspected his mother of being a lesbian but seemed reluctant to acknowledge it. Marion Cunningham, years later, noted in her diary follow-

ing a conversation with James that "he was puzzled about his suspicion of her lesbianism." Jones, *Epicurean Delight*, p. 40n.

33 **to travel upstate:** "Behind the Footlights," *San Francisco Examiner*, June 3, 1888.

33 **to Kansas City:** Beard, *Celebration Cookbook*, p. 18. Also "Personal," *Morning Oregonian*, May 19, 1889.

33 **John Brennan:** Beard, *Delights and Prejudices*, p. 11.

33 **the mahogany dressers:** *San Francisco Chronicle*, November 2, 1891.

34 **opened in 1892:** Scott Daniels, OHS, email message to author, April 13, 2019.

34 **speculating in real estate:** "Union Pacific Reorganization," *Morning Oregonian*, November 13, 1889.

34 **scarred lion of British politics:** In 1895, several affectionate tributes to Gladstone appeared in Portland newspapers.

34 **glimmer of Carpenter Gothic:** Beard, *Celebration Cookbook*, p. 19.

35 **a lady who drank:** Beard, *Delights and Prejudices*, p. 24.

35 **young men in Lownsdale Square Park:** Peter Boag, "Portland Vice Scandal (1912–1913)," *The Oregon Encyclopedia*, OHS, https://oregonencyclopedia.org/articles/portland_vice_scandal_1912_1913_/#.XYqSriV7ndQ. "Portland discovered that city parks (such as Lownsdale, Oaks, and Council Crest) . . . served as local hangouts for men interested in sex with other men."

35 **pocketing the silver nutcrackers:** During Elizabeth's tenure with her, Lizzie Curtis became entangled in a few cases of alleged staff theft, like this one regarding a chambermaid accused of stealing towels and nutcrackers. See "She Got Damages," *San Francisco Call*, Volume 75, Number 132, April 21, 1894.

35 **The Maxwells had "Charlie":** Based on an English phrasebook for Chinese house servants in Fat Ming Co., *Chinese and English Cook Book* (San Francisco, 1913), pp. 1–22.

36 **vegetable man Lam:** *Dreams of the West*, p. 37. Ching Lam was a Portland grocer who would make the rounds of white families in a horse-drawn cart.

36 **bloody massacres:** In 1890 and again in 1900, Portland had the second largest Chinese settlement in the United States, smaller only than San Francisco's. Before and after passage of the Chinese Exclusion Act in 1882, San Francisco and other West Coast cities saw white riots against the Chinese—Celestials, as they were known—and even bloody massacres. Until 1900, Portland was relatively hospitable to men from China, thanks to the political influence of elites like the Maxwells who depended on cheap Chinese labor: Jacqueline Peterson-Loomis, "Looks Like a Good Beginning: Immigration, Ethnicity, and Exclusion in Oregon, 1850–1910," lecture for *Oregon History 101*, Oregon Historical Society, February 2, 2015, http://www.ohs.org/events/looks-like-a-good-beginning.cfm.

37 **properly gelatinous terrapin stew:** Beard, *Delights and Prejudices*, pp. 17–18.

37 **had become fiercely expensive:** Joseph Mitchell, "Mr. Barbee's Terrapin," *The New Yorker*, October 28, 1939.

38 **a young man in Illinois:** Joseph Gaston, *Portland, Oregon, Its History and Builders*, Volume 2 (S. J. Clarke Publishing Co., 1911), p. 296.

38 **born in Scio:** US Bureau of the Census, "Andrew Francis Beard," 1880 United States Federal Census.

38 **figure she showed off:** Beard, *Celebration Cookbook*, p. 16. "She was full-busted and well corseted. I would say that she was very handsome."

39 **John's salary was $1,800:** US Treasury Department, *Customs Service: 1897, Volume 1.* "John A Beard, examiner, from Iowa; Oregon appointed by Multnomah; compensation: $1,800."

39 **plush yearly income:** In 1900, the average annual US salary was $438.

39 **The newspaper called it:** *Albany* [OR] *Democrat*, April 22, 1898.

39 **soon to leave:** Gaston, *History and Builders*, p. 296.

39 **fourteen dresses:** Beard, *Celebration Cookbook*, p. 20.

40 **slipped from her waist:** Ibid.

40 **renamed it the Hobart-Curtis:** "Hobart-Curtis Leased," *Sunday Oregonian*, November 28, 1909; Scott Daniels, OHS, email message to author, April 13, 2019.

40 **Mrs. Cornell and Miss Murphy:** Beard, *Delights and Prejudices*, p. 26.

40 **Main Street near Fifth:** US Bureau of the Census, "John A. Beard," 1900 United States Federal Census (data recorded June 8, 1900).

41 **Elizabeth began to sell:** "Real Estate Transfers," *Sunday Oregonian*, April 1, 1900; *Morning Oregonian*, April 2, 1902; *Morning Oregonian*, September 26, 1903; *Oregon Daily Journal*, December 23, 1904; *Sunday Oregonian*, September 3, 1905; *Morning Oregonian*, January 7, 1905.

41 **built rental cottages:** "For Sale or Rent," *Sunday Oregonian*, March 12, 1905; *Sunday Oregonian*, March 19, 1905; *Oregon Daily Journal*, March 20, 1905; *Sunday Oregonian*, April 2, 1905; *Sunday Oregonian*, May 7, 1905.

41 **a proper house:** Beard, *Celebration Cookbook*, p. 20.

CHAPTER 3: JUE LET'S TRUE ESSENCE OF CHICKEN

42 **Oaks Park:** Beard, *Delights and Prejudices*, p. 250. For the Chilcoot Pass, Whirlwind, and natatorium, see "The Oaks Amusement Park," PdxHistory.com, http://www.pdxhistory.com/html/oaks_park.html.

42 **White Mountain cake:** Beard, *James Beard's American Cookery*, pp. 662–63. "Blessed with an insatiable taste for coconut, I always wanted a cake piled high with it. And since my birthday came in May, there were usually hawthorn blossoms available to decorate the plate . . . usually a sunshine or moonshine cake or a white mountain cake."

43 **with multicolored layers:** Chester S. Benson, Portland, Oregon, to James Beard, May 14, 1969, JBP.

43 **Lester, Morris, and Virgil Coomer:** "Cards of Thanks," *Sunday Oregonian*, January 8, 1922.

43 **trolling in streams:** Beard, *Fish Cookery*, p. 300. "When I was about eight years old, my neighborhood contemporaries were always running off on fishing excursions and coming home with suckers—and I was never very much impressed."

43 **Elizabeth and John . . . read Dickens:** Jones, *Epicurean Delight*, p. 41.

44 **sexual transgressions:** Beard, *Celebration Cookbook*, p. 24. "There were a lot of people with unusual sexual lifestyles and my mother always seemed to attract them."

44 **inversion:** I use *inversion* here in a historical context, as a term more or less synonymous with homosexuality before the latter word was in wide use in the United States. According to Havelock Ellis, *Studies in the Psychology of Sex, Volume 2: Sexual Inversion* (1927): "Sexual inversion . . . means sexual instinct turned by inborn constitutional abnormality toward persons of the same sex."

44 **knew Mrs. Falt:** Beard, *Celebration Cookbook*, p. 21. [Barbara Kafka, who transcribed James's taped memoir, misspelled the name as "Fault."]

44 **famous for crawfish:** Anderson, *Portland: A Food Biography*, p. 196.

44 **"I suppose you've been":** Beard, *Celebration Cookbook*, p. 24.

44 **He had a temper:** Beard, *Celebration Cookbook*, pp. 23–24. "I was a large child and I was terrible to the other children. . . ."

44 **a regal friend:** Beard, "Cream and Schlag" (1983), in *The Armchair James Beard*, p. 145.

45 **Esther Kelly:** Esther K. Watson, Portland, Oregon, to Beard, May 23, 1984, Reed.

45 **Andrew Kan:** Elliott Robert Barkan, *From All Points: America's Immigrant West, 1870s–1952* (Indiana University Press, 2007), pp. 228–29.

45 **in Buster Brown style:** Beard, *Celebration Cookbook*, p. 24.

45 **in Chinese suits:** Beard, *Celebration Cookbook*, p. 20.

45 **Japanese loose-weave cotton:** Beard to Helen Evans Brown, May 14, 1955, LL. "I adore the shirt—[it] makes me think of a Japanese fabric that I used to wear when I was a kid. Pleasantly scratchy and cooling."

45 **his own collection:** Beard, *Celebration Cookbook*, p. 22.

45 **Elizabeth had begun collecting:** Ibid.

45 **a large American flag:** Historical photograph, "Andrew Kan and Co., China Store, Portland, Ore.," between 1895 and 1910, United States Library of Congress, Prints and Photographs Division, digital ID det.4a20691.

46 **Honolulu and the South Sea Islands:** "In a Talented Woman's Honor," *Woodland* [CA] *Daily Democrat*, September 25, 1908.

46 **a Chinese American boy:** Beard, *Celebration Cookbook*, p. 22.

46 **famous for his coleslaw:** Beard, *Delights and Prejudices*, p. 171.

46 **their cousin John Kan:** Beard, unpublished draft of his foreword to *Eight Immortal Flavors*, by Johnny Kan with Charles L. Leong (Howell-North Books, 1963), 1962, OHS. "[John Kan] was [in Portland] for a while and then went with his family to Eastern Oregon to a spot called Grass Valley."

46 **Andrew Junior:** "Chinese Student Attains Prominence," *Sunday Oregonian*, February 13, 1910.

46 **Mr. Kan . . . was beautiful:** Photo, date unknown, showing Andrew Kan at a party. He's remarkably handsome. [Source: Jackie Loomis-Peterson.]

46 **incubators for the disease:** "Can This Germ Climb?" *Oregon Daily Journal*, March 7, 1906.

47 **the Coomer boys:** Though the Coomers lived next door to the Beards, this is an imagined detail.

47 **Let appeared:** Beard, *Fowl and Game Cookery*, p. vii.

47 **whirl of his mother's dominion:** Beard, *Celebration Cookbook*, p. 16. "My mother was a magnificent rustle; she never quite stopped at anything. She rustled and she rushed."

48 **ponderous heap of masonry:** Historical photograph, Brück and Son Kunstverlag, Meissen, "U.S. Custom House, Portland, Ore.," 1906, Creative Commons, ID File:08269.

48 **pioneer roots:** Beard, *Celebration Cookbook*, p. 16. "I'm one generation from the covered wagon."

49 **After Summers died:** "Three Named for Appraiser," *Morning Oregonian*, March 27, 1911.

49 **didn't put forth:** "Customs Job Still Open," *Morning Oregonian*, March 8, 1911.

49 **On chicken mornings . . . ferociously with black pepper:** Beard, *Fowl and Game Cookery*, pp. 14–16.

50 **shape of legend:** Beard, *Delights and Prejudices*, p. 277.

50 **with natives on the Plains:** Beard, *Celebration Cookbook*, p. 24.

50 **Emma Clifford Biggers:** US Bureau of the Census, "John A. Beard," 1890 United States Federal Census.

50 **the Santa Claus suit:** Beard, *Delights and Prejudices*, pp. 164–65.

51 **delight in turning them out:** Beard, *Delights and Prejudices*, p. 25.

51 **men's retreats:** *Morning Oregonian*, July 17, 1901. "Deputy Health Commissioner William J. Beutelspacher and Customs Examiner John A. Beard have returned from an outing to St. Martin's Springs, much improved in health, and with appetites that scare their friends."

51 **Multnomah Camp No. 77:** "Lodge Continues Growth," *Sunday Oregonian*, December 4, 1921.

51 **mystical pioneer values . . . "Dum Tacet Clamet":** Lisa Hix, "Goat Rituals and Tree-Trunk Gravestones: The Peculiar History of Life Insurance," *Collectors Weekly*, https://www.collectorsweekly.com/articles/the-peculiar-history-of-life-insurance/.

52 **dollop of egg-butter-sugar batter:** Beard, "Tasteful Holiday Buffets," in *James Beard's Simple Foods*, p. 201.

52 **sailed south with James:** Beard, *Delights and Prejudices*, p. 182.

52 **stayed at the Palace . . . veal chops and sand dabs:** Beard, *Delights and Prejudices*, pp. 183–86.

52 **farming town of Woodland:** "Reception to Talented and Charming Woman," *Woodland Daily Democrat* (Woodland, California), September 30, 1912.

52 **Elizabeth spotted a woman:** Beard, in Jones, *Epicurean Delight*, p. 40. "I remember her riding in a black satin tailor-made suit with beautiful shoes."

53 **James ate by himself:** Beard, *Celebration Cookbook*, p. 21.

53 **cream wallpaper with red polka dots:** Beard, "The Stomach, Heart, and Spirit of the House" (1968), in *The Armchair James Beard*, pp. 4–5.

53 **tin baby's bathtub:** Beard, *Fish Cookery*, p. 157.

53 **He sent trays up:** Beard, "The Stomach, Heart, and Spirit of the House" (1968), in *The Armchair James Beard*, p. 5. "He made it known that he would prefer fixing breakfast and sending it upstairs on trays rather than have any company."

54 **Elizabeth took possession:** Ibid.

54 **wild sour grass:** Beard, *Cook It Outdoors*, p. 127.

54 **In spring, the lilac:** Beard, "The Stomach, Heart, and Spirit of the House" (1968), in *The Armchair James Beard*, p. 4.

54 **lacy mass of pinkish blossoms . . . as many as eighty!:** Beard, "Quince, a Forgotten Fruit" (1982), in *The Armchair James Beard*, pp. 148–49.

54 **branches on the Lambert:** Beard, *Celebration Cookbook*, p. 26.

54 **Three large Gravenstein:** Beard, *Celebration Cookbook*, p. 28.

54 **where it shimmered:** Beard, "The Joys of Jams, Jellies, and Preserves," in *James Beard's Simple Foods*, p. 135.

55 **ghostly white with field mushrooms:** Beard, *American Cookery*, p. 524. Also Beard, *Cook It Outdoors*, p. 148. "Nothing better grows on this earth."

55 **how to pluck:** Beard, *Celebration Cookbook*, p. 31.

55 **"Look at this, waiter":** Ian Hay Beith, "The Crimson Cocoanut," in *The Crimson Cocoanut and Other Plays* (Walter H. Baker and Company, 1913), p. 17.

55 **"It's only a fly":** Ibid.

55 **"Take your fingers out":** Ibid.

56 **"Confound and dash it!":** Beith, *Crimson Cocoanut*, p. 18.

56 **"James Beard nearly rivaled":** *Oregon Daily Journal*, May 25, 1919.

56 **The students raised $250:** Ibid.

56 **dark halls and four flights:** Billie Fenimore, *The Lens* (Washington High School periodical), June 1919. "[W]e love your old, dim halls, your clanging bells and your wearying flights of steps. We love every gray stone you are made of. . . ."

56 **future doom:** "High School Blaze Is Laid to Firebug," *Morning Oregonian*, October 26, 1922. On October 25, 1922, two and a half years after James graduated, fire destroyed Washington High. Fortunately, there were no fatalities.

56 **influenza outbreak in Boston:** Ivan M. Woolley, "The 1918 'Spanish Influenza' Pandemic in Oregon," *Oregon Historical Quarterly*, vol. 64, no. 3 (September 1963), pp. 247–49.

57 **ordered the schools closed:** Bessie Ford, *The Lens*, December 1918.

57 **"How everybody laughed":** J.B. [James Beard], *The Lens*, December 1918.

57 **"the 'most' sergeant-at-arms":** *The Lens*, April 1919.

58 **"Actors," James wrote:** *The Lens*, January 1920.

58 **"Knowledge is power":** Ethel Watts Mumford, Oliver Herford, and Addison Mizner, *The Entirely New Cynic's Calendar of Revised Wisdom for 1905* (Paul Elder and Company, 1905), p. 15.

58 **"You may lead":** Mumford et al., *Cynic's Calendar*, p. 22.

58 **"Tell the truth":** Mumford et al., *Cynic's Calendar*, p. 11.

58 **"Actresses will happen":** Mumford et al., *Cynic's Calendar*, p. 25.

58 **he liked boys:** Beard, *Celebration Cookbook*, p. 24. "By the time I was seven, I knew that I was gay."

58 **"Hard on the Eyes":** *The Lens*, December 1919.

58 **Edwin Booth:** Ibid.

CHAPTER 4: CECIL FANNING'S TEA CAKE

60 **one of eighty-five first-year students:** "Reed College Is Fit for Big Work Beginning Monday," *Oregon Daily Journal*, September 12, 1920.
61 **perfect for each other:** "Where College Boys Prefer Study to Baseball," *New York Times*, April 15, 1917.
61 **Simeon Gannett Reed:** "Reed, Simeon Gannett (1830–1895)" in "The New (Olde) Reed Almanac," ed. Chris Lydgate, *Reed Magazine*, vol. 90, no. 4, December 2011.
61 **with millions:** "Where College Boys Prefer Study to Baseball," *New York Times*, April 15, 1917.
61 **William Trufant Foster:** Ibid.
62 **"had made no mistakes":** Ibid.
62 **"regular provision for religious thought":** *Quest* [Reed College student newspaper], March 23, 1921.
62 **"Glance at the old":** *Griffin* yearbook, 1921, p. 3.
62 **"You are entering Reed":** "Welcome, Class of 1924," *Quest*, September 5, 1920.
63 **"And when you have":** Ibid.
63 **freshman class treasurer:** "Frosh Nominate," *Quest*, September 21, 1920.
63 **interclass tug-of-war:** "Crystal Springs Envelopes [*sic*] Frosh," *Quest*, October 13, 1920.
63 **"the rope pulled taut":** Ibid.
64 **campus straw poll:** "Harding Elected by Reed Students," *Quest*, October 27, 1920.
64 **stretching beyond campus lines:** Carol Summerfield and Mary Elizabeth Devine, eds., *International Dictionary of University Histories* (Fitzroy Dearborn Publishers, 1998), p. 346.
64 **Comrades of the Quest:** "Where College Boys Prefer Study to Baseball," *New York Times*, April 15, 1917.
65 **"Reed college opens":** "Reed College Is Fit for Big Work Beginning Monday," *Oregon Daily Journal*, September 12, 1920.
65 **head of the new German department:** *Oregon Daily Journal*, September 5, 1920.
65 **House I . . . Herman Kenin:** An undated [1972?], handwritten note by Florence W. Lehman ["FWL"], Reed class of 1941 (director of alumni relations from 1963 to 1986; later college archivist), summarizing a letter from James to Gladys Blaine Chambers (class of 1922), dated April 16, 1972, reveals that James was a resident of House I, and that Kenin and Bechtold were his close neighbors in the men's dorm. Herman D. Kenin (1901–1970) became a well-known West Coast bandleader and union organizer.
66 **a resident parrot:** "House I," *Griffin* yearbook, 1921, p. 45.
66 **"mystic lair":** Ibid.
66 **Kansas farm town:** *Advocate and Democrat* [Marysville, KS], July 1, 1920.
66 **German dramatic club:** *Jeffersonian Gazette* [Lawrence, KS], November 29, 1911.
66 **Columbia University and a brief flirtation:** *Oregon Daily Journal*, September 5, 1920.
66 **Pocatello, Idaho:** *Advocate and Democrat* [Marysville, KS], July 1, 1920.
66 **"He has the reputation":** *Oregon Daily Journal*, September 5, 1920.
66 **"Becky" Bechtold:** "House I," *Griffin* yearbook, 1921, p. 45.
67 **old chap:** "Great Words of Great Pedagogs," *Griffin* yearbook, 1921, p. 97. [Bechtold is misspelled as "Becktold."]
67 **an audition call:** "Reed Men Signed for Grand Opera," *Quest*, September 29, 1920.
68 **"It is said":** "Enormous Salary Rewards Reed Men," *Quest*, October 6, 1920.
68 **"naughty children":** "Halloween Guests Scum of the Earth," *Quest*, November 3, 1920.
68 **a rebel:** Beard, *Celebration Cookbook*, p. 34.
68 **He'd come to Portland:** "Cecil Fanning, Noted Baritone, Sings Monday," *Oregon Daily Journal*, January 2, 1921.
68 **could be toneless:** "H. J. K.," *Musical Times*, July 1, 1922.
68 **One afternoon:** *Oregon Daily Journal*, January 23, 1921.
69 **finding a teacher:** " 'Jimmy' Beard Sings for New York Artist," *Quest*, January 19, 1921.
69 **"DANCE DRAMA":** "Dance Drama Is Bechtold Plan," *Quest*, March 16, 1921.

69 **"Edmund C. Bechtold"**: "Dance-Drama Is Slated," *Sunday Oregonian*, March 13, 1921.

70 **"After surveying the location"**: "Dance Drama Is Bechtold Plan," *Quest*, March 16, 1921.

70 **"The production will have"**: "Three-Act Play to Be Presented," *Quest*, March 24, 1921.

70 **"Lohengrin, born on the lake"**: "Reed Attempts Something New in Fun," *Morning Oregonian*, May 22, 1921.

71 **"The announcement"**: *Quest*, May 18, 1921.

71 **"Mr. Bechtold's Reed friends"**: Ibid.

72 **a new president:** "Reed President Named by Board of Regents," *Quest*, February 23, 1921.

72 **Dr. Richard Frederick Scholz:** Ibid.

72 **night of November 8:** Peter Boag, *Same-Sex Affairs*, p. 1.

72 **local subculture of homosexuals:** Ibid. "Trout nervously detailed to authorities the contours of a local homosexual subculture and connected it to others that apparently were flourishing in major cities up and down the West Coast."

72 **"Rotten Scandal Reaches"**: *Portland Daily News*, December 11, 1912.

72 **the so-called Vice Clique:** George Painter, *The Vice Clique: Portland's Great Sex Scandal*, pp. 47–50.

73 **brand of Republican populism:** According to Boag, "Certain working-class forces associated degeneracy and homosexuality with big business, corporate capitalism, and the wealthier elements of society." It would re-ignite Portlanders' worst suspicions about Reed under Foster. The iron legacy of the 1912 Vice Clique scandal was that "homosexuality could be used as a powerful tool for prosecuting local political struggles." As James put it to a reporter in 1978, "Portland has always been a city of pleasant homes and what I might call reactionary living."

73 **"Our Morals Are Better Than Europe's"**: *Oregon Sunday Journal*, October 20, 1912.

73 **all the way to New York City:** Men who fled the scandal included Hermann Schmidt, who changed his name to Herman Smith, opened a restaurant, and wrote a food memoir: *Stina, the Story of a Cook* (M. Barrows and Company, 1942).

73 **A Hungarian violinist:** Painter, *The Vice Clique*, p. 3.

74 **"I am innocent"**: Painter, *The Vice Clique*, p. 51.

74 **"Sexual Hygiene and Morals"**: Boag, *Same-Sex Affairs*, p. 197.

75 **whether he ever masturbated:** Beard, *Celebration Cookbook*, p. 24.

75 **passed a eugenics law:** Boag, *Same-Sex Affairs*, pp. 208–13.

75 **an act of oral indecency:** Billy Cross, who met James in the early 1970s, recalls James telling him, "I got thrown out of Reed College for getting caught giving a blowjob."

76 **the case of a facilities engineer:** "Our Reed Jean Valjean," *Quest*, September 15, 1920.

76 **James's expulsion:** Beard, quoted in Minahan, introduction to *James Beard's Simple Foods*, pp. xx–xxi. "I went to Reed College . . . and got myself *very* well kicked out. . . . I was *too* progressive. I broke all the rules. There weren't many rules, but I broke them. I made new rules to break."

76 **Dr. Scholz embarked:** "Dr. Scholz Will Visit Colleges," *Quest*, April 27, 1921.

76 **The Rockefeller Foundation:** Summerfield and Devine, eds., *Dictionary of University Histories*, p. 346.

76 **stayed in Portland:** Bechtold remained a bachelor until 1936, fifteen years after leaving Reed. He was forty-three on his wedding day. (His bride, who worked as a stenographer, was twenty-eight.) He died in 1970.

76 **president of the Portland Players:** *Oregon Daily Journal*, October 9, 1921.

77 **He told her everything:** Beard, *Celebration Cookbook*, p. 24. James suggests his mother knew he was gay long before he entered Reed, so hearing of his incident with the professor would not have come as a complete shock. Referring to his sexual orientation, James says, "She was completely accepting about it."

77 **for the rest of his life:** Carl Jerome, email message to author, October 25, 2017: "It was something Jim alluded to but certainly never detailed," Carl says of James's expulsion from the college, which James related to him in the 1970s. "He talked about Reed as an [alumnus] would, like it was his school. But there was a scare there, a pretty deep scare, in fact."

CHAPTER 5: EARLY PEAS AND OTHER PRIVATE PLEASURES

79 **Washington's finest apples:** Gordon R. Newell, *The H.W. McCurdy Marine History of the Pacific Northwest* (Superior Publishing Company, 1966), p. 335.

79 **hauled beef from Argentina:** "Highland Heather," Caledonian Maritime Research Trust, http://www.clydeships.co.uk/view.php?ref=16087.

79 **John V. Bennes Jr.:** *Highland Heather* passenger manifest, February 1, 1923, via Ancestry. com.

79 **well-known Portland architect:** "John V. Bennes (1867–1943)," *The Oregon Encyclopedia*, OHS, https://oregonencyclopedia.org/articles/bennes_john_v_1867_1943_/#.XY6P_SV7ndQ.

79 **George Natanson:** Natanson was a baritone who began his career in comic opera. He founded the Theatre Guild to give music and drama students experience on the professional stage. ["The Portland Theatre Guild," *Music and Musicians*, Volume VI, No. 1, February 1920, pp. 18–19.] James and John Bennes Jr. appeared with Natanson at Portland's Turn Verein Hall on December 7, 1922, in the Red Lantern Players production of *Hedda Gabler*. [E. C. B., "Stage Gossip and Film News," *Oregon Daily Journal*, November 17, 1922.]

79 **the Royal Academy of Music:** On his passenger declaration, James states that his reason for traveling to London is to enroll in the academy.

80 **highway between Portland and Seaside:** "New Pavement Soon to Reach Sea at Seaside," *Oregon Daily Journal*, August 28, 1921.

80 **he strolled at night:** There's no evidence James went cruising at Strawberry Knoll, though later he suggested to John Schaffner that it was a common spot (including for James) to be initiated into sex. ". . . I'm sure people still lose their virginity on Strawberry Knoll as most of us did. . . ." [Beard, Surf Pines, Oregon, to Schaffner, May 31, 1968, JSP.]

80 **skinny-dipping with Gearhart boys:** This is speculative, though James certainly bathed in the river many times with other boys.

81 **Other men had equipment:** James had an extremely small penis, which, especially in connection with his height and physical bulk, affected not only his experience of sex but his broader feelings of desirability. The chef Jeremiah Tower, recalling the sight of James's almost-naked body through an open bathrobe, hints at this in his memoir. (Tower, *California Dish* [Free Press, 2003], pp. 100–101.) I got a frank description from Carl Jerome, James's assistant for five years in the 1970s. "[Jim] had a medical condition [phimosis]. . . , a very, very tight foreskin that stopped his penis from growing. So, he had an inch-long penis, and this really over-rode his whole idea of who he was and what he could do sexually and who he could do it with and what kind of person would be attracted to him. And he mentioned it too many times to me for me not to think that it was probably his entire life. It was a problem for him. . . . I think his entire life was dominated by the problems of his sexuality. . . ." [JBI with Carl Jerome, February 16, 2017.] John P. Carroll, who met James in 1981 and saw him naked, said James tried to blame the small size of his penis on what he called "a botched operation." [JBI with John P. Carroll, Session #2, May 9, 2017.] I include this fact of James's body not to feed morbid or prurient curiosities, but as a key to understanding his mind. His penis affected both his intimate relationships and his fundamental conception of himself.

81 **a tour of customs houses:** "Beard Finishes Valuation for Dutiable Imports," *Oregon Daily Journal*, December 30, 1921.

81 **The Joy Club:** *Oregon Daily Journal*, March 13, 1921.

81 **a dance for young people:** "Society News," *Morning Oregonian*, November 10, 1921.

81 *A Sinner Beloved*: "Pageant from Hosea Thrills Large Audience," *Oregon Daily Journal*, September 20, 1922.

82 *Nothing But the Truth*: "Red Lantern Drama Holds Interest on Evening Show List," *Oregon Daily Journal*, May 4, 1922.

82 **Carl Denton:** *Sunday Oregonian*, July 9, 1922. "Portland's representative of the Royal Acad-

emy of Music of England, Carl Denton, conductor of the Portland Symphony Orchestra, has received his invitation to be present for the centenary celebrations of the academy. . . ."

83   **St. Thomas in the Virgin Islands . . . dim dining room:** Beard, *Delights and Prejudices*, pp. 57–58.

84   **goading an unfazed donkey:** This and other details are from a short travel reel on St. Thomas. United States Department of the Interior, "In the Wake of the Bucka-neers" (1936), Periscope Film LLC Archive, YouTube.com, https://www.youtube.com/watch?v=FiU24umiArc.

84   **small pickling cucumbers:** Beard, *Delights and Prejudices*, p. 58.

84   **Charles Woodhouse:** *Highland Heather* passenger manifest, February 1, 1923, via Ances-try.com.

85   **sold by poor women:** Beard, *Delights and Prejudices*, p. 58. "I felt at home at once in that marketplace, as crude as it was, and it was there that I first discovered my affinity for mar-ket folk and first sensed the character of a country through its food."

85   **on the day he had to sing . . . James became flustered:** A reconstruction of likely events.

85   **John Bennes's audition:** After graduating from the Royal Academy of Music, and per-forming in London for a few years, John Bennes Jr. would have a successful singing career in New York City and Los Angeles. His son, John V. Bennes III (1933–2018), was a charac-ter actor who, strangely enough, sometimes went by the stage name "James Beard." "[My father] did many Broadway musicals [*Don't Drink the Water*; *Hello, Dolly!*; *The Egg*] and a couple of movies [*Tell Me That You Love Me, Junie Moon*] under the name 'James Beard,'" says Adam Bennes, his son. "When he told his father he had changed his name to 'James Beard,' his father couldn't believe it, because he already knew a James Beard of course." (Adam Bennes, email message to author, November 8, 2018.)

86   **downstairs bar at the Ritz:** In *Delights and Prejudices*, James doesn't say where he first meets Helen Dircks, the woman who becomes his sherpa for London's pleasures, and his very silence makes me think there's a good reason he doesn't. The worldly, older Dircks is an unlikely connection for an unsophisticated twenty-year-old from Oregon. Clearly, she takes James under her wing in order to tutor him in worldly pleasures, including (though James isn't explicit about this, naturally) the queer subculture of the metropolis. I've placed their meeting at the downstairs bar at the Ritz, a discreet but well-known watering hole for gay men, fashionable enough to dazzle a glamour-starved young queer from Portland. "The downstairs bar at the Ritz Hotel was . . . appropriated by men from metropolitan high society. Exclusive and unequivocally respectable, it was affectionately nicknamed l'Abri—the shelter." Matt Houlbrook, *Queer London: Perils and Pleasure in the Sexual Metropolis, 1918–1957* (University of Chicago Press, 2006), p. 71.

86   **Helen Dircks:** Helen, the Palladium's publicist, was the author of two books of Imagist poetry: *Finding* (1918) and *Passenger* (1920). Helen's marriage to Frank Arthur Swinner-ton (James, in *Delights and Prejudices*, erroneously refers to Helen's husband as "Ralph Goome") ends about the time James meets her. (In 1931, she would marry Sir James Sutherland, a professor of English literature who went on to teach at UCLA.) "This woman was a great force in my London life," James writes. "It was she who . . . guided me to restaurants, theaters, and interesting places." (Beard, *Delights and Prejudices*, p. 190.)

87   **his first London dry martini:** Beard, *Delights and Prejudices*, p. 190.

87   **They ate sole Rendezvous:** Lieutenant-Colonel Newnham-Davis, "The Rendezvous," in *The Gourmet's Guide to London* (Brentano's, 1914), pp. 255–60.

87   **London's discreet queer subculture:** Houlbrook, *Queer London*, pp. 68–69. "[T]he world men forged in cafés and bars, meeting friends and creating temporary sites of queer socia-bility. . . . Particularly if they were discreet, men could find such opportunities anywhere; socializing alongside other Londoners in backstreet pubs or the most fashionable night-spots they attracted little, if any, attention."

88   **marble bar at the Trocadero:** Houlbrook, *Queer London*, p. 74.

88   **basement bar at the Criterion Hotel:** Houlbrook, *Queer London*, p. 71.

88 **where men found each other:** Florence Tamagne, *A History of Homosexuality in Europe: Berlin, London, Paris 1919–1939* (Algora Publishing, 2004), p. 62.

88 **drily roasted them:** Beard, *Delights and Prejudices*, p. 59. "I love the Cockney and his drily bitter attack on things."

88 **Early Warwick peas:** *Farmer's Magazine*, vol. 15, January to June 1859 (Rogerson and Tuxford), p. 179.

88 **never once saw them:** Beard, *Delights and Prejudices*, p. 58.

89 **a questionable past:** In the 1920s, Loria (1877–1946) touted his connection to Enrico Caruso, though his actual history with the Neapolitan tenor was far less amiable. It didn't hurt that Caruso, who died in 1921, wasn't around to challenge Loria's claims that he'd been the great star's vocal coach.

89 **Giachetti sued Caruso:** Enrico Caruso Jr. and Andrew Farkas, *Enrico Caruso: My Father and My Family* (Amadeus, 1997), p. 183.

89 **The trial exposed Loria:** Caruso Jr. and Farkas, *Enrico Caruso*, pp. 198–201.

89 **officer cadets at Sandhurst Military College:** Gaetano Loria obituary, *New York Times*, May 1, 1946.

90 **a studio above Wigmore Hall:** *Observer* (London), October 1, 1922.

90 **a dancer in Milan:** Beard, *Delights and Prejudices*, p. 192.

91 **Mattia Battistini . . . Beniamino Gigli:** Ibid.

91 **a chilled tomato:** Ibid. James calls this dish "Eggs Gennaro."

91 **she'd booked passage:** *Melita* passenger manifest on arrival in Southampton, UK, June 1, 1923, via Ancestry.com.

91 **about a dozen baritone roles:** Waleson, "Beard on Opera," *Opera News*, July 1983.

92 **currant-studded buns:** Beard, "In Praise of English Food" (1958), in *The Armchair James Beard*, p. 309.

92 **the port town of Folkestone:** *Melita* passenger manifest on arrival in Southampton, UK, June 1, 1923, via Ancestry.com.

92 **"LONDON HEARS PORTLAND BOY IN CONCERT":** *Oregon Sunday Journal*, July 28, 1923.

92 **James had sung five numbers:** *Oregon Sunday Journal*, July 28, 1923.

92 **James . . . wasn't one of them:** The Wigmore Hall program for July 18, 1923, matches the notice for the concert in the *Observer*. ["Vocal Concert," *Observer* (London), July 15, 1923.] James is not listed among the eleven performers. Emily Woolf, Wigmore Hall's archivist, says it's possible that James was a last-minute substitute, but the claim that he sang five pieces makes that dubious. Although one student did perform six songs—two plus "*Vier ernste Gesänge*" ("Four Serious Songs") by Brahms—the others sang no more than three numbers each. It's highly unlikely that a hastily arranged sub would have sung more numbers than every other student but one. Nor does James's name appear on any other concert program that summer. (Emily Woolf, email message to author, November 14, 2018.)

92 **the role of Wolfram:** Waleson, "Beard on Opera," *Opera News*, July 1983.

93 **Helen Dircks had told him:** That Helen was James's connection to friends in Paris (as she was in London) is speculative but entirely likely.

93 **the rue Jacob:** Beard, *Delights and Prejudices*, p. 195.

93 **dinner at Maxim's:** Ibid.

93 **James preferred the food:** Beard, *Delights and Prejudices*, pp. 195–96.

94 **Plessis-Robinson, a forested suburb:** Beard, *Delights and Prejudices*, p. 197. The first arboreal guinguette (named Le Grand Robinson, for the treehouse at the center of *Swiss Family Robinson*) opened in 1848 in the commune then known as Plessis-Piquet. As more guinguettes sprouted, the area became simply "Robinson" and eventually changed its official name to Plessis-Robinson.

94 **early train back to Paris:** Ibid. "I finally took the milk train back to Paris, and it was past dawn when I crawled into my pension on the rue Jacob."

94 **queer brothel in Pigalle:** In the 1970s, James told his assistant Carl Jerome that he'd vis-

ited gay brothels in Europe in the 1920s and recalled masked men. "Back in the '20s—he talked about going into brothels where they would just wear masks. . . ." (JBI with Carl Jerome, February 16, 2017.) Other details in this scene come from descriptions of contemporaneous gay brothels in Paris (particularly one on the rue de la Folie-Méricourt) described by historian Florence Tamagne. (Tamagne, *Homosexuality in Europe*, pp. 73–74.)

94 **on the SS *Paris*:** *Paris* passenger manifest, September 7, 1923, via Ancestry.com.

94 **with a boxer:** In 1956, James recalled to John Schaffner his youthful fling in Paris with a fighter (James described him as an "affair"), a "heavyweight star of French boxing. . . . [I]n his day he was a choice morsel for consumption along the boulevards." (Beard, Palamós, Spain, to John Schaffner, August 2, 1956, JSP.)

95 **furnished room in Chelsea:** Beard, in *James Beard's Simple Foods*, p. xxi.

95 **awed by its grandeur:** James Beard, *Beard on Food*, p. 113.

95 **the apples were mealy:** Ibid.

95 **Astor Hotel and its bar:** Chauncey, *Gay New York*, pp. 350–51.

96 **James found he preferred:** Beard, *American Cookery*, p. 71.

96 **cold boiled-beef salad:** Ibid.

96 ***Cyrano de Bergerac:*** John Corbin, "The Play," *New York Times*, November 2, 1923.

96 **taking it on the road:** Beard, in *James Beard's Simple Foods*, p. xxi.

96 **populate his spectacle:** "Drama," *St. Louis Post-Dispatch*, October 14, 1924.

96 **large but not colossal:** Ibid.

96 **an eight-car train:** Arthur Pollock, "Notes About the Players," *Boston Globe*, November 9, 1924.

96 **child actors and stage mothers:** Beard, in *James Beard's Simple Foods*, p. xxi.

96 **Majestic Theatre on December 1:** Arthur Pollock, "About the Theater," *Brooklyn Daily Eagle*, November 23, 1924.

96 **a large soup plate:** Beard, "New Year Remedies" (1982), in *The Armchair James Beard*, pp. 213–14.

97 **to make bathtub gin:** Beard, *The Armchair James Beard*, "Gin" (1960), pp. 195–96. "Then Prohibition came. Gin, being a white eau-de-vie, was found to be one of the easiest liquors to prepare at home from alcohol, a few aromatics, and distilled water. . . . Sunday afternoons were spent making gin in the bathtub, then rolling it around the floor in a wooden cask to 'age.' Several hours later it was served in our Sunday night's cocktails. I may say that after two years of this, I became quite deft as a gin maker."

97 **package wrapped in paper:** Beard, *The Armchair James Beard*, "The Vogue for Vodka" (1956), p. 191.

98 **his father had kept a mistress:** Beard, *Celebration Cookbook*, p. 20.

98 **an iron partition between their lives:** Beard, *Celebration Cookbook*, p. 16.

98 **appreciate his mother more:** Beard, *Celebration Cookbook*, p. 20.

98 **felt sorry for him:** Beard, *Celebration Cookbook*, p. 16.

98 **Paul Claude Fielding:** Chater Genealogy, "Armenians in India: Behind the Scenes Forgotten History," http://chater-genealogy.blogspot.com/2015/08/armenian-something-vivien -leigh-and-her_12.html.

98 **a small part:** "Claude Fielding (1904–1973)" Internet Movie Database, https://www.imdb .com/name/nm0276123/?ref_=tt_cl_t9.

99 **John Ashby Conway:** Martha Holmberg podcast interview, "6 Seasons | Why Salmon Matters | James Beard On Film," *The Four Top* by Katherine Cole, Oregon Public Broadcasting, May 22, 2017, https://www.opb.org/news/article/four-top-podcast-episode-19 -seasons-salmon-james-beard-film/.

CHAPTER 6: THE DUCHESS OF WINDSOR'S
CORNED BEEF HASH BALLS

103 **hominy spoon breads:** Beard, *Cook It Outdoors*, p. 161. Headnote for "Dora's Boiled Dressing": "Her lemon meringue pie is something for the gods and her hominy spoon bread is another prize."

103 **prize herd of Pennsylvania Guernseys:** Various entries, *The Herd Register of the American Guernsey Cattle Club*, vol. 34, April 1922.

103 **charity balls at the Ritz-Carlton:** "Dinner Dance Held for House of Rest," *New York Times*, April 24, 1935.

103 **Viennese Roof Garden:** "Danish Financier Honored at Party," *New York Times*, May 21, 1937.

103 **the Young Republicans:** "Party Regulars Triumph," *New York Times*, November 18, 1939.

104 **ringed with porches and gardens:** J. Robert Zane, *This Was My Pottsville: Life and Crimes During the Gilded Age* (iUniverse, 2005) [unpaginated].

104 **sent him to West Point:** "James B. Cullum, Jr." in "Class of 1920," *Biographical Register of the Officers and Graduates of the U.S. Military Academy at West Point, New York*, Supplement, vol. VI-B, 1910–1920, p. 2138.

104 **train to Reno and divorced:** January 1931 family-tree entry for Anne Porter Milliken, Ancestry.com.

104 **14 Washington Place:** "July Leasing Heavy in Apartment Field," *New York Times*, July 8, 1936.

104 **Cullum asked James Beard:** Beard, *Delights and Prejudices*, p. 279.

104 **cushiony annual four grand:** US Bureau of the Census, "James B. Cullum Junior," 1940 United States Federal Census.

104 **got him a position:** Beard, *Delights and Prejudices*, p. 279.

104 **Hattie Hawkins:** Robert Clark, *The Solace of Food*, p. 103.

104 **Cullum's front:** Ibid. "[Cullum's] 'girlfriend' [was] a fashionably dressed woman named Peggy Martin."

105 **new rules for conduct:** George Chauncey, *Gay New York: Gender, Urban Culture, and the Making of the Gay Male World, 1890–1940* (BasicBooks, 1994), pp. 336–37.

105 **"silver and china queens":** Charles Kaiser, *The Gay Metropolis 1940–1996* (Houghton Mifflin, 1997), p. 7.

105 **apartment parties:** Chauncey, *Gay New York*, pp. 278–79.

105 **every evening at five:** Otis Bigelow (recalling New York City in the early 1940s), quoted in Charles Kaiser, *The Gay Metropolis 1940–1996* (Houghton Mifflin, 1997), p. 8. "There were a number of places where wealthy, youngish men had duplex apartments . . . , and pretty much any day if you dropped by at five o'clock there would be [gay men] there for cocktails. . . ."

106 **James became Papa:** Crosby Gaige, *Dining with My Friends* (Crown, 1949), pp. 7–8. Gaige quotes James describing his host persona as "Papa."

106 **fried squab pieces:** Gaige, *Dining with My Friends*, p. 11.

106 **Horace ended up:** Horace Gibson, *Good Afternoon Mr. Gibson* (self-published memoir, 2010), pp. 144–45.

106 **Herbert Weinstock:** Biographical overview, Herbert Weinstock Collection, Music Division, The New York Public Library Archives and Manuscripts, http://archives.nypl.org/mus/20135.

106 **making jam:** Gibson, *Good Afternoon Mr. Gibson*, p. 145.

106 **tray of radishes:** Beard, *Hors D'Oeuvre and Canapés*, p. 65.

107 **Bill Rhode:** Beard, *Delights and Prejudices*, pp. 279–80.

107 **Princess Hilda of Nassau:** Scott Mehl, "Hilda of Nassau, Grand Duchess of Baden," *Unofficial Royalty*, http://www.unofficialroyalty.com/hilda-of-nassau-grand-duchess-of-baden/.

107 **a doctorate in chemistry:** Irma Rhode obituary, *New York Times*, February 16, 1982.

107 **fleeing the Weimar Republic and hyperinflation:** JBI with Mike Rhode, March 21, 2018.

107 **a photographic memory:** Ibid.

107 **Society of Amateur Chefs:** "Society Is Formed by Amateur Chefs," *New York Times*, October 14, 1938.

108 **Queen Victoria of Sweden's:** William Rhode, *Of Cabbages and Kings* (Stackpole Sons, 1938), p. 138.

108 **King Nikita of Montenegro's:** Rhode, *Of Cabbages and Kings*, pp. 139–40.

108 **fried corned beef hash balls:** Rhode, *Of Cabbages and Kings*, p. 141.

108 **rich pheasant:** Rhode, *Of Cabbages and Kings*, p. 113.

108 **pressed duck:** Rhode, *Of Cabbages and Kings*, p. 123.

108 **Prince Charles of Belgium:** Rhode, *Of Cabbages and Kings*, p. 86.

108 **King Manuel of Portugal:** Rhode, *Of Cabbages and Kings*, p. 91.

109 **Hors d'Oeuvre, Inc.:** Beard, *Delights and Prejudices*, p. 281.

109 **Oliver Payne carriage house:** Tom Miller, "The Oliver H. Payne Carriage House: No. 126 East 66th St.," *Daytonian in Manhattan*, December 15, 2016, http://daytoninmanhattan .blogspot.com/2016/12/the-oliver-h-payne-carriage-house-no.html.

109 **large old-fashioned icebox:** Beard, *Delights and Prejudices*, p. 281.

110 **vichyssoise:** Rhode, *Of Cabbages and Kings*, pp. 151–52. [Rhode misspells it as "Vichysoisse."]

110 **King George VI and Queen Elizabeth:** "A Royal Invitation to the 'World of Tomorrow,'" 1939 New York World's Fair, https://www.1939nyworldsfair.com/worlds_fair/wf_tour/ zone-1/King_Queen.htm.

110 **Mack Shinn:** Beard, *Delights and Prejudices*, pp. 286–87.

111 **"turtle livers flown in":** Lucius Beebe, "This New York," *New York Herald Tribune*, April 29, 1939.

111 **"It's a brand new sort":** Ibid.

111 **sprang up in London:** "More History," The International Wine and Food Society, https:// www.iwfs.org/about/history/more.

112 **"Does he once think":** Ira Wolfert, "French Gourmet Pities Hurried Americans Who Miss Delights of Eating," *Hartford* [CT] *Courant*, May 26, 1935.

112 **"This gang of eating":** Alice Hughes, "A Woman's New York," *Poughkeepsie* [NY] *Journal*, August 18, 1945.

113 **She was French:** Dust-jacket copy, *A Wine Lover's Cook Book* by Jeanne Owen (M. Barrows and Company, 1940).

113 **Diana Trapes:** "Polly," October 10, 1925, to November 1925, Internet Broadway Database, https://www.ibdb.com/broadway-production/polly-9927.

113 *Just Relax:* "Goings On About Town: On the Air," April 29, 1933, *The New Yorker*.

113 **"Miss Owen's blithe wool-gatherings":** Cyrus Fisher, "Radio Reviews: Scalawag Stations and Fall Whirligig," *Forum*, October 1933, pp. 254–76.

113 **Mrs. Malaprop:** Ben Gross, "Listening In," *Daily News*, January 8, 1940.

114 **Brotherhood of Bachelor Cooks:** Jeanne Owen, *A Wine Lover's Cook Book*, p. 132.

114 **Philip set before them:** Bill Rhode, "Spécialités de la Maison: The Club 21," *Gourmet*, May 1945.

115 **member of the Thursday Club:** Lucius Beebe, "This New York," *New York Herald Tribune*, March 12, 1939.

115 **Born in Paris:** Jeanne Owen, *Jeanne Owen's Book of Sauces* (M. Barrows and Company, 1941), p. 34.

115 **Watch Hill Farm:** Owen, *A Wine Lover's Cook Book*, p. 141.

115 **producing hit shows:** Simon Loxley, "Frederic Warde, Crosby Gaige, and the Watch Hill Press," *Printing History*, no. 4, July 2008.

115 **cellared thousands of wines:** Ibid.

116 **Frederic Warde:** Ibid.

116 **"an exquisite enigma":** Rudolph Ruzicka, letter to Paul Bennett, August 26, 1963, quoted in Loxley, *Printing History.*

116 **mumble, and arch his eyebrows:** Tom Margittai, James's longtime friend, described James's knack for appearing to pass judgment on a wine while remaining noncommittal. JBI interview with Tom Margittai, March 14, 2018.

117 **"Flushing-on-the-Commode":** Gibson, *Good Afternoon Mr. Gibson*, p. 124.

117 **Mayor Fiorello La Guardia:** Chauncey, *Gay New York*, p. 182.

117 **"Hardly a loafer lingered":** Carleton Smith, "Roulades and Cadenzas," *Esquire*, May 1939.

117 **two hundred cows:** Ibid.

117 **the Borden Rotolactor:** Paul M. Van Dort, "The Food Zone," 1939 *New York World's Fair*, https://www.1939nyworldsfair.com/worlds_fair/wf_tour/zone-3/borden.htm.

117 **Westinghouse's planned electric kitchen:** "World's Fair 1939, New York, USA," Prelinger Archives, San Francisco, www.prelinger.com.

118 **The French government:** Gibson, *Good Afternoon, Mr. Gibson*, p. 146.

118 **was not impressed:** Beard, in Evan Jones, *Epicurean Delight*, p. 98. "Nothing but a maître d'."

118 **High above Constitution Mall:** Beard, *Hors D'Oeuvre and Canapés*, pp. 170–71.

118 **rode out with Jim Cullum:** Jones, *Epicurean Delight*, pp. 99–100.

118 **baked pigs' knuckle:** Menu for Ballantine Three Ring Inn, May 26, 1939, "What's On the Menu?" New York Public Library, 1939–0108_wotm.

119 **Olsen challenged James:** Jones, *Epicurean Delight*, p. 102.

CHAPTER 7: BRIOCHE EN SURPRISE

120 **the past few months:** Mrs. John A. Beard obituary, *Oregon Daily Journal*, August 17, 1940. "Mrs. John A. Beard, known to many Portlanders as the founder and proprietress of the old Gladstone residential hotel, died Friday morning after a long illness."

121 **Hamilton Bodil and Hobart Bosworth:** Beard, *Celebration Cookbook*, p. 18.

121 **might have been great friends:** Beard, in Jones, *Epicurean Delight*, p. 102.

122 **"hors d'oeuvre man":** Danton Walker, "Broadway," *Daily News* [New York, New York], December 3, 1940.

122 **a release party:** A copy of *Hors D'Oeuvre and Canapés* in James's possession (now in the collection at Reed College) served as a party guest book, with signatures of all who attended, starting with Hub Olsen.

123 **"gives the palate":** Clementine Paddleford, *Daily Herald*, June 16, 1939.

123 **parsley for freshness:** Craig Claiborne, "No Savoury Dish Without an Onion," *New York Times*, August 10, 1958. "The parsley is an excellent foil for the onion."

123 **Irma Rhode would admit:** Craig Claiborne, "Onion Sandwiches: A Memorable Whimsy of Humble Origin," *New York Times*, June 9, 1976.

124 **the specialty of a madam:** Ibid. "In the twenties, in a Parisian establishment described by Polly Adler [a famous New York City madam] as 'a house that's not a home,' two slices of leftover breakfast brioche spread with mayonnaise and filled with a slice of onion, were served with the aperitifs to my brother Bill."

124 **"Some famous French hostess":** Beard, *Hors D'Oeuvre and Canapés*, p. 98.

124 **"a famous English hostess":** Beard, *Hors D'Oeuvre and Canapés*, p. 67.

124 **Mary Hamblet's method:** Beard, *Cook It Outdoors*, p. 23.

124 **Harold Grossman:** Beard, *Cook It Outdoors*, p. 26.

124 **Charlotte Adams:** Beard, *Cook It Outdoors*, p. 68.

124 **Nancy Dorris:** Beard, *Cook It Outdoors*, p. 101.

125 **"one of the really great":** Beard, *Cook It Outdoors*, p. 86.

125 **"Game in the Goo":** Beard, *Cook It Outdoors*, p. 50.

125 **"chichi":** Beard, *Cook It Outdoors*, p. 65.

125 **"doodadery":** Beard, *Cook It Outdoors*, p. 75.

125 **"practically everything but":** Beard, *Cook It Outdoors*, pp. 117–18.

125 **"Grand Duchess What What":** Beard, *Cook It Outdoors*, p. 157.

125 **"No refinement here":** Beard, *Cook It Outdoors*, p. 25.

125 **"The authors of cookbooks":** Jessamyn Neuhaus, *Manly Meals and Mom's Home Cooking*, p. 93.

125 **"Primarily," he writes:** Beard, *Cook It Outdoors*, p. vii.

125 **"our old recipe":** Beard, *Cook It Outdoors*, pp. 35–36.

125 **"two girls [who] wanted":** Beard, *Cook It Outdoors*, pp. 18–21.

126 **produced and directed theater:** Leslie Bennetts, "Cheryl Crawford, Theatrical Producer," *New York Times*, October 8, 1986.

126 **7 Middagh Street:** Hugh Ryan, "The Queer Commune in WWII Brooklyn That Became a Cultural Epicenter," *Them*, https://www.them.us/story/themstory-the-queer-commune -in-wwii-brooklyn-that-became-a-cultural-epicenter.

126 **through Janet Flanner:** Milly S. Barranger, *A Gambler's Instinct: The Story of Broadway Producer Cheryl Crawford* (Southern Illinois University Press, 2010), p. 104.

126 **stuffed with books:** Ibid.

126 **She became possessive:** Beard, in Jones, *Epicurean Delight*, pp. 96–97. "[Jeanne's] great faults were her possessiveness and her jealousy."

128 **Rodgers and Hammerstein's *Oklahoma!*:** Beard, in Jones, *Epicurean Delight*, p. 117.

129 **reacquainted with Horace Gibson:** Gibson, *Good Afternoon Mr. Gibson*, p. 204.

130 **on a PanAm flight:** Pan American Airlines passenger manifest, "bound for Antigua and ports beyond."

130 **a woman named Manuela:** Jones, *Epicurean Delight*, p. 120.

130 **"twenty young kids":** Beard, in Jones, *Epicurean Delight*, p. 121.

130 **the old cog railway:** Beard, *Celebration Cookbook*, p. 28.

130 ***banana d'oro, banana pronto***: Ibid.

130 **New York to Casablanca:** Beard, *Delights and Prejudices*, pp. 298–99.

131 **"The people who cook":** Beard, quoted in Dana Polan, "James Beard's Early TV Work," *Gastronomica*, vol. 10, no. 3, Summer 2010.

131 **"It takes a little":** Ibid.

131 **"Yes!" he'd roar:** Ibid.

132 **makeup man Dick Smith:** Dick Smith, "Dick Smith Interview Part 6 of 14," Archive of American Television, EmmyTVLegends.org, https://www.youtube.com/ watch?v=Cb53lJIxxSA. "He was a sweater, and the lights were hot. I would pencil with a black pencil more hairs, and I'd powder him down, and then he'd get sweaty and I'd mop him off and so forth. . . ."

132 **"Chicken, I've got you":** Beard, quoted in Polan, "James Beard's Early TV Work."

133 **"The female contingent":** Ibid.

133 **"Men," James said:** Ibid.

133 **he spent an evening out:** Gibson, *Good Afternoon Mr. Gibson*, p. 207.

133 **Truman Capote at his apartment in Brooklyn:** Ibid.

133 **Duplaix migrated from Paris:** Leonard S. Marcus, *Golden Legacy: The Story of Golden Books* (Golden Books, 2007), p. 18.

134 **upstart publisher:** Marcus, *Golden Legacy*, p. 27.

134 **Within five months:** Marcus, *Golden Legacy*, p. 51.

134 **Albert Rice Leventhal:** Marcus, *Golden Legacy*, pp. 29–30.

134 **Sandpiper Press:** Marcus, *Golden Legacy*, p. 75.

134 **black market restaurant:** Beard, *Delights and Prejudices*, p. 132. "I recall feasting on *grives* in Marseille in a small but excellent black-market restaurant. It was not unlike speakeasy days in New York."

135 **an elaborate backyard setup:** Beard, "Come and Cook It! Part One," *Gourmet*, June 1948.

135 **refused to rise:** Emilie Keyes, *Palm Beach Post-Times*, January 18, 1948.

136 **imported from France:** Nicole Duplaix, email message to author, June 13, 2018.

CHAPTER 8: THE COUNTRY OMELET OF
NEW CANAAN, CONNECTICUT

137 **at the Restaurant Mayan:** Marcus, *Golden Legacy*, p. 30.

137 **a national bestseller:** Daniel Immerwahr, "The Books of the Century, 1940–1949," University of California Berkeley, http://booksofthecentury.com/.

138 **forgo all future royalties:** Years later, Alice Provensen, co-illustrator of *The Fireside Cook Book*, recalled Sandpiper as "one of the cheapest, [most] wicked publishers that ever was. . . . They didn't pay you anything, and they didn't give you the royalties, either." (Peter Larsen, O.C. "Children's Book Illustrator Busy as Ever at 91," *Orange County* [CA] *Register*, October 9, 2009.)

138 **would make his reputation:** JWI with Irene Sax, April 29, 2009. "[James Beard] would tell me how, when he did *The Fireside Cook Book*, he got a flat fee for it, but it didn't matter because it made his reputation. . . ."

138 **stupendous and exhilarating:** Beard, quoted in Jane Nickerson, "News of Food," *New York Times*, October 29, 1949.

138 **hired a deputy:** Marcus, *Golden Legacy*, pp. 77–78.

139 **They restored the boat:** Amy Sohn, "The Star-Studded Life of Ms. Dorothy Bennett," *JSTOR Daily*, JSTOR.org, https://daily.jstor.org/dorothy-bennett/.

139 **resulted in cost overruns:** Marcus, *Golden Legacy*, p. 77.

139 **a small estate:** Cheryl Crawford, *One Naked Individual*, pp. 169–70.

140 **wrote about chayote:** Beard, *Fireside*, p. 166.

140 **Golden Bantam and Golden Cream:** Ibid.

141 **"Not since the appearance":** E. J. Kahn Jr., "The Coming of the Big Freeze," *The New Yorker*, September 14, 1946.

141 **twenty-two shops:** Ibid.

141 **A 1949 survey:** "Demand Surveyed in Frozen Foods," *New York Times*, March 8, 1949.

141 **strawberries in January:** *Birds Eye Cook Book: Tempting Recipes for Good Meals!* (Frosted Foods Sales Corporation, 1941), p. 3.

141 **"I am obliged":** Beard, *Fireside*, p. 264.

141 **Birds Eye frozen raspberries:** Jeanne Owen, "Pêches Cabaret," *Lunching and Dining at Home*, p. 55. Owen first included the recipe in *A Wine Lover's Cook Book* (1940), but there she specifies fresh raspberries, or frozen—not specifically Bird's Eye.

142 **Birds Eye marketing points:** Recipes, too. James's Asparagus and Shrimp Platter (*Fireside*, p. 268) seems to be an adaptation of a Birds Eye recipe, Asparagus with Parmesan Cheese. [*Birds Eye Cook Book*, p. 11.] And his Vegetable Plate (*Fireside*, p. 267) is most likely an adaptation of Birds Eye's Busy Day Vegetable Plate. [*Birds Eye Cook Book*, p. 10.]

142 **cheese croquettes:** Beard, *Fireside*, p. 29. The acknowledgment misspells the title of the source: "*Hors d'Oeuvres and Canapés*," instead of *Hors D'Oeuvre and Canapés*.

142 **a refined new draft:** Beard, *Cook It Outdoors*, pp. vii–viii. "Our sometime ancestors," he wrote in *Cook It Outdoors*, "crashing through jungles or sloshing through marshes and soggy fields, were most enthusiastic diners-out." In *Fireside*: "Our ancestors, after a day's hunting in the forest or sloshing through marshes and soggy fields, were most enthusiastic outdoor eaters." [Beard, *Fireside*, p. 252.]

142 **Mabelle's Turkey Casserole:** Beard, *Fireside*, p. 89; Beard, *Fowl and Game Cookery*, pp. 105–6.

142 **marinated steak and steak sandwiches:** Beard, *Fireside*, p. 253; Beard, *Cook It Outdoors*, pp. 65–67.

142 **venison burgers:** Beard, *Fireside*, p. 99; Beard, *Fowl and Game Cookery*, pp. 175–76.

142 ***Fireside*'s squab recipes:** Beard, *Fireside*, p. 95; Beard, *Fowl and Game Cookery*, pp. 151–53.

142 **Vichyssoise is identical:** Beard, *Fireside*, p. 42; Beard, *Fowl and Game Cookery*, pp. 11–12.

143 **the way Jeanne Owen:** Owen, *Lunching and Dining at Home*, p. 88.

143 **his mother's rustic original:** James would refine clam chowder even more in *James Beard's Fish Cookery*, and once again in *Delights and Prejudices* (where he implied that his newly refined version was his mother's original).

143 **Braised Beef, Peasant Style:** Beard, *Fireside*, p. 107.

143 **Country Omelet:** Beard, *Fireside*, p. 146.

144 **"Friends are like melons":** Beard, *Fireside*, p. 37; Claude Mermet, "Epigram on Friends," in Kate Louise Roberts, *Hoyt's New Cyclopedia of Practical Quotations* (Funk and Wagnalls, 1922), p. 299.

144 **"Four persons are wanted":** Beard, *Fireside*, pp. 194–95; Spanish proverb quoted in John Gerard, *The Herbal, or General History of Plants*, 1636.

144 **Plain Chicken Sauté . . . followed by variations:** Beard, *Fireside*, pp. 69–71.

144 **It was a revolutionary:** The master recipe with variations would become a standard feature for cookbooks edited by the influential Judith Jones for the Alfred A. Knopf publishing house.

145 **backlash against queers:** Chauncey, *Gay New York*, p. 358.

145 **strict gender expectations:** Neuhaus, *Manly Meals*, pp. 73–97.

145 *Wolf in Chef's Clothing*: "Post–World War II cookbooks for men regularly mentioned the seductive powers of a man in the kitchen. Indeed, [*Esquire* food and drinks editor Rob] Loeb's stated purpose in *Wolf in Chef's Clothing* was to provide recipes for bachelors interested in wooing women with the aid of home-cooked meals." [Neuhaus, *Manly Meals and Mom's Home Cooking*, p. 200.]

145 **Alice Twitchell met Martin Provensen:** Shannon Maughan, "Obituary: Alice Provensen," *Publishers Weekly*, May 1, 2018.

145 **worked for Walt Disney:** Frank Thomas and Ollie Johnston, *The Illusion of Life: Disney Animation* (Disney Editions, 1995), p. 511.

146 **introduced the LA transplants:** Marcus, *Golden Legacy*, pp. 112–13.

146 **winked at Dorothy Bennett:** Beard, *Fireside*, p. 281.

146 **a leering troubadour:** Beard, *Fireside*, p. 155.

146 **Cubist collages:** Beard, *Fireside*, pp. 54–55.

146 *Dinner for Threshers*: Beard, *Fireside*, pp. 216–17.

147 **poster-size illustrated chart:** Marketing a book with a bonus accessory was classic Simon and Schuster. The publishing house's first-ever title, *The Cross Word Puzzle Book* of 1924, included a free pencil, and in 1940 Dorothy Kunhardt's *Pat the Bunny* had pages glued up with interactive props, including a mirror, a squeaky ball, sandpaper, and a seductively tactile wad of cotton. [Marcus, *Golden Legacy*, p. 28.]

147 **a piece on carving:** Beard, "Carving Is an Art," *Gourmet*, November 1948.

147 **"those whose first idea":** Beard, "Spécialités de la Maison," *Gourmet*, April 1949.

148 **"as beautiful and elaborate":** No byline [Sheila Hibben], "Briefly Noted," *The New Yorker*, December 10, 1949.

148 **"Mr. Beard simply doesn't":** Ibid.

148 **Who else but Jeanne:** Beard to Helen Evans Brown, August 1953, LL.

148 **Bennett's rare mistake:** Beard, *Fireside*, pp. 273, 277.

148 **"Mr. Beard said":** Nickerson, "News of Food," *New York Times*, October 29, 1949.

CHAPTER 9: PHEASANT SOUVAROFF, AN AMERICAN DISH

153 **Duke Ellington Orchestra:** Carl Hällström, "Duke Ellington Itinerary: 1950," *The Duke Ellington Chronicle: Duke Ellington's Working Life and Travels*, ellingtonweb.ca.

153 **in record time:** "Quick Flight to Paris," *New York Times*, April 9, 1950.

153 **Also on his flight:** Air France passenger manifest, April 28, 1950, Ancestry.com.

153 **Arthur Hornblow Jr.:** Though Hornblow produced for MGM at the time, Arthur Freed was credited as the producer of *An American in Paris*.

153 **two-thousandth birthday:** Naomi Jolles Barry, "Party for Paris," *New York Times*, June 24, 1951.

154 **streaming into Paris:** John E. Booth, "The Whole of France Welcomes the Tourist," *New York Times*, February 19, 1950.

154 **Sam Aaron was a Francophile:** JBI with Peter Aaron, August 1, 2017.

154 **1955 ad in *The New Yorker*:** Air France advertisement, *The New Yorker*, April 19, 1955, p. 55.

155 **greenish claires oysters:** Beard, "Vintage Tour—1949, Part Two" *Gourmet*, February 1950.

157 **his friend Jack Cowan:** JBI with Alastair Fiddes Watt, March 16, 2018. "[Sandy] and Jack Cowan took to the road, and basically, as dashing young men but with no money at all, just energy and charm, cut a swathe into France and Switzerland."

157 **squalid beehive of ateliers:** Alexander Watt, *Art Centres of the World: Paris* (Michael Joseph Ltd., 1967), p. 14.

157 **"Before the war":** Alexander Watt, *Paris Bistro Cookery* (MacGibbon and Kee, 1960), p. 14.

157 **visitors' map of Paris:** Jane Nickerson, "The Flavor of Paris," *New York Times*, May 18, 1952.

158 **"Our recipes wear":** Advertisement for *The Gourmet Cookbook*, *Gourmet*, October 1956.

158 **virtually intact, physically:** "Paris, unlike so many other cities of Europe, has been miraculously preserved under the conflict of six years. Her wounds are slight, and far from her heart." Gibson Parker, "Paris on the Seine (1950–1955)", short film directed by J. C. Bernard, British Pathé, https://www.youtube.com/watch?v=2L2OEf4FuIA.

159 **"The fashion in guidebooks":** Samuel Putnam, "Guide to France," *New York Times*, December 5, 1948.

159 **roundup of old-fashioned chophouses:** Beard, "Spécialités de la Maison," *Gourmet*, February 1950.

159 **talked too freely:** JBI with Ruth Reichl, March 13, 2019. According to Reichl, who joined *Gourmet* as editor-in-chief in 1999, the story of MacAusland firing Beard for an indiscretion over drinks was a kind of heirloom at the magazine, passed down from one generation of the staff to the next.

160 **the Oak Room was well known:** George Chauncey, *Gay New York*, p. 350.

160 **that month in *Gourmet*!:** Beard, "Vintage Tour 1949, Part One," *Gourmet*, January 1950; Beard, "Vintage Tour 1949, Part Two," *Gourmet*, February 1950.

160 **alcoholism and yearly dry-outs:** Beard to Helen Evans Brown, May 18, 1953, LL.

161 **performing at Baptist Church suppers:** *Sunday Oregonian*, February 1, 1920.

161 **theater department of a women's school:** "Mills Girls to Give Play," *Oakland Tribune*, October 13, 1932.

161 **James fixed a snack:** Mark Beltaire, "Jim's 300 Pounds Prove His Trade," *Detroit Free Press*, May 18, 1959.

161 **directed James in a few performances:** Wood Soanes, *Oakland Tribune*, November 8, 1936.

161 **radio series for the Natural History Museum:** "Museum Wins Citation for Educational Program," *Chicago Tribune*, December 18, 1944.

162 **changed his recipes:** Beard to Helen Evans Brown, May 23, 1952, LL.

162 **like the beer they sent:** Beard to Helen Evans Brown, May 23, 1952, LL. "The beer is good—in fact to my mind, one of the best."

162 **"under the age of seventy-nine":** M. F. K. Fisher, "An Alphabet for Gourmets, A-B," *Gourmet*, December 1948.

163 **"cooked within half an hour":** Beard, "On the Fire," *Argosy*, September 1951.

163 **Grete was an au pair:** JBI with Alastair Fiddes Watt, March 16, 2018.

163 **"the great, gray Préfecture":** James Baldwin, "Equal in Paris: An Autobiographical Story," *Commentary* magazine, March 1955, p. 254.

164 **"rasait les murs"**: Julian Jackson, *Living in Arcadia: Homosexuality, Politics, and Morality in France from the Liberation to AIDS* (University of Chicago Press, 2009), pp. 39–40.

164 **a massive scouring**: Watt, *Art Centres of the World*, pp. 11–12.

164 **"Capitale du non-conformisme"**: "Saint-Germain-des-Prés: Capitale du non-conformisme," *Futur* magazine, October 1952, quoted in Georges Sidéris, "Des folles de Saint-Germain-des-Prés au fléau social," http://semgai.free.fr/contenu/textes/sideris_folles.htm.

165 **"The art quarters of Paris"**: Osborne Putnam Stearns, *Paris Is a Nice Dish* (Henry Regnery Company, 1952), p. 75.

165 **"It doesn't take long"**: Ibid.

165 **but suggestively so**: Richard Olney, *Reflexions* (Brick Tower Press, 1999), pp. 13–14. Olney, introduced to the Reine Blanche a year or so after Beard, described it as "a deep tunnel, lit brightly and crudely. . . . The bar, thickly populated by trade [hustlers], was cruising territory."

165 **sex-starved farm boys**: Beard, *Delights and Prejudices*, p. 95.

166 **exclusively male realm**: Ibid.

166 **Ate de Boer**: Hoping to open a restaurant with Ruth Norman and Cheryl Crawford, James told Helen that his friend, a bar steward on the *Maasdam*—Ate de Boer, I suspect—might want to go in with them. [Beard to Helen Evans Brown, January 20, 1954, LL.]

166 **his first trip to Paris**: Horace Gibson, *Good Afternoon Mr. Gibson*, p. 228.

166 **a morning tryst**: Gibson, *Good Afternoon Mr. Gibson*, p. 237.

166 **Charpentier's verismo opera Louise**: Gibson, *Good Afternoon Mr. Gibson*, p. 234.

166 **both preferred Grace Moore's**: Ibid.

166 **choucroute garnie à l'alsacienne**: Gibson, *Good Afternoon Mr. Gibson*, p. 234.

167 **on an Air France flight**: Air France passenger manifest, November 7, 1950, Ancestry.com.

167 **Chope Danton**: James A. Beard and Alexander Watt, *Paris Cuisine*, pp. 91–94.

168 **Brasserie Lipp**: Beard and Watt, *Paris Cuisine*, pp. 95–98.

168 **kitchens at Orly**: Beard and Watt, *Paris Cuisine*, pp. 256–59.

168 **Paul Burke-Mahony**: Beard and Watt, *Paris Cuisine*, p. 265. The acknowledgments page names "Paul Burke-Mahony, for eating his way through practically every page of this book." Also Gibson, *Good Afternoon Mr. Gibson*, p. 299. "As a neighbor Paul had been frequently called in by the master to the testing of the recipes."

168 **Paint Your Wagon**: *Paint Your Wagon* (opened November 12, 1951), Internet Broadway Database, https://www.ibdb.com/broadway-production/paint-your-wagon-1974.

168 **"You will not get the same flavor"**: Beard and Watt, *Paris Cuisine*, p. 178.

169 **air-ship samples to New York**: Beard and Watt, *Paris Cuisine*, p. 47.

169 **"The fresh butter"**: Nickerson, "The Flavor of Paris," *New York Times*, May 18, 1952.

170 **"I'm giving a birthday party"**: Gibson, *Good Afternoon Mr. Gibson*, p. 298.

170 **a flash of shapely bare legs**: Ibid.

170 **John F. Kennedy**: Gibson, *Good Afternoon Mr. Gibson*, p. 299.

170 **had never seen a cookbook**: John Ferrone, introduction to James Beard, *Love and Kisses and a Halo of Truffles: Letters to Helen Evans Brown*, John Ferrone ed. (Arcade Publishing, 1994), p. vii.

171 **"with real delight"**: James Beard, jacket copy for *Helen Brown's West Coast Cook Book* (Little, Brown, 1952).

172 **James thought it was pretty**: Beard to Helen Evans Brown, May 23, 1952, LL.

172 **a book-release party**: Ibid.

172 **"The Flavor of Paris"**: Nickerson, "The Flavor of Paris," *New York Times*, May 18, 1952.

172 **"The transcription of the recipes"**: Charlotte Turgeon, "Parisian Dinners at Home," *New York Times*, June 29, 1952.

172 **"Such bitchery I cannot"**: Beard to Helen Evans Brown, January 20, 1953, LL.

172 **"Osborne Stearn's [sic] rather naïve"**: Turgeon, "Serving Them Up Hot and Cold," *New York Times*, December 7, 1952.

173 **"A very reliable"**: No byline [Sheila Hibben], *The New Yorker*, August 23, 1952.

173 **"Dear Sheila Hibben"**: Beard to Helen Evans Brown, August 1953, LL.

CHAPTER 10: PISSALADIÈRE AT THE HAMBURGER STAND

174 **"Thanks to frozen foods":** E. W. Williams, *Quick Frozen Foods* magazine, quoted in "Rapid Gains Seen for Frozen Foods," *New York Times*, June 3, 1954.

174 **four billion pounds:** Ibid.

174 **more than five billion:** Ibid.

174 **twenty-five billion dollars:** Ibid.

174 **first frozen breaded fish sticks:** Jane Nickerson, "News of Food," *New York Times*, May 20, 1954.

175 **nine million pounds:** Ibid.

175 **"The industry looks on":** Ibid.

175 **"I think it is the most":** Beard to Helen Evans Brown, February 4, 1953, LL.

176 **"They are worth adding":** Beard to Helen Evans Brown, February 4, 1953, LL. "[T]he books from the department of the interior written by Rachel Carson . . . are worth adding to your collection for the information as well as the writing. And I'm afraid those days in Washington are gone when thy [*sic*] will have someone like Carson to do a job like that."

176 **"This rich land of ours":** Beard, *James Beard's Fish Cookery*, p. vii.

176 **"I am writing on":** Beard to Helen Evans Brown, February 4, 1953, LL.

177 **"The best bread I ever ate":** June Platt and Sophie Kerr, *The Best I Ever Ate: A Practical Home Cook Book* (Rinehart and Company, 1953), p. 115.

177 **"Stories and recipes and gaiety":** Beard to Helen Evans Brown, February 26, 1953, LL.

177 **"The question the scientists":** Platt and Kerr, *The Best I Ever Ate*, p. 3.

178 **sat down with the family:** Beard, datebook entry for April 24, 1953, JBP.

178 **James described the lunch:** Beard, "A Fine Kettle of Fish," *Argosy*, June 1953.

178 **Eleanor Peters's rental mansion:** Maxim Gershunoff and Leon Van Dyke, *It's Not All Song and Dance: A Life Behind the Performing Arts* (Limelight Editions, 2005), p. 34.

178 **Eleanor Hirsch:** Obituary for Eleanor Sophie Peters, *Los Angeles Times*, June 24, 2005.

178 **Robert Joffrey and Gerald Arpino:** Gershunoff and Van Dyke, *It's Not All Song and Dance*, p. 34.

179 **James made celery root rémoulade:** Beard, datebook entry for May 5, 1953, JBP.

179 **cocktails at the beach bungalow:** Beard, datebook entry for May 7, 1953, JBP.

179 **women with scarves.** Cisco Family Film, "Nantucket 1934–1935," NHA Research Library Film Collection, Nantucket History, FC-26, https://www.youtube.com/watch?v=CdICBbPdZTE.

179 **a sculptor and ceramicist:** Anne Whelan, "Westport's Kathi Urbach Revives Art of the Pharoahs," *Bridgeport* [CT] *Telegram*, June 17, 1951.

180 **Kathi's kitchenware line:** Promotional brochure, "Potluck Cooking Ware for the Gourmet: Designed by Kathi Urbach with Recipes by James Beard," undated [1952], JBP.

180 **meet them for drinks:** Beard, datebook entry for February 22, 1953, JBP.

180 **The menu listed:** Lucky Pierre menu advertisement, *This Week in Nantucket*, June 22, 1953, posted in Jan Whitaker, "Between Courses: Beard at Lucky Pierre's," *Restaurant-ing Through History*, https://restaurant-ingthroughhistory.com/2009/05/18/between-courses -beard-at-lucky-pierres/.

180 **in their absence:** Beard to Helen Evans Brown, February 26, 1953, LL.

180 **"Did I tell you":** Beard to Helen Evans Brown, March 29, 1953, LL.

181 **"It is one of those nights":** Beard to Helen Evans Brown, June 19, 1953, LL.

181 **James pushed a teacart:** Mary Cremmen, "TV Notebook," *Boston Daily Globe*, February 25, 1954.

181 **"This is *octopus!*":** Ibid.

182 **stuffed squab or a burger:** Maxwell's Plum café dinner menu, 1974, Culinary Institute of America Menu Collection; George Lang Menu Collection, menu 2–1666, http://ciadigitalcollections.culinary.edu/digital/collection/p16940coll1/id/6433.

182 **fabulous garlicky hamburger:** Beard, *Cook It Outdoors*, p. 82.

182 **drown in a cistern:** Beard, *The James Beard Celebration Cookbook*, p. 32. "I used to drown kittens when I was a child."

183 **"I am certainly astonished":** Schaffner to Helen Evans Brown, July 27, 1953, JSP.

183 **"I certainly must take back":** Schaffner to Helen Evans Brown, August 3, 1953, JSP.

183 **interviewed college boys:** Beard, datebook entry for April 15, 1953, JBP.

183 **Irwin "Win" Chase:** Beard, *James Beard's Fish Cookery*, p. 53. Beard describes him as "an excellent Yankee cook."

184 **blueberry pies and hamburger buns:** Beard, Nantucket, to Helen Evans Brown, undated [July 1953], LL.

184 **his favorite was Win Chase's:** Beard, Nantucket, to Helen Evans Brown, undated [July 1953], LL. "Did I tell you that our chowder is a sensation. Win brought it with him and I love it."

184 **James turned fish heads:** Beard, Nantucket, to Helen Evans Brown, undated [July 1953], LL.

184 *Délice au Chocolat*: Beard, Nantucket, to Helen Evans Brown, undated [July 1953], LL.

184 **chocolate rolls:** Beard, Nantucket, to Helen Evans Brown, undated [July 1953], LL.

184 **pizzas:** Ibid.

184 **pissaladières:** Ibid.

184 **topped burgers with green peppers:** Beard, Nantucket, to Helen Evans Brown, undated [July 1953], LL.

184 **Nantucket's sweet, delicate romaine:** Beard, Nantucket, to Helen Evans Brown, undated [summer 1953], LL.

184 **corn on the cob:** Ibid.

184 **local fish were commercially extinct:** Beard, *James Beard's Fish Cookery*, pp. 155–56.

184 **"We are becoming known":** Beard, Nantucket, to Philip S. Brown, July 10, 1953, LL.

185 **"That boy is wonderful":** Beard, Nantucket, to Helen Evans Brown, undated [July 1953], LL.

185 **"I have made about five":** Beard, Nantucket, to Helen Evans Brown and Philip S. Brown, undated [summer 1953], LL.

185 **Claude confronted James:** Evan Jones, *Epicurean Delight*, p. 178.

185 **"The natives resent":** Beard, Nantucket, to Helen Evans Brown, undated [July 1953], LL.

185 **"I guess he's afraid":** Beard, Nantucket, to Helen Evans Brown, undated [July 1953], LL.

185 **He took sleeping pills:** Beard, Nantucket, to Helen Evans Brown, undated [July 1953], LL.

186 **"I am so fed up":** Beard, Nantucket, to Helen Evans Brown, undated [July 1953], LL.

186 **ran to a men's shop:** Marge Burns, Boston, Massachusetts, to Beard, September 19, 1976, JBP.

186 **"Packed on individual-portion":** June Owen, "News of Food," *New York Times*, October 7, 1953.

187 **"Television's influence is revising":** "Television Spurs Trends to 'Heat 'n' Eat' Meals," *New York Times*, June 10, 1954.

187 **First Lady Mamie and President Eisenhower:** Stephen E. Ambrose, *Eisenhower: The President, Volume II* (Touchstone, 1984), p. 89.

187 **"old-fashioned fried chicken":** Swanson TV Dinner advertisement, *Life*, June 1955.

187 **James sailed from New York:** Beard to Philip S. Brown, September 21, 1953, LL.

188 **Alexis Lichine at Château Lascombes:** Beard, datebook entry for October 9–10, 1953, JBP.

188 **Pillsbury Paris:** "Europe's Recipes to Be Used in U.S.," *New York Times*, October 19, 1953. The event was something of a promotional stunt for the press. Baking authentic French bread from American flour in a home oven was the Great White Whale of US cookbooks on French food—it would take until 1970, with Julia Child and Simone Beck's ten-page recipe for baguettes in Volume Two of *Mastering the Art of French Cooking*, that many Americans would even muster the courage to take it on.

188 **"Ideas for articles":** Beard, datebook entry for November 21, 1953, JBP.

188 **"Wine is for the people":** Beard, datebook entry for November 24, 1953, JBP.

189 **Freeman "Doc" Lewis:** John Schaffner to Sam Aaron, June 14, 1963, JSP.

189 **stuffed oxtail recipe:** Beard, *How to Eat Better for Less Money*, p. 27.

190 **pigs' feet St. Menehould:** Beard, *How to Eat Better for Less Money*, p. 46.

190 **cassoulet from *Paris Cuisine*:** Beard, *How to Eat Better for Less Money*, p. 83.

190 **Jeanne Owen's Poulet:** Beard, *How to Eat Better for Less Money*, pp. 201–2

190 **"He constantly had to cut back":** John Schaffner to Helen Evans Brown, July 2, 1954, JSP.

190 **"It is a challenge":** Beard to Helen Evans Brown, undated [August 1953], LL.

190 **"A much misunderstood word":** Beard, *How to Eat Better for Less Money*, p. vi.

191 **"giant haul" of recipes:** dust jacket, *James Beard's Fish Cookery*.

191 **"an invaluable aid":** Beard, *James Beard's Fish Cookery*, p. vii.

191 **"Like other kinds":** Beard, *James Beard's Fish Cookery*, p. 3.

191 **the lust of the throngs:** Beard, *James Beard's Fish Cookery*, p. 202.

191 **The baby's bathtub:** Beard, *James Beard's Fish Cookery*, p. 157.

191 **Harry Hamblet frying oysters:** Beard, *James Beard's Fish Cookery*, p. 394.

191 **carp he saw in France:** Beard, *James Beard's Fish Cookery*, p. 276.

191 **added Scotch to a crab soup:** Beard, *James Beard's Fish Cookery*, p. 55.

191 **"Jim Beard is considered":** Charlotte Turgeon, "Add a Pinch of Exotic," *New York Times*, August 22, 1954.

192 **Newspaper Food Editors Conference:** "Jim Beard's Fish Cook Book Introduced by Fishing Industry at Food Editors Conference," J. Walter Thompson Company press release, September 27, 1954, OHS.

CHAPTER 11: AMERICAN CHEESE

193 **beneath a dangling welter:** Author photo by Serisawa Studio for *Helen Brown's West Coast Cook Book* (Little, Brown, 1952).

193 **born in Brooklyn in 1904:** Helen Evans Brown obituary, *New York Times*, December 7, 1964.

194 **Pierre Blot's . . . Urbain Dubois':** Philip S. Brown Books Catalog, spring 1949, JSP.

194 **writing radio scripts and recipes:** Schaffner to Burroughs Mitchell, Charles Scribner's Sons, New York, February 26, 1953, JSP.

194 **Robert Balzer:** Elaine Woo, "Robert Lawrence Balzer Dies at 99: L.A. Times Wine Writer," *Los Angeles Times*, December 9, 2011.

195 **"which several of us here":** Ned Bradford, Boston, to Helen Evans Brown, August 17, 1949, JSP.

195 **It stood apart:** Elizabeth David, "West Points," *An Omelette and a Glass of Wine*, p. 138; reprinted from *The Spectator*, December 8, 1961. "Mrs. Brown makes short work of substitutes, makeshifts, and synthetics and her lists of ingredients . . . are very far removed from those interminable recipes of American magazine cookery."

196 **chafing dish cooking:** Helen Evans Brown, *Chafing Dish Book* (The Ward Ritchie Press, 1950).

196 **patio cooking:** Helen Evans Brown, *Patio Cook Book* (The Ward Ritchie Press, 1951).

196 **"like bananas in England":** Helen Evans Brown to Beard, undated [March 1952], JBP.

196 **"*too* darned attractive":** Helen Evans Brown to Ned Bradford, January 11, 1950 (erroneously marked 1949), JSP.

196 **312 East Fifty-Third Street:** Tom Miller, "The 1866 Wooden Houses at Nos. 312 and 314 East 53rd Street," October 11, 2011, http://daytoninmanhattan.blogspot.com/2011/10/1866-wooden-houses-at-nos-312-and-314.html.

196 **Schaffner, thirty-five:** John V. Schaffner obituary, *New York Times*, November 30, 1983.

196 **called them Perdita's "mummies":** Schaffner to Beard, Hotel de France et Choiseul, Paris, January 22, 1955, JSP.

197 **Stein and Toklas's adored succession of poodles:** Ibid.
197 **worked for the OSS:** Schaffner to Helen Evans Brown, January 25, 1953, JSP.
197 **did most of the cooking:** JBI with Tim Schaffner, March 11, 2018.
197 **a quiet gay one in private:** Ibid.
197 **one of Helen's recipes:** Schaffner to Helen Evans Brown, August 3, 1953, JSP. "[T]he little pie I chose from the tray was one made from a Helen Evans Brown recipe, a lemon cream tart."
197 **James took a bus to Siasconset:** Beard, datebook entry for August 1, 1953, JBP.
198 **"I'm only writing this":** Schaffner to Helen Evans Brown, August 3, 1953, JSP.
198 **"Your banana lunch":** Helen Evans Brown to Beard, undated [March 1952], JBP.
198 **"an esoteric sheet":** Beard to Helen Evans Brown, undated [August 4, 1952], LL.
198 **"quaint and eccentric":** Helen Evans Brown to Schaffner, September 29, 1948, JSP.
199 **"She believes passionately":** M. F. K. Fisher, introduction to *Helen Brown's Holiday Cook Book*, p. xi.
199 **"I have no doubt":** Ned Bradford to John Schaffner, March 13, 1951, JSP.
199 **"I don't know quite where":** Schaffner to Helen Evans Brown, March 11, 1953, JSP.
200 **"In some respects":** Geraldine Rhoads to John Schaffner, March 31, 1953, JSP.
200 **"Jim Beard":** Helen Evans Brown to Schaffner, April 27, 1953, JSP.
200 **"The idea is that":** Ibid.
200 **"A West Coaster transplanted":** Ibid.
201 **"You and I know":** Beard to Helen Evans Brown, May 18, 1953, LL
201 **"I have returned here":** Ibid.
201 **"The wonderful times":** Ibid.
201 **He'd planned a dinner:** Beard to Helen Evans Brown, January 11, 1954, LL.
202 **called his closest friends:** Ibid.
202 **late into the night:** Ibid.
202 **"I haven't slept enough":** Ibid.
202 **travel guide for all of Europe:** John Schaffner to William H. Hanna, January 21, 1954, JSP.
202 **a scheme called Data-Guide:** Beard to Helen Evans Brown, undated [January 18, 1954], LL.
203 **"They pay a royalty":** Ibid.
203 **A publicity woman for Crosley:** Eloise Davison to Beard, January 28, 1954, LL.
203 **"I am about to go":** Beard to Helen Evans Brown, March 3, 1954, LL.
203 **The Browns invited James:** Helen Evans Brown to Beard, December 14, 1953, LL.
203 **"This is the last gasp":** Beard to Helen Evans Brown, March 28, 1954, LL.
204 **Harold A. Bartron:** L. Burr Belden, "Retired Commander of Air Depot Turns Lifetime Hobby into Profitable Manufacturing Project," *San Bernardino* [CA] *Sun*, April 17, 1949.
204 **the Skotch Grill:** Jane Nickerson, "News of Food," *New York Times*, February 20, 1954. "The grill looks like a plaid-covered bucket. The round steel surface is [finished] in vinyl plastic in a handsome Scotch plaid design; the firepot is recessed inside."
204 **Abercrombie and Fitch:** The company became a fashion retailer only in the late 1980s. Before that, from its founding in 1891, the New York–based company sold high-end outdoor and sporting-goods gear and clothing.
204 **Smoke Cookery, Inc.:** June Owen, "Tips on Smoke Cooking with Tin Apparatuses Constructed at Home," *New York Times*, June 19, 1954.
204 **"The subject turns out":** Helen Evans Brown to Hildegarde Popper, *House & Garden*, May 10, 1953, JSP.
205 **cookbook publishing was surging:** Jessamyn Neuhaus, *Manly Meals and Mom's Home Cooking*, pp. 164–66. "In the 1950s specialty cookbooks started to make significant inroads into the cookbook market and seriously challenged the market share held by a select few 'kitchen bibles.' "
205 **"She is very much":** Schaffner to Helen Evans Brown, August 17, 1953, JSP.

205 **returned from France:** Beard, datebook entry for November 8, 1953, JBP.

205 **open a kitchen shop:** For years, James hoped to convince the Browns to move to New York City so he and Helen could go into business together. In July 1955, he signed a lease for a storefront at 68 Fifth Avenue and wanted to call it Boutique Gastronomique. Helen said emphatically that she wasn't interested in moving east. James got out of the lease.

206 **westbound red-eye flight . . . one of only four:** Beard, datebook entry for April 4, 1954, JBP.

206 **Fly Trap . . . sand dabs:** Beard, datebook entry for April 4, 1954, JBP.

206 **stationery in his room:** Beard to the Browns, undated [April 5, 1954], LL.

206 **luncheon of poulet sauté:** Beard, datebook entry for April 6, 1954, JBP.

206 **Frank Timberlake:** Beard, datebook entry for April 7, 1954, JBP.

206 **a trip to San Jose:** Beard, datebook entry for April 8, 1954, JBP.

206 **Bess Whitcomb:** Ibid.

207 **to the Napa Valley:** Beard, datebook entry for April 12, 1954, JBP.

207 **lunched with a winery publicist:** Ibid.

207 **Elena Zelayeta:** Beard, datebook entry for April 11, 1954, JBP.

207 **Tomales . . . first taste of Teleme:** Beard to Helen Evans Brown, undated [August 1954], LL. "What is the address of the place where we bought the Teleme the first day out." Beard, datebook entry for April 9, 1954, JBP. "Teleme/Baby Teleme, Louis Bononci, Tomales, California."

207 **lunched on abalone:** Beard, datebook entry for April 13, 1954, JBP.

207 **Langlois, Oregon:** Beard, datebook entry for April 15, 1954, JBP.

207 **Langlois Blue Vein Cheese:** Hans Hansen produced Langlois Blue Vein Cheese until 1957, when the factory burned. At the same time that they were working with Hansen in Langlois, Iowa State University microbiologists Clarence Lane and Bernard W. Hammer worked with Frederick L. Maytag II and Robert Maytag to produce a similar cheese from homogenized cows' milk, which unlike Langlois has survived as the cheese we know today as Maytag Blue. See "Langlois Blue Vein Cheese: A Little Taste of History," Langlois city website, worldfamouslanglois.com.

208 **Reedsport . . . Tillamook:** Beard, datebook entry for April 15–16, 1954, JBP.

208 **The backseat around James filled up:** Beard quoted in Jerome Beatty Jr., *Collier's* magazine, June 22, 1956. "[T]he three of us did a long auto tour of twelve western states, through the cheese and wine districts and to the fish and oyster centers. We never brought a lunch the whole time. The back seat was so full of food samples that all we had to buy was a loaf of bread and we'd have the grandest picnic lunches you can imagine."

208 **Mabelle and Ralph Jeffcott:** Beard, datebook entry for April 16, 1954, JBP.

208 **at the Crab Broiler:** Beard, datebook entry for April 19, 1954, JBP.

208 **Harvey Welch:** Ibid.

208 **the Pancake House:** Beard, datebook entry for April 18, 1954, JBP.

209 **John Conway:** Beard, datebook entry for April 23, 1954, JBP.

209 **would use one:** In fact, Doubleday did.

209 **cube steak, cottage cheese:** Beard, datebook entry for April 25, 1954, JBP.

209 **Templin's Grill:** Ibid.

210 **"biscuits light as a feather":** Beard, datebook entry for April 26, 1954, JBP.

210 **Star Valley Swiss Cheese Factory:** Beard, datebook entry for April 27, 1954, JBP.

210 **Virginia City:** Beard, datebook entry for April 30, 1954, JBP.

210 **Lucius Beebe . . . Chuck Clegg:** John Gruber, *Beebe and Clegg: Their Enduring Photographic Legacy* (Center for Railroad Photography and Art, 2018).

210 **"Drinks, Steaks, Drinks!":** Beard, datebook entry for April 30, 1954, JBP.

210 **home to Pasadena:** Beard, datebook entry for May 4, 1954, JBP.

211 **"The trip is one":** Beard, Pasadena, to Schaffner, May 4, 1954, JSP.

211 **"I suppose you might":** Helen Evans Brown to Schaffner, undated [June 29, 1954], JS

211 **"one energetic":** Ibid.

CHAPTER 12: WOO HIM WITH CALF'S HEAD

212 **by the end of February:** Beard to Helen Evans Brown, January 18, 1954, LL.

212 **her mysterious ailments:** Schaffner to Clara Claasen, May 15, 1954, JSP. Also Helen Evans Brown to Schaffner, February 11, 1954, JSP. "[N]ow that Eddie (he's our charming doctor Mauer) has let me off the dope I am thinking more clearly."

213 **"THE HELEN EVANS BROWN":** James Beard and Helen Evans Brown, unpublished proposal for *The Complete Book of Outdoor Cookery*, February 1954, JSP.

213 **"big garden crushes":** Ibid.

213 **"how to make a transcontinental trip":** Ibid.

213 **"to really romanticize":** Ibid.

213 **"How to use the hibachi":** Ibid.

213 **"This is for the person":** Beard and Brown, proposal for *The Complete Book of Outdoor Cookery*, February 1954, JSP.

214 **"Complete, yes":** Helen Evans Brown to Schaffner, February 11, 1954, JSP.

214 **"As for the managing":** Ibid.

214 **"I don't get it":** Ibid.

214 **"I think I have become":** Beard to Helen Evans Brown, undated [December 13, 1953], LL.

214 **"We can afford to be a little chichi":** Beard to Helen Evans Brown, January 18, 1954, LL.

214 **James and Helen's contract:** Schaffner to Helen Evans Brown, March 24, 1954, JSP.

215 **sprawling Skotch Grill party:** Beard to Myron Piker, Hamilton Metal Products, New York, June 7, 1954, OHS.

215 **She served rumaki:** Beard, datebook entry for June 8, 1954, JBP.

215 *Mike Roy's Cooking Thing:* Beard, datebook entry for June 9, 1954, JBP.

216 **"Jim and I work":** Helen Evans Brown to Schaffner, undated [May 1954], JSP.

216 **"The book is going slowly":** Beard, Pasadena, to Schaffner, May 13, 1954, JSP.

216 **"Philip knows much more":** Helen Evans Brown to Schaffner, undated [June 1954], JSP.

216 **Maco Magazine Corporation:** Beard to Helen Evans Brown, February 9, 1954, LL. "Jerry Mason . . . used to be my Argosy man—he does paper bounds and they are all automatically given hard cover publication by Bobbs Merrill."

217 **a book on outdoor cookery:** James Beard, *Jim Beard's Complete Book of Barbecue and Rotisserie Cooking* (Maco Magazine Corporation, 1954).

217 **"You know," Schaffner noted:** Schaffner to Helen Evans Brown, January 19, 1954, JSP.

217 **"I won't go into any more":** Schaffner to Helen Evans Brown, February 7, 1955, JSP.

217 **"It is [Claasen's] idea":** Schaffner to Helen Evans Brown, August 18, 1954, JSP.

218 **Helen nixed James's recipes:** Helen Evans Brown to Schaffner, August 9, 1954, JSP.

218 **"What Doubleday—":** Beard to Helen Evans Brown, January 20, 1954, LL.

218 *Jim Beard's Complete Cookbook for Entertaining:* James Beard, *Jim Beard's Complete Cookbook for Entertaining* (Maco Magazine Corporation, 1954).

218 **Josephine von Miklos:** Josephine B. von Miklos obituary, *New York Times*, November 3, 1972.

219 **Bacon and Egg Salad:** Beard, *Complete Cookbook for Entertaining*, p. 13; Helen Evans Brown and James A. Beard, *The Complete Book of Outdoor Cookery*, p. 183.

219 **Shrimps Beard:** Beard, *Complete Cookbook for Entertaining*, p. 48. Shrimps Pierre: Brown and Beard, *Outdoor Cookery*, pp. 129–30.

219 **Escabêche de Pescado:** Beard, *Complete Cookbook for Entertaining*, pp. 14–15; Helen Evans Brown, *Helen Brown's West Coast Cook Book*, p. 175.

219 **"To be perfectly honest":** Helen Evans Brown to Beard, January 5, 1955, JBP.

219 **"He not only used innumerable":** Helen Evans Brown to Schaffner, undated [January 1955], JSP.

219 **"When the mss was typed":** Helen Evans Brown to Schaffner, January 22, 1955, JSP.

220 **"Jim dear":** Helen Evans Brown to Beard, January 19, 1955, JBP.

220 **General Bartron:** Brown and Beard, *Outdoor Cookery*, p. 24.

220 **Jorge Ramirez:** Ibid.

220 **Hugo Hammer:** See Hugo Hammer's Spareribs, Brown and Beard, *Outdoor Cookery*, p. 109.

220 **"You and I have never":** Helen Evans Brown to Beard, January 5, 1954 [*sic*] [1955], JBP.

221 **The numbers for 1955:** Doubleday and Company royalty statement for *The Complete Book of Outdoor Cookery*, October 31, 1955, JSP.

221 **the first half of 1956:** Beard to Helen Evans Brown, August 22, 1956, LL.

221 **"They didn't do a fucking":** Ibid.

221 **urged Helen to scrap it:** Helen Evans Brown to Schaffner, undated [August 21, 1954], JSP.

222 **"Saturday I am having":** Beard to Helen Evans Brown, February 9, 1954, LL.

222 **Ken Zwerin was a lawyer:** James Thomas Sears, *Behind the Mask of the Mattachine: The Hal Call Chronicles and the Early Movement for Homosexual Emancipation* (Routledge, 2006), p. 364. "The San Francisco attorney [1911–1991] had been advising gay clients caught in compromising situations, apprehended by the vice squad, or victimized by blackmail. In exchange for these Mattachine referrals, he consulted on the *Mattachine Review* for two years. The glib and articulate Zwerin was an embodiment of contradictions: insecure and aggressive, a homophile activist and a closeted homosexual, generous yet possessive."

222 **As a youth, he studied:** "History," Congregation Beth Jacob, Redwood City, California, bethjacobrwc.org. It's not clear whether Zwerin was ever actually ordained as a rabbi.

222 **the Mattachine Society:** Jonathan [Ned] Katz, *Gay American History: Lesbians and Gay Men in the U.S.A.*, pp. 406–20.

223 **wasn't purely altruistic:** Joe Baron, oral history in Nan Alamilla Boyd, *Wide Open Town: A History of Queer San Francisco to 1965* (University of California Press, 2003), p. 106. "[Zwerin] specialized, as he put it, in 'gay law.' . . . He came down to the police station and talked to my friend [who had been charged with grand vagrancy] and said, 'I'll take care of it. It ain't cheap, but I'll take care of it.'"

223 **"the holy of holies":** Beard to Helen Evans Brown, February 15, 1954, LL.

223 **a menu Zwerin requested:** Beard to Helen Evans Brown, undated [February 9, 1954], LL.

223 **The choucroute was superb:** Beard to Helen Evans Brown, undated [February 15, 1954], LL.

223 **James and Zwerin met:** Beard, datebook entry for April 9, 1954, JBP. "Vince's Vallejo St / Zwerin / Elver."

223 **Vince's Garden Restaurant:** Menu for Vince's Garden Restaurant, undated [September 1944], California Menu Collection, California Historical Society, San Francisco.

224 **Elver Barker:** Tyler Alpern, "Elver Barker a.k.a. Carl B. Harding," http://www.tyleralpern.com/ElverBarker.html. Barker served on the editorial board of the *Mattachine Review*, the Mattachine Society's publication, launched in 1955. He wrote under the pen name "Carl B. Harding."

224 **The Kate Smith Hour . . . army training films:** "Play to Have Tryout Tomorrow at Deal," *Asbury Park* [NJ] *Press*, October 9, 1947.

224 **Freddie Shrallow:** Vivian Brown, "Pierced Hardboard Will Prove Useful in Multiple Ways," *Tucson* [AZ] *Daily Citizen*, February 15, 1964.

224 **The Merry Widow . . . Mexican Hayride:** Entry for Aleks Bird, Internet Broadway Database, https://www.ibdb.com/broadway-cast-staff/aleks-bird-481231.

224 **hung up his tights to write:** Aleks Bird, "There's a Man in the Kitchen," *American Home* magazine, June 1949.

225 **cottage in Connecticut:** Philip Nell, *Crockett Johnson and Ruth Krauss: How an Unlikely Couple Found Love, Dodged the FBI, and Transformed Children's Literature* (University Press of Mississippi, 2012), p. 85.

225 **reader for Dell Books:** JWI with John Ferrone, Session 1, March 3, 2009.

225 **Ferrone's first assignment:** Ibid.

225 **looked up Coward:** Ibid.

225 **go on to Harcourt, Brace and World:** Bruce Weber, "John Ferrone, Editor of Eclectic Stable of Writers, Dies at 91," *New York Times*, April 16, 2016.

226 **James received a gift:** Kenneth C. Zwerin to William Lambert, *ONE* magazine, Los Angeles, July 14, 1958, *ONE* Archives at the USC Libraries, University of Southern California.
"I am enclosing herewith my check for $10.00. . . . [K]indly enter a subscription for James
A. Beard. . . . I would appreciate if you would drop Mr. Beard a note advising him that this
is a gift from me."

226 **gay-rights magazine *ONE*:** "History," ONE Archives Foundation website, https://www
.onearchives.org/about/history/.

226 **deemed it obscene:** "Timeline," ONE Archives Foundation website, https://www
.onearchives.org/about/history/.

226 **cover story on gay beaches:** Frank Golovitz, "Gay Beach, *ONE: The Homosexual Viewpoint*, July 1958, ONE Archives at the USC Libraries, University of Southern California.

226 **James had arrived in Mexico:** Beard, Mexico City, to Helen Evans Brown, undated [July
1955], LL.

227 **layover in New Orleans:** Beard, datebook entry for July 13, 1955, JBP.

227 **Basque piperade for Marilyn Monroe:** Beard to Helen Evans Brown, undated [August
1955], LL.

227 **She was so quiet:** Beard to Helen Evans Brown, undated [July 1955], LL.

227 **a little over thirty:** Jane Nickerson, "News of Food: How to Eat Well," *New York Times*,
March 25, 1953.

227 **he was an investor:** Ibid.

228 **Paul et Virginie in Paris:** Ibid.

228 **rock lobsters flamed:** Ibid.

228 **land crab asopao:** Ibid.

228 **lunch in Havana:** Ibid.

228 **colonia San Ángel:** Beard, San Angel Inn, Mexico City, to Helen Evans Brown, undated
[July 1955], LL. "San Angel Inn is a residential section where [the Guths] live."

228 **a Continental steakhouse:** Pepe Romero, *My Mexico City (and Yours)* (Dolphin Books,
1962), pp. 100–101.

228 **"I've always wanted":** Ibid.

228 **a dinner for thirty:** Beard, datebook entry for July 14, 1955, JBP.

228 **He declared it marvelous:** Beard, San Angel Inn, Mexico City, to Helen Evans Brown,
undated [July 1955], LL. "[E]veryone is trying to get the name of [Guth's] supplier and it
is simply that he knows how to buy and what to do with the meat when he has it."

229 **Alan Taulbee:** James Beard, address book entry for Alan Taulbee, undated [1962?], JBP.
"Mr. Alan Taulbee, Penthouse, Hotel Prince [Principe], Luis Moya 12, Mexico DF."

229 **former radio announcer:** "Advertising, Agencies, Stations," *Billboard*, August 8, 1942.
"WQXR chief announcer Arch Kepner and staff announcer Alan Taulbee have been
sworn into the navy for aviation cadet training."

229 **road race on the Pan-American Highway:** "Drisdale Swerves to Miss Car, But Regains
Road," *El Paso* [TX] *Herald-Post*, November 21, 1952. "Alan Taulbee, [Pan American road
race] publicity director. . . ."

229 **Turkish baths:** Beard, datebook entry for July 21, 1955, JBP. "T Bath." There were many
bathhouses operating in Mexico City in this period. (Víctor M. Macías-González, Professor of History and Women's, Gender, and Sexuality Studies, University of Wisconsin–La
Crosse, email message to author, May 5, 2018.) Macías-González has studied male bathhouses in the Mexican capital as far back as 1880. He's identified a widespread culture
of male queer sexuality, whether or not the participants identified as homosexuals. See
Macías-González, "Scrubbing the Queer Away, or Homosexuality and Mexico City Bathhouses, 1880–1920," a paper delivered before the Primer Congreso Mexicano de Historia
LGBTT, Monterrey, Mexico, October 2001.

229 **José Jorge Carlos de Jesús Palomino y Cañedo:** In 1931, at age twenty-two, Jorge met the
Soviet avant-garde filmmaker Sergei Eisenstein. Eisenstein had come to Mexico in 1930 to
shoot a film about the grand sweep of Mexican history, bankrolled by Upton Sinclair and

other American progressives, *¡Que viva México!* There were many obstacles, and Eisenstein eventually abandoned the project, but not before he'd captured about fifty hours of footage in various locations. The young Jorge was the filmmaker's guide and translator in Colima and Jalisco. The men had an affair. Eisenstein, who'd expressed no prior physical interest in men, wrote to his future wife that with Jorge he was finally able, at age thirty-three, to "go all the way" sexually. Masha Salazkina, *In Excess: Sergei Eisenstein's Mexico* (University of Chicago Press, 2009), p. 130.

229 **went to the bullfights:** Beard, datebook entry for July 17, 1955, JBP.

229 **the Mauna Loa:** Ibid. See Romero, *My Mexico City*, pp. 102–3. "[A]n enormous Cantonese-Polynesian luxury eating place."

229 **everything tasted atrocious:** Ibid.

230 **good and ripped:** Queer poet Robert Nichols Hunt, in a 1953 letter to his longtime partner, the writer Witter Bynner, described a night out in Mexico City with Jorge Palomino: an all-night marathon of drinking, in bars, nightclubs, and at house parties (one with 150 guests, all men). Jorge was capable of interesting conversation when not too drunk. ("He's likeable when he is [sober]," Hunt wrote, "and really most intelligent.") Robert Nichols Hunt, Guadalajara, to Witter Bynner, Santa Fe, New Mexico, August 27, 1953, Houghton Library, Harvard University.

230 **Guth was translating it:** Beard, Mexico City, to Helen Evans Brown, undated [July 1955], LL.

230 **"These are family recipes":** Ibid.

231 **six-hour trip to Acapulco:** Beard to Helen Evans Brown, undated [July 1955], LL. Also Richard W. Wilkie, "The Drive to Acapulco," in *Adventures into Mexico: American Tourism Beyond the Border* (Rowman and Littlefield Publishers, 2006), ed. Nicholas Dagen Bloom, pp. 106–7.

231 **carnitas, tamales, and avocado soup:** Beard, datebook entries for July 23 and July 24, 1955, JBP.

231 **went to the baths again:** Beard, datebook entry for July 22, 1955, JBP.

231 **The original plan:** Helen Evans Brown to Schaffner, June 28, 1955, JSP.

231 **"It is definitely off":** Ibid.

231 **James saw Jorge again:** Beard, datebook entry for September 6, 1955, JBP.

231 **Johnny Johnston's Charcoal Room:** Ibid. For the Charcoal Room, see Jane Nickerson, "News of Food," *New York Times*, October 11, 1954.

232 **three days with Jorge:** Beard, datebook entries for January 10, 12, and 20, 1956, JBP.

232 **"Worth the price":** Beard, datebook entry for January 12, 1956, JBP.

232 **Felice De Gregorio:** Clementine Paddleford, "Waiters, Diners, Even the Owner Sing for Their Supper at Felix's," *New York Herald Tribune*, October 11, 1947.

232 **Felice had sung:** Ibid.

233 **"middle price, middle good":** Ibid.

233 **Ralph, the baritone waiter:** Ibid.

233 **At their table:** Peter Kump, "In Memory" [obituary for Gino Cofacci], *News from the Beard House* newsletter, Volume 3, Number 5, May 1989. "[Gino] met James Beard at a Greenwich Village restaurant, Chez Felix." James had fabricated a romantic story about meeting Gino one night in Rome, on the Spanish Steps. Clark Wolf, who, as a young queer, met James in the early 1980s, recalls James telling this anecdote. In the story, James and Gino walked to the bar at the Hotel d'Inghilterra for Bronx cocktails. They fell in love, and James asked Gino to move to New York. The story had a punch line, according to Wolf: "[James] referred to [Gino] as the most expensive cocktail in Roman history." It's not clear why James would invent the story, unless he thought the truth—meeting in a semi-reputable gay establishment on West Thirteenth with mediocre Italian food—was unbecoming to the image of James Beard. JBI with Clark Wolf, January 15, 2017.

233 **Harrison & Abramovitz:** Kump, "In Memory," *News from the Beard House*, May 1989.

233 **immigrated to the United States:** US Bureau of the Census, "Stefan Taussig," 1940 United

States Federal Census. "Pasquale Cofacci," twenty-six, is classified as a "guest" in the household.

233 **School of Architecture:** "Former Ithacan in Pacific," *The Ithaca* [NY] *Journal*, February 20, 1945.

233 **Gino was inducted:** "Another Ordered Inducted," *The Ithaca* [NY] *Journal*, July 22, 1941.

233 **interned to a relocation camp:** the terminology for these internment camps has been controversial; they fit the definition of concentration camps.

233 **Technician Fourth Grade:** "Former Ithacan in Pacific," *The Ithaca* [NY] *Journal*, February 20, 1945.

233 **returned to Ithaca:** "Men Discharged," *The Ithaca* [NY] *Journal*, July 17, 1945.

233 **became a Gargoyle:** "Cornell Class to Include 14 Ithacans," *The Ithaca* [NY] *Journal*, February 2, 1948.

234 **had Gino to dinner:** Beard, datebook entry for April 25, 1956, JBP.

234 **had Gino over again:** Beard, datebook entry for April 28, 1956, JBP.

234 **cold hors d'oeuvres:** Ibid.

234 **meat and tongue served first:** Beard, *Delights and Prejudices*, pp. 117–18.

CHAPTER 13: PERDITA BAKES A LAYER CAKE

237 **Frank Schoonmaker:** Thomas Pinney, *The Makers of American Wine: A Record of Two Hundred Years* (University of California Press, 2012), pp. 149–70.

238 **"I have always admired":** Beard to Helen Evans Brown, February 17, 1956, LL.

238 **under contract with Random House:** Beard to Helen Evans Brown, June 13, 1956, LL.

238 **newest international beach resort:** Barbara Probst Solomon, "Before the Tourists," *New York Times*, July 14, 1985.

238 **his wife, Marina:** Marina Villar grew up in Santander, Spain, and immigrated to the United States to study at Columbia University. She married Frank Schoonmaker in New York City in June 1945. "Marina Villar a Bride," *New York Times*, June 28, 1945.

238 **canceled at the last minute:** According to his datebook, James flew to Madrid on June 29, 1956, and spent a few days before taking the train to the Costa Brava. He noted somewhat cryptically in his datebook, "Madrid is so beautiful and so clean—it's perfectly kept—for the rich—and normal."

238 **Palamós was picturesque:** "1950s Costa Brava, Spain, Rare Colour Home Movie Footage," Kinolibrary Archive Film collections, Clip ref. KLR254.

239 **"I am not the person":** Beard, Palamós, Spain, to John Schaffner, July 11, 1956, JSP.

239 **"Marina is a boring bitch":** Ibid.

239 **"Marina came over here":** Beard, Palamós, Spain, to John Schaffner, July 22, 1956, JSP.

239 **"As you remember":** Beard, Palamós, Spain, to John Schaffner, July 11, 1956, JSP.

239 **early at the market:** Bettina McNulty, quoted in Evan Jones, *Epicurean Delight*, p. 248.

240 **"We have just finished":** Beard, Palamós, Spain, to John Schaffner, July 22, 1956, JSP.

240 **"I wish you could visit":** Ibid.

240 **James escaped to Barcelona:** Beard, datebook entry for July 16, 1956. JBP. "To Barcelona—crowded train."

240 **Bel y Cía:** Ibid. "Fittings for shirts."

240 **Jack Raglin:** James Beard, address book entry for Jack Raglin, undated [1962?], JBP. The caption for a 1969 photo from the *Denver Post* identifies Raglin as Conoco's assistant director of public affairs. https://www.gettyimages.com/detail/news-photo/oil-was-not-the-subject-speaker-at-a-conoco-political-news-photo/161915525.

240 **"the slums":** Beard, Palamós, Spain, to John Schaffner, August 2, 1956, JSP.

240 **"You sit on the street":** Ibid.

240 **"I have seen a sofa":** Beard, Palamós, Spain, to John Schaffner, August 3, 1956, JSP.

241 **"I find myself":** Beard, Palamós, Spain, to John Schaffner, August 2, 1956, JSP.

241 **Robert Tyler Lee:** "Robert Tyler Lee (1910–1987)," Internet Movie Database, https://www

.imdb.com/name/nm0498135/. Beard, Palamós, to Helen Evans Brown, July 14, 1956, LL. "Bob Lee whom you have met at Eleanors [*sic*] is coming next week for a few days. He has been all over the continent and I guess is coming here for a complete rest and relaxation."

241 **"I fell upon the idea":** Beard, Palamós, Spain, to John Schaffner, July 22, 1956, JSP.

241 **"I hope he isn't":** Robert Tyler Lee, Palamós, Spain, to John Schaffner, July 26, 1956, JSP.

242 **"It is going to be revolutionary":** Beard, Palamós, Spain, to John Schaffner, August 2, 1956, JSP.

242 **the empty apartment:** Beard to Helen Evans Brown, undated [September 4, 1956], LL.

242 **"rather a swell guy":** Ibid.

242 **took on the assignment:** Gino Cofacci to Isabel Callvert, Detroit, May 11, 1958, OHS.

242 **unworthy of their friend:** JWI with John Ferrone, Session 1, March 3, 2009. "[Gino] would enter, and the whole atmosphere would change to one of fussing, anxiety, complaints."

243 **André Surmain:** Frank J. Prial, "Surmain, Still the Restless Restaurateur," *New York Times*, September 2, 1981.

243 **founded Aziza Cosmetics:** Gael Greene, "Au Revoir, André Surmain," *Insatiable*, January 23, 1973.

243 **changed his name to Surmain:** Jeremy Josephs, *Murder on the Menu: On the French Riviera*, p. 48.

243 **running a catering company:** Josephs, *Murder on the Menu*, pp. 100–101.

243 **Les Ambassadeurs du Bien Manger:** Prial, "Surmain, Still the Restless Restaurateur," *New York Times*, September 2, 1981.

243 **oversaw the conversion:** Josephs, *Murder on the Menu*, p. 97. In 1961, the Surmains would open their celebrated French restaurant Lutèce—overseen by the young chef André Soltner—in the brownstone where they lived.

243 **teaching a cooking class:** Beard to Helen Evans Brown, April 26, 1955, LL. James urged Helen about collaborating on a bicoastal cooking school with Surmain, offering classes both in New York and Los Angeles.

244 **"If Dione":** Ibid.

244 **"Mrs. Hibben is now begging":** Beard to Helen Evans Brown, February 17, 1956, LL.

244 **O'Quin's Charcoal Sauce:** Beard to Helen Evans Brown, undated [June 22, 1956], LL. O'Quin's was a barbecue sauce flavored with liquid smoke. An application at the US Patent Office describes it as useful for "steaks, chops, sea foods, gravies, soups, etc." Official Gazette of the United States Patent Office, Volume 684, July 13, 1954, p. 266.

244 **"He divides himself":** Schaffner to Helen Evans Brown, June 1, 1956, JSP.

244 **"I . . . wish he would decide":** Helen Evans Brown to Schaffner, June 11, 1956, JSP.

245 **P.S. from Paris:** Art Buchwald was best known for Paris After Dark, his column in the Paris Edition of the *New York Herald Tribune*, launched in 1949. In the early 1950s, Buchwald's column became syndicated under the name P.S. from Paris.

245 **"The gourmet vintage 1956":** Beard met Buchwald in Paris for the interview on January 10, 1956, according to Beard's datebook. The column appeared a few weeks later.

246 **appeared on the masthead:** Beard, Palamós, Spain, to Helen Evans Brown, July 6, 1956, LL.

246 **"We shall have a test kitchen":** Ibid.

246 **"We are giving":** Beard to Helen Evans Brown, undated [September 1956], LL.

246 **"JAMES BEARD and ANDRE SURMAIN":** Postcard notice addressed to Mr. and Mrs. John Schaffner, postmarked September 19, 1956, JSP.

247 **"Not exciting but":** Beard to Helen Evans Brown, October 7, 1956, LL.

247 **"You will be fascinated":** Schaffner to Helen Evans Brown, October 13, 1956, JSP.

247 **Perdita asked James:** Beard to Helen Evans Brown, October 11, 1956, LL.

247 **"I think the class":** Schaffner to Helen Evans Brown, October 13, 1956, JSP.

CHAPTER 14: CORONATION CHICKEN

248 **he paid a visit:** Beard, datebook entry for January 15, 1955, JBP.

249 **James cooked choucroute:** Henry McNulty, "James Andrews Beard: A Personal Memoir," *Petits Propos Culinaires*, vol. 19, March 1985.

249 **She wore the clothes:** M. Cameron Grey, recalling Alice during this period in "Miss Toklas Alone," *Virginia Quarterly Review*, Autumn 1976. "I can only guess that she never changed her appearance nor deviated from her apparel of a beige blouse, wool skirt, stout brown wool stockings, and sandals which were the soul and essence of all sandals."

249 **"She is really a darling":** Beard, Hotel de France & Choiseul, Paris, to Schaffner, January 16, 1955, JSP.

249 **she was a fan . . . also of Helen's:** Ibid. "She happens to be a fan of Helen's and of mine which floored me completely."

249 **"She has one now":** Ibid. After Schaffner wrote to her, saying he'd be delighted to try and place her article in a magazine, Alice demurred. "Mr. Beard was too indulgent." [Alice B. Toklas, 5 rue Christine, Paris, to John Schaffner, April 18, 1955; quoted in Edward Burns, editor, *Letters of Alice B. Toklas: Staying On Alone*, 1973, p. 320.]

249 **Montfort-l'Amaury:** Beard, datebook entry for May 19, 1957, JBP.

250 **"I never face the view":** McNulty, *Petits Propos Culinaires*, March 1985.

250 **"a fine duckling pâté":** James Beard, "Picnicking Can Be a Gourmet's Delight," *James Beard's Simple Foods*, p. 153.

250 **"crispy brown, not overcooked":** Ibid.

250 **private cooking lessons:** Beard to Helen Evans Brown, undated [August 14, 1958], LL.

250 **Brown's seemed majestic:** Alice B. Toklas, 5 rue Christine, Paris, to James Beard, Brown's Hotel, London, February 17, 1959, JBP.

251 **dinner at Café Chambord:** Beard, datebook entry for March 22, 1955, JBP.

251 **charming and flamboyant:** JWI with John Ferrone, Session #1, March 3, 2009, NYU.

251 **It was astronomical:** Beard to Helen Evans Brown, undated [March 28, 1955], LL. "The dinner for four of us was so astronomical in price I guess I have to do two books to make up for it."

251 **book advance would be $3,000:** Schaffner to Isabel Callvert, April 29, 1955, JSP.

251 **she didn't think:** JWI with John Ferrone, Session #1, March 3, 2009, NYU.

251 **first published in 1896:** Farmer's book was a follow-up to Mary Lincoln's *Mrs. Lincoln's Boston Cook Book* of 1884.

251 **James Beard's Basic Cook Book:** Schaffner to Isabel Callvert, April 29, 1955, JSP.

252 **"Buy good food":** Beard, *The James Beard Cookbook*, p. 9.

252 **deliver fresh eggs:** Beard, *The James Beard Cookbook*, p. 7.

252 **"narrative type of recipe":** "James Beard and His Successful Cook Books," *Publishers Weekly*, May 18, 1959.

252 **Braised Beef, Bordeaux Fashion:** Beard, *The James Beard Cookbook*, p. 232.

252 **Polynesian Stuffed Leg of Lamb:** Beard, *The James Beard Cookbook*, p. 287.

252 **how to boil water, an echo of Mary Lincoln's:** Beard, *The James Beard Cookbook*, p. 287. "[Boiling] is one of the most generally used, and abused, forms of cooking." [Mrs. D. A. (Mary) Lincoln, *Boston Cooking School Cook Book: A Reprint of the 1884 Classic* (Dover Publications, 1996), p. 8.]

252 **photo by George Lazarnick:** Dell had doubts about using the photo of James for the cover. "A lot of people thought the cover was gross—too much meat, too much fat, *yecch*!" John Ferrone, quoted in David Kamp, *The United States of Arugula*, p. 61.

253 **"We are definitely":** James Beard, Drake Hotel, Chicago, to Isabel Callvert, undated [May 1959], OHS.

253 **"not a gastronomic cliché":** Craig Claiborne, "New Cookbook Covers Everything But the Kitchen Sink," *New York Times*, April 16, 1959.

253 **sold 150,000 copies:** JWI with John Ferrone, Session #1, March 3, 2009, NYU.

253 **first hardcover edition:** Beard, *The James Beard Cookbook* (E. P. Dutton and Co., 1961).

The hardcover edition included new illustrations but was otherwise identical to the 1959 Dell paperback.

253 **Dell's *Anatomy of a Murder*:** "James Beard and His Successful Cook Books," *Publishers Weekly*, May 18, 1959.

253 **"shut off its telephones":** Ibid.

254 **"Everyone seems stunned":** Beard, Cincinnati, to Helen Evans Brown, undated [May 1959], LL.

254 **the future of cookbooks:** Beard to Helen Evans Brown, February 26, 1953, LL.

254 **his fifth party:** Beard to Helen Evans Brown, undated [January 1, 1960], LL.

254 **"Living across from":** Beard to Helen Evans Brown, October 3, 1959, LL.

255 **even Eleanor Roosevelt:** "Eleanor Roosevelt's Margarine Commercial (1959)," in "Leftovers," *History of the World in 1000 Cookbooks*, http://www.leftovershistory.com/eleanor -roosevelt-margarine-commercial/.

255 **"all manner of junk":** Beard to Helen Evans Brown, undated (September 1959), LL.

255 **vermillion Formica:** Beard, "The Stomach, Heart, and Spirit of the House" (1968), in *The Armchair James Beard*, p. 7.

256 **a 1746 engraving:** Aubrey Gaby Miller, American Museum of Natural History, New York, email to author, July 31, 2017.

256 **seven-armed Italian candelabra:** Beard to Helen Evans Brown, undated [January 1, 1960], LL.

257 **tangerine sections marinated:** Ibid.

257 **"That's nerve":** Ibid.

257 **"handsomely styled and spacious":** Craig Claiborne, "Cooking Classes to Have International Flavor," *New York Times*, January 14, 1960.

258 **"I shall write a memoir cookbook":** Beard to Helen Evans Brown, undated [January 1, 1960], LL.

258 **"Yes," Helen wrote back:** Helen Evans Brown to Beard, January 8, 1960, JBP.

258 **interviewed two candidates:** Beard to Helen Evans Brown, undated [December 1959], LL.

258 **assumed it was a woman:** KSI with Clayton Triplette, August 12, 2013.

258 **baggy, pleated suit pants:** This description is based on a small, unsigned portrait of Clayton in the private collection of the James Beard Foundation, tagged "Clay at 32." JBF.

258 **Judith Garden:** "Judith Garden, Flower Arranger, Dies at 81," *New York Times*, November 2, 1988.

259 **Miss Crawford's penthouse:** KSI with Clayton Triplette, August 12, 2013. See also "New York City: 2 East 70th Street at Fifth Avenue, 1957 to 1967," *The Best of Everything: Joan Crawford Geography*, ed. Stephanie Jones, https://www.joancrawfordbest.com/geo5thave .htm.

259 **On his father's side:** José Wilson, "Cooking with Mr. Triplette," *New York Post*, May 2, 1979.

259 **his mother was something else:** Clayton Triplette, "JBF Staff Profile," unpublished questionnaire, James Beard Foundation private archives, undated. "Mom was something else."

259 **"Do you want me":** KSI with Clayton Triplette, August 12, 2013.

259 **"You're not!":** Ibid.

259 **Guerlain Impériale eau de cologne:** JBI with Neil O'Donnell, February 8, 2018.

259 **"My mother says":** KSI with Clayton Triplette, August 12, 2013.

259 **"If I told you":** Ibid.

260 **in a pine box:** JBI with Renée Davis (Clayton Triplette's niece), July 10, 2017. "He said the only time he'd come back to Buffalo is to die, and that's what he did."

260 **He took him on:** Beard, datebook entry for December 21, 1959. "Houseman."

260 **on the Lower East Side:** James Beard, address book entry for Clayton Triplette, undated [1962?], JBP. "231 Eldridge Street."

260 **his mother's fried chicken:** Wilson, *New York Post*, May 2, 1979.

260 **additional chicken or goose fat:** Ibid.

260 **never tasted finer:** Beard, *Beard on Food*, p. 122. "My housekeeper, Clayton Triplette, who is an expert at southern cooking even though he isn't southern, always adds a good bit of cinnamon, as well as salt and pepper, to the flour in which he dips chicken before frying it, which gives his fried chicken the most haunting, subtle, and delicate flavor."

260 **James sailed without Gino:** Undated travel itinerary [April 1960] for James A. Beard by Nancy Surmain, Travel Consultant, 1960, JSP.

261 **"strangely exhilarating city":** Beard, Gritti Palace-Hotel, Venice, to Schaffner, April 27, 1960, JSP.

261 **"Certainly it is blessed":** Ibid.

261 **"Give Gino a call":** Beard, Gritti Palace-Hotel, Venice, to Isabel Callvert, undated [April 1960], OHS.

261 **"I really have had it":** Beard to Helen Evans Brown, February 1960, LL.

261 **"I loved this trip":** Beard, MS *San Marco*, to Helen Evans Brown, May 9, 1960, LL.

261 **"I find I don't want":** Ibid.

261 **"gets increasingly busy":** Ibid.

261 **"There is really no one":** Ibid.

262 **birthday in Istanbul:** Beard, datebook entry for May 5, 1960, JBP.

262 **tarama, stuffed vine leaves:** Ibid.

262 **"Very tired for 57 years!":** Beard, datebook entry for May 4, 1960, JBP.

262 **Miltowns during the day:** Beard to Helen Evans Brown, January 16, 1959, LL.

262 **"my first picnic memory":** Beard, Gritti Palace-Hotel, Venice, to Isabel Callvert, undated [April 28 or 29, 1960], OHS.

262 **"The ladies brought salads":** Beard [Jerry Mason], *James Beard's Treasury of Outdoor Cooking*, p. 214.

263 **"an imposing culinary angel":** Craig Claiborne, "Three for the Chef," *New York Times Book Review*, October 16, 1960.

263 **"suited to the parlor":** Ibid.

263 **"I think you are right":** Beard, MS *San Marco*, to Helen Evans Brown, May 9, 1960, LL.

CHAPTER 15: "MORE CAKES, MORE TASTES"

264 **"An analysis of good eating":** James Beard to John Schaffner, January 15, 1961, JSP.

264 **"uninhibited without being bitter":** Ibid.

265 **"Make notes":** Ibid.

265 **"SUGGESTIONS FOR A BOOK":** Beard [and Schaffner], prospectus for *Delights and Prejudices*, unpublished manuscript, January 1961, OHS.

265 **"I could branch out":** Ibid.

265 **"While I do not":** Ibid.

266 **"I would here give":** Ibid.

266 **scratched out the word:** Ibid.

266 **"I now have an offer":** Beard to Helen Evans Brown, undated [January 9, 1961], LL.

266 **James signed the contract:** Beard to Helen Evans Brown, undated [February 21, 1961], LL.

266 **would have necessitated approval:** Alfred Knopf Jr. to Schaffner, March 3, 1961, JSP.

266 **gave him $3,500:** Schaffner to Beard, February 9, 1961, JSP.

266 **James sailed alone:** Beard, datebook entry for May 12, 1961, JBP.

266 **"I'm getting some work":** Beard to Helen Evans Brown, June 7 [1961], LL.

267 **met up with Alexis Lambelet:** Lambelet, who lived in an apartment block on Lausanne's Chemin de Primerose, probably worked in Nestlé's public relations department. It's likely he and James had an affair. [Beard, address book entry for Alexis Lambelet, undated (1962?), JBP.]

267 **"Peasanty and fabulous":** Beard, datebook entry for June 3, 1961, JBP.

267 **"Last Saturday we went":** Beard to Helen Evans Brown, June 7, 1961, LL.

267 **braised pigs' feet:** Beard, datebook entry for June 2, 1961, JBP.

267 **small Saturday market:** Beard, *Delights and Prejudices*, p. 59.

267 **"about sixty pages":** Beard, Hotel Central-Bellevue, Lausanne, to Schaffner, undated [June 10, 1961], JSP.

268 **"It depresses me":** Alfred Knopf Jr. to Schaffner, December 11, 1961, JSP.

268 **all rather sad:** Beard, Hotel Ritz, Barcelona, to Helen Evans Brown, undated [July 20, 1961], LL.

268 **"a remarkable manuscript":** SBFI with Judith Jones, April 22, 2013.

269 **"He seemed intrigued":** Judith Jones, *The Tenth Muse: My Life in Food* (Alfred A. Knopf, 2007), p. 69.

269 **The publisher noted:** Publisher's note in Louisette Bertholle, Simone Beck, and Helmut Ripperger, *What's Cooking in France* (Ives Washburn, Inc., 1952).

269 **"He just devoured it":** SBFI with Judith Jones, April 22, 2013.

269 **"falls flat on its face":** Beard to Helen Evans Brown, undated [October 15, 1961], LL.

269 **he wished he'd written:** SBFI with Judith Jones, April 22, 2013.

270 **James invited Julia:** Beard to Helen Evans Brown, November 1, 1961, LL.

270 **teetered on the brink:** Though an experienced cooking teacher and TV host, Dione sometimes seemed overwhelmed. "She drank a little bit too much," Judith Jones told Sara B. Franklin. [SBFI with Jones, April 22, 2013.] But in a 2011 profile, Jeanne Schinto challenged the rumors of Lucas's alcoholism, citing instead her frequent migraines and use of prescription drugs to manage them. [Schinto, "Remembering Dione Lucas," *Gastronomica*, vol. 11, no. 4 (Winter 2011).]

270 **"Dinner was held":** Beard to Helen Evans Brown, December 16, 1961, LL.

270 **"look she gave me":** Ibid.

271 **"Dione told me":** Ibid.

271 **"Shy—shit":** Ibid.

271 **The Four Seasons:** Ibid.

271 **the rights were his:** Thomas McNamee, *The Man Who Changed the Way We Eat: Craig Claiborne and the American Food Renaissance* (Free Press, 2012), p. 66.

271 **nearly thirty thousand copies:** Beard to Helen Evans Brown, undated [December 16, 1961], LL.

271 **"I wonder if some":** Alfred Knopf Jr. to Schaffner, January 8, 1962, JSP.

271 **"This is a work":** Schaffner to Alfred Knopf Jr., January 11, 1962, JSP.

272 **"John Ferrone is doing":** Beard to Helen Evans Brown, undated [January 7, 1962], LL.

272 **"most sensitive open secret":** Robert C. Doty, "Growth of Overt Homosexuality in City Provokes Wide Concern," *New York Times*, December 17, 1963.

272 **"In Greenwich Village":** Ibid.

272 **"A New York homosexual":** Ibid.

273 **"just a clump":** JWI with John Ferrone, Session #3, April 1, 2009, NYU.

273 **"Ah," he said:** Ibid.

273 **James's favorite bildungsroman:** Heidi Waleson, "Beard on Opera," *Opera News*, July 1983.

273 **"As I told Jim":** Alfred Knopf Jr. to Schaffner, March 19, 1962, JSP.

274 **"placement of the exact years":** Ibid.

274 **monthlong tour of Asia:** "Itinerary of James Beard," unpublished memorandum, undated [1962], JSP.

274 **"involving themselves too much":** Alfred Knopf Jr. to Schaffner, May 24, 1962, JSP.

274 ***Pepperidge Farm Cookbook:*** Margaret Rudkin, *The Margaret Rudkin Pepperidge Farm Cookbook* (Atheneum, 1963).

274 **"I certainly feel that":** Beard, Peninsula Hotel, Hong Kong, to Schaffner, June 8, 1962, JSP.

275 **"Your objection is":** Schaffner to Knopf, August 7, 1962, JSP.

275 **"Pat Knopf insists":** Beard to Helen Evans Brown, undated [September 30, 1962], LL.

275 **"to extend the book":** Beard to Helen Evans Brown, undated [October 14, 1962], LL.

275 **Lou Barcarès:** John Ferrone, "With Beard in Provence: A Gastronomic Memory," unpublished manuscript, JBP.

276 **a gravel terrace:** Ibid.

276 **"I go struggling on":** Beard, Lou Barcarès, Saint-Rémy-de-Provence, to Schaffner, June 19, 1963, JSP.

276 **"My mood is becoming":** Beard to Helen Evans Brown, December 29, 1962, LL.

276 **He found dark-crusted:** Ferrone, "With Beard in Provence," JBP.

276 **"Ate like a nut":** Beard, datebook entry for May 17, 1963, JBP.

277 **"think I have finished":** Beard, datebook entry for May 15, 1963, JBP.

277 **"Sonnez la trompette!":** Beard, datebook entry for May 16, 1963, JBP.

277 **went to a party:** Beard, datebook entry for May 10, 1963, JBP. "Jean de Beucken here, what a talker!"

277 **"The gigot is beautiful":** Ibid.

277 **"Our meat is much":** Beard, datebook entry for May 13, 1963, JBP.

277 **"sent to the hospital":** Beard, Lou Barcarès, Saint-Rémy-de-Provence, to Schaffner, June 19, 1963, JSP.

277 **a cerebral hemorrhage:** Artemis Cooper, *Writing at the Kitchen Table: The Authorized Biography of Elizabeth David* (The Ecco Press, 1999), p. 225.

277 **"has been so much change":** Beard, Lou Barcarès, to Schaffner, June 19, 1963, JSP.

277 **"John seems to feel":** Ibid.

278 **"an art as transitory":** James Beard, in the appreciation in M. F. K. Fisher, *The Art of Eating* (The Macmillan Company, 1954), p. xviii.

278 **"The ability to recall":** James Beard, *Delights and Prejudices*, p. 8.

278 **"Not all taste memory":** Ibid.

278 **"I think I developed":** Beard, *Delights and Prejudices*, p. 9.

279 **"For Beard, food was":** Ferrone, *The Armchair James Beard*, p. 316.

279 **"When Proust recollected":** Beard, *Delights and Prejudices*, p. 3.

CHAPTER 16: COLD SICILIAN ROULADE WITH THE MASTER

281 **organizing cooking demonstrations:** Beard to Helen Evans Brown, January 12, 1964. "I'm glad you decided to come back via New York and that you will be a star guest at the Fair. It just wouldn't have been right to have everybody else who is important and not you of whom we are most fond."

281 **a stay at Doctors Hospital:** Beard to Helen Evans Brown, undated [February 17, 1964], LL.

282 **Goodner surmised:** JBI with Charles Goodner, June 15, 2017.

282 **"Certainly after all":** Beard, Lou Barcarès, Saint-Rémy-de-Provence, to Helen Evans Brown, undated [August 14, 1964], LL.

282 **"I understand the feeling":** Ibid.

282 **"Lights are still out":** Ibid.

282 **Helen died that December:** Helen Evans Brown obituary, *New York Times*, December 7, 1964.

283 **"I must say":** Schaffner to Beard, June 10, 1965, JSP.

283 **For ghost-authoring:** Schaffner to Beard, Paris, France, May 18, 1965, JSP.

283 **not get a credit:** Ibid.

284 **"Like almost all great":** Nika Hazelton, "Suited to All Tastes," *New York Times*, December 5, 1965.

284 **"I have a predilection":** Beard, *James Beard's Menus for Entertaining*, p. 136.

284 **"cooking in the nude":** Ibid.

285 **"Dear Reader":** Draft included in a letter from Richard L. Williams, Time-Life Books, to Schaffner, November 25, 1968, JSP.

285 **"It is past midnight":** Beard to Helen Evans Brown, undated [June 23, 1955], LL.

286 **met Gino at the airport:** Beard, datebook entry for May 24, 1965, JBP.

286 **next day, they traveled:** Beard, datebook entry for May 25, 1965, JBP.

286 **"The trip has been":** Beard, Hotel Ritz, Paris, to Schaffner, May 18, 1965, JSP.

286 **"Gino decides he prefers":** Beard, Nîmes, France, to John and Perdita Schaffner, undated [May 1965], JSP.

286 **"Showed Gino his first":** Beard, datebook entry for June 1, 1965, JBP.

286 **clutter and exuberant tiles:** Ibid.

286 **shopped for old tinware:** Beard, datebook entry for June 4, 1965, JBP.

286 **James saw Elizabeth David:** Beard, datebook entry for June 12, 1965, JBP.

286 **took Gino to a supper party:** Ibid.

287 **Fannie Merritt Farmer's niece:** Uncredited, "Wilma Lord Perkins Dead; Editor of Cookbooks for 45 Years," *New York Times*, December 1, 1976.

287 **"comprehensive James Beard cookbook":** John Schaffner to Ned Bradford, November 9, 1965, JSP.

287 **"big ultimate book":** Schaffner to Beard, December 3, 1965, JSP.

287 **"really comprehensive cookbook":** Ibid.

287 **"at last the essence":** Schaffner to Bradford, March 21, 1966, JSP.

288 **"I'm hungry":** John Skow, "If I Had to Practice Cannibalism . . . ," *Saturday Evening Post*, July 30, 1966.

288 **untimely death in January:** "Henri Soulé of Le Pavillon Dies," *New York Times*, January 28, 1966.

288 **"Eight or ten people":** Skow, *Saturday Evening Post*, July 30, 1966.

289 **"It says something":** Ibid.

289 **"The pupils listened":** Ibid.

289 **"The chatter hushed":** Ibid.

289 **"thinly sliced, larded sausage":** Ibid.

290 **"Dr-r-r-rape it in bacon":** Ibid.

290 **"who think of cooking":** Ibid.

290 **"the size of the man":** Ibid.

291 **"didn't make the cover":** Beard, 25 De Vere Gardens, London, to Schaffner, July 20, 1966, JSP.

291 **Schaffner enlisted Alvin Kerr:** Schaffner to Beard, 25 De Vere Gardens, London, July 27, 1966, JSP.

291 **"great army of people":** "The Man Who Wears the No. 1 Apron," *Business Week*, April 4, 1970.

291 **"average man's wish":** Nika S. Hazelton, "Cooking: Plain and Fancy," *New York Times*, June 6, 1965.

291 **"healthy, able-bodied men":** Ibid.

292 **he had a secret:** JBI with Alfred Rosenthal, November 17, 2017.

292 **bouquets of flowers:** Ibid.

292 **pledged to keep James:** Ibid.

292 **A tape recorder:** Beard to Schaffner, May 1, 1966, JSP.

292 **"We are very excited":** Martha Lehtola, Little, Brown and Co., Boston, to Earl Thollander, San Francisco, May 19, 1966, JSP.

292 **"a tome of American cookery":** Beard, 25 De Vere Gardens, London, to Schaffner, July 20, 1966, JSP.

293 **"[We] have a good deal":** Ibid.

293 **"how many nude bodies":** Beard, 25 De Vere Gardens, London, to Schaffner, July 28, 1966, JSP.

293 **an exhausting summer:** Beard, 25 De Vere Gardens, London, to Schaffner, September 30, 1966, JSP. "[I] find I don't have the stamina I used to have."

293 **"I only wish I":** Beard, 1141 Armada Drive, Pasadena, to Schaffner, undated [October 1966], JSP.

293 **"Isn't it a shame"**: Beard, Surf Pines, Oregon, to Schaffner, undated [October 1966], JSP.

294 **"I realize, though"**: Ibid.

294 **"I can feel age"**: Ibid.

294 **shirt of olive-colored plaid:** Photo in the James Beard Collection, JBP.

294 **The sandy blond:** Photo in the James Beard Collection, JBP.

295 **wealthy clients in Portland:** JBI with Jill Stanford (Harvey Welch's former assistant), February 5, 2018.

295 **"I'm fairly happy"**: Beard, La Pitchoune, Plascassier, France, to Schaffner, May 6, 1967, JSP.

295 **"darling little butcher"**: Ibid.

296 **"You wheel your little"**: Ibid.

296 **"Elizabeth David and Renée Fedden"**: Ibid.

296 **"has an endless collection"**: Beard, La Pitchoune, to Schaffner, May 18, 1967, JSP.

296 **Julia and Paul had told him:** Schaffner to Beard, La Pitchoune, May 22, 1967, JSP.

296 **"consolidate your position"**: Ibid.

296 **"glorious sun and air"**: Beard, La Pitchoune, to Schaffner, May 27, 1967, JSP.

296 **"I'm quite sure"**: Ibid.

297 **"I sit upon"**: Beard, La Pitchoune, to Schaffner, June 15, 1967, JSP.

CHAPTER 17: SHATTERED GLASS AND SCHNECKENOODLES

301 **"I have moments of wondering"**: Beard, La Pitchoune, Plascassier, France, to Schaffner, May 24, 1967, JSP.

302 **take two years:** Noël Riley Fitch, *Appetite for Life: The Biography of Julia Child* (Doubleday, 1997), p. 325.

302 **hundreds of pounds:** Fitch, *Appetite for Life*, p. 326.

302 **"Simca has enough energy"**: Beard, La Pitchoune, Plascassier, France, to Schaffner, June 15, 1967, JSP.

302 **"such a dear person"**: Ibid.

302 **Simon and Schuster told Schaffner:** Richard Olney, *Reflexions*, p. 102.

302 **Surely James:** Beard, La Pitchoune, to Schaffner, May 24, 1967, JSP.

302 **had met Olney:** Olney, *Reflexions*, p. 102.

302 **crawling with Americans:** Olney, *Reflexions*, p. 73. Olney recalled the June 1961 party as a reception marking the publication of *Mastering the Art of French Cooking*, but since the book didn't appear until October 1961, it's unlikely.

302 **James pleaded with him:** Beard, La Pitchoune, to Schaffner, July 25, 1967, JSP.

302 **He'd pay him:** Schaffner to Beard, Finistère, France, September 1, 1967, JSP.

303 **"Ned is just going"**: Beard, La Pitchoune, to Schaffner, July 25, 1967, JSP.

303 **"I'm in love!"**: Beard, Anglais Hotel, Stockholm, to Schaffner, August 4, 1967, JSP.

303 **"I know it needs"**: Ibid.

303 **"I take a very dim"**: Beard, Pasadena, to Schaffner, May 9, 1968, JSP.

303 **"What I should do"**: Ibid.

303 **"It seems to me"**: Schaffner to Beard, Pasadena, May 16, 1968, JSP.

304 **a significant book:** Ibid.

304 **"The climax of all"**: Schaffner to Beard, Pasadena, June 19, 1968, JSP.

304 **"Coming here to Gearhart"**: Beard, Surf Pines, Oregon, to Schaffner, May 31, 1968, JSP.

304 **"It's amazing to think"**: Ibid.

304 **By June 1970:** Schaffner to Beard, June 23, 1970, JSP.

304 **saw an old friend:** Beard, datebook entry for June 28, 1969, JBP.

305 **At the Stonewall Inn:** Martin Duberman, *Stonewall* (Dutton, 1993), pp. 192–94.

305 **drag queens and trans women:** Duberman, *Stonewall*, pp. 198–99.

305 **rolled by blackmailers:** William McGowan, "The Chickens and the Bulls," *Slate*, July 11, 2012, https://slate.com/human-interest/2012/07/the-chickens-and-the-bulls-the-rise

-and-incredible-fall-of-a-vicious-extortion-ring-that-preyed-on-prominent-gay-men-in-the
-1960s.html.

305   **outside the paper's offices:** David Carter, *Stonewall: The Riots That Sparked the Gay Revolution* (St. Martin's Griffin, 2004), pp. 201–2.

306   **everything to lose:** JBI with Andrew Zimmern, August 7, 2017. "It's hard for people to
understand the nature of what it meant to be a gay man in America in the 1960s," says
Zimmern, whose father, Robert, was gay, lived in the Village, and was a friend of James's.
"At a point in time when the counter culture was exploding, you were hoping for accep-
tance but at the same time Stonewall was thrown in your face."

306   **"Their new militancy":** "The Homosexual in America," *Time*, October 31, 1969.

306   **"national climate of openness":** Ibid.

306   **"We are . . . a people":** Ronald Forsythe [Donn Teal], "Why Can't 'We' Live Happily Ever
After, Too?" *New York Times*, February 23, 1969.

306   **"We must create":** Donn Teal, "How Anguished Are Homosexuals?" *New York Times*,
June 1, 1969.

307   **"63% of the nation":** "The Homosexual in America," *Time*, October 31, 1969.

307   **an aspiring young chef:** Mayukh Sen, "The Gay Man Who Brought Tapas to America,"
Taste, October 18, 2018, https://www.tastecooking.com/gay-man-brought-tapas-america/.

307   **"Peruvian Adonis":** Olney, *Reflexions*, p. 129.

307   **chefs' jackets custom made:** Olney, *Reflexions*, p. 177.

307   **walked out of:** Henry Giniger, "Paris Peace Talks Reopen with Hope on Secret Parley,"
New York Times, April 28, 1972.

308   **Operation Linebacker:** Bernard C. Nalty, "1972: Operation Linebacker," in *Air War
Over South Vietnam, 1968–1975*, posted on April 27, 2011, Air Force Historical Support Division, https://www.afhistory.af.mil/FAQs/Fact-Sheets/Article/458990/operation
-linebacker-i/.

308   **the Watergate burglars broke:** Tom van der Voort, "Watergate: The Break-In," June
17, 1972, Miller Center, University of Virginia, https://millercenter.org/the-presidency/
educational-resources/watergate/watergate-break.

308   **slipped a rock hammer:** Paul Hofmann, "Pieta Damaged in Hammer Attack," *New York
Times*, May 22, 1972.

308   **items in the Oakland Museum:** "Gallery of California History," Oakland Museum of
California.

308   **collection of thrift-store finds:** Earl Thollander, Calistoga, California, to Beard, April 5,
1972.

309   **"favorite great ladies":** Beard, *James Beard's American Cookery*, dedication.

309   **The Hall of Presidents:** "The Hall of Presidents Story," *D23: The Official Disney Fan
Club*, https://d23.com/the-hall-of-presidents-story/

309   **Blushing Bunny and Tyler Pie:** Beard, *American Cookery*, pp. 118, 629.

310   **had other sources:** Eier Kringel (Beard, *American Cookery*, pp. 714–15; *Mary Cullen's
Northwest Cook Book* [Binfords and Mort, 1946], ed. Cathrine C. Laughton, p. 215); Lebkuchen (Beard, p. 719; Laughton, p. 216); Gingerbread Men (Beard, p. 717; Laughton, p.
212); Chocolate Potato Cake (Beard, p. 675; Laughton, p. 171); Old-Fashioned Six-Layer
Cake (Beard, p. 660; Laughton, p. 173); Lazy Daisy Cake (Beard, pp. 657–58; Laughton, p.
178).

310   **such as Génoise:** Beard, *American Cookery*, pp. 680–81; Paula Peck, *The Art of Fine Baking* (Simon and Schuster, 1961), pp. 64–66.

310   **Melting Tea Cake:** Beard, *American Cookery*, p. 684.

310   **source of the Snickerdoodles:** Beard, La Pitchoune, to Robert Stevenson, Chillingsworth
Inn, Brewster, Massachusetts, May 20, 1967, JBP.

310   **"a brilliant cook":** Beard, *American Cookery*, p. 792.

311   **Slaw with Egg Dressing:** Beard, *American Cookery*, p. 499.

311   **Lemon Cake Pudding:** Beard, *American Cookery*, p. 727.

311 **Lentil Soup with Chard . . . Kibbeh Naye:** Beard, *American Cookery*, pp. 96, 390–91.

311 **"believed to be typically":** Beard, *American Cookery*, p. 91.

311 **"came from Provence":** Beard, *American Cookery*, p. 519.

312 **"There is something":** Beard, unpublished draft, "France," undated [1955], OHS.

312 **France was the model:** Richard Olney had come to a similar conclusion, although he was interested in preserving authentic dishes in the French canon. "Good and honest cooking," he writes in *The French Menu Cookbook*, "and good and honest French cooking are the same thing . . . It is comforting to realize that the principles of good cooking do not change as one crosses frontiers or oceans, and that the success of a preparation depends on nothing more than a knowledge of those principles plus personal sensibility." [Olney, *The French Menu Cookbook* (Simon and Schuster, 1970), p. 17.]

312 **"I spent most of":** Alfred Knopf Jr. to Beard, May 5, 1972, JBP.

312 **"For certain it will":** Elizabeth David, 24 Halsey Street, London, to Beard, May 16, 1972, JBP.

312 **"A stupendous achievement":** Julia Child, La Pitchoune, Plascassier, France, to Beard, May 12, 1972, JBP.

313 **"You have definitely":** M. F. K. Fisher, Bouverie Ranch, Glen Ellen, California, to Beard, July 19, 1972, JBP.

314 **"An alternative to super-market":** Dust-jacket copy for Sandra Oddo, *Home Made* (Atheneum, 1972).

314 **"[Oddo] thinks":** Raymond Sokolov, "America in the Kitchen: As 3 Cookbook Authors See It," *New York Times*, May 25, 1972.

314 **"simply a record":** Beard, *American Cookery*, p. 6.

314 **American food's "grotesqueries":** Beard, *American Cookery*, p. 7.

314 **"A rather quick note":** Julia Child, La Pitchoune, Plascassier, France, to Beard, June 9, 1972, JBP.

314 **"I am a long":** Raymond Sokolov, *New York Times*, to Beard, undated [spring 1972], JBP.

315 **"You've got the":** Avis DeVoto, Cambridge, Massachusetts, to Beard, May 16, 1972, JBP.

315 **"Dear Mr. Beard":** Benson Eschenbach, Marshall, California, to Beard, November 5, 1972, JBP.

CHAPTER 18: SALMON QUICHE À LA CARL

316 **Oxford dress shirt:** Carl Jerome, email to author, August 31, 2017.

316 **brunch at the Eagle:** Ibid.

317 **raised in the South:** JBI with Carl Jerome, February 16, 2017.

317 **Carl arrived in Manhattan:** Ibid.

317 **the adrenaline rush:** Ibid.

317 **his coeur à la crème:** Fred Sparks, "Jackie's a Bit Rough on the Hired Help," *Quad City Times-Democrat* (Davenport, Iowa), February 4, 1973.

317 **spread a little dirt:** Maxine Cheshire, "Very Interesting People," *State Journal* (Lansing, Michigan), October 6, 1972.

317 **work for a famous cook:** JBI with Carl Jerome, February 16, 2017.

318 **a London shop, Floris:** Ibid.

318 **the operatic wallpaper:** Ibid.

318 **kiss him good-bye:** JBI with Carl Jerome, October 20, 2018.

319 **slip his tongue inside:** Ibid. "As I recall it, as I was leaving, he was sitting on a sofa. He said, 'Can I kiss you, goodbye.' I thought it would be two gay men . . . a peck on the cheek. I felt I didn't know what was happening. I left feeling kind of molested, but not like I was raped. I felt that I'd been violated. He was trying to make it into a French kiss and I was trying to move back."

319 **said it was terrible:** JBI with Carl Jerome, February 16, 2017.

320 **dozens of classes:** Raymond Sokolov, "Anyone for Cooking Lessons in the Long, Cold Winter Ahead?" *New York Times*, September 7, 1971.

320 **regional Northern Italian:** Ibid.

320 **tamales and mole Poblano:** Ibid.

320 **Lydie Marshall's renovated brownstone:** Ibid.

320 **"reasons-behind-the-recipes":** Ibid.

320 **Meyers captured the mood:** Perla Meyers, *The Seasonal Kitchen: A Return to Fresh Foods* (Holt, Rinehart and Winston, 1973), p. 3.

321 **"able co-star":** Carolyn Flournoy and Marilee Harter, "Beard Stresses Perfection," *Shreveport* [LA] *Times*, September 24, 1975.

321 **"bearded young associate":** Ibid.

321 **"in the kitchens of":** Ibid.

321 **"computer bank mind":** Ibid.

321 **waiting list of five hundred:** Jane Howard, "Passionate Pasha of Food," *Life*, June 16, 1972.

321 **no waiting list:** JBI with Carl Jerome, May 30, 2017. "I wanted to dispel the idea that the [James Beard] Cooking School ever had a waiting list: It did not. Ever."

322 **to have a social life:** JBI with Carl Jerome, February 16, 2017.

323 **crossing out recipes:** The collection of some of James's books at the Reed College Library includes the 1954 copy of *James Beard's Fish Cookery* that James marked up for revisions in 1975, RCP.

323 **"lobsters are so damn":** Avis DeVoto, Cambridge, Massachusetts, to Beard, May 16, 1972, JBP.

324 **did not want organization:** JBI with Carl Jerome, February 16, 2017.

324 **"I'm bored":** JBI with Carl Jerome, October 20, 2018.

324 **The actor Van Johnson:** Johna Blinn, "Van Johnson: Orange Cook," *Sun-Telegram* (San Bernardino, California), May 7, 1978.

325 **James undid the tie:** JBI with Carl Jerome, October 20, 2018. "I remember he made the bathrobe pass to me in Miami. I have a visual with the cotton robe—it was his standard. He wasn't mobile, there wasn't any way for him to approach you. So the bathrobe, him sitting on the bed in the bathrobe, was the routine."

CHAPTER 19: LATE RASPBERRIES FOR CHRISTMAS

326 **no-goods, libertines, and queers:** Justin Spring, *Secret Historian: The Life and Times of Samuel Steward, Professor, Tattoo Artist, and Sexual Renegade* (Farrar, Straus and Giroux, 2011), p. 194. The Stanford Court's basement apartments were a favorite with queer men. Samuel Steward paid fifty dollars a month for a room with wall-to-wall carpeting and communal showers where sex was commonplace.

326 **$17 million remodel:** William Rice, "Chain Reaction," *Chicago Tribune*, January 24, 1989.

327 **carpets were wool:** Marian Burros, "The 24-Hour-a-Day Hotelkeeper," *New York Times*, January 6, 1985.

327 **Comtesse chocolates from the Godiva boutique:** Ibid.

327 **It never revealed its guest lists:** JBI with Jim Dodge, February 21, 2017.

327 **its own entrance:** Ibid.

328 **James received a letter:** Michael Z. Kay, Stanford Court, San Francisco, to Beard, July 31, 1972, JBP.

328 **"In a Christmas note":** *Oregonian*, January 7, 1973.

328 **Thai silk bow tie:** Carl Gohs, "James Beard at Seaside," *Northwest Magazine*, September 30, 1973.

329 **there were sixteen students:** Ibid.

329 **the kitchen was organized:** Yvonne Rothert, "Cajoling, Frowning, Beard Whips Class into Shape," *Oregonian*, June 25, 1973.

329 **"I hope no one came":** Gohs, "James Beard at Seaside," *Northwest Magazine*, September 30, 1973.

329 **a dozen big crates:** Ibid.

329 **"Everyone was giving classes":** Yvonne Rothert, "Guru of Cookery Remains Friendly Giant," *Oregonian*, July 15, 1981.

330 **Perla Meyers was teaching:** Raymond Sokolov, "Anyone for Cooking Lessons in the Long, Cold Winter Ahead?" *New York Times*, September 7, 1971.

330 **He caught Antoinette Hatfield:** Rothert, "Cajoling, Frowning, Beard Whips Class into Shape," *Oregonian*, June 25, 1973.

330 **"You'll just have to":** Ibid.

330 **"There are only about":** Ibid.

330 **"Cooking is very simple":** Ibid.

331 **a working-class family:** Marion Cunningham, "Marion Cunningham: An Oral History," conducted by Suzanne Riess, 2001–2002, Regional Oral History Office, Bancroft Library, University of California, Berkeley, 2012.

331 **Fruit and nut trees clustered:** Bernard Clayton, *Bernard Clayton's Cooking Across America* (Simon and Schuster, 1993), p. 170.

331 **dreaded crossing bridges:** Cunningham, "Marion Cunningham: An Oral History," by Suzanne Riess, Bancroft Library, University of California, Berkeley.

331 **Elevators terrified her:** Ruth Reichl, "Celebrating America's Mom," *Los Angeles Times*, March 5, 1992.

331 **drive to San Francisco:** Cunningham, "Marion Cunningham: An Oral History," by Suzanne Riess, Bancroft Library, University of California, Berkeley.

332 **urged Marion to go:** Ibid.

332 **her son told her:** Reichl, "Celebrating America's Mom," *Los Angeles Times*, March 5, 1992.

332 **didn't interest her:** Cunningham, "Marion Cunningham: An Oral History," by Suzanne Riess, Bancroft Library, University of California, Berkeley.

333 **He saw the fun in her:** Ibid. "He knew he had more fun when I was around."

333 **stop being so nice:** Ibid. "James Beard didn't like people who were too nice. When I was nice, he wanted to kick me."

333 **"I try new restaurants":** Marion Cunningham, Walnut Creek, California, to Beard, January 6, 1975, JBP.

333 **two weeklong sessions:** "Learning to Cook Like Jim": *San Francisco Examiner*, January 15, 1975.

334 **for men only:** Ibid.

334 **"We're not here":** Helen Civelli Brown, "The Class of James A. Beard," *San Francisco Examiner*, April 30, 1975.

334 **wore a plaid shirt:** Ibid.

334 **"the new boys":** Ibid.

334 **He showed the class:** Ibid.

335 **an antiques dealer:** JBI with Elizabeth Randal, September 29, 2017.

335 **English oak furniture and Staffordshire:** William Warren, *Merchant of Sonoma: Chuck Williams, Pioneer of the American Kitchen* (Weldon Owen, 2011), p. 104.

335 **New England boiled dinner:** Ibid., pp. 86–87.

335 **Gerald Asher took James:** JBI with Gerald Asher, September 27, 2017.

335 **1900 wood-frame house:** Jack Shelton, Chez Panisse review, *Jack Shelton's Private Guide*, May 1972, Chez Panisse Collection, Bancroft Library, University of California, Berkeley.

335 **this co-op venture:** James Beard, syndicated food column, *The San Francisco Examiner*, Deember 30, 1974.

335 **a party Marion threw:** JBI with Jeremiah Tower, April 30, 2017.

336 **bowls of mangoes:** JBI with Jim Dodge, February 21, 2017.

336 **raspberries (James's favorite):** Beard, "Whatever Happened to Breakfast?" (1978), *The Armchair James Beard*, pp. 29–30.

336 **In the 1960s:** Warren, *Merchant of Sonoma: Chuck Williams, Pioneer of the American Kitchen*, p. 114.

337 **twenty-five young men:** Chris Lenwell, "Male Order Fulfillment," *From Ellis Island to the Ellis Act*, December 1, 2014, https://ls2lsblog.com/2014/12/01/male-order-fulfillment/.

337 **Chris Lenwell was one:** JBI with Chris Lenwell, July 17, 2017.

337 **made them laugh:** Ibid.

337   **"wasn't a dry seat":** Ibid.

337   **the Rolling Mincer:** Lenwell, "Male Order Fulfillment," *From Ellis Island to the Ellis Act.*

337   **muscled and solid:** Carl Jerome, email to author, September 18, 2017. "He was a beautifully attractive young man, exactly Jim's type. And Jim was very open about his infatuation with him—at least in SF."

338   **working for a temp agency:** JBI with Louie Worden, September 10, 2017.

338   **make sure to be on:** Ibid.

338   **asked Louie to join them:** Ibid.

338   **cold poached snapper:** Chez Panisse menu, "A Birthday Dinner à la James Beard," May 5, 1978, Chez Panisse Collection, Bancroft Library, University of California, Berkeley.

339   **to wrap his legs:** JBI with Louie Worden, September 10, 2017.

339   **recommended self-help books:** Ibid.

339   **Michael Butusov:** Michael was a student of Jim Dodge—Stanford Court's pastry chef—at Tante Marie's Cooking School in San Francisco. As a line cook at Hayes Street Grill in San Francisco in 1987, I met Michael and heard his story of meeting James and the incident of the bathrobe.

CHAPTER 20: RAISIN BREAD REDEMPTION

341   **disdained the world of cookbooks:** SBFI with Judith Jones, Session #1, March 30, 2013.

342   **"box-top books":** Ibid.

342   **so jealous of them:** SBFI with Judith Jones, Session #3, April 22, 2013.

342   **The Skotch Bucket!:** SBFI with Judith Jones, Session #4, May 13, 2013.

342   **the Bread Basket:** Jean Hewitt, "From Rolls to Loaves: 113 Varieties," *New York Times,* February 11, 1970.

343   **"MAGICAL MYSTERIES OF MAKING BREAD":** Mary Daniels, *Chicago Tribune,* August 30, 1971.

343   **"Currently there's a revival":** Ibid.

343   **Shambhala, a hippie publisher:** Jonathan Kauffman, *Hippie Food* (William Morrow, 2018), pp. 124–25.

343   **bunch of counterculture kids:** SBFI with Judith Jones, Session #6, June 28, 2013. Judith Jones: "I decided that somebody should do a bread book, because all these sixties counterculture people were making their own bread!"

343   **bread-and-soup cookbook:** Yvonne Young Tarr, *The New York Times Bread and Soup Cookbook* (Quadrangle/The New York Times Book Co., 1972).

343   **series of monthly lunches:** SBFI with Judith Jones, Session #6, June 28, 2013.

343   **James would deliver:** Schaffner to Ned Bradford, Little, Brown, Boston, April 8, 1971, JSP.

343   **"I hope you will":** Judith Jones, Knopf, to Schaffner, March 11, 1971, JSP.

343   **"The craze for bread-making":** Knopf editorial fact sheet for *Beard on Bread,* undated [1973], JBP.

344   **"I have to say":** Schaffner to Judith Jones, October 2, 1973, JSP.

345   **three weeks in Norway:** "Norway Itinerary for Mr. James A. Beard," Export Council of Norway, unpublished transcript, June 1972, JBP.

345   **Norway had decriminalized:** William N. Eskridge Jr. and Darren R. Spedale, *Gay Marriage: For Better or for Worse? What We've Learned from the Evidence* (Oxford University Press, 2006), pp. 62–63.

345   **folk museum at Bygdøy:** "Norway Itinerary for Mr. James A. Beard," Export Council of Norway, unpublished transcript, June 1972, JBP.

345   **they watched Elizabeth Ovenstad:** Ibid.

345   **Gohs scoured boulangeries:** Carl Gohs, "Friends, Associates Fondly Recall Beard," *Oregonian,* January 24, 1985.

346   **"I grew up on this":** Beard, unpublished draft for "Mother's Raisin Bread" recipe, undated [1972], JBP.

346   **"appeared in the columns":** Beard, *Beard on Bread,* p. 88.

346 **a 1968 *Times* feature:** Craig Claiborne, "Bread: Winners," *New York Times*, April 28, 1968.

346 **"JB," she wrote:** Sourdough Rye recipe test sheet, undated, JBP.

348 **"World-renowned culinary authority":** Ellen Mandleberg, Atheneum, to editor of the Reed College Alumni Bulletin, Portland, Oregon, May 21, 1971, RCP.

348 **Lehman noted his address:** Handwritten notes in James Beard file, undated [1972], Reed College Papers.

348 **reported back to Lehman:** Handwritten notes in James Beard file signed FW [Florence Walls Lehman], undated [1972], RCP.

349 **to write the foreword:** Thomas Vaughan, Oregon Historical Society, Portland, Oregon, to Beard, January 3, 1973, JBP.

350 **perfected the dacquoise:** Cookbook author Madhur Jaffrey—who lived on the same block on West Twelfth Street where James and Gino were to move—found Gino's fragile, meticulous dessert "scrumptious." [JBI with Madhur Jaffrey, August 24, 2017.]

351 **or Tom Margittai:** JBI with Tom Margittai, September 23, 2017.

352 **tweaked so much:** Andrew Scott Dolkart, "The James Beard House, 167 West 12th Street: A House History," unpublished transcript, September 1992, JBF.

352 **bed alcove with mirrors:** JBI with Jerry Lamb, April 11, 2017.

353 **Gino drew up plans:** Dolkart, "The James Beard House," September 1992, JBF.

353 **Knoll table . . . McGuire chairs:** JBI with Jerry Lamb, April 11, 2017.

354 **"Kiddo," he said:** JBI with James Villas, February 28, 2017.

355 **dropped to one knee:** Ibid.

355 **to say into her tape recorder:** Barbara Kafka, "A James Beard Memoir," *The James Beard Celebration Cookbook*, p. 15. Though Kafka didn't provide dates for the recordings, it's clear from James's references they were done between February and August 1978. Carl Jerome believes Kafka recorded a total of four tapes with James. [JBI with Carl Jerome, May 30, 2017.]

355 **time to come clean:** Beard, *The James Beard Celebration Cookbook*, Barbara Kafka ed., p. 24. "By the time I was seven, I knew that I was gay. I think it's time to talk about that now."

355 **no promise to let her publish:** JBI with Carl Jerome, May 30, 2017. "[Jim] would never speak to anyone the way he would open up to Barbara [Kafka]. She was the one person on that level that he would be intimate with."

356 **Mary Goodbody and Irene Sax:** JBI with Mary Goodbody, September 22, 2017; JBI with Irene Sax, July 11, 2017.

356 **go through stacks of old *Gourmet* magazines:** JBI with Nick Malgieri, March 29, 2017.

356 **"whose impact on society":** "Citation: Honorary Degree, Reed College Doctor of Humane Letters," unpublished transcript, May 16, 1976, RCP.

357 **called it *Delights and Pleasures*:** Ibid.

357 **above three hundred pounds:** Carl Winston, "All the Way Down to a Svelte 270," *San Francisco Examiner*, August 9, 1976.

358 **"Go have a good life":** JBI with Carl Jerome, February 16, 2017.

358 **draw up the will:** JBI with Morris Galen, April 10, 2017.

358 **James shrugged:** Ibid. Morris Galen: "I was preparing his will and I said, 'What do you want me to do?' [Beard] said, 'I don't know, what charity?' I said, 'We have Reed. . . .' We discussed it. I suggested Reed because I was on the board, and he said, 'Fine.' "

359 **"I don't want a monument":** JBI with Jerry Lamb, April 11, 2017.

359 **or a memorial:** JBI with Tom Margittai, September 23, 2017.

EPILOGUE: MISS LEWIS'S BISCUITS FOR THE DEAD

361 **something historic would unfold:** Marian Burros, "A Tribute to American Cooking," *New York Times*, June 2, 1985.

361 **Union Square Café and Arizona 206:** Bryan Miller, "Restaurants," *New York Times*, January 24, 1986; also Miller, "New and Notable," *New York Times*, July 11, 1986.

361 **rock stars all:** Ruth Reichl, "Chefs as the Star Ingredients," *Los Angeles Times*, October 08, 1985. "They roll into town like rock stars, roadies in their wake."

362 **eighty-second birthday party:** Gael Greene, "The Father of Us All," *New York*, June 3, 1985.

362 **the old man died:** Albin Krebs, "James Beard, Authority on Food, Dies," *New York Times*, January 24, 1985.

362 **The gala would still:** Nancy Jenkins, "A Feast in Memory of James Beard," *New York Times*, June 5, 1985.

363 **the seductive young lions:** Karen MacNeil, "Superchefs Acquire a Taste for Stardom," *USA Today*, May 22, 1985.

363 **had maneuvered his way:** Jeremiah Tower, *California Dish: What I Saw (and Cooked) at the American Culinary Revolution* (Free Press, 2003), p. 195.

363 **its most bombastically trendy:** Jeff Weinstein, "Faith, Hope and Buffet," *Village Voice*, June 18, 1985. "Most women [at the gala] shared a collective dream: *Dynasty/Dallas*."

364 **"The present lionization":** Ibid.

364 **On the cover:** Milton Glaser, illustration for the event program "A Celebration of James Beard," June 3, 1985.

364 **scattered on the beach:** JBI with Jerry Lamb, April 11, 2017.

364 **bowls of bread dough:** Jim Dodge, February 21, 2017.

365 **organized a New York party:** JBI with Tom Margittai, September 23, 2017.

365 **Brooke Astor . . . Marian Anderson:** Clayton Triplette, "JBF Staff Profile," unpublished questionnaire, James Beard Foundation private archives, undated, JBF.

365 **They commissioned Arbit Blatas:** JBI with Tom Margittai, September 23, 2017.

365 **"I think I have onions":** Triplette, "JBF Staff Profile," James Beard Foundation private archives, undated, JBF.

365 **he despised the portrait:** JBI with Tom Margittai, September 23, 2017. In 1998, after Margittai and Paul Kovi sold The Four Seasons, new owners Julian Niccolini and Alex von Bidder took the portrait down and donated it to the James Beard Foundation. [James Barron, Alex Kuczynski, and Joyce Wadler, "Public Lives," *New York Times*, September 25, 1998.]

365 **turn his face to the wall:** JBI with Tom Margittai, September 23, 2017. "In 1985 Jim was in the hospital again, this time it was very serious. We talked on the phone and he told me that he [was] tired of living and 'wanted to turn himself to the wall and leave.' He said he did not want any memorial service or any other celebration of his life. (He was always some kind of a rebel.)"

365 **lifted thirty-nine recipes:** Olney, *Reflexions*, pp. 264–68.

366 **crossed out in red felt-tip pen:** JBI with John P. Carroll, Session #3, May 9, 2017.

367 **shook his head:** JBI with Irene Sax, July 11, 2017.

367 **relieved Richard of that:** JBI with Robert Carmack, March 1, 2017.

368 **"just wouldn't believe it.":** KSI with Clayton Triplette, August 12, 2013.

SOURCES

Interviews (including email and telephone)

Aaron, Peter. August 1, 2017.
Asher, Gerald. September 27, 2017.
Batterberry, Ariane. August 17, 2017.
Baum, Hilary. July 21, 2017.
Bennett, John. April 3, 2017; May 26, 2017.
Bricke, Ron. August 17, 2017.
Brown, Diane Harris. August 2, 2017.
Carmack, Robert. March 1, 2017.
Carroll, John P. April 24, 2017; May 9, 2017.
Clark, Robert. August 11, 2017.
Cross, Billy. September 30, 2017.
Davis, Mitchell. January 12, 2017.
Davis, Renée. July 10, 2017.
Dodge, Jim. February 21, 2017.
Galen, Morris. April 10, 2017.
Goodbody, Mary. September 22, 2017.
Goodner, Joe. June 15, 2017.
Greenburg, Dan. July 12, 2018.
Jaffrey, Madhur. August 24, 2017.
Jerome, Carl. February 16, 2017; May 30, 2017; August 29, 2017; September 18, 2017; October 25, 2017.
Kaiser, Charles. August 21, 2017.
Kamp, David. July 25, 2017.
Karpfinger, Barney. May 14, 2018.
Katz, Jonathan Ned. July 19, 2017.
Kramer, Matt. October 24, 2017.
Lamb, Jerry. April 11, 2017.
Lenwell, Chris. July 17, 2017.
Lobrano, Alec. July 12, 2017.

Malgieri, Nick. March 29, 2017; September 17, 2017.
Margittai, Tom. September 23, 2017; March 14, 2018.
Mellgren, Jim. November 20, 2017.
O'Donnell, Neil. February 8, 2018.
Olney, Judith. February 22, 2017.
Peterson-Loomis, Jacqueline. November 3, 2017.
Poley, Madeline. July 18, 2017.
Randal, Elizabeth. September 29, 2017.
Reichl, Ruth. March 13, 2019.
Rhode, Mike. March 21, 2018.
Roden, Claudia. September 27, 2017.
Rosenthal, Alfred. November 17, 2017.
Sax, Irene. July 11, 2017.
Schaffner, Tim. March 11, 2018.
Sokolov, Raymond. July 17, 2017.
Stanford, Jill Charlotte. February 5, 2018.
Stuart, Caroline. March 23, 2017; August 19, 2017.
Tower, Jeremiah. April 30, 2017.
Unterman, Patricia. April 3, 2017.
Villas, James. February 28, 2017.
Waters, Alice. September 29, 2017.
Watt, Alastair Fiddes. March 16, 2018.
Weiss, Golda. July 25, 2017.
Whiteman, Michael. April 29, 2017.
Wolf, Clark. January 21, 2017; June 24, 2017.
Worden, Louie. September 10, 2017.
Zimmern, Andrew. July 28, 2017.

BOOKS, FILMS, ORAL HISTORIES, AND ARTICLES

1950s Costa Brava, Spain. Home movie footage. Kinolibrary Archive Film collections, Clip ref. KLR254.

Adams, Charlotte. *The Four Seasons Cookbook.* James Beard, special consultant. New York: Holt, Rinehart and Winston, 1971.

Alpern, Tyler. "Elver Barker/Carl B. Harding." Tyler Alpern blog, tyleralpern.com.

America's First Foodie: The Incredible Life of James Beard. Documentary film, directed and produced by Beth Federici, coproduced by Kathleen Squires. Federici Films and Thirteen Productions, 2017.

Anderson, Heather Arndt. *Portland: A Food Biography.* Lanham, MD: Rowman and Littlefield, 2015.

Barkan, Elliott Robert. *From All Points: America's Immigrant West, 1870s–1952.* Bloomington: Indiana University Press, 2007.

Barr, Luke. *Provence, 1970: M.F.K. Fisher, Julia Child, James Beard, and the Reinvention of American Taste.* New York: Clarkson Potter, 2013.

Barranger, Milly S. *A Gambler's Instinct: The Story of Broadway Producer Cheryl Crawford.* Carbondale: Southern Illinois University Press, 2010.

Beachy, Robert. *Gay Berlin: Birthplace of a Modern Identity.* New York: Vintage Books, 2015.

Beard, James. *Beard on Bread.* New York: Alfred A. Knopf, 1973.

———. *Beard on Pasta.* New York: Alfred A. Knopf, 1983.

———. "Come and Cook It! Part One." In *Gourmet,* June 1948.

———. *Cook It Outdoors.* New York: M. Barrows, 1941.

———. *Delights and Prejudices.* New York: Atheneum, 1964.

———. "Foreword." In *Dining with Marcel Proust,* by Shirley King. London: Thames and Hudson, 1979.

———. *Fowl and Game Cookery.* New York: M. Barrows, 1944.

———. *Hors D'Oeuvre and Canapés, with a Key to the Cocktail Party.* New York: M. Barrows, 1940.

———. *Hors D'Oeuvre and Canapés.* Revised edition, with a new foreword by James Beard. New York: M. Barrows, 1963.

———. *James Beard's American Cookery.* Boston: Little, Brown, 1972.

———. *James Beard's Menus for Entertaining.* New York: Delacorte Press, 1965.

———. *James Beard's Treasury of Outdoor Cooking.* New York: Golden Press and The Ridge Press, 1960.

———. *The New James Beard.* New York: Alfred A. Knopf, 1981.

———. "A Tribute to Eleanor Lowenstein." In *Petits Propos Culinaires 7.* London: Prospect Books, March 1981.

———. "Vintage Tour 1949, Part One." In *Gourmet,* January 1950.

———. "Vintage Tour 1949, Part Two." In *Gourmet,* February 1950.

Beard, James A. "Appreciation." In M. F. K. Fisher, *The Art of Eating.* New York: Macmillan, 1954.

———. *The Fireside Cook Book.* New York: Simon and Schuster, 1949.

———. "A Gourmet's Beginnings." In Dale Brown and the Editors of Time-Life Books, *American Cooking: The Northwest.* Alexandria, VA: Time-Life Books, 1970.

———. *James Beard's Fish Cookery.* Boston: Little, Brown, 1954.

———. *James Beard's New Fish Cookery.* Boston: Little, Brown, 1976.

Beard, Jim. *The Casserole Cookbook.* Indianapolis: Bobbs-Merrill, 1955.

———. *Jim Beard's Complete Cookbook for Entertaining.* New York: Maco Magazine Corporation, 1954.

———. *Jim Beard's New Barbecue Cookbook.* New York: Maco Magazine Corporation, 1958.

———. "Manhattan Market Place." In *Harper's Bazaar,* February 1955.

———. "On the Fire." Column in *Argosy,* May 1951.

———. "On the Fire." Column in *Argosy,* July 1951.

———. "On the Fire." Column in *Argosy,* August 1951.

———. "On the Fire." Column in *Argosy,* September 1951.

Beard, James. Hal Kendig, ed. *James Beard's Simple Foods.* New York: Macmillan, 1993.

Beard, James, and Milton Glaser and Burton Wolf, eds. *The Cooks' Catalogue.* New York: Harper and Row, 1975.

Beard, James A., and Alexander Watt. *Paris Cuisine.* Boston: Little, Brown, 1952.

Beard, James, in collaboration with Isabel E. Callvert. *The James Beard Cookbook.* New York: Dell, 1959.

———. *The James Beard Cookbook.* New York: E. P. Dutton, 1961.

Beard, James, assisted by José Wilson. *Beard on Food.* New York: Alfred A. Knopf, 1974.

Beard, James, with the assistance of Gino P. Cofacci. *How to Eat (and Drink) Your Way Through a French (or Italian) Menu.* New York: Atheneum, 1971.

Beard, James, in collaboration with José Wilson. *James Beard's Theory and Practice of Good Cooking.* New York: Alfred A. Knopf, 1977.

Beard, James A., and Sam Aaron. *How to Eat Better for Less Money.* New York: Appleton-Century-Crofts, 1954.

———. *How to Eat Better for Less Money.* Revised edition. José Wilson, ed. New York: Simon and Schuster, 1970.

Beard, James. John Ferrone, ed. *Love and Kisses and a Halo of Truffles: Letters to Helen Evans Brown.* New York: Arcade Publishing, 1994.

Beck, Simone, and Suzanne Patterson. *Food and Friends: Recipes and Memories from Simca's Cuisine.* New York: Penguin Books, 1991.

Beith, Ian Hay. *The Crimson Cocoanut and Other Plays.* Boston: Walter H. Baker, 1913.

Bennett, Dorothy A. *Sold to the Ladies! Or, the Incredible but True Adventures of Three Girls on a Barge.* Chicago: Cadmus Books, 1940.

Berger, Frances de Talavera, and John Parke Custis. *Sumptuous Dining in Gaslight San Francisco, 1875–1915.* Garden City, NY: Doubleday, 1985.

Bérubé, Allan. *Coming Out Under Fire: The History of Gay Men and Women in World War Two.* New York: The Free Press, 1990.

Betty Crocker's Picture Cook Book. McGraw-Hill and General Mills, 1950.

Birds Eye Consumer Service Department. *Birds Eye Cook Book.* New York: Frosted Foods Sales Corporation, 1941.

Boag, Peter. *Same-Sex Affairs: Constructing and Controlling Homosexuality in the Pacific Northwest.* Berkeley: University of California Press, 2003.

Boe, Eugene, with recipes by June Roth. *Edith Bunker's All in the Family Cookbook*. New York: Popular Library, 1971.

Boyd, Nan Alamilla. *Wide Open Town: A History of Queer San Francisco to 1965*. Berkeley: University of California Press, 2003.

Brown, Helen Evans. *A Book of Appetizers*. With drink recipes by Philip S. Brown. Los Angeles: Ward Ritchie Press, 1958.

———. *Chafing Dish Book*. Los Angeles: Ward Ritchie Press, 1950.

———. *Helen Brown's Holiday Cook Book*. Boston: Little, Brown, 1952.

———. *Helen Brown's West Coast Cook Book*. Boston: Little, Brown, 1952.

———. *Patio Cook Book*. Los Angeles: Ward Ritchie Press, 1951.

Brown, Helen Evans, and Philip S. Brown. *Shrimp and Other Shellfish Recipes*. Los Angeles: Ward Ritchie Press, 1966.

Brown, Helen Evans, and James A. Beard. *The Complete Book of Outdoor Cookery*. Garden City, NY: Doubleday, 1955.

Brown, Helen Evans, and Philip S. Brown, Katharine Best, and Katharine Hillyer. *The Virginia City Cook Book*. Los Angeles: Ward Ritchie Press, 1953.

Burns, Edward, ed. *Staying on Alone: Letters of Alice B. Toklas*. New York: Vintage Books, 1975.

Callahan, Genevieve. *The California Cook Book for Indoor and Outdoor Eating*. New York: M. Barrows, 1946.

Carmack, Robert, and Gino Cofacci. *Cooking with Spirit!* Introduction by James Beard. New York: Atheneum, 1985.

Carroll, John P. "John P. Carroll Reminisces About James Beard and Time with Him." Blog, jamesbeardrevisited.wordpress.com.

Carter, David. *Stonewall: The Riots That Sparked a Gay Revolution*. New York: St. Martin's Press, 2004.

Caruso Jr., Enrico, and Andrew Farkas. *Enrico Caruso: My Father and My Family*. Abridged ed.. Portland, OR: Amadeus Press, 1997.

Cather, Willa. *The Song of the Lark*. New York: Oxford University Press, 2000.

Chan, April. "The Untold Story of San Francisco's Greatest Chinatown Restaurateur." Online essay. Medium.com, June 11, 2016. medium.com/food-ink/johnnykan-9b228d396e5b.

Chapman Publishing Company. *Portrait and Biographical Record of Western Oregon*. Chicago: Chapman Publishing Company, 1904.

Chauncey, George. *Gay New York: Gender, Urban Culture, and the Making of the Gay Male World, 1890–1940*. New York: BasicBooks, 1994.

Child, Julia, Louisette Bertholle, and Simone Beck. *Mastering the Art of French Cooking*. New York: Alfred A. Knopf, 1961.

Child, Julia, and Simone Beck. *Mastering the Art of French Cooking: Volume Two*. New York: Alfred A. Knopf, 1970.

Child, Julia, with Alex Prud'homme. *My Life in France*. New York: Anchor Books, 2006.

Chinese Consolidated Benevolent Association. *Dreams of the West: A History of the Chinese in Oregon, 1850–1950*. Portland, OR: Ooligan Press, 2007.

City of Gearhart, Historic Landmarks Commission. "Gearhart, Oregon, Historic Context Statement, Second Edition, Revised." September 1999.

Claiborne, Craig. *Craig Claiborne's A Feast Made for Laughter: A Memoir with Recipes*. Garden City, NY: Doubleday, 1982.

———. *The New York Times Cook Book*. New York: Harper and Row, 1961.

Clark, Robert. *James Beard: A Biography*. New York: HarperCollins, 1993.

Clayton, Bernard. "Today's Farmer: Marion Cunningham." In *Cooking Across America*. New York: Simon and Schuster, 1993.

Collins, Kathleen. "A Kitchen of One's Own: The Paradox of Dione Lucas." In *Camera Obscura: Feminism, Culture, and Media Studies* 27, No. 2 80, 2012.

Cooper, Artemis. *Writing at the Kitchen Table: The Authorized Biography of Elizabeth David*. New York: The Ecco Press, 1999.

Council of Jewish Women. *The Neighborhood Cook Book*. Portland, OR: Bushong, 1912.

Coward, Noel. Gilbert Millstein, ed. *Short Stories, Short Plays and Songs by Noel Coward*. New York: Dell, 1955.

Crawford, Cheryl. *One Naked Individual: My Fifty Years in the Theatre*. Indianapolis: Bobbs-Merrill, 1977.

Cunningham, Marion. "Marion Cunningham: An Oral History." Conducted by Suzanne Riess, 2001–2002. Regional Oral History Office, Bancroft Library, University of California, Berkeley, 2012.

David, Elizabeth. *An Omelette and a Glass of Wine*. New York: Elizabeth Sifton Books/Viking, 1985.

———. *Elizabeth David Classics*. Foreword by James A. Beard. New York: Alfred A. Knopf, 1980.

———. *English Bread and Yeast Cookery*. American edition, with notes by Karen Hess. New York: Penguin Books, 1980.

De Gouy, Louis. *The Gold Cook Book*. New York: Greenberg, 1947.

Dolkart, Andrew Scott. "The James Beard House, 167 West 12th Street: A House History." Unpublished transcript, September 1992.

Duberman, Martin. *Stonewall*. New York: Dutton, 1993.

Editors of American Heritage. Helen McCully, recipes ed. *The American Heritage Cookbook*. New York: Penguin Books, 1967.

Fat Ming Co. *Chinese and English Cook Book*. Shanghai: Fat Ming Co., 1916.

Ferrone, John, ed. *The Armchair James Beard*. New York: The Lyons Press, 1999.

———. *Voices from the Food Revolution: People Who Changed the Way Americans Eat*. An oral history project conducted by Judith Weinraub. Session #1, March 3, 2009. Fales Library and Special Collections, New York University.

———. *Voices from the Food Revolution: People Who Changed the Way Americans Eat*. An oral history project conducted by Judith Weinraub. Session #2, March 5, 2009. Fales Library and Special Collections, New York University.

———. *Voices from the Food Revolution: People Who Changed the Way Americans Eat*. An oral history project conducted by Judith Weinraub. Session #3, April 1, 2009. Fales Library and Special Collections, New York University.

Fitch, Noël Riley. *Appetite for Life: The Biography of Julia Child*. New York: Doubleday, 1997.

Florence Crittenton League. *Specialty of the House: 100 Favorite Recipes from 100 Favorite Cooks*. New York: The Florence Crittenton League, 1955.

Fussell, Betty. *Masters of American Cookery: M. F. K. Fisher, James Andrews Beard, Raymond Craig Claiborne, Julia McWilliams Child*. New York: Times Books, 1983.

Gaige, Crosby. *Dining with My Friends: Adventures with Epicures*. New York: Crown, 1949.

Gaston, Joseph. *Portland, Oregon, Its History and Builders, Volume 2*. Chicago: S. J. Clarke, 1911.

Gershunoff, Maxim, and Leon Van Dyke. *It's Not All Song and Dance: A Life Behind the Performing Arts*. Pompton Plains, NJ: Limelight Editions, 2005.

Gibson, Horace. *Good Afternoon Mr. Gibson: Memoirs of Horace Gibson*. Lexington, KY: Horace Gibson, 2010.

Golovitz, Frank. "Gay Beach, 1958." In *ONE: The Homosexual Viewpoint*, July 1958.

Gourmet. *The Gourmet Cookbook*. New York: Gourmet Distributing Corporation, 1950.

Greene, Gael. *Insatiable: Tales from a Delicious Life of Excess*. New York: Warner Books, 2006.

Hess, John L., and Karen Hess. *The Taste of America*. New York: Penguin Books, 1977.

Hibben, Sheila. *American Regional Cookery*. Boston: Little, Brown, 1946.

Houlbrook, Matt. *Queer London: Perils and Pleasures in the Sexual Metropolis, 1918–1957*. Chicago: University of Chicago Press, 2006.

Jackson, Julian. *Living in Arcadia: Homosexuality, Politics, and Morality in France from the Liberation to AIDS*. Chicago: University of Chicago Press Books, 2009.

Jacobs, Jay. "James Beard, An American Icon: The Early Years." In *Gourmet*, January 1984.

———. "James Beard, An American Icon: The Later Years." In *Gourmet*, February 1984.

James Beard Foundation. Barbara Kafka, ed. *The James Beard Celebration Cookbook*. New York: William Morrow and Company, Inc., 1990.

Jones, Evan. *Epicurean Delight: The Life and Times of James Beard*. New York: Alfred A. Knopf, 1990.

Jones, Judith. *The Tenth Muse: My Life in Food*. New York: Alfred A. Knopf, 2007.

Josephs, Jeremy. *Murder on the Menu: On the French Riviera*. BookBaby, 2013.

Kahn Jr., E. J. "The Coming of the Big Freeze." In *The New Yorker*, September 14, 1946.

Kaiser, Charles. *The Gay Metropolis, 1940–1996*. New York: Houghton Mifflin, 1997.

Kamp, David. *The United States of Arugula: How We Became a Gourmet Nation*. New York: Broadway Books, 2006.

Kan, Johnny, and Charles L. Leong. Foreword by James A. Beard. *Eight Immortal Flavors*. Berkeley: Howell-North Books, 1963.

Katz, Jonathan [Ned]. *Gay American History: Lesbians and Gay Men in the U.S.A.* New York: Harper Colophon, 1985.

———. *The Invention of Heterosexuality*. New York: Dutton, 1995.

Kauffman, Jonathan. *Hippie Food: How Back-to-the-Landers, Longhairs, and Revolutionaries Changed the Way We Eat*. New York: William Morrow, 2018.

Kerr, Graham. *The Complete Galloping Gourmet Cookbook*. New York: Grosset and Dunlap, 1972.

Kerry, Katherine. *Look What's Cooking*. San Francisco: Filmer Brothers and Cooperative Bindery, 1950.

Koler/Morrison Preservation and Planning Consultants. "A Survey and Inventory of Historic Resources, City of Seaside, Oregon." Oregon City, OR, 1987.

Kump, Peter. "In Memory. In *News from the Beard House*, Vol. 3, No. 5, May 1989.

Laughton, Cathrine C., ed. *Mary Cullen's Northwest Cook Book*. Portland, OR: Binfords and Mort, 1946.

Lenwell, Chris. "Male Order Fulfillment." Blog post at *From Ellis Island to the Ellis Act*, ls2lsblog.com, December 1, 2014.

Lincoln, Mrs. D. A. [Mary], *Boston Cooking School Cook Book: A Reprint of the 1884 Classic*. Mineola, NY: Dover, 1996.

Macías-González, Víctor M. "Scrubbing the Queer Away, or Homosexuality and Mexico City Bathhouses, 1880–1920." Paper delivered to the Primer Congreso Mexicano de Historia de la Comunidad LGBTT, Monterrey, Mexico, October 2001.

Mann, William J. *Behind the Screen: How Gays and Lesbians Shaped Hollywood, 1910–1969*. New York: Viking, 2001.

Marcus, Leonard S. *Golden Legacy: The Story of Golden Books*. New York: Golden Books, 2007.

McNamee, Thomas. *Alice Waters and Chez Panisse: The Romantic, Impractical, Often Eccentric, Ultimately Brilliant Making of a Food Revolution*. New York: Penguin Press, 2007.

———. *The Man Who Changed the Way We Eat: Craig Claiborne and the American Food Renaissance*. New York: Free Press, 2012.

McNulty, Henry. "James Andrews Beard: A Personal Memoir." In *Petits Propos Culinaires 19*. London: Prospect Books, March 1985.

Mendelson, Anne *Stand Facing the Stove: The Story of the Women who Gave America the Joy of Cooking*. New York: Scribner, 1996.

Meyers, Perla. *The Seasonal Kitchen: A Return to Fresh Foods*. New York: Holt, Rinehart and Winston, 1973.

Minahan, John. "Introduction." In James Beard, Hal Kendig, ed , *James Beard's Simple Foods*. New York: Macmillan, 1993.

———. *The Music of Time: An Autobiography*. iUniverse, 2001.

Mitchell, Joseph. *Up in the Old Hotel and Other Stories*. New York: Vintage Books, 1993.

Mumford, Ethel Watts, with Oliver Herford and Addison Mizner. *The Entirely New Cynic's Calendar of Revised Wisdom for 1905*. San Francisco: Paul Elder, 1905.

Muscatine, Doris. *A Cook's Tour of San Francisco: The Best Restaurants and Their Recipes*. New York: Charles Scribner's Sons, 1963.

Nantucket 1954–1955. Cisco family home movies. NHA Research Library Film Collection: Nantucket History, FC-26.

Neuhaus, Jessamyn. *Manly Meals and Mom's Home Cooking: Cookbooks and Gender in Modern America*. Baltimore: Johns Hopkins University Press, 2003.

Newnham-Davis, Nathaniel. *The Gourmet's Guide to London*. New York: Brentano's, 1914.

Newspaper Comics Council. Introduction by James A. Beard. *The Cartoonist Cookbook*. New York: Hobbs, Dorman, 1966.

Oddo, Sandra. *Home Made: An Alternative to Supermarket Living*. New York: Galahad Books, 1972.

Olney, Richard. *The French Menu Cookbook*. New York: Simon and Schuster, 1970.

———. *Reflexions*. New York: Brick Tower Press, 1999.

———. *Simple French Food*. New York: Atheneum, 1974.

The Open Road: London (1926). Film travelogue. Produced and directed by Claude Friese-Greene. BFI National Archive.

Owen, Jeanne. *A Wine Lover's Cook Book*. New York: M. Barrows, 1940.

———. *Jeanne Owen's Book of Sauces*. New York: M. Barrows, 1941.

———. *Lunching and Dining at Home*. New York: Alfred A. Knopf, 1942.

Painter, George. *The Vice Clique: Portland's Great Sex Scandal*. Portland, OR: Espresso Book Machine at Powell's, 2013.

Paris on the Seine (1950–1955). Documentary short film. Photographed in Technicolor by Jack Cardiff, assisted by Geoff Unsworth, recorded by P. Handford, commentary by Gibson Parker, directed by J. C. Bernard. British Pathé. Undated [1956].

Peck, Paula. *The Art of Fine Baking*. New York: Simon and Schuster, 1961.

Perkins, Wilma Lord. *The Fannie Farmer Cookbook*. Eleventh edition. Boston: Little, Brown, 1965.

Peters, Erica J. *San Francisco: A Food Biography*. Lanham, MD: Rowman and Littlefield, 2013.

Peterson-Loomis, Jacqueline. "Looks Like a Good Beginning: Immigration, Ethnicity, and Exclusion in Oregon." Lecture, online video. Oregon Historical Society, ohs.org.

"Pillsbury, Ann," ed. *300 Pillsbury Prize Recipes*. New York: Dell, 1952.

———. *Ann Pillsbury's Baking Book*. New York: Pocket Books, 1950.

Pinney, Thomas. *The Makers of American Wine: A Record of Two Hundred Years*. Berkeley: University of California Press, 2012.

Platt, June, and Sophie Kerr. *The Best I Ever Ate: A Practical Home Cook Book*. New York: Rinehart and Company, 1953.

Polan, Dana. "James Beard's Early TV Work." In *Gastronomica*, Vol. 10, No. 3, Summer 2010.

"Potluck Cooking Ware for the Gourmet: Designed by Kathi Urbach with Recipes by James Beard." Promotional brochure, undated [1952].

Randall, Michael. *Westbury in Old Photographs*. London: Alan Sutton, 1988.

Reed College Quest, Vol. 9, No. 1. Portland, OR: September 15, 1920.

———. Vol. 9, No. 4. Portland, OR: October 6, 1920.

———. Vol. 9, No. 5. Portland, OR: October 13, 1920.

———. Vol. 9, No. 7. Portland, OR: October 27, 1920.

———. Vol. 9, No. 8. Portland, OR: November 3, 1920.

———. Vol. 10, No. 1. Portland, OR: February 2, 1921.

———. Vol. 10, No. 6. Portland, OR: March 9, 1921.

Rhode, William. *Of Cabbages and Kings*. New York: Stackpole Sons, 1938.

Rieser, Andrew C. *The Chautauqua Moment: Protestants, Progressives, and the Culture of Modern Liberalism.* New York: Columbia University Press, 2003.

Roden, Claudia. *Everything Tastes Better Outdoors.* New York: Alfred A. Knopf, 1984.

Rombauer, Irma S. *The Joy of Cooking.* New York: Simon and Schuster, 1931.

———. *The Joy of Cooking,* Philadelphia: Blakiston, 1943.

Romero, Pepe. *Mexican Jumping Bean.* New York: G. P. Putnam's Sons, 1953.

———. *My Mexico City (and Yours).* Garden City, NY: Dolphin Books, 1962.

Root, Waverley. *The Food of France.* New York: Alfred A. Knopf, 1958.

Rudkin, Margaret. *The Margaret Rudkin Pepperidge Farm Cookbook.* New York: Atheneum, 1963.

Ryan, Hugh. *When Brooklyn Was Queer.* New York: St. Martin's Press, 2019.

Salazkina, Masha. *In Excess: Sergei Eisenstein's Mexico.* Chicago: University of Chicago Press, 2009.

San Grael Society of the First Presbyterian Church. *The Web-Foot Cook Book.* Portland, OR: W. B. Ayer and Company, 1885.

Sax, Irene. *Voices from the Food Revolution: People Who Changed the Way Americans Eat.* An oral history project conducted by Judith Weinraub. Session #1, April 29, 2009. Fales Library and Special Collections, New York University.

Scarpaci, Vincenza. *The Journey of the Italians in America.* New Orleans: Pelican, 2008.

Schoonmaker, Frank. *Frank Schoonmaker's Encyclopedia of Wine.* New York: Hastings House, 1964.

Sears, James Thomas. *Behind the Mask of the Mattachine: The Hal Call Chronicles and the Early Movement for Homosexual Emancipation.* New York: Routledge, 2006.

Shapiro, Laura. *Julia Child: A Life.* New York: Penguin Books, 2007.

Sheraton, Mimi. *Eating My Words: An Appetite for Life.* New York: William Morrow, 2004.

Simon, André L. *A Concise Encyclopædia of Gastronomy.* New York: Harcourt, Brace, 1952.

Skow, John. "If I Had to Practice Cannibalism . . . ." In *Saturday Evening Post,* July 30, 1966.

Smith, Andrew F., ed. *Savoring Gotham: A Food Lover's Companion to New York City.* New York: Oxford University Press, 2015.

Sohn, Amy. "The Star-Studded Life of Ms. Dorothy Bennett." In *JSTOR Daily,* JSTOR.org, https://daily.jstor.org/dorothy-bennett/.

Spitz, Bob. *Dearie: The Remarkable Life of Julia Child.* New York: Alfred A. Knopf, 2012.

Spring, Justin. *The Gourmands' Way: Six Americans in Paris and the Birth of a New Gastronomy.* New York: Farrar, Straus and Giroux, 2018.

———. *Secret Historian: The Life and Times of Samuel Steward, Professor, Tattoo Artist, and Sexual Renegade.* New York: Farrar, Straus and Giroux, 2011.

Stanish, Rudolph. *Omelets, Crêpes, and Other Recipes.* New York: Harbor Press, 1970.

Stearns, Osborne Putnam. *Paris Is a Nice Dish: Its Recipes and Restaurants.* Chicago: Henry Regnery, 1952.

Students of Reed College, The. *The Griffin of 1921*. Reed College yearbook. Portland, OR, 1921.

Summerfield, Carol, and Mary Elizabeth Devine, eds. *International Dictionary of University Histories*. Chicago: Fitzroy Dearborn, 1998.

Sunset Books and Sunset Magazine. *Sunset Barbecue Cook Book*. Menlo Park, CA: Lane Publishing, 1950.

Sunset Editorial Staff, Annabel Post, ed. *The Sunset Cook Book: Food with a Gourmet Touch*. Menlo Park, CA: Lane Book Company, 1960.

Tamagne, Florence. *A History of Homosexuality in Europe: Berlin, London, Paris, 1919–1939*. New York: Algora Publishing, 2004.

Tarr, Yvonne Young. *The New York Times Bread and Soup Cookbook*. New York: Quadrangle/The New York Times Book Co., 1972.

Thelin, Emily Kaiser. *Unforgettable: The Bold Flavors of Paula Wolfert's Renegade Life*. Berkeley: M&P, 2017.

Timmons, Stuart. *The Trouble with Harry Hay: Founder of the Modern Gay Movement*. Boston: Alyson Publications, 1990.

Toklas, Alice B., with introduction and comments by Poppy Cannon. *Aromas and Flavors of Past and Present*. New York: Harper and Brothers, 1958.

———. *The Alice B. Toklas Cook Book*. New York: Harper and Brothers, 1954.

Tower, Jeremiah. *California Dish: What I Saw (and Cooked) at the American Culinary Revolution*. New York: Free Press, 2003.

Triplette, Clayton. Kathleen Squires interview, unpublished transcript. August 12, 2013.

Villas, James. *Between Bites: Memoirs of a Hungry Hedonist*. New York: John Wiley and Sons, 2002.

Voss, Kimberly Wilmot. *The Food Section: Newspaper Women and the Culinary Community*. Lanham, MD: Rowman and Littlefield, 2014.

Warren, William. *Merchant of Sonoma: Chuck Williams, Pioneer of the American Kitchen*. San Francisco: Weldon Owen, 2011.

Washington High School, Portland, OR. *The Lens*, Vol. 15, No. 1, November 1918.

———. *The Lens*, Vol. 15, No. 2, December 1918.

———. *The Lens*, Vol. 15, No. 3, January 1919.

———. *The Lens*, Vol. 15, No. 4, March 1919.

———. *The Lens*, Vol. 15, No. 5, April 1919.

———. *The Lens*, Vol. 16, No. 1, November 1919.

———. *The Lens*, Vol. 16, No. 2, December 1919.

Waters, Alice, in collaboration with Linda P. Guenzel. *The Chez Panisse Menu Cookbook*. New York: Random House, 1982.

Watt, Alexander. *Art Centres of the World: Paris*. London: Michael Joseph, 1967.

———. *The Art of Simple French Cookery*. Garden City, NY: Doubleday, 1962.

———. *Paris Bistro Cookery*. London: MacGibbon and Kee, 1957.

White, Florence, ed. *Good Things in England: A Practical Cookery Book for Everyday Use, Containing Traditional and Regional Recipes Suited to Modern Tastes*. London: The Cookery Book Club, 1968.

Wilkie, Richard W. "The Drive to Acapulco." In *Adventures into Mexico: American Tourism Beyond the Border*. Lanham, MD: Rowman and Littlefield, 2006.

Willan, Anne, with Amy Friedman. *One Soufflé at a Time: A Memoir of Food and France.* New York: St. Martin's Press, 2013.

Zane, J. Robert. *This Was My Pottsville: Life and Crimes During the Gilded Age.* iUniverse, 2005.

Zelayeta, Elena. *Elena's Secrets of Mexican Cooking.* Englewood Cliffs, NJ: Prentice-Hall, 1958.

———. *Elena's Fiesta Recipes.* Los Angeles: Ward Ritchie Press, 1952.

INDEX

ABOUT THE AUTHOR

John Birdsall grew up near San Francisco and learned to cook at Greens Restaurant in that city. He spent the next seventeen years in professional kitchens there and in Chicago, and did some writing as a side gig, including food stories and restaurant reviews for the *San Francisco Sentinel*, a pioneering LGBTQ weekly. After leaving the kitchen, he was a restaurant critic and features writer at the *Contra Costa Times* and *East Bay Express*, and the editor of *SF Weekly*'s food blog. In 2014, he won a James Beard Award for food and culture writing for "America, Your Food Is So Gay" in *Lucky Peach*, and another in 2016 for "Straight-Up Passing" in the queer food journal *Jarry*. He's written for *Food & Wine*, *Bon Appétit*, the *San Francisco Chronicle*, and *Los Angeles Times*, and taught culinary writing at the San Francisco Cooking School. He's married to Perry Lucina, an artist and designer.

Twitter @John_Birdsall
Instagram @john_birdsall
Website john-birdsall.com